About the Authors

RICHARD BIERNACKI is Associate Professor of Sociology at the University of California–San Diego. He is the author of *The Fabrication of Labor: Germany and Britain, 1640–1914* (University of California Press, 1995).

WILLIAM BRUSTEIN is Professor and Chair of Sociology at the University of Minnesota. He is the author of *The Logic of Evil: The Social Origins of the Nazi Party, 1925 to 1933* (Yale University Press, 1996).

MICHAEL DONNELLY is Professor of Sociology at the University of New Hampshire. His recent publications include "From Political Arithmetic to Social Statistics," in *The Rise of the Social Sciences*, edited by J. Heilbron et al. (Kluwer, forthcoming).

JOHN R. HALL, Professor of Sociology at the University of California–Davis, has written on countercultural social movement organizations, theory, culture, and political economy. He is currently completing a book on methodologies of sociohistorical inquiry.

J. CRAIG JENKINS, Professor of Sociology and Faculty Associate, Mershon Center for International Security, Ohio State University, is author most recently (with Bert Klandermans) of the volume *The Politics of Social Protest: Comparative Perspectives on States and Social Movements* (University of Minnesota Press, 1995, and has published articles on social movement theory, collective action, and comparative studies of conflict and violence.

PATRICK JOYCE is Professor of History at Manchester University, England. He has published on the history of class, politics, and work; his books include *Visions of the People: Industrial England and the Question of Class* (Cambridge University Press, 1991).

MICHÈLE LAMONT is Associate Professor in the Department of Sociology, Princeton University. A Guggenheim Fellow, she is completing a book on class and racial communities in France and the United States.

KEVIN T. LEICHT is Associate Professor of Sociology at the University of Iowa. His most recent published work (with J. Craig Jenkins) is an article titled "Direct Intervention by the Subnational State: The Development of Public Venture Capital Programs in the American States," appearing in *Social Problems*.

SONYA ROSE is Professor of History and Sociology at the University of Michigan–Ann Arbor, and author of *Limited Livelihoods: Gender and Class in Nineteenth-Century England* (University of California Press, 1992).

JAN C. C. RUPP is Senior Fellow at the Amsterdam School for Social Science Research, University of Amsterdam, the Netherlands. His publications include "Ethnic Background: Social Class or Status?" in the *Journal for Ethnic and Racial Studies* 15 (1992): 284–303.

MARGARET R. SOMERS is Associate Professor of Sociology at the University of Michigan–Ann Arbor. Her publications include "Narrating and Naturalizing Civil Society and Citizenship Theory: The Place of Political Culture and the Public Sphere," *Sociological Theory* 13, 3 (1995): 229–274, and *The People and the Law: The Making of Modern Citizenship Rights* (Cornell University Press, forthcoming).

GEORGE STEINMETZ is Associate Professor of Sociology at the University of Chicago. He is the author of *Regulating the Social: The Welfare State and Local Politics in Imperial Germany* (Princeton University Press, 1993).

DALE TOMICH is Associate Professor of Sociology at Binghamton University and author of *Slavery in the Circuit of Sugar: Martinique in the World Economy, 1830–1848* (Johns Hopkins University Press, 1990).

JOHN WALTON is Professor of Sociology and Anthropology at the University of California–Davis and author of *Western Times and Water Wars: State, Culture, and Rebellion in California* (University of California Press, 1992).

ERIK OLIN WRIGHT is C. Wright Mills Professor of Sociology, University of Wisconsin. His most recent publication is *Class Counts: Comparative Studies in Class Analysis* (Cambridge University Press, 1996).

Acknowledgments

CHAPTER 1, "RETHINKING, ONCE AGAIN, THE CONCEPT OF CLASS STRUCTURE," by Erik Olin Wright is an abridged version of the chapter by the same title, pp. 269–343 in Erik Olin Wright et al., *The Debate on Classes* (New York: Verso, 1989), reprinted by permission of Verso Editions. Chapter 2, "Deconstructing and Reconstructing Class Formation Theory: Narrativity, Relational Analysis, and Social Theory," by Margaret R. Somers, is a modified version of her article "Narrativity, Narrative Identity, and Social Action: Rethinking English Working-Class Formation," which appeared in *Social Science History* 16, 4 (1992): 591–630, copyright Social Science History Association, 1992, reprinted by permission of Duke University Press. Portions of the text and the four figures in Chapter 5, "Work and Culture in the Reception of Class Ideologies," by Richard Biernacki, first appeared in his book *The Fabrication of Labor: Germany and Britain, 1640–1914* (Berkeley: University of California Press, 1995), copyright © 1995 The Regents of the University of California, and are reprinted with the permission of the University of California Press.

Reworking Class

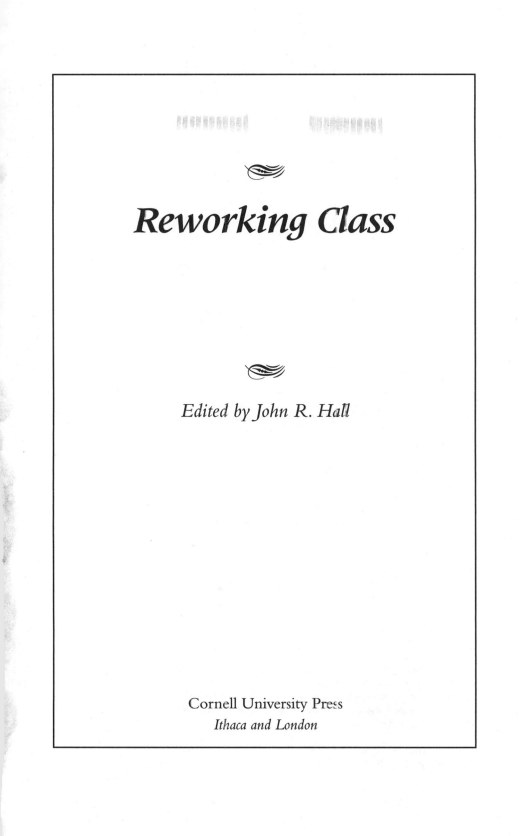

Reworking Class

Edited by John R. Hall

Cornell University Press
Ithaca and London

First published 1997 by Cornell University Press.

Printed in the United States of America.

Library of Congress Cataloging-in-Publication Data

Reworking class / edited by John R. Hall.
     p. cm.
   Includes index.
   ISBN 0-8014-3242-1 (cloth : alk. paper). — ISBN 0-8014-8321-2
(paper : alk. paper)
    1. Social classes. I. Hall, John R.
  HT609.R45 1997
   305.8—dc21   97-18765

Cornell University Press strives to utilize environmentally responsible
suppliers and materials to the fullest extent possible in the publishing
of its books. Such materials include vegetable-based, low-VOC inks
and acid-free papers that are also either recycled, totally chlorine-free,
or partly composed of nonwood fibers.

Cloth printing   10 9 8 7 6 5 4 3 2 1
Paperback printing 10 9 8 7 6 5 4 3 2 1

Contents

About the Authors   vii

Acknowledgments   ix

Foreword   xi
Patrick Joyce

INTRODUCTION   **The Reworking of Class Analysis**   I
John R. Hall

PART I
Changing Cultures of Class Analysis

CHAPTER I   **Rethinking, Once Again, the Concept of**   41
Class Structure
Erik Olin Wright

CHAPTER 2   **Deconstructing and Reconstructing Class**   73
Formation Theory: Narrativity, Relational
Analysis, and Social Theory
Margaret R. Somers

CHAPTER 3   **Statistical Classifications and the Salience**   107
of Social Class
Michael Donnelly

CHAPTER 4   **Class Formation and the Quintessential**   133
Worker
Sonya O. Rose

PART II

Cultural Structurings of Class Identities

CHAPTER 5   **Work and Culture in the Reception of**   169
             Class Ideologies
             Richard Biernacki

CHAPTER 6   **The Meaning of Class and Race: French**   193
             and American Workers Discuss Differences
             Michèle Lamont

CHAPTER 7   **Rethinking Cultural and Economic Capital**   221
             Jan C. C. Rupp

CHAPTER 8   **Cannery Row: Class, Community, and the**   243
             Social Construction of History
             John Walton

PART III

The Economic, the Social, and the Political Agencies of Class

CHAPTER 9   **World of Capital / Worlds of Labor:**   287
             A Global Perspective
             Dale Tomich

CHAPTER 10   **Class Location versus Market Interests**   313
             in Macropolitical Behavior: The Social
             Origins of the German Nazi Party
             William Brustein

CHAPTER 11   **Social Class and the Reemergence of the**   335
             Radical Right in Contemporary Germany
             George Steinmetz

CHAPTER 12   **Class Analysis and Social Movements:**   369
             A Critique and Reformulation
             J. Craig Jenkins and Kevin Leicht

             Index   399

Foreword

Patrick Joyce

THIS BOOK REGENERATES CLASS, ENABLING IT TO BE THOUGHT ABOUT IN new kinds of ways. It is a very welcome book. The welcome, above all, must be for the book's contribution to rethinking the economic in relation to culture, agency, the social, and the political. Through this rethinking, the concept of social class comes to have renewed use. A conception of social class without the economic becomes a contradiction in terms, and many existing conceptions of social class—in relation to which the book positions itself—are seen to have a limited understanding of the economic that renders them well-nigh useless. Thus, *Reworking Class* resuscitates a concept that was almost dead on its feet. Yet like all good books, it poses as many questions as it answers

John R. Hall's Introduction identifies the twin processes that have led to "the end of class as a historical subject" and "the deconstruction of class as a theoretical object." With the latter he associates what he calls "the postmodern crisis of knowledge," and with the former the transforming economic and political changes of recent times. The problem of the "historical subject" may be said to turn both on class (or "group") as a collective actor and on the narratives that write the movement of this actor in history. The problem of class as a "theoretical subject" may be said to involve the question of structure; it evinces, in Hall's words, "the need to theorize in nonstructuralist ways." To meet this need, Hall replaces "class structure" with "class action," thereby avoiding the theoretical bind of the action-structure and culture-economy dualisms. This is the cue for the particularly revealing contributions of Margaret Somers and Richard Biernacki, and for Sonya Rose's employment of Sartre's existentialist concept of seriality as linked social locations, obviously pertinent to the notion of class formation. What is so interesting about concepts like seriality is that they exemplify the deeply felt need to think not only in nonstructuralist but in antistructuralist and processual ways about the nature of the social. Responding to this need, Somers develops the idea of "relational setting" to replace "society." The relational setting, she indicates, is involved in long-term patterns of change, the historicity of her approach disclosing an understanding of origins.

"Relational setting" displaces "society," and "narrative" displaces "interest" (but also "group"). The result, in Somers's work, is an account of historical change in which class formation is driven not by the economy but by "the long-term consequences of the legal revolutions of medieval England." In fact, the economy itself is inseparable from notions of law and rights, and is not an autonomous entity. Somers's discussion opens the way for Biernacki's more direct assault on the idea of the separability of the economic from culture and politics—as he frames it, the specious separability of "practice" and "culture." Again, the general thrust is to supplant dualistic modes of thought. The other contributors also have valuable things to say about developing new notions of the economic, but I will exercise a foreword writer's prerogative in concentrating on Biernacki, since what he has to say lies at the heart of this book.

Biernacki certainly goes to the center of things in showing how the foundational concepts of class analysis are inseparable from culture. There is no more foundational concept than "labor." In developing his case he criticizes my work, among others, for talking of culture as if it were *of* or *for* work, instead of *in* work (if I may use this shorthand). Whether or not his charge is just, his exploration of the cultural definition of labor in Germany and England represents an advance of considerable magnitude. If there is any doubt among historians of the value of historical sociology, this contribution (and the book) should allay it: the account of how "labor" in Germany was materialized and embodied—and in England related to its product and to the effort expended in it—is very telling. These cultural constructions of labor are then seen to be involved in patterns of labor relations and trade union practice.

It is here that this contribution and the volume as a whole begin to suggest questions as well as answer them. A certain absence of the European tradition of politico-philosophical social analysis is forcibly felt. In this tradition, the object of study is subject to critical scrutiny, in the twin senses of the bodies of knowledge that analysis produces and the critique of power and social relations. In both senses, Foucault has been a pivotal figure. His work also signals possibilities for a series of self-reflexive intellectual procedures concerned with the constitution, on the one hand, of the concept of "the social" as an object of knowledge and, on the other, of the nature of "sociality" (through a concern with the creation of subjectivities). Among historians, a concern with class as an object of discursive practice has tended to concentrate on "discourse" rather than on "practice." A concentration on *both*, following Foucault, points to an understanding of "sociality" as well as "the social," and signals one purposeful way of linking practice and representation, "structure" and "action" (it is indeed one way of *transcending* these distinctions). Even if they lean more to discourse and representation than to practice and "social context," the historians' uses of what may be termed the "language of class" approach are suggestive (they receive some attention here, but not a great deal).[1] They point to the necessity of looking at the historical conditions in which discourses about classification emerge. These are very often framed in terms of "political" as opposed to "economic" conjunctures.

The understanding of "the economic" in this collection points to the importance of this concept for social class and simultaneously suggests the illusion of the economic as a sphere isolable from culture and politics. In drawing on historians' work, this understanding can in turn enrich it. But if, as my opening remarks suggest, social class without the economic is a contradiction in terms, it also follows that because the economic is not autonomous, its study opens onto the vast field of the modes and manners of human classification. Here the study of social class unreservedly aligns itself with the broad study of classification, as practiced by many disciplines from anthropology and literary criticism to philosophy (including the self-other classifying binary that informs poststructuralism and the philosophy of Jacques Derrida). The challenge then becomes thinking about the nature of "the economic" in new ways. It is a tribute to *Reworking Class* that this challenge can be taken up with renewed urgency and increased clarity. Responses to it surely lie in the dissolution of those boundaries between disciplines and traditions of thought that have for so long hindered our understanding of class and the nature of society.

Department of History
University of Manchester   *May 1996*

1. Patrick Joyce, ed., *The Oxford Reader on Class* (Oxford: Oxford University Press, 1995), sec. C, F.

Reworking Class

The Reworking of Class Analysis

John R. Hall

D URING THE CONSOLIDATION OF CAPITALIST SOCIETY OVER THE LAST TWO centuries, social theorists have debated the question of classes to the point where, in its modernist terms, the argument now seems exhausted. The once dominant Marxist theory that predicted a historically deci- sive struggle in the capitalist world between two classes—workers and owners—is widely recognized as inadequate. Yet abiding interests in issues of class continue unabated. So it is important to "rework" class analysis in ways that bear promise under new historical and intellectual conditions. That is the project of the present volume.

In this Introduction, I initiate this project by working as something of an underlaborer who frames a "neo-Weberian" and "institutionalist" way of construing class analysis in relation to the broader study of political economy. This is a self-conscious effort to claim for Max Weber a stronger relevance than is often recognized by contemporary political economists. As a reading of subsequent chapters in this volume will show, other inter- esting and fruitful directions of inquiry about class are emerging from

The research for this chapter was supported by the Graduate Research Council, University of California–Davis. I wish to thank Stephen P. Turner and the Committee on Conceptual and Terminological Analysis of the International Sociological Association for early support of the entire project, and Marc Steinberg, Sonya Rose, Christopher L. Tomlins, Fred Block, and the readers for Cornell University Press for thoughtful comments on earlier versions of this essay.

diverse sources, ranging from feminist studies to revisionist world-systems theory. In relation to this diversity, I do not claim some grand new synthesis. Instead, it is my thesis that a neo-Weberian institutionalist standpoint offers a useful alternative to synthesis, by thematizing the debates on class in a way that brings the most promising and diverse strands of class analysis into productive dialogue with one another.

The approach to classes I describe in this Introduction entails abandoning dialectical class conflict as the metanarrative that gives History its shape and meaning. To some people (e.g., Wood 1986), this may seem too high a cost for reworking class analysis. But the opposite is the case. Only by abandoning the myth of a bipolar class struggle can we hope to understand the socially constructed and historically contingent ways in which economic interests are articulated and pursued in the everyday capitalist world—through individual and collective action, within and beyond orientations of class. In turn, because class analysis has been a mainstay of both radical and "mainstream" sociohistorical inquiry, reworking class analysis can have broader ramifications: it amounts to a prototype for a more general rethinking of inquiry in the wake of recent critical-theoretical, cultural, and poststructuralist challenges.

The revolutions that have swept across the intellectual world during the late twentieth century establish new conditions for sociohistorical inquiry. Three great modern models must now be transcended: (1) historicism that avoids social theory altogether, (2) universal history that arranges history in relation to a master theory, and (3) the theoretical formalism that undergirds the social sciences in their positivist (and now postpositivist) vein. On the one hand, no understanding of history is "theory free"; on the other hand, neither "classes" nor any other theoretical construct can any longer be conceived as a "structure" in its own terms, constituted as either a historical subject—"the" engine of history—or a theoretical representation of "objective" empirical dynamics. Instead, the relation is far more complex. As Patrick Joyce (1995) puts it, "the 'social' is itself a 'discursive' product of history." This would include the social production of theory.

What then will be left of class as a concept? In a postpositivist world, in the absence of compelling evidence, we no longer can presume to "represent" social phenomena "objectively," that is, in a way that captures some supposedly essential dynamic of classes. Nevertheless, it still seems possible to analyze classes on the basis of rigorous theoretical distinctions that speak to issues of social significance. I pursue this possibility in the remainder of this Introduction by elaborating a neo-Weberian strategy for reworking class analysis, beginning by briefly sketching the (1) historical and (2) intellectual developments that have undermined modernist class analysis. I then (3) locate the reworking of class analysis within a broader neo-Weberian practice of political economy. In this reworking, I define class in relation to social actors' shared interests in economic markets, and I sketch how these class interests come to be structured by:

- institutional and cultural patterns of market formations,
- extramarket processes that directly affect how markets operate, and
- broader organizational and interorganizational political-economic formations.

This introductory orientation opens out toward subsequent chapters that address three broad issues of class analysis: questions about how we conceptualize classes and class relations, considered in Part I; how cultural, historical, and institutional processes construct class identities, the focus of Part II; and the conditions of class mobilization, taken up in Part III. As befits inquiry at the beginning of the third millennium, the boundaries among the three parts of the book are blurred; each chapter spills beyond its textual location by addressing questions that connect with other chapters.

The focus on theoretical puzzles about class conceptualization, identity formation, and mobilization is meant to inspire further research on historical and contemporary class developments on a global basis. Nevertheless, there is an important caveat: it is beyond the scope of the present project to offer a comprehensive analysis of world, national, or regional class formations. The collection is shaped by its contributors' interests and expertise, and the majority of chapters are centrally concerned with industrialized nations in the West. Other regions of the global capitalist economy are considered most directly in two chapters: Dale Tomich's reexamination of labor forms in the world economy, and J. Craig Jenkins and Kevin Leicht's chapter on the differential prospects of class-based social movements in the industrial West versus former state socialist, newly industrializing, and third-world countries. Because class processes are structured in part by international trade and power relations, and indeed, because whole new economic formations may emerge from developments centered outside the West, it is my hope that future empirical research analyzing class processes, not only in the West but globally and in nonwestern regions of the world economy, will benefit from the approaches to class analysis developed here.

The End of Class as a Historical Subject

In some quarters, a world-historical dynamic of class relations is still considered the central engine that organizes and changes the fundamental conditions of social life. But in the course of the twentieth century, this view has become less and less tenable. Over the past half-century, the political left largely abandoned either economistic Marxism or any narrow thesis anticipating a proletarian revolution, and in recent years the ideologues of capitalism have pointed to the failed communist regimes as exemplars of societal dystopia on a monumental scale.

The developments on the ground that challenge the adequacy of a class-ordered model of contemporary society are diverse and well known. On the economic front in industrialized societies, working-class radicalism has been largely blunted; labor-management conflict has become increasingly institutionalized; and a capital-financed mass-media culture has overwhelmed any authentic working-class culture in most countries. Claims about the structuration of classes in an industrial organization of production have become increasingly confounded by a broad tendency long linked with modernization (and now postmodernization), namely, *differentiation* in the social organization of both production and consumption (Berger, Berger, and Kellner 1973; Kumar 1978; Schluchter 1981, 70–77; 1989, 73–78). When the consequences of differentiation driven by technological innovation are identified as a qualitative change rather than an incremental process, the result is something like Daniel Bell's (1973) thesis about the rise of *postindustrial society*, marked by emerging new classes and the growing importance of cross-cutting "situses" (institutional sectors like business, government, health care, education, and the military). Initially, class analysts mostly opposed Bell's thesis, though now it seems almost prophetic. Even so, the postindustrial and "new class" studies of the 1970s and 1980s that sought to account for the emergence of highly skilled and relatively successful occupational groups are now challenged by unforeseen empirical developments. Economies of the advanced societies increasingly undergo dramatic *reorganizations of production*, marked by deindustrialization, "downsizing" of large firms and the proliferation of small firms, the rise of de-skilled service businesses, and "post-Fordist" decentralized and demand-driven production (often of services or hybrid service products, rather than mass-produced objects). More and more, the new economic arrangements employ a "flexible" (read part-time and occupationally unstable) workforce (Myles and Turegun 1994). During the same time period, capitalist markets and commodity flows have continued to become subjected to *global integration*. In turn, new *global forms of production* connect core and periphery nation-states via commodity chains and highly differentiated trade networks (Gereffi 1989) that change the circumstances of labor around the world.

On the side of consumption, the *commodification of experience* and the relentless extension of ever more differentiated products into the final activities of consumption (e.g., convenience foods, VCRs, and personal computers) have reorganized the fabric of everyday life. In turn, the experiential expansion of consumption (Hall and Neitz 1993, chap. 5) has amplified the already salient issue of *consumption as a class interest*—for example, in product quality, product liability and other consumer rights movements.

Apart from purely economic considerations, it has become obvious that class mobilizations and political struggles cannot be presumed to follow neatly from "objectively" shared class situations—either at present or in the past. Instead, as Craig Calhoun (1982) shows for the early phases of industrialization in England, and as Ronald Aminzade (1993) shows for Republican politics in three nineteenth-century French cities, the relationships of industrialization's structurations of classes to political mobilization have been contingent, complex, and often theoretically perverse. Indeed, social movements based in self-conscious class have not necessarily had emancipatory consequences. As Randall Collins (1986, 127) evidences on a general basis and as William Brustein (Chapter 10) shows by analyzing who joined the Nazi Party in Weimar Germany, workers are not always unified in their interests, nor are their interests always at odds with those of their employers. Today, direct class actions—organizing campaigns, strikes, boycotts, union shop elections—continue to be undertaken, and union organizations project a new dynamism, but at least in the United States, unions have lost much of their membership and their moral appeal as the representatives of a broader social class. Under these circumstances, some scholars seriously debate whether we have arrived at the *end of class political mobilization* (Clark and Lipset 1991; Hout, Brooks, and Manza 1993; Pakulski 1993; Clark, Lipset, and Rempel 1993).

However, any conclusion about class mobilization seems premature; rather, it seems that the conditions and processes have shifted. As George Steinmetz shows for Germany today (see Chapter 11), a post-Fordist regime of production significantly changes the calculus of political mobilization, in the case at hand, for proletarians moving to the far right. More generally, Craig Jenkins and Kevin Leicht argue in Chapter 12 that globalized production has shifted the circumstances whereby social actors' experiences in class situations translate (or fail to translate) into class-based social movements. In developed capitalist countries, the fault lines fragment old class loyalties by "new class" and "new right" emergences, whereas in third-world and state-socialist societies, rapid industrialization tied to repressive state regimes has tended to increase labor militancy.

Beyond the question of political mobilization, the collapse of the Soviet Union and other Cold War era socialist states marks the probable *end of communism as a world-historical social movement*, and the collapse has unleashed deep crises of nationalism in Eastern Europe and the former Soviet Union. These crises, together with ethnic conflicts over economic issues in other parts of the world, are strong evidence that social organization has not completely shifted from primordial and particularistic ties to the rationalized, universalistic social relations—including class relations—anticipated by modern theories. *"Modernization" has been uneven, incomplete, and fragile.* This circumstance is salient in the economic sphere because *markets are incompletely autonomous.* From one direction, surviving socialist states (China, Cuba) have modified their planned economies by incorporating market mechanisms. But the opposite tendency is also important: capitalist economies are extensively planned, not organized solely by some "hidden hand" of the "free market." Indeed, we had best acknowledge an old historical lesson: capitalism as an economic form can operate in a wide variety of state contexts. In the contemporary situation, alliances between states and the economic enterprises operating within their boundaries are sometimes best understood as coordinated ventures of political capitalism.

All in all, acknowledging the contemporary capitalist transformations, the collapse of the world-historical communist movement, the semi-marketization of ideologically communist states, and the extra-economic structurings of economies yields a straightforward conclusion: capitalist and state-capitalist organizations operating in relation to incompletely rational economic markets are likely to be the central structures of economic activity for the foreseeable future. It is to an understanding of the dynamics of classes under these conditions that research on the contemporary situation ought to be directed. In turn, our awareness of contemporary complexities ought to raise questions about how to understand the past. Despite some lingering nostalgia for a neat theory of history, treating capitalist development as a teleological materialistic dialectic is rapidly being overtaken by a recognition that the world is unevenly pocked with social struggles over material and ideal, social and cultural interests that do not always look like the surface manifestations of a dialectical class struggle.

The Deconstruction of Class as a Theoretical Object

The present (but not necessarily ultimate) historical realities mean that the future of class analysis has slipped off the charts of radical social theory, along with any self-assurance about how to use class analysis to understand the past. The simple truths are: that many scholars sympathetic to Marxist analysis (for example, Sewell 1993) now question the adequacy of a materialist history of class conflict, that social theory with emancipatory interests is no longer well served by invoking a Marxism predicated on an industrial capitalist mode of production, and that value commitments of intellectuals to workers and the improvement of their conditions no longer yield any single point of departure for class analysis. The long-awaited world-historical communist revolution predicted by Marx a century and a half ago seems ephemeral, a cohesive working class seems highly implausible as the vanguard of social change, and for the near term, political economies are likely to be ordered by the market and organizational dynamics of broadly capitalist society. It is time to bring our practices of conceptualization into alignment with our sense of past historical complexity and future historical possibilities.

To pursue this task I first briefly review intellectual developments that have led to the deconstruction of class as a theoretical object. These developments are connected to a wider postmodern shift of knowledge, signaled especially by Jacques Derrida's practice of deconstruction and by feminist critiques of scientism (e.g., Alcoff and Potter 1993). Without repeating the wider critiques here, certain implications for class analysis can be identified, namely, that "class," like any other concept, is a *social construct* used to describe aspects of the social world. As Max Weber argued long ago, whatever ontological status we grant to social reality in some down-to-earth way, efforts to characterize reality always involve choices of "cultural significance" that cannot be derived directly from the "nature" of phenomena (Hall, forthcoming, chap. 2). Weber, in short, evidenced deconstructionist sensibilities before the word. Social constructionist and deconstructionist perspectives remain controversial because they often are taken to imply that we lack the capacity to create objective knowledge about the social world. But rather than rejecting them out of hand, we are better served if we pursue Weber's thesis about cultural significance by investigating specific historical and intellectual constructions of class and asking how they shape inquiry. As Michael Donnelly shows in Chapter 3, basic ideas about class vary by national context, and they are informed in part by official statistical indices, sometimes constructed on the basis of issues distant from political economy. On a different front, in Chapter 8, John Walton's study of the fishing industry of Monterey, California, shows how class as a meaningful interpretation of history lives—or dies —in socially organized popular memory. Overall, social constructionist analyses fortify the long-standing call of critical theory to abandon any "objective" conception of class as either (1) an independent structure identified by formal theory, or (2) a historical Subject that gives to historical inquiry its central metanarrative (cf. Benhabib 1986).

The challenge is substantial. Both formal social theories (Marxism, structural-functionalism, positivist approaches to stratification) as well as the sort of history championed by E. P. Thompson (1963) have been central to modern class analysis in the post–World War II era. Epistemologically these approaches are founded—for example, in the contention between Thompson (1978) and Louis Althusser—on the assumption of a *division* between history and theory. Thompson (1963, 10–11) rejected structuralist theorizing, warning against "a static view of class" and emphasizing that "class is a relationship, not a thing." *The Making of the English Working Class* thus describes class as a cultural achievement of a living historical community. As an avatar of the new left, Thompson succeeded politically at breaking with Third-International Marxism and intellectually at avoiding the sort of universal history that would write class conflict from an already theorized dialectic. Unfortunately, however, Thompson's study, although brilliant and inspirational, is a product of the intellectual bifurcation that dominated its era. His admonitions against structuralism invoke a deep historicism that comes close to denying the utility of any analytic constructs and thus deepens the gulf between history and theory. In its repression of theory, Thompson's historicism thus offers no help in sorting through the alternative conceptual approaches to class analysis, even though his critique of theoreticism is a useful antidote to theoretical reification.

The two modes of inquiry, historical and theoretical, now face parallel challenges. On the one hand, especially with the decline of the working class in the most economically developed nation-states, the subject and metanarrative of labor history have become increasingly matters of dispute (Lembcke 1995). On the other hand, class theory, particularly in its structuralist variants, is subject to poststructuralist critique because of its inability to incorporate understandings of historicity, culture, agency, and social difference. To come to terms with these challenges, it is necessary to avoid the twin modernisms—the Charybdis of historicism and the Scylla of reified formal theory. We need to acknowledge the role of theory in providing language that makes analytic discussion of classes possible, yet account for classes in their historicities.

The journey to theorizing the historicity of class dynamics, I believe, can be more effectively guided by developing better analytic markers of theory than by trying to steer through the shifting whirlpools of class histories. In this Introduction I therefore take a theoretical tack. Specifically, I first show that Marxist and other structuralist conceptualizations of class share theoretical assumptions of "structural holism." These assumptions, of course, are precisely the object of poststructuralist critique, which identifies slippage between the empirical world and any "structures" presumed to undergird or represent it. In the remainder of the Introduction, I sketch an alternative, neo-Weberian approach that substitutes "action" for "structure." This approach acknowledges that any conceptualization is a cultural construction; it conceptualizes classes as something other than elements of a totalized structure; and it emphasizes the meaningful and

discursive bases of social action and organization that themselves yield
socially constructed meanings of class in unfolding social life. This tack
keeps sight of poststructuralist and deconstructionist critiques yet avoids
the extreme postmodern notion that we are lost in a morass of floating
signifiers, incapable of analyzing the world in which we live.

In central ways, modern class analysis traces to Marx. But Marx was
notoriously brief about directly conceptualizing class. In *The Eighteenth
Brumaire of Louis Bonaparte*, he wrote, "insofar as millions of families live
under economic conditions of existence that divide their mode of life,
their interests and their culture from those of the other classes, and put
them in hostile contrast to the latter, they form a class" (Marx 1978 [1852],
608). Later, in the third volume of *Capital*, Marx identified "the three big
classes of modern society based on the capitalist mode of production" to
be "the owners merely of labour-power, owners of capital, and landowners, whose respective sources of income are wages, profit and ground-
rent, in other words, wage-labourers, capitalists and landowners." When
discussing England—the paragon of capitalist development of his day,
Marx noted, "even here the stratification of classes does not appear in
its pure form" (1978 [1887], 441). In Chapter 2 of the present volume,
Margaret Somers shows that conceptually pure "denarrativized" Marxist concepts of class have bedeviled debates on class by drawing reality
into question for failing to conform to theory, and she proposes an alternative methodology for exploring English working-class formation in
terms of "narrative identities" and "relational settings." Somers thus boldly
breaks with any overarching construct of "society" or any structuralist
concept of "class," and thereby finesses dilemmas created by modernist
"correspondence" approaches to concept formation. But in his day, Marx
had written off any problematic relation between concepts and empirical reality as "immaterial" because of what he described as a "continual
tendency and law of development" toward divisions between labor, capital and capitalist landed property "corresponding to the capitalist mode
of production." It was at this point in the text, however, that the abyss
opened up for Marx: he acknowledged that the interests of the three great
classes could become divided based on interests deriving from more differentiated sources of income among laborers, capitalists, and landowners. Precisely where Marx (1978, 442) saw the empirical possibility "of
the infinite fragmentation of interest and rank," we find the editor's enig-
matic note: "here the manuscript breaks off."

Two characteristics of Marx's formulation are reflected in a wide range of subsequent scholarship, Marxist and otherwise. First, Marx treated classes as historically emergent *groups* with bases in the objective character of capitalism; although he recognized the existence of "intermediate strata," he dismissed this empirical circumstance as "immaterial" on the presumption of a developmental tendency toward a "pure form" of capitalism. Second, in describing "the infinite fragmentation of interest and rank into which the division of social labor splits" class groups, Marx invoked a conception of the division of labor as an integrated *totality* of positions and ranks. These two presuppositions—about bounded class groups and the division of labor as an organic totality—are foundational metaphors that have shaped a wide range of modernist approaches to class. On the one hand, historicist versions of them give the history of classes its Subject, its metanarrative about a moral material struggle that transcends and gives meaning to the flux of empirical phenomena. On the other hand, for Marxist social theorists, the holistic constructs variously termed the "class system" or the "class structure" focus debate on a constructed object of analysis, namely, the structure of the theorized totality, its subdivisions, and their character and interrelations. Of course, not all Marxist theorizing is structuralist. John Roemer (1982) and Jon Elster (1985), for example, embrace the Marxist commitment to theorizing exploitation under a thesis of historical materialism while employing more Weberian analytic strategies of methodological individualism. But overall, totality is a strong motif in the alternation between Marxist class theory and Marxist historicism (Sayer 1987).

Conversely, structuralism has not dominated Marxism alone. It has also served as a foundational assumption in modern social science alternatives to Marxism concerned with "socioeconomic status" (SES). By this construct, modern sociologists deemphasized individuals' interests based on their class situations and emphasized their economic interests in occupational mobility and their political interests in an "open" occupational structure. Thus, structural-functionalists Kingsley Davis and Wilbert Moore (1945) conceptualized the stratification system as a totality, but in place of the Marxist thesis of class conflict, they proposed that socially unequal rewards for work function to sustain an overall division of labor by efficiently allocating skills to systemic needs. Other sociologists developed the metaphor of stratification as a structural totality in the direction of statistical description, conceived as a matrix of individuals in a hierarchical framework of positions. Their studies of socioeconomic status, occupational prestige, and social mobility (Duncan 1961; Blau and Duncan 1967) and related Wisconsin-school studies of status attainment (Sewell and Hauser 1972) depend, explicitly or implicitly, on the assumption that stratification has a "structure" that locates all occupational positions within it.[1] Thus, Robert Hodge and his collaborators (1966) and Peter Blau and Otis Dudley Duncan (1967) talk of "the occupational structure," and W. G. Runciman (1974)—perhaps borrowing a Parsonian metaphor—posits a "stratification system." The criticism that Patrick Horan (1978) advances about status-attainment research has a broader relevance: models of stratification share an intellectual heritage in one or another structural-functionalist conception of a bounded theoretical object. Questions about individual positions and careers thus became isolated from issues of family circumstance that more recently have been theorized in relation to class by Heidi Hartman (1981) and Annemette Sørensen (1994). Moreover, stratification analysis represses questions about whether individuals in various occupational positions have shared economic interests and about how those interests are contextually shaped or played out in collective action.

Since the 1970s, a number of neo-Marxist theorists have challenged SES approaches that downplay class divisions. However, many of these formulations were based on structuralist assumptions, the subject of strong critique from a socialist perspective (Connell 1979). In slightly different ways, Louis Althusser and Etienne Balibar (1970), and more substantively Nicos Poulantzas (1975), worked toward incorporating class within a more encompassing theorized totality. Other revisions of Marx have sought to analyze empirical diversity—especially of "new" classes, while maintaining the class structure as a totality of relationships among class positions. The most developed effort—the typology developed by Erik Olin Wright (1985, 88)—identifies twelve class positions that are differentiated by (1) ownership of the means of production, (2) "organizational assets"—the individual's authority over a span of organized production, and (3) for nonowners (wage laborers), "skill" and/or "credential" assets. Owners are divided into the bour-

---

1. Some of these approaches, e.g., Blau and Duncan 1967, 5–6, incorporated Weberian ideas about status groups—transformed into "prestige strata." But insofar as the shift from "status groups" to "prestige strata" created an "objective," as opposed to social, measure of prestige, it relocated Weber's ideas within an alien framework.

geoisie, small employers, and the petty bourgeoisie. Nonowner positions are theorized in a three-by-three typology that ranges from the high-skill, high-organizational-assets position of expert managers to low-skill, low-organizational-assets proletarians.

More than one commentator (e.g., Waters 1991) has suggested that because Wright incorporates skill and credential assets best defined as market capacities and organizational resources, he shifts from Marxism toward an alternative, Weberian approach to class analysis. At the least, it seems to me, Wright tries to inoculate neo-Marxism against Weber by incorporating Weberian themes within a structuralist Marxist edifice. But in Chapter 1 of this volume, Wright refuses "the Weberian temptation," partly because he argues that a Weberian approach would not place exploitation of labor at the center of class analysis, and partly because he remains committed to a structuralist approach to concept formation and a Marxist theory of history. These are issues that I engage below, by suggesting how exploitation within organizations can be theorized from a Weberian as well as a Marxian framework. But for his part, Wright is unwavering in his intellectual commitment: he affirms a theoretical structuralism in the styles of Althusser and Poulantzas that yields a Marxian alternative to a conventional sociology of occupational structure, mobility, and status attainment (Kamolnick 1988).

Other scholars also remain resolutely Marxist in their commitments to theorizing capitalism as a totality, but in new ways. Perhaps the most promising recent effort is that of Moishe Postone, who identifies not class conflict but a historically specific form of labor as the central mediating relationship of capitalism. Postone (1993, e.g., 314–24) locates class conflict within capitalism in conflicts over wages, job security, and conditions of work, but he disputes the supposed historically transformative role of the working class.

The centrality of structuralism is also evidenced both by ambivalent stances and by rejections of it. In the ambivalent vein, Immanuel Wallerstein (1979) shifted away from the Marxist analysis of class conflicts in relation to modes of production, and toward a historical analysis of markets in a world economy. Yet this move imposed a holistic world-system theory on more complex events (Hall 1984, 1991). The substance of the theory shifted, but its logic remained structuralist. In Chapter 9 of the present volume, Dale Tomich suggests how to transcend both Wallerstein and critic Robert Brenner by totalizing neither wage relations nor market positions in a world system; like Weber (1978, 125–38, 165–66), Tomich emphasizes that wage labor is only one possible basis of labor exploitation in capitalist profit seeking, but Tomich moves beyond Weber's nationalistic and modern Western frame by emphasizing the emergent, postindustrial global interdependences of wage and non-wage labor that link differentially developed regions of the world economy.

As for rejections of structuralism, they force the question of what it might mean to theorize about class. Some of the most promising scholarship in the past quarter century recognizes the limitations of a theoreticist "reading off" of class formation from objective structures, yet proceeds differently than the pure historicism of Thompson. Thus, in the late 1970s, Adam Przeworski (1985) theorized an important opening for comparative histories by showing how two key historical processes of capitalist development—the separating of workers from control over the means of production, and the processes of proletarianization that organize workers' locations within production—have separate trajectories that cannot be derived from capitalism as a totality, and thus are theoretically "indeterminate" and historically contingent. In tandem with this move, other scholars have displaced social theory in favor of conceptual thematization and comparative historical explanation. Thus, Charles Tilly sidesteps the explication of class as a concept, yet identifies "capital concentration" and "proletarianization" as the "twin processes" that "were transforming the organization and interests of most groups in western Europe from 1750 to 1914" (1981, 17–18). Similarly, Ira Katznelson (1986, 14) shifts from theorizing capitalism as a totality to designating four "layers" of class—"structures, ways of life, dispositions, and collective action"; this approach yields a rich set of questions for historical and comparative analysis of class formations—for example, in relation to nation-states (Katznelson and Zolberg 1986), concerning tensions between working class and social identities of male workers (Halle 1984), and in the existential circumstances of class solidarity (Fantasia 1988). These studies offer deep substantive understandings of classes and their contexts. But because they display a discomfort with Marxist structuralist theorizing, they implicitly raise the question of how to build up alternative forms of theorizing rather than resorting to empiricism.

Indeed, in some quarters structuralism has become so identified with theory that efforts to break away from it have tended to eclipse class theory altogether, and shifted inquiry on classes to a radicalized program of discourse analysis and cultural studies (cf. Becker 1989). Certain observers (Wood 1986; Palmer 1990) assail these developments as the substitution of wishful and fuzzy thinking for any serious emancipatory project. But these judgments seem premature, narrow-mindedly doctrinaire, and defensive. Radical endeavors are now being renewed both politically—by aligning workers' interests with feminism, struggles for ethnic equality, environmental movements, and other wellsprings of progressive change, and theoretically—by establishing new analytic practices. Thus, "post-Marxists" Ernesto Laclau and Chantal Mouffe (1985) have promoted a radical politics that no longer privileges class in relation to gender, ethnicity, and other bases of inequality, and which emphasizes the role of discourse and subjectivity in forging political mobilization. The latter approach has been further developed, among others, by Marc Steinberg (1991), who critiques the discursive turns of Gareth Stedman Jones and Joan Scott in order to bring a less structuralist and more processual discourse analysis to the study of class formation.

The recent contingently historical and discursive analyses of classes are promising, precisely because they disavow what Jan Pakulski (1993, 282) identifies as key features of "the Marxist conceptual and theoretical tradition," namely, (1) "economic determinism," (2) "structural determinism and the assumption of necessary correspondence" between socioeconomic inequality and culture, consciousness and identity, and (3) the "logic of capitalism" argument. But there is a cost to the historical and discursive turns. When Pakulski's three features of Marxism are abandoned, the problem is how to theorize about class at all. Avoiding totalizing and essentializing elements of Marxist theory runs the risk of rejecting the practice of political economy in favor of (1) an atheoretical historicism, (2) discursivism, (3) the search for a metanarrative that grips many labor historians of our day, (4) an undertheorized comparative historical sociology, or (5) an alternative semiotic theoretical totalization—of signs—to be substituted for the former totalization of class structure. Because Marxist theory has been so resolutely structuralist, its practitioners have not responded very effectively to the challenge of how to theorize in nonstructuralist ways. The reactions against structuralist theory have tended to discredit theory altogether, and thus to undermine any theoretically coherent conceptualization of class and, by extension, any theoretically informed practice of political economy.

Reworking Class into an Institutionalist Political Economy

Overall, the conjuncture of events on the ground and intellectual debates undermines the persuasiveness of a structuralist conceptualization of class, but without yielding any theoretically coherent alternative. The challenge is to work up an alternative theorization of classes in relation to a broader project of political economy. The approach that I propose here is neo-Weberian and institutionalist. By invoking institutionalism, I mean to emphasize how practices that become socially established structure ever new conditions under which individual and group class meanings, interests, and actions develop (cf. Friedland and Alford 1991). Given its focus on historically emergent and culturally specified phenomena, an institutionalist approach cannot presume to totalize social structure or class structure as its proxy. Institutionalist analysis, in other words, denies any supposedly necessary relations between class positions and interests and a dynamic of social change driven by class conflict.

But how, then, can classes be conceptualized at all? I submit that a neo-Weberian approach yields a conceptualization of classes appropriate to institutionalist analysis. I use the term "neo-Weberian" with some hesitation, first because some scholars (Jones 1976, 301–3; Przeworski 1985, 64; Katznelson 1986, 5) do little more than caricature Weber in ways that amplify misunderstandings of his approach to class, and second because some Weberian approaches to stratification (e.g., Parkin 1979) leave the approach incompletely developed, while other approaches borrow Weberian categories of class to analyze a posited "occupational" or "class structure" of the sort that I have already criticized. Indeed, some characterizations of studies as neo-Weberian are refused by their authors (Erikson and Goldthorpe 1992, 37). The Weber relevant to class analysis is better located within an agenda of political economy deeply shared with Marx (Sayer 1991). Sketching a neo-Weberian institutionalist approach is a step in this direction.

Rather than trying to explain "class structure" as an autonomous theorized object, the neo-Weberian approach shifts from materialistic causality to a sociology predicated on meaningful action. This approach identifies "cultural structures" (Hall 1988) of capitalist organization as the contexts of economically interested action in general, and class action in particular. It theorizes the historical interplays of class actions with gender, ethnicity, and other bases of social inequality, and it investigates how these processes occur within complex, differentiated organizational and extraorganizational fields, power complexes, and state formations, on the basis of culturally available embedded and emergent patterns of meaning. This Weberian political economy can take as its point of departure the well-known reinterpretation of Weber on class offered by Anthony Giddens in the 1970s (1971, 163–65).

Since Giddens, Weber's emphasis on *market interests* as defining bases of classes has become widely recognized as an alternative to a Marxist definition of classes tied to modes of production (e.g., Poulantzas 1975; Hindess and Hirst 1975). Weber's concepts are based on a "methodological individualism" that acknowledges the relationships between social arrangements and the actions of individuals. Weber also held to a broadly neo–Kantian recognition that concepts are shaped by issues of cultural significance. Yet despite his presciently postmodern sense about the perspectival character of concepts, Weber sought to examine "structural" features of social formations, including their cultures, in a macro-comparative fashion. Thus his dilemma: because he repudiated organicism, Weber needed to reconcile structural analysis with methodologically individualist and culturally perspectivist strategies of concept formation. The study of classes raised the dilemma in a particularly acute way. To discuss "class" in any systemic terms would seem tantamount to assuming the existence of a totality that structures the orientations of individuals and groups—thus exceeding the bounds of Weber's antiorganicist methodological individualism. Weber resolved the issue in different ways at different stages of writing his magnum opus, *Economy and Society*. Late in his life, he supplemented his earlier "situational" conceptualization of classes with a more objectively constructed classification.

The earlier approach to class, contained in part 2 of *Economy and Society*, hinges on identifying a class on the basis of circumstances in which "a number of people have in common a specific causal component of their life chances," based on shared economic interests in relation to a particular *market*, whether that market be concerned with commodities or labor. (Life chances also may be affected by many other than purely economic circumstances.) So far as class situations are concerned, the distribution of *property* is the central defining fact. Those who possess property have far greater flexibility by virtue of their access to "profitable deals" and their capacities to play the market, whereas the propertyless "have nothing to offer but their labor or the resulting products, and . . . are compelled to get rid of these products in order to subsist at all" (Weber 1978, 927). Possession of property (and wealth more generally) is a gradient, of course, but at any given level of entry into a market, whether it be for real estate, commodities, jobs, education, or whatever, individuals who lack sufficient resources simply are unable to participate.

It is the hard reality of differential purchasing capacities in the face of prices that undergirds William Reddy's intriguing analysis in *Money and Liberty in Modern Europe* (1987) of "monetary exchange asymmetry" between the rich and the poor. Unfortunately, Reddy is so antagonistic toward analytic distinctions about classes that he fails to theorize the types of exchange that his analysis suggests. To do so, he would do well to return to Weber, who shows that the basic distinction between the propertied and the propertyless can be further differentiated by the kinds of property or services they have available to use in making money. "The propertied, for instance, may belong to the class of rentiers or to the class of entrepreneurs." Weber ties this distinction to a "generic connotation of the concept of class": "that the kind of chance in the *market* is the decisive moment which presents a common condition for the individual's fate. Class situation is, in this sense, ultimately market situation" (1978, 928). In other words, the kind of property—e.g., commodity, capital, factory, livestock, land, slaves, labor, etc.—distinguishes heterogeneous class situations that arise in distinct markets (cf. Giddens 1971, 165).

Emphasizing the existential moment of facing the market as defining class situation suggests that (1) a given person may orient action toward more than one market and hence may face multiple, potentially reinforcing or incongruent class situations at different moments in his or her life; (2) a shared class situation does not translate directly into common interest, much less into collective action (thus, Weber warned, "to treat 'class' conceptually as being equivalent to 'group' leads to distortion"); and (3) cultural conditions rather than objective circumstances alone affect whether individuals jointly perceive their situations as deriving from a common external cause (Weber 1978, 927–32). Given the open-ended possibilities, Weber wrote, "not much of a general nature can be said about the more specific kinds of antagonism between classes (in our meaning of the term)." Only "at a cost of some precision" would it be possible to discuss large-scale historical shifts in predominant forms of class struggle—in Weber's day, "toward wage disputes on the labor market" (1978, 930–31).

Toward the end of his life, in what is now part 1 of *Economy and Society*, Weber streamlined his treatment of classes.[2] He retained the individual's "situation" as the basis of class, and, *contra* Marx, he refused to theorize a holistic, long-term developmental dynamic of class conflicts. But Weber (1978, 302) now defined "class situation" in less existential terms, as "the typical probability of (1) procuring goods, (2) gaining a position in life, and (3) finding inner satisfactions, a probability which derives from the relative control over goods and skills and from their income-producing uses within a given economic order." He also presented a new, more "objective," categorization of (1) property classes, (2) commercial classes, and (3) social classes.

Social classes represented the most substantial change from Weber's earlier formulation. A class of this type he defined as making up "the totality of those class situations within which individual and generational mobility is easy and typical." As examples, Weber listed the working class, the petty bourgeoisie, "the propertyless intelligentsia and specialists," and "the classes privileged through property and education" (1978, 305). Social classes, in this formulation, have historical existences, but they are not predicated in any straightforward way on a given mode of production, since ethnic and racial distinctions, social constructions of gender, education, occupational mobility, religion, and other phenomena that shape rigid or diffuse boundaries among social classes and their cultures may not have a solely economic basis. In effect, the concept of social class identified a potential for the formation of class-based status groups that have deeper connections to cultural, educational, neighborhood, and community solidarities and distinctions than do purely self-interested economic classes (Weber 1978, 307; Collins 1986, 127–29). This social-class formulation aligns well with Marxist conceptions that emphasize classes as historically formed and relatively enduring (but not always politically class-conscious) social groups (e.g., Thompson 1963). Both enterprises shift away from the search for a totalized structure of class locations that is presumed to be predictive of class interests, and toward the analysis of contingent class situations and

---

2. The reasons for this shift are open to debate. Wolfgang Schluchter (1989, 462) holds that the two parts of *Economy and Society* are "two mutually independent drafts." Yet he does not discuss why Weber made significant emendations. Guenther Roth (1988–89, 145) argues that Weber's shift embraced the "new objectivity" popular at the time; it was a "continuation of his political war with other means."

actions. But Weber refused historicism, instead formulating a conceptual apparatus for class analysis. In particular, he underscored the difference between *social* class situations—grouped by ease of social mobility—and *economic* class situations—defined by markets or property.[3] Three important points about this formulation underscore the alternative that Weber offers to Marxist conceptions of classes. They have to do with (1) Weber's approach to markets, (2) his way of linking classes to institutional arrangements of political economy, and (3) the economic aspects of extramarket social relations. I will take up each in turn.

Classes and the Heterogeneity of Markets

Despite his late objectivist turn, Weber continued to tie class interests to social actors' situations in relation to specific markets. If this logic is pursued with some vigor, it yields a conceptualization of class that avoids the deterministic and reductionist difficulties of totalized approaches. The key difference lies in how Weber construed markets. A "modern market economy," in Weber's formulation, "essentially consists in a complete network of exchange contracts, that is, in deliberate planned acquisitions of powers of control and disposal" (1978, 67). Within a market economy, the " 'market situation' for any object of exchange" is defined as "all the opportunities of exchanging it [the object] for money which are known to the participants in exchange relationships and aid their orientation in the competitive price struggle" (1978, 82). This approach neither reduces classes to strata of occupational positions with posited similar interests nor assumes an overall matrix of class interests, relations, or structure in relation to production. Instead, Weber's formulation allows for the possibility that there will be multiple "objects of exchange" (labor, credit, commodities, and so on) and multiple and heterogeneous markets around which class interests arise.

Class interests, for instance, come into play in a small factory town owned by a lumber company, where one large employer is pitted in the

---

3. In an interesting review of the theoretical issues, Barry Barnes (1995, 188–89) argues that class reduces to a form of status group, and therefore that its use "as a key *theoretical* concept should be discontinued." There is something to this argument so far as *social* class is concerned. But Barnes (174–75) presumes a binary opposition between an interest-based model of economic class mobilization and an interactional model of social class mobilization. Thus, in my view, his analysis does not give enough consideration to the reflexive and interactional aspects of economic classes that I sketch below, and therefore prematurely dismisses the status of class as a theoretical concept.

labor market against a relatively solidary community. Here, on the one hand, the position of workers in the *labor market* is undermined both by the company's ability to seek sources of labor outside the community and by the near monopoly that the company holds on opportunities in the labor market in the town. On the other hand, the capacity of workers to exact concessions also derives from market position. Specifically, the company has a fixed investment in a particular mill, and a solidary community of workers may be able constrain market availability of labor by strikes, picket lines, and other interventions. But there are other class interests in play as well. The enterprise that owns the lumber mill must attend to competitive struggles in *commodity markets* for raw and milled lumber. For their parts, mill workers, along with other individuals outside that particular labor market, may share class interests as participants in retail consumer markets, or as owners of real estate, stocks, retirement fund investments, and so forth.

This conceptualization of class has several obvious implications.

First, individuals are not *members* of a class; they *engage* in various class *actions*—both individually and collectively, in everyday life and in relation to extraordinary events, and not just in relation to production and occupations. In these acts, individuals may have multiple, overlapping, sometimes contradictory, sometimes reinforcing interests based on their participation in multiple, heterogeneous markets. Second, as scholars such as Przeworski (1985) argue, the play of class interests in any market situation is historically contingent, in part on developments that lie outside the market arena proper. (For instance, with the recent emergence of ethanol as a fuel, the class interests of petroleum producers and refiners have become pitted against those of farmers growing corn used to produce ethanol—a class conflict that had no previous basis.) Third, given the multiplicity of individuals' interests at stake in multiple markets, the empirical play of class alliances and interests can be expected to range from ongoing local class struggles that are the stuff of everyday economic activity to much more unusual occasions in which a broad range of unified and opposed interests come to a head in "political" events that break out of any institutionalized framework. Fourth, not all class action necessarily involves direct conflict; instead, a cohesive class group may pursue its interests by taking actions that are not necessarily the target of opposition yet that have the potential of becoming institutionalized class advantages—for example, restricting access to a market by outsiders. This possibility bears emphasis because, to take one case, in recent years the United States has seen a great deal of class action but not much struggle. The tendency of academicians to glorify "class struggle" has focused on dramatic conflicts, whereas important stakes in the play of class interests may get settled in ways that are relatively uncontested, and have the potential of becoming historically obscure or "naturalized."

Overall, once the *multiple-market* formulation of specifically economic class is taken in a direction that replaces either "structure" or "the" (essentialized) market, class analysis opens into a multifaceted enterprise that acknowledges the historical emergences of multiple and overlapping interests of actors in relation to a variety of market situations. As individuals and groups reckon these situations, they pursue complex pathways of actions and social movements to realize shared class interests.

Classes and Structurations of Political Economy

The tendency to focus on class structure as an abstracted and isolated totality has left obscure an important additional aspect of how Weber theorized classes. Namely, Weber located the concepts of class, situation, and market within a wider battery of *verstehende* concepts of political economy that transcend the structure/agency dichotomy without essentializing "the" economy as a thing with laws unto itself. Here, Anthony Giddens's analysis is helpful but incomplete. Giddens (1981, 105) has argued that "the most important blank spots in the theory of class concern the processes whereby 'economic classes' become 'social classes,' and whereby in turn the latter are related to other social forms." For this question, Giddens focuses on what he terms the "structuration" of social classes, that is, their temporal and spatial patterned forming-up in relation to social-mobility closure, social constructions of identity, class-as-status-group cultures, processes of inclusion and exclusion in relation to group boundaries, and cross-cutting versus aligned solidarities in relation to ethnic, racial, gender, and other social distinctions. These foci, when applied to empirical data on social constructions of status boundaries and social mobility, begin to identify relatively coherent social classes and their cultural structurations in relation to other dimensions of inequality (Waters 1991; for an earlier research tradition that anticipates empirical structuration analysis, see Warner et al. 1963; Davis, Gardner, and Gardner 1941). They thus empirically map the social classes that Weber (1978, 302) defined on the basis of "easy and typical" individual and intergenerational mobility.

Giddens shifted to social classes because he reasoned that Weber's definition of *economic* classes in terms of market situations tends to give rise to "a cumbersome plurality of classes." Regarding economic classes, he correctly observed, "There would appear to be as many 'classes,' and as many 'class conflicts,' as there are differing market positions" (1981, 104). Yet if this condition turns out to be empirically central to how class situations play out, reduction of complexity would unduly narrow the analysis. In the first place, as William Brustein shows for the Nazi party (see Chapter 10), when the Weberian precept about market situation is taken seriously, a rational-choice analysis of economic market class situations can yield understandings about political mobilization that would be obscured by restricting analysis to *social* classes, however defined. Second, in Giddens's more elaborated idea of structuration (1984), economic institutions represent structures of domination that involve resource allocation. In these terms—and in contrast to Giddens's analysis in *The Class Structure of Advanced Societies*, to concentrate on *social* classes would leave a blank spot on a topic to which Weber devoted considerable attention, namely, the structuration of *economic* markets as class situations.

To examine economic structuration, a neo-Weberian approach must look to Weber's less widely cited typological distinctions about economic action and organization. Two points bear mention. First, in Part 1 of *Economy and Society*, Weber locates the concept of market within an array of other concepts that identify potentially important social, organizational, cultural, and institutional sources of market structurations. This approach yields important analytic leverage by directly tying the play of class interests to the political economy of how markets are structured.

In part, economic structurations involve actions that undermine the *formal* rationality of decisions in markets; that is, they operate *against* decision making in purely calculable terms of value defined in relation to price. Specifically, economic actors often employ criteria of *substantive* rationality that take into consideration other factors than economic value—affection or tradition, discrimination or solidarity, friendship or politics, and so on. They thereby infuse economic action with motives that are not fully subject to monetary valuations (Weber 1978, 85, 108,

161). Thus, market interests may become patterned through practices of inclusion and exclusion on the basis of other social distinctions—gender, ethnicity, status group, religion, credentials, "social" class, and so forth— which become institutionally constitutive of market conditions (on this point see Barth 1970; Collins 1979; Hartman 1983; Dex 1985; Lockwood 1986). Such status-distinction-oriented actions are constitutive of the widely noted phenomenon of split labor markets (Bonacich 1972), and the consequence is a "cultural division of labor" that yields ethnic- and gender-concentrated and -excluded occupations (Hechter 1978). Here, Weber's emphasis on meaningful action reminds us that classes cannot be understood by an autonomous class analysis, for any action may be heterogeneous in its motives and hybrid in its significance. A given action may simultaneously have formally rational, market-oriented aspects and nevertheless weigh substantively rational "political" or "status group" considerations. Clearly, Giddens's formulation about structuration in the *social* classes that circumscribe boundaries of mobility is incomplete. Much structuration—for example, closure on the basis of race or gender, the exercise of credential exclusion, split labor markets, and similar processes—occurs in labor markets themselves.

It is in everyday life, through networks of family, friendship and acquaintance, neighborhoods, communities, and education to obtain skills and credentials, for example, that class situation is structured in the specifically social—rather than economic—domain. Even here, the processes of social class formation are complex and varied in relation to other social and cultural patterns. For example, David Roediger (1991) shows for the industrializing United States that class consciousness, insofar as it developed among white workers, often became structured on the basis of a culturally marked exclusion of blacks. Through consideration of scholarship on diverse intersections among class, race, and gender, Sonya Rose (in Chapter 4) broadens this argument, emphasizing that there is no "quintessential worker," only specific workers who live in their specific social circumstances. To theorize this situation, Rose invokes a famous critic of deterministic Marxism, Jean-Paul Sartre, whose concept of "seriality" she uses to underscore the potentialities of class formation that emerge in existential moments of social life—in families, neighborhoods, religious groups, and so forth. Michèle Lamont's analysis of French and American workers (Chapter 6) can be read as identifying empirical traces of seriality. As Lamont's interviews reveal, the kinds of boundaries that individuals invoke between themselves and people in other classes get drawn on the basis of other than purely economic distinctions. In effect building on Weber's analytic distinction between economic and social classes and his treatment of social classes as based on status-group distinctions of exclusion, both Rose and Lamont show that structurations of social classes have stakes other than economic interests narrowly construed.

Beyond clarifying the economic versus social contexts of class structuration, we must also scrutinize the relation of power to market structuration. In the Weberian approach, this analysis unfolds from the understanding that modern market economies are "networks of exchange contracts." They therefore depend on the existence of law "external" to markets that regulates such contracts. In turn, law presumes an "organization enforcing a formal [economic] order," that is, a state. And there are empirical possibilities of other "economically regulative organizations" such as labor unions, cartels, and real estate associations (Weber 1978, 67). Here, Weber's agenda resonates with the neo-Marxist regulation theory applied by George Steinmetz to post-Fordist Germany (Chapter 11). As Steinmetz holds, regulation theory abandons teleology and functionalism, instead positing that struggles to sustain profit rates result in historically contingent institutional structurations of economic activity.

The modern emergences of legal, organizational, and institutional regulation of economic activities establish arenas where class interests can be pursued by actions that are not strictly speaking class actions—that is, actions that are not directly oriented toward immediate market situations (and may involve interests beyond strictly market ones). States may pursue foreign trade policies, occupational safety policies, environmental policies, and other regulation, either in alliance with business sectors or for other political purposes (cf. Weber 1978, 194). Realtors' associations will attempt to exclude access to property markets that circumvent association members. Business associations and labor unions will pursue legislation favorable to their clients' direct market interests, as well as regulation of economic activity that affects market situations in less direct ways (e.g., product safety requirements, environmental health, and safety). Importantly, business associations may pursue state policies that limit the effectiveness of labor organizations, and partly for this reason, labor unions face considerably different organizing climates in various nation-states (Voss 1993; Golden and Wallerstein 1995). Just as actions *within* a market may incorporate substantively rational considerations that undermine formal economic rationality, so too, markets may be structured through *extra*market pursuits of class interests, as well as in other social arenas—of family life, politics, the state, cultural domination—in short, the entire gamut of public and private social relationships. As John Walton shows in Chapter 8, just these kinds of complexities account for the historical emergence of classes in the Monterey, California, fishing industry and, in turn, today submerge earlier class relations in a romanticized local tourist metanarrative that socially constructs remembrance—and forgetting—by blurring history and popular culture.

Overall, when class situation is unambiguously conceptualized in relation to markets, it yields an important conclusion: many of the actions that structure class situations are not purely class actions. They are hybrid actions that permeate class with social and political as well as formally rational economic considerations.

Extramarket Economics: Quasi-Markets, Organizations, and Exploitation

In turn, it is important to consider an entirely different possibility, namely, of economic actions that are not class actions at all. As Weber (1978) pointed out, individuals and social groups—from families to ethnic groups to bureaucracies and states—allocate labor, services, and resources in nonmarket circumstances. Indeed, as Karl Polanyi affirmed in *The Great Transformation* (1944), market society itself is a historical creation achieved only by institutional transformations of social relationships. A continuum helps to specify the possibilities. At one hypothetical extreme, no social allocation of resources is monetized. Conversely, in a hypothetical completely marketized society, all resource allocation—including household labor, child care, government services, and so on—would occur through markets that are fully monetized, hence "rationalized" in the formal sense of calculability. Under these conditions, all markets would be equilibrated relative to one another through markets for the exchange of different types of money, credit instruments, and other kinds of quasi-money. In relation to this continuum, in contemporary societies, social and economic "exchange" is incompletely rationalized in the specific sense that utilities of alternative resource allocation are not always calibrated by reference to a socially rationalized standard, for example, money (Weber 1978, 81; for the interesting case of children, see Zelizer 1985). In the absence of such calibration, judgments about allocations remain incommensurate. This recognition yields two different directions of theoretical development—the analysis of "quasi-markets" and the analysis of organizational structuration and its relation to exploitation.

First, the possibility of incompletely calculable equilibration of values suggests that there may be "quasi-markets" in which "capital" and "exchange" have metaphorical qualities. Here it is important to consider "cultural capital" as the basis of "distinction," and to begin to think about "social capital" (Bourdieu 1984, 114) and "moral capital" (Lamont 1992). Pushing this line of analysis suggests that people may undertake exchanges involving cultural, social, and moral capital in heterogeneous markets. Thus, Pierre Bourdieu (1984) in effect transposes class analysis from the economic realm to the social domain, where the "habitus" of structured practices in everyday life and the accumulation and deployment of cultural capital dialectically structure, in Weber's (1978, 303–5) terms, class-based status groups, or "social" classes. Bourdieu's formulation is powerful, yet the metaphoric quality of cultural capital points to social and theoretical ambiguities. Specifically, for cultural capital, the absence of rationalization of exchange through some formalized medium of calculability such as money accentuates the proliferation of multiple signifying systems of value, and it leaves open the empirical question of whether any status group (e.g., an elite) can succeed in imposing its cultural valuations; moreover, by concentrating on class-based status groups, Bourdieu leaves undertheorized the production of cultural capital by nonelite classes, by ethnic and racial groups, and on the basis of gender distinctions (Collins 1992; Hall 1992). Jan Rupp builds on this line of critique in Chapter 7 of this book. As Rupp argues, "capital" may be too high-class a term for the cultural and economic "investments" pursued by working-class people in the Netherlands.

Other extensions of capital theory suggest that the play of "class" interests can build up on the basis of the most heterogeneous domains of value. Thus, a moral "class" interested in promoting particular standards of conduct or ethics of action (i.e., a status group) may seek to define "legitimate" moral capital (Gusfield 1963). In a different way, in societies where substantial property differentials emerge, marriage "markets" are central to the maintenance of patriarchy and the monopolization and focusing of assets by propertied classes (Lewin 1987; Adams 1994).

More central to class analysis conventionally understood, the thesis of incomplete rationalization points to a second broad issue: the interplay of market interests and other social phenomena within (and among) organizations (e.g., Powell 1991, 184–85). It is here that the Weberian approach locates issues of exploitation. Weber (1978, 114–40) distinguished various possible arrangements of production in relation to technical and social aspects of the division of labor, including the appropriation of managerial functions and the expropriation of the means of production from workers. His wide-ranging discussions defy any brief summary, but they underscore the point that class struggles unfold on multiple fronts and have outcomes that structure the organization of production in variable ways, even within a capitalist market economy. In general, Weber (1978, 930) held that capitalist enterprise presupposes the power of property holders to dispose of their assets as they choose, and by implication, it depends on a legal order that guarantees these rights. Under such conditions, "the expropriation of workers from the means of production"—the hallmark of large-scale industrial capitalism—is favored, among other factors, "by the sheer bargaining superiority which in the labor market any kind of property ownership grants vis-à-vis the workers" (Weber 1978, 138; cf. Roemer 1982). Workers divested of the means of production are disadvantaged in the marketplace, and hence are vulnerable to exploitation of their labor for profit in the organization of capitalist activity. In other words, organizational exploitation depends on differential market situations in relation to assets (capital, commodities, skills). Careful analysis of empirical findings (e.g., Wright 1996) may help unravel these complex relations.

Following Weber's formulation, three broad circumstances of exploitation within capitalist organizations can be identified. First, insofar as the technical and rational dictates that maximize return are unproblematic for workers as they construe their interests, the organization operates unfettered by political mobilization around issues of exploitation. Second, when workers have some capacity to affect an organization's access to labor markets, either through solidary monopolization of skills, via maintenance of a closed shop, or by political means, the organization is forced to negotiate with labor to address and ameliorate conditions of exploitation. Third, exploitation remains unameliorated when a capitalist organization is both strongly advantaged relative to the labor market and unconstrained by law in relation to specific exercises of power; under these circumstances the organization can define and orchestrate the conditions of work in thoroughgoing and nonnegotiable ways. In short, the (variable) organizational capacity for exploitation derives from the lack of an effective market power on the part of labor. This situation is sustained on the basis of the pervasive and multifaceted power of property, and it is challenged most directly when workers restrict market availability of labor and when political movements achieve state and interstate regulation.

The social definitions and organizational struggles over exploitation are empirically open as to their content, and content may shift over time, if institutional, legal, or contractual resolution of one set of issues gives way to searches for profit by other devices. To be sure, workers have interests at stake in the most fundamental aspects of their class situations, that is, in the definition of their labor as a commodity. Yet as Richard Biernacki demonstrates in Chapter 5, social constructions of meaning haunt Marxist theoretical discourse. The definition of labor time, which is after all a central basis for the extraction of profit from the organization of labor, is in part shaped by different national cultural contexts of the struggle over the calculation of workers' compensation—in Biernacki's study, in Germany and England.

Under conditions of market advantage, management will seek to benefit not only from labor compensation but also from organization of work processes (Burawoy 1979) and the promotion of industrial divisions among gendered and racialized labor forces (Janiewski 1991). Increasingly in recent years, similar interests encourage the use of part-time and temporary workers. But at higher skill levels, individuals may develop proprietary knowledge that effectively reappropriates certain aspects of the means of production, and groups may appropriate rights (e.g., in the form of legal credentials) of professional practice. Such moves differentiate—even fragment—the labor market and thus undermine the emergence of broader class interests among workers, even if those workers "share" an overall class location defined in structural terms. In short, class interests of employees and owners are at stake in the very organization of the capitalist workplace—the factory, the plantation, the store, the information-processing bureaucracy, the service center.

When classes are conceptualized in relation to markets, however, it becomes evident that not all economic activities within organizations are purely class phenomena. Propertied classes have advantages in market position, as Weber observed, yet sometimes their pursuit of class interests is played out in the contexts of power, authority, hierarchy, and organization—at some remove from direct market situations (cf. Dahrendorf 1959). But these empirical possibilities should not persuade us to conflate class with power and authority. The reason is simple: power can be exercised in manifold ways that cannot be reduced to any simple matrix of opposed class interests (Weber 1978, 942).

Weber did not seek to isolate capitalism as a single theoretical form with its own developmental dynamic; he was more interested in distinguishing alternative structurations of economic interests *within* various economic orders. He identified a number of such possibilities, including state socialism, patrimonial capitalism (Hall 1984, 1991), and most generally, the play of economic interests in modern bureaucracy. The general point is that markets and organizations interface in complex ways that cannot be reduced to a structural determination of class interests, but which precisely for this reason warrant extended analysis. This point has been pursued with new vigor in recent years.

Oliver Williamson (1975) argues that capitalist firms face tradeoffs in the efficiency of satisfying their needs for labor and intermediate products either through external transactions or internal (hierarchical) organization. A variety of contingencies, he suggested, affect both the optimal mode of labor utilization as well as the structuring of enterprises through vertical integration, conglomerates, or interfirm contracting. Mark Granovetter (1985) criticizes Williamson and expands the domains in which we understand economic activity to be "socially embedded" from "hierarchies" to other kinds of transactional situations. Among others, Gary Hamilton and Nicole Biggart (1988) extend this line of analysis by showing how alternative national political economies develop in the countries of East Asia. Although firms adopt rational strategies meant to reduce transaction costs, as Williamson would expect, Hamilton and Biggart find that alternative structurations of capitalism in East Asia are also shaped by distinctive relationships of enterprises to one another, to the state, and to privately held wealth. As Marco Orrù, Biggart, and Hamilton put it, "The business organizations found in each of these economies are not corruptions of technically ideal organizational forms, but represent qualitatively distinct conceptualizations of what constitutes appropriate economic activity" (1991, 363; see also Hamilton and Feenstra, forthcoming). By showing that the social fabric of capitalist activity is quite differently structured in a region of the world far from the industrialized West where modern capitalism originated, such research demonstrates a central implication of the present discussion—that "capitalism" is not a uniformly ordered "mode of production." There is not one capitalism but many. The class situations of individuals and groups and their capacities to pursue collective interests are in part shaped by diverse institutional structurations of capitalism as organized economic activity.

In the present era, we have witnessed the triumph of "market economy" *ideology* and the explosion of what may be called *"semi-market" economies*— that is, diverse hybrid complexes of organized and regulated markets tied to other forms of social organization. Because these complexes are themselves differentially linked by world trade yet also structured by hierarchical, interorganizational, and political relationships, the neo-Weberian program reworks class analysis within a broader practice of political economy that investigates the interplay of economic interests with markets, economic organizations, political power, and cultural distinctions.

Marxists might well say, we are already doing this. Indeed, once the totalization of historical processes is dropped as a theoretical motif, Marxian and Weberian approaches to political economy tend to converge (Sayer 1991). But one point bears mentioning. Marxian analysis sometimes retains the Marxian concept of class "in the breach." Insofar as Marxian formulations about classes tied to "modes of production" are defined in structuralist terms (that is, insofar as they are Marxist in theoretical construction as well as in political commitment), they remain analytically underdeveloped in their capacity to make distinctions in the very terms (action, closure, status groups, organization, power, etc.) that enhance the Weberian capacity to develop a nontotalizing analysis of differentially connected alternative forms of capitalist organizations on the ground. Once it is acknowledged that market capacities, class interests, and organizational exploitation become structured in diverse ways within capitalism, the theoretical gaps between Marxian and Weberian approaches are largely erased, and the Weberian analysis of structurations within capitalism becomes ever more salient. Under these conditions, new directions of political intervention emerge, for example, through reorganization of markets and economic institutions (Block 1992). In the reworking described here, the dialectic of class conflict no longer can be identified as the engine of history. But once the myth of a heroic and triumphant class struggle is abandoned, inquiry less encumbered by moral presuppositions can acquire central political significance for emancipatory praxis under ever shifting historical conditions.

References

Adams, Julia. 1994. "The Familial State: Elite Family Practices and State-Making in the Early Modern Netherlands." *Theory & Society* 23: 505–39.

Alcoff, Linda, and Elizabeth Potter, eds. 1993. *Feminist Epistemologies*. New York: Routledge.

Althusser, Louis, and Etienne Balibar. 1970 [1968]. *Reading Capital*. London: NLB.

Aminzade, Ronald. 1993. *Ballots and Barricades*. Princeton: Princeton University Press.

Barnes, Barry. 1995. *The Elements of Social Theory*. Princeton: Princeton University Press.

Barth, Fredrick. 1970. *Ethnic Groups and Boundaries*. Bergen, Norway: Universitets Forlag.

Becker, Ewe. 1989. "Class Theory: Still the Axis of Critical Social Scientific Analysis?" In Erik Olin Wright et al., *The Debate on Classes*. New York: Verso.

Bell, Daniel. 1973. *The Coming of Post-Industrial Society*. New York: Basic.

Benhabib, Seyla. 1986. *Critique, Norm, and Utopia*. New York: Columbia University Press.

Berger, Peter L., Brigitte Berger, and Hansfried Kellner. 1973. *The Homeless Mind*. New York: Random House.

Blau, Peter M., and Otis Dudley Duncan. 1967. *The American Occupational Structure*. New York: Wiley.

Block, Fred. 1992. "Capitalism without Class Power." *Politics and Society* 20: 277–303.

Bonacich, Edna. 1972. "A Theory of Ethnic Group Antagonism: The Split Labor Market." *American Sociological Review* 37: 547–59.

Bourdieu, Pierre. 1984. *Distinction*. Cambridge: Harvard University Press.

Burawoy, Michael. 1979. *Manufacturing Consent*. Chicago: University of Chicago Press.

Calhoun, Craig. 1982. *The Question of Class Struggle*. Chicago: University of Chicago Press.

Clark, Terry Nichols, and Seymour Martin Lipset. 1991. "Are social classes dying?" *International Sociology* 6: 397–410.

Clark, Terry Nichols, Seymour Martin Lipset, and Michael Rempel. 1993. "The declining political significance of social class." *International Sociology* 8: 293–316.

Collins, Randall. 1979. *The Credential Society*. New York: Academic Press.

——. 1986. *Weberian Sociological Theory*. New York: Cambridge University Press.

——. 1992. "Women and the Production of Status Cultures." In Michèle Lamont and Marcel Fournier, eds., *Cultivating Differences*. Chicago: University of Chicago Press.

Connell, R. W. 1979. "A Critique of the Althusserian Approach to Class." *Theory & Society* 8: 303–45.

Dahrendorf, Ralf. 1959 [1957]. *Class and Class Conflict in Industrial Society*. Stanford: Stanford University Press.

Davis, Allison, Burleigh B. Gardner, and Mary R. Gardner. 1941. *Deep South*. Chicago: University of Chicago Press.

Davis, Kingsley, and Wilbert Moore. 1945. "Some Principles of Stratification." *American Sociological Review* 50: 242–49.

Dex, Shirley. 1985. *The Sexual Division of Work*. Brighton, England: Harvester Press.

Duncan, Otis Dudley. 1961. "A Socio-Economic Index for All Occupations." In Albert J. Reiss, Jr., ed., *Occupations and Social Status*. New York: Free Press.

Elster, Jon. 1985. *Making Sense of Marx*. New York: Cambridge University Press.

Erikson, Robert, and John H. Goldthorpe. 1992. *The Constant Flux*. Oxford: Clarendon Press.

Fantasia, Rick. 1988. *Cultures of Solidarity*. Berkeley: University of California Press.

Friedland, Roger, and Robert R. Alford. 1991. "Bringing Society Back In." In Powell and DiMaggio 1991.

Gereffi, Gary. 1989. "Rethinking Development Theory." *Sociological Forum* 4: 505–33.

Giddens, Anthony. 1971. *Capitalism and Modern Social Theory*. New York: Cambridge University Press.

——. 1981 [1973]. *The Class Structure of the Advanced Societies*. London: Hutchinson.

——. 1984. *The Constitution of Society*. Berkeley: University of California Press.

Golden, Miriam, and Michael Wallerstein. 1995. "Unions, Employers, and Collective Bargaining: A Report on Data for 16 Countries from 1950 to 1990." Working paper 95-2 (March), Institute of Industrial Relations, University of California–Los Angeles.

Granovetter, Mark. 1985. "Economic Action and Social Structure: The Problem of Embeddedness." *American Journal of Sociology* 91: 481–510.

Gusfield, Joseph R. 1963. *Symbolic Crusade.* Urbana: University of Illinois Press.

Hall, John R. 1984. "World System Holism and Colonial Brazilian Agriculture." *Latin American Research Review* 19: 43–69.

———. 1988. "Social Organization and Pathways of Commitment." *American Sociological Review* 53: 679–92.

———. 1991. "The Patrimonial Dynamic in Colonial Brazil." In Richard Graham, ed., *Brazil and the World-System.* Austin: University of Texas Press.

———. 1992. "The Culture(s) of Capital: A Non-Holistic Approach to Status Situations, Class, Gender and Ethnicity." In Michèle Lamont and Marcel Fournier, eds., *Cultivating Differences.* Chicago: University of Chicago Press.

———. forthcoming. *Cultures of Inquiry.*

Hall, John R., and Mary Jo Neitz. 1993. *Culture: Sociological Perspectives.* Englewood Cliffs, N.J.: Prentice-Hall.

Halle, David. 1984. *America's Working Man.* Chicago: University of Chicago Press.

Hamilton, Gary G., and Nicole Woolsey Biggart. "Market, Culture and Authority." *American Journal of Sociology* 94: S52–S94.

Hamilton, Gary G., and Robert Feenstra. Forthcoming. "The Organization of Economies." In Victor Nee and Mary Brinton, eds., *The New Institutionalism in Economic Sociology.*

Hartman, Heidi. 1981. "The Family as the Locus of Gender, Class, and Political Struggle." *Journal of Women in Culture and Society* 6: 366–94.

———. 1983 [1976]. "Capitalism, Patriarchy and Job Segregation by Sex." In Elizabeth Abel and Emily K. Abel, eds., *The Signs Reader.* Chicago: University of Chicago Press.

Hechter, Michael. 1978. "Group Formation and the Cultural Division of Labor." *American Journal of Sociology* 84: 293–318.

Hindess, Barry, and Paul Q. Hirst. 1975. *Pre-Capitalist Modes of Production.* Boston: Routledge and Kegan Paul.

Hodge, Robert W., Donald J. Treiman, and Peter H. Rossi. 1966. "Occupational Prestige in the United States 1925–1963." In Reinhard Bendix and Seymour M. Lipset, eds., *Class, Status and Power.* 2d ed. New York: Free Press.

Horan, Patrick M. 1978. "Is Status Attainment Research Atheoretical?" *American Sociological Review* 43: 534–41.

Hout, Mike, Clem Brooks, and Jeff Manza. 1993. "The Persistence of Classes in Post-industrial Societies." *International Sociology* 8: 259–77.

Janiewski, Delores. 1991. "Southern Honor, Southern Dishonor: Managerial Ideology and the Construction of Gender, Race and Class Relations in Southern Industry." In Ava Baron, ed., *Work Engendered*. Ithaca, N.Y.: Cornell University Press.

Jones, Gareth Stedman. 1976. "From Historical Sociology to Sociological Theory." *British Journal of Sociology* 27: 295–305.

Joyce, Patrick. 1995. "The End of Social History?" *Social History* 20: 73–91.

Kamolnick, Paul. 1988. *Classes: A Marxist Critique*. Dix Hills, N.Y.: General Hall.

Katznelson, Ira. 1986. "Working-Class Formation: Constructing Cases and Comparisons." In Katznelson and Zolberg 1986.

Katznelson, Ira, and Aristide R. Zolberg, eds. 1986. *Working-Class Formation: Nineteenth-Century Patterns in Western Europe and the United States*. Princeton: Princeton University Press.

Kumar, Krishan. 1978. *Prophecy and Progress: The Sociology of Industrial and Post-industrial Society*. New York: Penguin.

Laclau, Ernest, and Chantal Mouffe. 1985. *Hegemony and Socialist Strategy*. London: Verso.

Lamont, Michèle. 1992. *Money, Morals and Manners*. Chicago: University of Chicago Press.

Lembcke, Jerry. 1995. "Labor History's 'Synthesis Debate': Sociological Interventions." *Science and Society* 59: 137–73.

Lewin, Linda. 1987. *Politics and Parentela in Paraíba*. Princeton: Princeton University Press.

Lockwood, David. 1986. "Class, Status and Gender." In Rosemary Crompton and Michael Mann, eds., *Gender and Stratification*. Cambridge: Polity Press.

Marx, Karl. 1978. *The Marx-Engels Reader*. Ed. Robert C. Tucker. 2d ed. New York: Norton.

Myles, John, and Adnan Turegun. 1994. "Comparative Studies in Class Structure." *Annual Review of Sociology* 20: 103–24.

Orrù, Marco, Nicole W. Biggart, and Gary G. Hamilton. 1991. "Organizational Isomorphism in East Asia." In Powell and DiMaggio 1991.

Pakulski, Jan. 1993. "The Dying of Class or of Marxist Theory?" *International Sociology* 8: 279–92.

Palmer, Bryan D. 1990. *Descent into Discourse*. Philadelphia: Temple University Press.

Parkin, Frank. 1979. *Marxism and Class Theory: A Bourgeois Critique*. New York: Columbia University Press.

Pawson, Ray. 1989. *A Measure for Measures*. New York: Routledge.

Polanyi, Karl. 1944. *The Great Transformation*. New York: Farrar and Rinehart.

Postone, Moishe. 1993. *Time, Labor, and Social Domination*. New York: Cambridge University Press.

Poulantzas, Nicos. 1975 [1974]. *Classes in Contemporary Capitalism*. London: NLB.

Powell, Walter W. 1991. "Expanding the Scope of Institutional Analysis." In Powell and DiMaggio 1991.

Powell, Walter W., and Paul DiMaggio, eds. 1991. *The New Institutionalism in Organizational Analysis*. Chicago: University of Chicago Press.

Przeworski, Adam. 1985. *Capitalism and Social Democracy*. New York: Cambridge University Press.

Reddy, William M. 1987. *Money and Liberty in Modern Europe*. New York: Cambridge University Press.

Roediger, David R. 1991. *The Wages of Whiteness*. New York: Verso.

Roemer, John. 1982. *A General Theory of Exploitation and Class*. Cambridge: Harvard University Press.

Roth, Guenther. 1988–89. "Weber's Political Failure." *Telos*, no. 78 (winter): 136–49.

Runciman, W. G. 1974. "Towards a Theory of Social Stratification." In Frank Parkin, ed., *The Social Analysis of Class Structure*. London: Tavistock.

Sayer, Derek. 1987. *The Violence of Abstraction*. New York: Basil Blackwell.

———. 1991. *Capitalism and Modernity: An Excursus on Marx and Weber*. New York: Routledge.

Schluchter, Wolfgang. 1981. *The Rise of Western Rationalism*. Berkeley: University of California Press.

———. 1989. *Rationalism, Religion and Domination: a Weberian Perspective*. Berkeley: University of California Press.

Sewell, William H., and Robert M. Hauser. 1972. "Causes and Consequences of Higher Education: Models of the Status Attainment Process." *American Journal of Agricultural Economics* 54: 851–61.

Sewell, William H., Jr. 1993. "Toward a Post-materialist Rhetoric for Labor History." In Lenard R. Berlanstein, ed., *Rethinking Labor History*. Urbana: University of Illinois Press.

Sørensen, Annemette. 1994. "Women, Family and Class." *Annual Review of Sociology* 20: 27–47.

Steinberg, Marc W. 1991. "The Re-making of the English Working Class?" *Theory and Society* 20: 173–97.

Thompson, E. P. 1963. *The Making of the English Working Class*. New York: Pantheon.

———. 1978. *The Poverty of Theory and Other Essays*. New York: Monthly Review Press.

Tilly, Charles. 1981. "Introduction." In Louise A. Tilly and Charles Tilly, eds., *Class Conflict and Collective Action*. Beverly Hills, Calif.: Sage.

Voss, Kim. 1993. *The Making of American Exceptionalism*. Ithaca, N.Y.: Cornell University Press.

Wallerstein, Immanuel. 1979. *The Capitalist World-Economy*. New York: Cambridge University Press.

Warner, W. Lloyd, J. O. Low, Paul S. Lunt, and Leo Srole. 1963 [1941–1961]. *Yankee City*. Abridged edition. New Haven: Yale University Press.

Waters, Malcolm. 1991. "Collapse and Convergence in Class Theory." *Theory and Society* 20: 141–72.

Weber, Max. 1978. *Economy and Society*. Berkeley: University of California Press.

Williamson, Oliver E. 1975. *Markets and Hierarchies*. New York: Free Press.

Wood, Ellen Meiksins. 1986. *The Retreat From Class*. London: Verso.

Wright, Erik Olin. 1985. *Classes*. New York: Verso.

———. 1996. *Class Counts*. New York: Cambridge University Press.

Zelizer, Viviana. 1985. *Pricing the Priceless Child*. New York: Basic Books.

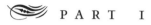 PART I

Changing Cultures of Class Analysis

CHAPTER I

Rethinking, Once Again, the Concept of Class Structure

Erik Olin Wright

*A*T THE CORE OF MARXIAN CLASS ANALYSIS IS THE CLAIM THAT CLASS IS a fundamental determinant of social conflict and social change. In trying to defend and deepen this intuition, contemporary Marxist theorists have been torn between two theoretical impulses. The first is to keep the concept of class structure as simple as possible, perhaps even accepting a polarized version, and then to remedy the explanatory deficiencies of such a simple concept by introducing a range of other explanatory principles. The second impulse is to increase the complexity of the concept in the hope that such complexity will more powerfully capture the explanatory mechanisms embedded in class relations.

My work on class has pursued this second strategy. In my theoretical discussions of class structure I have been preoccupied with the "middle class," with elaborating a class structure concept that would give a coherent and systematic theoretical status to nonproletarian employees. My conviction has been that conceptually clarifying the structural location of the middle class is essential for understanding class formation and the

This abridgment of Wright 1989 is by Maureen Sullivan. Interested researchers may wish to consult the complete text. I would like to express my thanks to Julia Adams, Ron Aminzade, Robin Blackburn, Sam Bowles, Johanna Brenner, Lisa Brush, Michael Burawoy, Val Burris, Ira Katznelson, Lane Kenworthy, Michael Mann, Scott McNall, John Roemer, Joel Rogers, Ivan Szelenyi, and Philippe Van Parijs for their extraordinarily helpful comments on an earlier draft of this essay.

formation of coalitions of classes and segments of classes around radical democratic and socialist political projects within contemporary capitalism. This led to the introduction of the concept of "contradictory locations within class relations" and, subsequently, to the reformulation of that concept in terms of a multidimensional view of exploitation. The theoretical aspiration was that these reconstructions of the concept of class structure would enhance its explanatory power by more adequately representing the complexities of class interests in capitalist societies and, accordingly, making it possible to map more systematically the variations in class structures across capitalist societies and the impact of those variations on processes of class formation.

In what follows I try to lay out a general agenda for the further development of the concept of class structure, which I hope will help to bring us closer to this goal. The first section briefly situates the concept of class structure within the broader agenda of class analysis and examines some metatheoretical considerations that affect the analysis of class structure. The next section discusses what it is that classes have in common that justifies calling them "classes." In particular, I will defend the decision to treat objective material interests as the central commonality of class. A third section then assesses the strengths and weaknesses of constructing a concrete map of class structure grounded in class interests. The upshot of this discussion is that neither of my two proposed strategies provides a completely satisfactory solution to the conceptual problem of the middle class. The following section briefly explores the attractions and limitations of the neo-Weberian alternative to the enterprise of reconstructing a Marxist concept of the middle class. In the fifth section I explore a new way of adding complexity to the concept of class structure that differs from those embodied in my various typologies. My previous approaches treated class structure as a structure of "empty places" filled by people. Here I want to examine something different, namely, the various ways in which individual lives are tied to such a structure of positions. The last section then returns to the problem of the middle class.

Class Structure in Class Analysis

The concept of "class structure" is only one element in a broader theoretical enterprise that can be called "class analysis." Other elements include class formation (the formation of classes into collectively organized actors), class struggle (the practices of actors for the realization of class interests) and class consciousness (the understanding of actors of their class interests). This essay will be largely restricted to discussing the problem of class structure because this concept is pivotal to clarifying the overall logic of class analysis. To speak of class formation or class struggle as opposed to simply group formation or struggle implies that we have a definition of "class" and know what it means to describe a collective action as an instance of class formation, or a conflict as a class conflict instead of some other sort of conflict. Elaborating a coherent concept of class structure therefore, is an important conceptual precondition for developing a satisfactory theory of the relationship between class structure, class formation, and class struggle.

Underlying this preoccupation with clarifying the concept of class structure is a particular view of the relationship between concept formation and theory construction. My assumption is that the explanatory capacity of the theories we construct depends to an important extent on the coherence of the concepts we deploy within them. The central thrust of my work on class structure has been to try to produce, within a broadly Marxist theoretical framework, a class structure concept capable of being used in analyses of micro–level processes at a relatively low level of abstraction. It has been driven by two overarching questions: first, how can we best explain the empirical variations in patterns of class formation across advanced capitalist societies? and second, under what conditions are class formations likely to embody projects of radical social change? My assumption is that any viable democratic socialist politics in advanced capitalist societies must contend with the formation of durable political coalitions between segments of the "middle class" and the working class. Overly abstract and macro-level concepts of class structure do not seem to provide the categories necessary for exploring such coalitions. In order to study class formation in a politically relevant way, therefore, I felt it was necessary to produce a class structure concept that was much less abstract than existing concepts and more suitable for micro-level analysis.[1]

While all concepts are abstract in the sense that they are mental constructions distinct from the "real objects" that they attempt to represent, concepts nevertheless differ in their degree of abstraction or concreteness.

1. For discussions of class formation that do not emphasize class structure, see Burawoy 1985, 1989; Przeworski 1985, 1989.

Within a given conceptual hierarchy, a more abstract concept is one that constitutes a classification of the variable forms of the less abstract concepts; concrete concepts are nested within abstract concepts. Within the Marxist tradition, at the most abstract level, the concept of class structure attempts to differentiate distinct modes of production—for example, capitalism and feudalism. More concrete concepts attempt to capture the ways in which class structures vary over time and place within a given type of society.[2] The micro/macro distinction is also important for class structure analysis, as it refers to the level of aggregation of social phenomena which the concept attempts to describe. As a macro-level concept, class structures are meant to describe a crucial property of whole societies. As a micro-level concept, on the other hand, class structures define a set of "locations" filled by individuals subjected to a set of mechanisms that impinge directly on their lives as they make choices and act in the world.

The Marxist concept of class structure has traditionally been constructed most systematically as a highly abstract macro-structural concept. Class structures have been defined in terms of pure modes of production (slavery, feudalism, capitalism, communism) and used to understand the broad, macro-structural dynamics of social development. Typically the class structure concept deployed in such analyses has tended to be unsuitable for concrete, micro-analysis. The overarching objective of my work on class structure has been to elaborate this concept in ways that would enhance its analytical power both in concrete analyses and in micro-analyses. My goal has been to generate a repertoire of class structure concepts that can be used both for comparative historical and institutional analyses of variations in the class structures of capitalist societies and for the analysis of the impact of class on the lives of individuals within those societies.

My ambition has been to achieve a high level of theoretical integration among these various class structure concepts so as to enhance the explanatory capacity of Marxist class analysis. I have attempted to apply systematic rules to the derivation of new class structure concepts from the abstract concepts at the core of Marxist theory. The basic strategy I adopted for moving from the *abstract* to the *concrete* is to see concrete class structures as consisting of different combinations of abstractly

---

2. Sometimes Marxists use the expression "social relations of production" to refer to the mode of production level of abstraction, and reserve the term "class structure" for more concrete levels of analysis. In this essay I use the term "class structure" to refer to the theoretical object of the structural analysis of classes at whatever level of abstraction.

defined social relations of production. The basic strategy for moving from *macro* to *micro* levels of analysis is to explore the ways these combinations of relations are embodied in *specific jobs*, since jobs are the essential "empty places" filled by individuals within the system of production. The traditional assumption of Marxian class analysis is that every location in the class structure falls within one and only one class. In contrast, I have argued that individual jobs can, in different ways, have a multiple, and sometimes even *contradictory*, class characters. Taking these two rules together in principle provides a way of linking the abstract macro-concept of class structure rooted in the analysis of modes of production to the concrete and micro concept of class structure rooted in the analysis of individual lives.

What Do Classes Have in Common That Makes Them Classes?

Class structures, for most Marxists anyway, are thought to designate real mechanisms, causal processes that exist independently of the theorist. Mechanisms are effect-generating processes.[3] One crucial aspect of the theoretical content of the concept of class thus concerns the specification of the kinds of direct effects that class structural mechanisms are thought to produce. Marxist treatments of class structure can be seen as emphasizing one or more of three types of effects: material interests, lived experience, and capacities for collective action. I will argue that of these three possible bases for the specification of class mechanisms, material interests provides the most coherent basis for the elaboration of concrete, micro-level concepts of class structure. Before explaining why I feel this is the case, it will be useful to briefly examine the logic of each of these mechanisms.

Material Interests

Class is sometimes viewed as an answer to the question, Who gets what and how do they get it? The social relations of production determine a

---

3. To say that mechanisms are effect-generating processes does not imply that mechanisms invariably generate empirically observable effects. Since, to use the formulation of Roy Bashkar (1975, 1979), the world is an open system consisting of many distinct mechanisms operating simultaneously, it is always possible that the presence of one mechanism can block the effects of another.

set of mechanisms through which people obtain access to material resources and the social product produced using those resources. Two critical kinds of material interests are bound up with these mechanisms: first, interests with respect to *economic welfare*, and second, interests with respect to *economic power*.

Economic welfare. Economic welfare refers to the total package of toil-leisure-income available to a person. People have an objective interest in having superior trade-offs between toil, leisure, and consumption. *Class* interests with respect to economic welfare are determined by what a person must *do* to achieve a given economic welfare; they are determined, that is, by the welfare-generating mechanisms, not by the outcome itself. To talk about common class interests, then, means that people in a given class, by virtue of their relationship to the underlying mechanisms embedded in the social relations of production, objectively face the same broad structure of choices and strategic tasks when attempting to improve their economic welfare—that is, the package of toil-leisure-income available to them.

Economic power. The social relations of production also distribute a crucial form of power: control over the surplus product. Loosely, we can define the surplus product as that part of the total social product that is left over after all of the inputs into production (both labor power and physical capital) have been reproduced. The control of the surplus product fundamentally determines the nature of economic investments, and because of the centrality of investments to a broad range of social goals, the control over the surplus can also be considered a central mechanism constraining social and political alternatives in general. As many commentators (e.g., Cohen and Rogers 1986) have stressed, the private, capitalist control over the surplus imposes a pervasive limit on the potential exercise of democratic political power in a capitalist society. As in the case of class interests with respect to economic welfare, class interests with respect to economic power are also based on the underlying mechanisms which determine access to the surplus, not simply on the outcomes themselves. As a dimension of the commonality of class interests, economic power is particularly salient for linking macro and micro levels, since the generation of economic power through the control over the surplus affects the overall, macro-structural development of a society, not simply the fate of the individual who exercises that power.

Material interests and exploitation. In Marxist theory, interests in securing the conditions for material welfare and interests in enhancing economic power are linked through the concept of exploitation. Exploitation generates both deprivations and powerlessness, and material interests are structured around both of these. By virtue of appropriating the surplus, exploiters are able both to obtain much higher levels of economic welfare (by consuming part of the surplus) and to have much higher levels of economic power (by retaining control over the social allocation of the surplus through investments). For the exploited, economic welfare is depressed by virtue of having surplus appropriated from them, and economic power drastically curtailed by their being excluded from control over the allocation of the surplus.

Marxism is not the only theoretical tradition which sees the essential commonality of classes as rooted in common material interests. The Weberian concept of members of a class sharing common "life chances" based on their common market capacities, for example, is a specific way of grounding classes in common material interests. Where the Marxist and Weberian concepts of class sharply diverge, however, is that Marxists, but generally not Weberians, analyze the linkage between class and material interests through the concept of exploitation.[4] Within the Marxist tradition, relationally defined classes do not simply have different material interests, as in the Weberian tradition; they have opposed material interests. While Weberians would certainly acknowledge that there are many circumstances in which class actors subjectively perceive their interests to be opposed, this perception is explained in terms of the particular construction of cultural meanings in the society, not in terms of inherent antagonism of interests.[5]

For Marxists, the objectively antagonistic character of the material interests of classes helps to explain why class structure should be associated with class conflict. If the material interests bound up with classes are inherently opposed to each other, then the divisions between structurally defined classes will have a tendency to become the basis for cleavages between conflicting groups.

Interests, trade-offs, strategies. In recent years Marxists and others have become increasingly suspicious of claims concerning the "objective"

4. Of course, there are theorists identified with the Weberian tradition—for example, Anthony Giddens (1973, 1982) and Michael Mann (1987)—who do talk about exploitation, but when they do so they are not drawing on the Weberian tradition itself.
5. The absence of a concept of exploitation and control over the surplus has also meant that the linkage between class structures and social power has not been a systematic concern in the Weberian concept of class.

interests of actors, interests that supposedly exist independently of the subjective understandings of those interests held by the actors themselves. This kind of criticism, however, misses the theoretical point that it is not the distributional outcomes of welfare or power as such which define the critical commonality of class interests, but the common material conditions which shape the available choices and strategies with respect to those outcomes.

The expression "available choices and strategies" in this formulation can refer either to choices faced by members of a class as individuals or to choices they face as potential members of organized collectivities. For the individual capitalist, economic welfare depends upon extraction of surplus labor from workers, technical innovation, successful investment strategies, market competition with rival capitalists; for the individual worker, economic welfare depends upon selling one's labor power to a capitalist and competing with other workers for better jobs. But both workers and capitalists also face distinctive structures of choices with respect to the collective pursuits of economic welfare. Workers, for example, face choices between various individualist market strategies (via training, promotions, geographical mobility) and various kinds of collective strategies (unionization, revolutionary politics). To describe members of a class as sharing common material interests, therefore, suggests that they share common dilemmas with respect to collective action as well as individual pursuit of economic welfare and power.

Lived Experience

Some Marxists have questioned the adequacy of grounding the concept of class in material interests. For them, common lived experience is the central, abstract content of the commonality of class membership. Instead of seeing class as an answer to the question, Who gets what and how? it is seen as an answer to Who does what and why? The social relations of production, in these terms, impose a set of practices on people within those relations. Those common practices systematically generate common experiences, which in turn are the basis for a common set of understandings about the world.

In the abstract model of the pure capitalist mode of production with a polarized relation between the bourgeoisie and the proletariat, there are three critical lived experiences that constitute the commonality of the working class. First, there are experiences of being forced to sell one's labor power in order to survive. Showing up at the factory gate, being unable to reproduce oneself without entering the labor market, does not simply define a set of material interests of actors, but a set of experiences as well. Second, within production itself there is the experience of being dominated, bossed around. Under a set of production conditions in which the critical task for employers is to extract surplus labor from their employees, experiences of domination will be an inherent aspect of the class relation. Third, the inability of workers to control the allocation of the social surplus also generates a certain kind of lived experience—the experience of powerlessness in the face of social forces that shape their destiny.

An objection might be raised against this characterization of working-class lived experiences on the grounds that this is a largely male characterization. Feminists have correctly pointed out that the lived experience of women in the working class is in many respects distinctively different from that of men. This issue is particularly striking for full-time housewives in the working class, whose lived experience of class is clearly not adequately characterized by saying that they are "forced to sell their labor power in order to survive" or that they are "bossed around within production."[6]

However, within a Marxist class structure concept, at the level of abstraction of the pure capitalist mode of production, there are no "housewives" of "male breadwinners" (and equally, there are no male breadwinners as such). At this level of abstraction, it is impossible to specify the crucial differences in lived experiences of men and women in the working class that are generated by the concrete intersection of class relations and gender relations. Thus, while it is legitimate to insist on the importance of gender for understanding and explaining the concrete lived experiences of people, it does not follow that gender must or can be incorporated in the abstract concept of class itself. Throughout this discussion, therefore, I will continue to assume that one can legitimately identify a set of lived experiences associated within abstractly defined common locations within class structures.

As in the case of interest-based concepts of the commonality of class, experience-based concepts are found in a variety of theoretical traditions besides Marxism. Most notably in contemporary social theory, Pierre

6. This objection was raised by Barbara Laslett (personal communication).

Bourdieu's (1984, 1985, 1987) theory of class relies heavily on such an approach. Bourdieu attempts to elaborate a view of class around the dual concepts of class habitus and capital. A class habitus is defined by a set of common conditions in everyday life which produce common conditionings experienced by people and which, in turn, generate a common set of internalized dispositions to act in particular ways. In Bourdieu's analysis, a class habitus is constituted not only within the workplace but in communities, schools, families, and other institutions as well.

Anthony Giddens's analysis of class structure (1973) also puts considerable emphasis on lived experience. For Giddens, classes are the outcome of a process through which economic categories (which he does not want to consider proper classes) defined by market capacities are transformed into collectivities sharing common lived experiences. He refers to this process as "class structuration." To the extent that various processes of structuration overlap and correspond to the "objective" divisions of market capacities, distinctive classes will be constituted in a class structure.[7]

Collective Capacity

The essential commonality of a class is sometimes seen as derived from its potential capacity for collective action. In particular, one of the central properties of the working class, it is often claimed, is that it has the potential capacity to organize collectively to overthrow capitalism and transform the social relations of production into socialism. In this view, the social relations of production do not merely distribute material interests or the pattern of lived experiences across classes; they also distribute various resources for collective action.

The working class was seen by Marx to have this capacity for collective struggle for two main reasons: first, workers were the direct producers of society's wealth, and thus they collectively possessed the necessary knowledge to organize social production; and second, the concentration and centralization of capital generated by capitalism brought masses of workers into contact and interdependency with one another, which generated the kind of solidarity and organizational capacity needed to challenge capitalist power.

---

7. Similar kinds of arguments are made by other theorists commonly regarded as working in the Weberian tradition. See Lockwood 1958 and Goldthorpe 1982.

Occasionally one does find this kind of argument outside of strictly Marxist approaches to class Alvin Gouldner's (1979) analysis of the "New Class" in capitalist societies, and George Konrad and Ivan Szelenyi's (1978) analysis of Eastern European intellectuals, both treat the potential for becoming a ruling class as an essential element in the claim that intellectuals should be treated as a class.

Levels of Abstraction and the Commonality of Class Locations

At the highest level of abstraction of class analysis, all three of these effects of class relations—material interests, lived experiences, and capacities for collective action—are credible candidates for the essential criteria defining the commonality of class locations. If we were exclusively interested in analyzing capitalism abstractly as a mode of production, then we could probably treat the concept of class structure as built simultaneously around all three of these commonalities. The problem occurs when we try to move to lower levels of abstraction, since at a relatively concrete, micro-level of analysis there is no longer necessarily a simple coincidence of material interests, lived experience, and collective capacity.

In light of this failure for interests, experiences, and capacities to coincide at the concrete level of analysis, class theorists face difficult choices. One possibility is simply to abandon the concept of an objectively given class structure altogether. This is essentially the position of Adam Przeworski, particularly in some of his more recent writings.[8] Classes are not structured prior to struggle; they are strictly the effects of the strategies of collectively organized actors, especially political parties.

A second general strategy would be to escalate the complexity of the concept of class structure at the concrete level of analysis by retaining all three aspects of the commonality of class location but allowing them to vary independently of one another. We could then define a kind of three-dimensional space consisting of class-interest structure, class-experience structure, and class-capacity structure. This solution risks adding more confusion than clarification. But there is an additional reason why

8. In Przeworski's (1985, 105) earlier writings on the working class, he seemed to suggest that classes had a structural foundation that existed independently of the strategies of parties and other collective actors. In the final version of this argument (Przeworski and Sprague 1986), this claim is dropped, and class definitions are viewed strictly as the outcome of the strategic choices of collective actors.

I do not think it is a viable general strategy for dealing with these problems. While there are a range of strategies for deriving concrete material interests from the abstract concept of class relations—for example, concrete class structures can be treated as specific combinations of different modes of production—I know of no parallel way of deriving concrete lived experiences and collective capacities. As far as I know, therefore, the only coherent way to generate concrete concepts of class structure from the abstract concept of mode of production is via the category of material interests.

Attempts at Building an Adequate Map of Class Structure

A wide variety of specific strategies for elaborating the substantive content of class structure and for developing the criteria for class structural analysis are consistent with the decision to ground the concept of class structure in relationally generated, antagonistic class interests. In my work, I have explored two different general approaches to this problem: the contradictory locations approach and the multidimensional exploitation approach. Both are attempts at providing a positive theorization to the category "middle class" within an essentially interest-based framework. Each of these solutions, in my judgment, has attractive features; but, alas, each has serious problems as well.

The First Solution: Contradictory Locations

Most class structure concepts are built on the unstated premise that there is a one-to-one mapping between "locations" in a class structure (the places filled by human individuals) and "classes" themselves: every location is in one and only one class. In capitalist society this implies that everyone must be located in the working class, the capitalist class, the petty bourgeoisie, or, perhaps, some entirely new class (appropriately called by some theorists, therefore, the New Class). The concept of contradictory locations within class relations was an attempt at breaking with this assumption: some locations in a class structure might be in two or more classes simultaneously. Managers, for example, could be understood as simultaneously in the working class and the capitalist class: they were in the working class insofar as they had to sell their labor power in order to obtain their livelihood; they were in the capitalist class insofar as they dominated workers within production. And since the class interests of workers and capitalists were inherently antagonistic, a dual class location that combined these two classes was dubbed a "contradictory location within class relations."[9]

How can a concrete location in a class structure simultaneously be in two classes? Within a relational concept of class, class locations are positions-within-relations. In order for it to make sense to see a "location" as simultaneously in two (or more) "classes," therefore, it must be the case that class relations themselves are multidimensional or multifaceted. The basic intuition underlying the conceptual strategy of contradictory locations is that the concept of "class relation" has two primary dimensions: property or ownership relations and possession or control relations. The former was linked to the concept of exploitation; the latter to the concept of domination. Managers occupied a capitalist location within control relations (they dominated workers), but a working-class location within ownership relations (they sold their labor power to capitalists). To talk about the multidimensionality of a relation, therefore, is equivalent to talking about the multidimensionality of the practices structured within that relation. What we call the "capital-labor relation" should thus be viewed as a package of relational practices.

This framework emerged as a specific solution to the problem of managers in the class structure. It was subsequently modified to accommodate the problem of professionals, experts, and credentialed specialists and technicians of various sorts. How should these jobs be located within a class structure? My solution was to consider these class locations as simultaneously working-class and petty-bourgeois. This means that they occupy a contradictory location that combines elements from two distinct kinds of production relations: capitalist relations and what is sometimes called petty commodity production relations. That is, experts and professional employees are petty-bourgeois insofar as they have direct control over their own labor process (self-direction or autonomy within work), but are proletarian insofar as they have to sell their labor power to

---

9. At roughly the same time as I was elaborating the concept of contradictory class locations, Guglielmo Carchedi (1977) was working on essentially the same underlying insight in his functional definition of the new middle class as being constituted by the simultaneous presence of the "functions" of capital and of labor.

an employer in order to work. For want of a better expression, I call such positions "semi-autonomous employees."

To complete the picture, small employers occupy a contradictory location that combines petty bourgeois and capitalist relations. Like the petty bourgeoisie, they are direct producers working alongside their employees, but like capitalists they are exploiters of workers.

This first strategy has a number of attractive features. First, the definitions of different class locations—both fundamental classes and contradictory locations—are all specified in *relational* terms. Second, the strategy suggested a particular set of experience-generating mechanisms linked to class. Domination and autonomy are aspects of work settings that are closely tied to daily experiences within production. The concept of contradictory locations thus manages to capture at a lower level of class structure analysis some notion of the lived experience embodied in the more abstract concept. Finally, the idea of contradictory locations introduces into class analysis a desirable kind of explanatory indeterminacy. One of the purposes of trying to develop a more refined class structural concept was to facilitate analyses of the relationship between class structure and class formation, in which class formations are not seen as simply derivative of class structures. The concept of contradictory locations helps to open up this theoretical space. Since many locations in the class structure have dual (and even contradictory) class logics, this implies that their translation into class formations will be contingent upon social processes that mobilize action around one or another of these poles. This gives a theoretically specific, rather than just an ad hoc, role for political and ideological determinants of class formation.

Nevertheless, in spite of these strengths, the concept of contradictory locations quickly runs into difficulties. First, exploitation is treated as the basic interest-generating mechanism within class structures, but it does not actually enter into the specification of the class map in a very systematic manner. The central novel categories of the analysis—managers and semi-autonomous employees—are both defined exclusively in terms of domination relations, not exploitation as such.

Second, the concept does not offer a satisfactory way of dealing with the state. The criteria used to define managers and semi-autonomous employees within the capital-labor relation are simply applied to state employment with no modification or justification. Given that classes are supposed to be defined within distinctive types of social relations of production, it is at best a weakness of the framework that state employment is simply amalgamated to capitalist relations. Also, the lack of systematic elaboration of classes within the state means that the framework is unable to define the specificity of classes in postcapitalist, "state socialist" societies.

Finally, at a practical level, it is exceptionally difficult to operationalize empirically one of the contradictory locations that figures in the general conceptual framework: the category "semi-autonomous employees." Autonomy within the labor process proves to be an extremely elusive concept all attempts at operationalizing it have a suspiciously gradational (rather than relational) quality, and all operationalizations seem relatively unreliable.

The Second Solution: Multiple Exploitations

The basic idea of the second solution is that different "modes of production" are based on distinctive mechanisms of exploitation, which can be differentiated on the basis of the kind of productive asset whose unequal ownership (or control) enables the exploiting class to appropriate part of the socially produced surplus. Building on the work of John Roemer, I distinguished four types of assets: labor power assets (feudal exploitation), capital assets (capitalist exploitation), organization assets (statist exploitation), and skill or credential assets (socialist exploitation) (Wright 1989a, 14–22). This opens up the possibility that people in certain locations in the class structure are simultaneously exploited through one mechanism of exploitation but exploiters through another mechanism. In capitalism, the key instances of such locations are managers (who are capitalistically exploited but organization exploiters) and experts (who are capitalistically exploited but skill/credential exploiters).

This second strategy, I felt, had a number of theoretical advantages over the earlier concept of contradictory locations within class relations. First, unlike in the earlier concept, exploitation-based interests occupy center stage. Different mechanisms of exploitation—exploitation-generating assets—define locations within a class structural matrix.

Second, the new formulation has a much stronger connection to the general Marxist theory of history, historical materialism. The sequence feudalism-capitalism-statism-socialism can now be characterized as a logical sequence of successive eliminations (or at least marginalizations) of specific forms of exploitation. This conceptual typology also gives the problem of the middle class a distinctive historical cast: the middle class of a society dominated by one mode of production is the principal contender for being the dominant class in the subsequent mode of production. The emergent bourgeoisie was the pivotal middle class of feudalism and the managerial-bureaucratic "class" is the central middle class of capitalism.

Third, this new formulation copes with the problem of the state more effectively: it is now possible to identify a specific form of exploitation (organization exploitation) and associated class relations with what is sometimes called a "statist mode of production."

Fourth, rather than trying to situate professionals and experts in the class structure via the slippery concept of their self-direction within work, they are now situated with respect to their capacity to appropriate the surplus due to their monopoly of certain skills, particularly when this monopoly is legally certified through credentials.

Finally, by introducing three distinct dimensions of the class structure—dimensions based on capital assets, organization assets, and skill assets—the new class concept provides a particularly nuanced empirical map for studying the relationship between class structure and class formation.

While these seemed like substantial theoretical gains, I recognized from the start that there were problems with the new concept.

Skill exploitation. There is a basic conceptual problem in treating surplus appropriation rooted in the ownership of skills or credentials as "exploitation," which does not exist for capitalist or feudal exploitation. An employee in a capitalist firm who has a high level of scarce skills (that is, skills which are scarce relative to their demand on the market), whether or not that scarcity is institutionalized through credentials, performs labor and thus contributes to the social surplus. When such an employee appropriates part of the social surplus through wages that are above the costs of reproducing labor power, instead of saying that this employee is an exploiter of unskilled labor power, it would make more sense to say that she or he is simply *less* exploited by capitalists.

The problem is that since this appropriation remains entirely contingent upon the actual performance of labor by the credential holder, there is no simple way of distinguishing those credential holders who are real exploiters from those who are simply "privileged" by virtue of being less exploited than other employees. In other words, one cannot distinguish the mechanisms through which the individual appropriates his or her own surplus and the surplus of others.

Another way of stating this problem with skill exploitation is that the idea of credential- or skill-based classes is less relational than the idea of capital-based classes. Knowing that a certain person owns capital intrinsically sets that person into a social relation with workers. In the case of skill owners, there is not necessarily an inherent social relation that binds them to the unskilled in the required way. Thus, credentials are a relatively ambiguous basis for defining a class relation, at least if we want the concept of class to be built around relations of exploitation.

Capitalist managers and statism. One of the implications of the multiple exploitations view that has aroused much skepticism concerns the alleged interests of managers within capitalism. If it is correct to claim that managers are simultaneously exploited by capitalists and yet organizational exploiters, then it follows that in principle they should have an objective material interest in the elimination of capitalist exploitation and the creation of a society within which organizational exploitation is the primary basis of class relations.

This characterization of managers flies in the face of most historical evidence. Undaunted, I have argued in the past that the obvious support of capitalism by managers in general, and by top managers and executives in particular, reflects the strength of capitalist "hegemony." A hegemonic class attempts to tie the interests of potential rival classes to its interests as a way of neutralizing their latent opposition. In the case of managers, this is accomplished through the organization of managerial careers and the ability of managers to buy their way into the bourgeoisie (through investments, stock ownership, etc.).

This kind of argument sounds very much like special pleading. While it is not unthinkable that historical circumstances could arise in which managers in general would adopt a statist critique of capitalism, this possibility seems like a weak basis for understanding the essential class character of managers in capitalism itself.

Organizational assets and the state. The multiple exploitation approach does not, in the end, solve the problems of state employment within capitalism generated by the concept of contradictory locations. In the map of class locations in capitalism, no account whatsoever is made of the institutional site of the organizational assets controlled by managers. Managers or bureaucrats in the state and in capitalist corporations are treated as situated in identical ways within the class structure because they bear a similar relation to their class-defining asset, organizational resources.

Operationalizations. One of the reasons for shifting away from the concept of contradictory locations was the enduring problems of operationalizing the concept of "semi-autonomy." In the end, however, this problem has simply been displaced onto the categories of skills and credentials, which are, if anything, more difficult to operationalize in a consistent and theoretically meaningful way.

The Weberian Temptation

Given these difficulties with the concepts of class structure built around contradictory class locations and around multiple exploitations, there are several broad choices about how to proceed. First, we could retain the abstract polarized concept of class structure but abandon the project of trying to develop a repertoire of more concrete, micro-level Marxist class concepts derived from it. One could, for example, adopt Weberian class concepts for the analysis of variations in individual consciousness while retaining the abstract polarized Marxist concept for understanding the structural dynamics of capitalism. It seems to me, however, that the explanatory force of the abstract, macro-level Marxist concept of class would be greatly compromised if it was unconnected to corresponding micro-level concepts, concepts that are closely tied to the lives and conditions of individuals.

A second possible response is to retain both the abstract class structure concept and the concrete derivations from it, and decide simply to live with a certain level of conceptual incoherence. This does not mean abandoning altogether the project of eliminating such inconsistencies, but it does mean adopting a certain pragmatic attitude toward research and not waiting until all conceptual problems are resolved.

There is, however, a third possible response. One can decide that these conceptual issues have been so persistent and intractable that they must reflect deeper problems in the larger theoretical framework of which they are a part. While there are still plenty of problems of operationalization within Weberian class structure analysis, many of the conceptual difficulties bound up with the middle class within a Marxist framework appear to vanish within the Weberian tradition of class analysis.[10] The Weberian

10. John Goldthorpe (1980, 39–42), for example, faces difficult problems in defining nonarbitrary criteria for operationalizing class distinctions. Nevertheless, the conceptual status of these distinctions poses no difficulties within the overall class structure concept.

concept of class structure is relieved of three theoretical burdens that a Marxist framework must contend with in one way or another:

Class, mode of production, and the theory of history. For Weberians, the concept of class structure does not have to be linked to an abstract concept of "mode of production." As a corollary, the concept does not have to figure in any general theory of history, as it generally does for Marxists. The absence of this concern means that the specific problem of conceptualizing classes in capitalist society does not have to meet any criteria of coherence with the analysis of class structures of precapitalist or postcapitalist societies.

Exploitation and antagonistic classes. While the Weberian concept of class is relational (it is grounded in economic exchange relations), it is not based on an abstract model of polarized relations. Weberians can admit an indefinite number of additional classes besides workers and capitalists without having to postulate any underlying conflicts of material interest. Marxists, on the other hand, have to produce concepts of specific class locations that are congruent with the underlying antagonistic logic of class relations based in exploitation.

Ambitiousness of the theoretical ordering of concepts. The neo-Weberian concept of class does not attempt to specify and defend a systematic hierarchy of conceptual elements. This means that Weberians can deploy a variety of criteria for defining aspects of class structures in a rather ad hoc manner without embarrassment. This lower level of aspiration of conceptual and theoretical integration within the Weberian tradition facilitates a rather pragmatic, empirical attitude toward the task of concept formation.[11]

The absence of these three theoretical constraints makes it much easier to locate categories like professionals, technical employees, and managers in the class structure. Given the fact that the middle class is so much easier to contend with in a Weberian framework, the question clearly arises: Why not simply jump ship and adopt the Weberian approach?

The reason for adopting a Marxist over a Weberian strategy has to rest on a commitment to precisely these theoretical constraints that Marxist theory imposes on class analysis. There is no reason to accept the difficulties that this abstract framework generates unless one sees the value of embedding the concept of class structure in an abstract model of

---

11. Val Burris (1987) suggests that the relatively low level of aspiration for theoretical integration of the distinct elements of class theory in the Weberian tradition is due to certain general properties of Weberian theory.

modes of production in which classes are fundamentally polarized around processes of exploitation. My personal commitment to these constraints is grounded on three broad considerations. One is political or normative, one theoretical, and one methodological. Politically, the Marxist tradition broadly understood continues to provide, in my judgment, the most comprehensive and compelling theoretical framework within which to understand the possibilities for and obstacles to emancipatory social change.[12] Theoretically, the concept of class structure within Marxism figures simultaneously and centrally in analyses of both epochal social change and systematically structured social conflict within given types of society. Methodologically, finally, I believe it is generally better to try to develop and reconstruct specific concepts within a clearly specified set of constraints than to do so in the absence of rigorously elaborated constraints. The Weberian tradition is generally characterized by quite ad hoc and diffuse conceptual specifications. If we want to gain knowledge not simply *about* a particular empirical problem, but *from* that problem, it is crucial that the concepts used in the analysis be as integrated as possible into a general conceptual framework.

Weberian solutions do represent a way of avoiding the conceptual knots generated by conceptualizing the middle classes within the Marxist tradition. But these solutions are purchased at the price of lowering one's theoretical ambitions and abandoning the attempt at consistency with the conceptual framework—a broadly conceived Marxism—that remains the most coherent general approach to radical, emancipatory social theory.

New Complexities

In the past, all of my work on class structure has treated class structures as sets of relationally defined "locations" filled by individuals, in which

---

12. Two points of clarification. First, the claim is about the Marxist tradition, defined in an ecumenical fashion, not about any particular theoretical position. Second, the claim is not that this tradition provides the most fruitful framework for analyzing every question of relevance to radical projects of social change, but simply that it provides the best overall framework for the general problem of understanding the obstacles to and opportunities for emancipatory transformation. Thus, for example, the Marxist tradition probably does not— and perhaps cannot—provide adequate tools for understanding many of the important issues bound up with gender oppression.

a location was basically equivalent to a "job." The class structure was thus essentially a relational map of the job structure. I now want to introduce three additional sources of complexity in the analysis of class structure. First, it must be recognized that individuals may occupy more than one formal job and, furthermore, that class-based material interests may not be associated with "jobs" as such. Second, the description of class structure needs to include what I call "mediated class locations": locations that are derived from various kinds of social networks rather than directly from individual participation in the relations of production. And third, an analysis of class structure must take account of the temporal dimension of material interests, especially as these are tied to careers.

Multiple Locations

Virtually all discussions of class structure, including my own, assume that individuals occupy one and only one location in the class structure. While I have argued that some locations have a dual class character, I have nevertheless assumed that individuals occupy unique locations. There are two contexts in which this description is clearly inadequate. First, and most obviously, many people have more than one job. Second, many people are both owners of capitalist property (and accordingly receive some of their income as returns on capitalist investment) and are employees in a job. There is a fairly wide spectrum of people—most notoriously, high-level executives in large corporations—who are employees in jobs with sufficiently high pay that they are able to convert some of their employment earnings into capitalist property through investments and savings. These kinds of situations define a specific kind of complexity in the class structure in which work and property ownership are partially uncoupled.[13]

Mediated Class Locations

The second new complexity concerns the various ways in which the class interests of people are conditioned by social relations other than their

---

13. Under certain circumstances, home ownership may also begin to function like a capitalist investment, if the rapid increase in housing prices gives the owner a substantial equity which they are able to use for investment purposes. Real estate speculation by workers is certainly not unheard in the contemporary United States, and when it occurs, it should be treated as a specific kind of change in their class location.

direct relation to the process of production (either through their jobs or their personal ownership of property). The most important of these "mediated" class locations are based in kinship networks and family structures, but in certain contexts the relation to the state also constitutes a mediated class location.

For certain categories of people in contemporary capitalism, location in the class structure is entirely constituted by mediated relations. This is most clearly the case for children. Mediated class relations also loom large in understanding the class interests of the unemployed, pensioners, students, and housewives not in the paid labor force.[14] In each of these cases an adequate picture of class interests cannot be derived simply from examining direct participation in the relations of production. A class structure at the concrete level of analysis, then, should be understood as consisting of the totality of direct and mediated class relations.

The concept of mediated class relations is particularly relevant to the interconnection of gender relations, family structure, and class. In conventional sociological discussions of social classes (e.g., Goldthorpe 1983), the family, rather than the individual, is treated as the fundamental "unit" within class structures. The class location of the family unit, in turn, is generally determined by the class location of the job of the "head of household"—typically, the male "breadwinner." This has the effect of deriving the class locations of all family members, including both housewives and wives in the paid labor force, from the class locations of husbands.

Many people have objected to the simple identification of the class location of wives with that of their husbands.[15] And yet, it also seems inappropriate to reduce the class of either husbands or wives in a family simply to their direct job class: should a school teacher married to a factory worker be seen as in the same class location as a fellow teacher mar-

14. To say that mediated class relations are particularly salient in understanding the class location of full-time housewives is not to prejudge the question of whether or not the gender relations between husbands and wives should be considered a form of "class relations." I do not think that this is a useful way of understanding gender relations within families. But even if one adopts this view, it would still be the case that mediated class relations would be salient for housewives. The class locations of a housewife married to a capitalist and one married to a factory worker are not the same, even if their status as "domestic workers" itself constitutes a gender-based class location. For a more extended discussion of the relevance of the concept of mediated class locations for understanding the class location of "housewives" and married women in the paid labor force, see my (1989c) essay, "Women in the Class Structure."

15. For critical commentaries on Goldthorpe's views, see Heath and Brittain 1984 and Stanworth 1984; also Goldthorpe's response (1984).

ried to a corporate manager or a capitalist? Some kind of differentiation between these two teachers is necessary.

The concept of mediated class locations provides one way of accom-
plishing this. The class location of husbands and wives should be treated
as a function of both their direct class location and their mediated location. The overall "class interests" of individuals, then, is formed out of some
kind of weighted combination of these direct and mediated locations.

Temporal Locations

One common objection to the kind of structural class analysis I have pursued is that it treats locations in an excessively static manner.[16] This temporal problem is particularly salient when one treats material interests as
the central commonality of class locations. The concept of "interests" is
inherently a forward-looking concept: to talk about interests is always
to imply something about future states, not simply present configurations.
Two individuals in identical working-class jobs—identical in terms of sta-
tically defined relational characteristics—would have very different material interests if one was certain to be promoted into a managerial position
and one was certain to remain for life in a working-class position.

Typically, analyses of the temporal dimension of class structures treat
this problem as one of intragenerational "mobility": individuals move
from one location to another, and thus the locations are definable independently of the movements. If, however, specific jobs are embedded in
careers, and certain kinds of careers cross class lines, then it probably does
not make sense to treat such movements as mobility at all. This line of
discussion suggests that it is important to distinguish between class careers
and mobility between careers. This distinction has generally been difficult to operationalize empirically because many careers are not orderly
or determinate. Individuals in specific jobs face a given probability of promotion across class lines, but the probability may be far less than certainty.
To put the matter somewhat differently, there may be a certain degree of
temporal indeterminacy in an individual's class location. The central point
here is that the class location of certain jobs cannot adequately be determined simply by looking at the relational properties of the job at one
point in time.

16. This objection specifically to my approach was first raised in Stewart, Prandy, and Blackburn 1980, 271–72.

Back to the Middle Class

With these new conceptual elements in hand we can return to the problem of the "middle class." I will focus on three categories that have provoked much discussion: professionals and experts, managers, and state employees.

Professionals and Experts

In many ways, experts and professionals of various sorts, particularly when they are not directly part of managerial hierarchies, constitute the category that has caused the most persistent difficulty in formulating a coherent Marxist concept of class structure. As indicated earlier, neither of the solutions I have offered—the concepts of skill exploitation and the semi-autonomous employee—is entirely satisfactory. Lurking behind both of these conceptual proposals is the basic assumption that the jobs filled by experts or professionals are not really working-class. In some sense or other they are "middle-class," and thus a conceptual justification for identifying their non-working-class location is needed. What I will argue, then, is that the basis for considering nonmanagerial professionals and experts as potentially part of the middle class is not a relational property of their jobs as such, but rather a temporal property of professional work.

Three considerations are particularly important in this regard. The first concerns the capacity of professionals and experts to capitalize their income. Holders of scarce skills, especially when these are legally certified through credentials, can be viewed as generally able to appropriate a "rent" component in their wage. When such rents are organized in careers in such a way that they are relatively large and increase over time, they generate a significant capacity for individuals to convert these credential rents into capitalist property: income-producing real estate, stocks, bonds, etc. Both in terms of interests in material welfare and in terms of interests in material power, professionals who accumulate significant savings and investments begin to share material interests with capitalists.

The second temporal issue concerns career trajectories that move into managerial hierarchies. To the extent that it is a normal part of an orderly career for professionals eventually to become supervisors and managers within their organizations, it might be appropriate to consider those professionals and experts who are outside the managerial hierarchy as nevertheless temporally inserted into the middle class.

The third temporal issue concerns what might be termed the petty-bourgeois shadow class of employees in many professional occupations. This is most clearly the case for the classic "free professions" such as doctors and lawyers, who in many capitalist countries have the relatively open option of self-employment. To the extent that such self-employment (and consulting) opportunities expand and are regularly available, they affect the class location even of those employee professionals who do not take advantage of them, since the availability of such opportunities affects the material interests of employee-professional locations in general (that is, it affects the trade-offs and dilemmas faced by people in such jobs). Given this way of analyzing the class character of professional employment, professionals and experts would generally be considered in "middle-class contradictory locations" by virtue of their capacity to capitalize their income and their career trajectories into managerial hierarchies and viable petty-bourgeois options.

This way of thinking through the issues, however, introduces a new kind of ambiguity into the analysis of class structures. How should we treat professionals who consume all of the credential rent in their income? Credential rents generate a capacity for acquiring capitalist property, but of course not all individuals who have that capacity will utilize it. Similarly, not all professionals or experts in careers that normally involve movement into the managerial hierarchy actually ever become managers. As I argued earlier, "material interests" should be understood as common material trade-offs and dilemmas in the choices people face concerning material welfare and power. Careers that generate sufficiently large credential rents to enable a person to capitalize their income define a set of alternatives unavailable to someone whose wages simply cover the costs of reproducing labor power. In a sense, therefore, whether or not the capitalist investments are actually made is a secondary matter; the primary issue is being in a position that makes such investments possible.

Nevertheless, it remains the case that as a result of the actual choices made by individuals in these kinds of careers, their material interests in the future change. In such cases we face a degree of indeterminacy or objective ambiguity in defining the location of individuals in the class structure. Class locations are partially indeterminate or ambiguous because they depend not simply upon observable properties of current jobs but also upon future states linked to those jobs, and these future states depend in part upon contingent choices and events. Thus, in addition to characterizing certain locations in the class structure as "contradictory locations within class relations," it now seems appropriate to characterize some as "objectively ambiguous locations."[17]

Managers

I previously advanced two basic rationales for shifting from the treatment of managers as constituting a contradictory combination of capitalist and working-class locations to the treatment of managers as organization asset exploiters. First, the difficulties with the category "semi-autonomous employees" seemed to indict the concept of contradictory locations when applied to managers as well. If, however, we no longer try to discover a single strategy capable of simultaneously solving all of the various conceptual problems posed by different categories of "nonproletarianized employees," then it may well be the case that the concept of contradictory locations within class relations is an appropriate way for theorizing managers, while some other strategy will be needed for other categories.

Second, the concept of organizational asset exploitation appeared to make it possible to link the analysis of managers within capitalism to the problem of classes in postcapitalist societies. However, this conceptualization makes sense only if it can be credibly argued that managers in capitalism, by virtue of their control over the organizational resources of production, have a material interest in a statist organization of production. Without contriving rather unlikely scenarios, this assertion seems implausible at best.

These two reasons for abandoning the treatment of managers as contradictory locations thus do not seem very compelling. While I think the class location of managers is best understood in terms of the original concept of contradictory locations, this does not mean that we should abandon the idea of organizational exploitation altogether. Organization exploitation, like "skill exploitation," generates employment-based rents in the earnings of managers. Because of the difficulty employers encounter insuring loyalty and responsible exercise of authority through

---

17. Allowing a certain degree of indeterminacy in the location of professionals and experts in the class structure may help to explain why this category of social actors is frequently characterized by such high levels of internal ideological heterogeneity. Much more frequently than is the case for other segments of the "middle class," nonmanagerial professionals and experts can be found all over the ideological map.

a purely repressive form of control over managerial activity, managerial careers have to be structured around a hierarchically organized "incentive structure," one that generates "loyalty rents" in managers' wages . As in the case of professionals and experts, this gives managers the capacity to capitalize their income. particularly when their careers involve movements into higher reaches of managerial hierarchies.

The State

State employment has always posed a serious problem for Marxist class structural analysis. If classes are defined by distinctive forms of social relations of production, how should employees within the state be treated in a class analysis? On the one hand, most employees in the state do not own any means of production and have to sell their labor power in order to acquire their subsistence. However, although they enter the labor market with the same kinds of resources as private sector employees, they leave the market for a very different kind of social relation: instead of entering a capital-labor relation, they enter a state-labor relation.

The issue here is how we should conceptualize the social relations of production within the state. Are there distinctive classes within the state in capitalist societies? Are the "locations" in the state outside of the class structure? Should the locations in the state simply be conceptually amalgamated with the corresponding classes of capitalism proper?[18]

One solution, of course, would be simply to argue that employees in the state are not in any class location; they are "outside" the class structure. After all, there are many people in capitalist society who do not have a *direct* location in the class structure: children, pensioners, permanently disabled, students, perhaps housewives. State employees—and employees in a variety of other noncapitalist institutions—could be treated in a similar fashion. Such a treatment of state employees might possibly be appropriate for those people who work in the political apparatuses of the state—the taxing authority, the courts, the police, the administrative apparatuses of the executive, the legislature, etc. However, a great deal of what the state does in capitalist societies involves the production and distribution of use-values such as education, health, fire protection, sanitation, transportation, and so forth.

18. Employment in certain other sites—churches, nonprofit organizations, voluntary associations, unions, even political parties—poses similar problems. Here I discuss only the state.

Once it is recognized that the state is a site of considerable social production, then it follows that the social relations within which such production takes place must be considered a variety of social relations of production. If these relations of production in the state involve processes of exploitation and domination, then they constitute the basis for a state-centered class structure.

This line of reasoning leads directly towards the concept of a "state mode of production" (or, at a minimum, "state relations of production"). Within state relations of production, the dominant class would be defined as those agents in the state who politically direct the appropriation and allocation of the surplus acquired by the state; the subordinate class would be defined as those agents who directly produce use-values (goods and services) within the state; and, in a way analogous to contradictory locations in capitalism, contradictory locations inside of the state would be defined as state managers/bureaucrats who control the activity of state workers while being, at the same time, subordinated to the state dominant class.

If we restrict our analysis to class locations defined directly by jobs—that is, to "direct" class locations—then these various locations within the state would be viewed as distinct classes from those in the private, capitalist sector. We would have a state working class and a capitalist working class, state contradictory locations and capitalist contradictory locations, etc.

But as I argued earlier, class structures should not be analyzed exclusively in terms of direct class locations; mediated class relations may be equally important in defining the contours of a class structure. An analysis similarly incorporating mediated relations is needed for the specification of the location of state employees in the class structure. Above all, state workers occupy mediated locations within the capitalist working class via the commodified relations of labor markets. Similarly, the ruling "elite" in the state—the political directorate of state production—is linked to the capitalist class through a variety of mediating social relations. For example, elite state employees follow career trajectories that move back and forth between the public and private sectors; state elites have the ability to capitalize surplus income, etc.

The implication of this analysis of classes within the state is that so long as state employment occurs within a society dominated by the capitalist mode of production, one cannot define the class location of state employees exclusively in terms of their locations within state production relations. To a greater or lesser extent, therefore, state employees occupy a kind of dualistic class location: a combination of direct locations within state classes and mediated locations within capitalist relations.[19]

This is, of course, not the only way to treat the problem of class relations within the capitalist state. Many theorists reject the concept of a state mode of production altogether; state production can be treated simply as a peculiar form of capitalist production—one organized by public authority rather than by private boards of directors. It is "capitalist" because it obtains its inputs from capitalist markets, it recruits its labor through these markets, it is constrained in myriad ways by the process of private capital accumulation, and its employment practices are largely shaped by capitalist practices of hierarchy and control. Just as the household should not be viewed as a residual form of some precapitalist "domestic mode of production" but rather as the domestic sphere of capitalist production, so, too, state production in capitalism should not be treated as the forerunner of some post-capitalist mode of production but rather as simply the "public sphere" of capitalist production.

This alternative view of state-based production relations in capitalist societies should certainly not be dismissed out of hand. Nevertheless, I feel that this view of state employment suffers from a kind of latent functionalism in its assessment of the relationship between state production and capitalist production. To describe state production as simply the public sphere of capitalist production suggests that its logic of development and internal organization is not just constrained by capitalism, but is strictly derived from the logic of capitalism. That is, there is something called the "logic of capitalism" which is embodied in a number of inter-connected spheres of production—domestic, capitalist proper, public/state. The articulation of such spheres, then, would be regulated by some kind of principle of functional integration.

Instead of such a functional derivation, it seems to me more plausible to treat the degree to which state production in capitalism is effectively subsumed under a capitalist logic as a variable rather than a constant. Thus, the statist character of state production, and accordingly the noncapitalist character of the class relations constituted within state production, will also vary across time and place.

19. I refer to this situation as "dualistic class locations" rather than "contradictory locations" because there is no inherent reason why the interests generated by the direct and mediated relations contradict each other.

Conclusion: Where Does This Leave Us?

I began this essay by arguing for the necessity of producing a repertoire of Marxist class structure concepts capable of effective deployment in concrete, micro-level analyses. The task was somehow to do this while remaining consistent with the abstract understanding of class relations in terms of interests, lived experience, and collective capacity. The most effective way of doing this, I argued, was to try to generate more concrete, micro-concepts of class structure on the basis of material interests and exploitation. Let me summarize the various lessons that can be drawn from this attempt:

Contradictory locations. The "middle class" in capitalist society should be understood as constituted by those contradictory locations within class relations which are simultaneously in the capitalist class and the working class.

Secondary exploitations. Skill exploitation and organization exploitation (or equivalently: skill-generated scarcity rents and organization-generated loyalty rents) are probably best viewed as the basis for strata within classes rather than for class divisions as such. Such strata, however, can constitute the material basis for the emergence of distinct class trajectories as individuals turn the surplus appropriated through credential and loyalty rents into capitalist investment.

Mediated locations and temporal trajectories. Class locations should not be understood simply in terms of the direct class relations within which jobs are immediately embedded. Class locations are also structured to a variable extent by mediated relations and temporal trajectories.

Professionals and experts. Temporal trajectories are particularly salient for understanding the class location of professionals, experts, and other categories of credentialed labor power since the careers of such occupations frequently involve (1) movement into management, (2) increasing capacity to capitalize employment rents, and (3) viable options of full-time or secondary self-employment. Such temporal trajectories, therefore, generally place professionals and experts into contradictory class locations (the "middle class") even if at a particular point in time they have not capitalized any of their income and are neither part of the managerial hierarchy itself nor self-employed. However, given the relatively underdetermined character of such trajectories for any given individual, professionals and experts may have what can be called objectively ambiguous class locations. In the lived experience of class relations, professionals and experts generally experience work in a much less alienated way than workers, and this contributes to the general perception that they are middle-class.

State employees. Although the direct class location of state employees can be seen as constituted within postcapitalist statist relations of production, to the extent that the conditions of production within the state are dominated by capitalist relations, it may be more fundamentally determined by the employees' mediated locations than by their direct locations.

At the core of Marxist theory is an elegant and simple abstract picture of classes in capitalist societies: a fundamentally polarized class structure which constitutes the basis for the formation of two collectively organized classes engaged in struggle over the future of the class structure itself. We have now journeyed far from that simple core. Instead of two polarized classes, we have contradictory locations within class relations, mediated class locations, temporally structured class locations, objectively ambiguous class locations, dualistic class locations. Instead of a simple historical vision of the epochal confrontation of two class actors, we have a picture of multiple possible coalitions of greater or lesser likelihood, stability, and power contending over a variety of possible futures.

References

Bashkar, Roy. 1975. *A Realist Theory of Science.* Brighton, England: Harvester Press.

———. 1979. *The Possibility of Naturalism.* Brighton, England: Harvester Press.

Bourdieu, Pierre. 1984. *Distinction.* Cambridge: Harvard University Press.

———. 1985. "The social Space and the Genesis of Groups." *Theory and Society* 14: 723–44.

———. 1987. "What Makes a Social Class?" *Berkeley Journal of Sociology* 32: 1–18.

Burawoy, Michael. 1985. *The Politics of Production.* London: Verso.

———. 1989. "Marxism without Microfoundations: A Review of Adam Przeworski's Work." *Socialist Review* 19: 53–86.

Burris, Val. 1987. "The Neo-Marxist Synthesis of Marx and Weber on Class." In Norbert Wiley, ed., *The Marx-Weber Debate.* Beverly Hills, Calif.: Sage.

Carchedi, Guglielmo. 1977. *The Economic Identification of Social Classes.* London: Routledge & Kegan Paul.

Cohen, Joshua, and Joel Rogers. 1986. *On Democracy.* New York: Penguin.

Giddens, Anthony. 1973. *The Class Structure of the Advanced Societies.* New York: Harper and Row.

———. 1982. *A Contemporary Critique of Historical Materialism.* Berkeley: University of California Press.

Goldthorpe, John. 1980. *Social Mobility in Modern Britain.* Oxford: The Clarendon Press.

———. 1982. "On the Service Class, Its Formation and Future." In Anthony Giddens and Gavin McKenzie, eds., *Social Class and the Division of Labour.* Cambridge: Cambridge University Press.

———. 1983. "Women and Class Analysis: In Defense of the Conventional View." *Sociology* 17: 465–88 .

———. 1984. "Women and Class Analysis: A Reply to the Replies." *Sociology* 18: 491–99.

Gouldner, Alvin. 1979. *Intellectuals and the Rise of the New Class.* New York: Seabury Press.

Heath, A., and N. Brittain. 1984. "Women's Jobs Do Make a Difference: A Reply to Goldthorpe." *Sociology* 18: 475–90.

Konrad, George, and Ivan Szelenyi. 1978. *Intellectuals on the Road to Class Power.* New York: Harcourt Brace Jovanovich.

Lockwood, David. 1958. *The Blackcoated Worker.* London: Routledge & Kegan Paul.

Mann, Michael. 1987. *The Sources of Social Power.* Cambridge: Cambridge University Press.

Przeworski, Adam. 1985. *Capitalism and Social Democracy.* Cambridge: Cambridge University Press.

———. 1989. "Class, Production and Politics: A Reply to Burawoy" *Socialist Review* 19: 87–111.

Przeworski, Adam, and John Sprague. 1986. *Paper Stones.* Chicago: University of Chicago Press.

Stanworth, M. 1984. "Women and Class Analysis: a reply to John Goldthorpe." *Sociology* 18: 161–69.

Stewart, A., K. Prandy, and R.M. Blackburn. 1980. *Social Stratification and Occupation.* London: Macmillan.

Wright, Erik Olin. 1989a. "A General Framework for the Analysis of Class Structure." In Erik Olin Wright et al., *The Debate on Classes.* New York: Verso.

———. 1989b. "Rethinking, Once Again, the Concept of Class Structure." In Erik Olin Wright et al., *The Debate on Classes.* New York: Verso.

———. 1989c. "Women in the Class Structure," *Politics & Society* 17: 35–66.

CHAPTER 2

Deconstructing and Reconstructing Class Formation Theory: Narrativity, Relational Analysis, and Social Theory

Margaret R. Somers

*T*HE NINETEENTH-CENTURY ENGLISH WORKING CLASS BEARS A MOST peculiar burden and embodies a most peculiar paradox. Like Auden's academic warriors who spar with "smiles and Christian names," historians, economists, and sociologists have pushed and prodded early nineteenth-century English working people into procrustean political positions to support or disconfirm Marx's predictions of revolutionary class conflict erupting from the contradictions of capitalism. A Manichaean concern locks the debate into an impasse: Were early nineteenth-century workers revolutionary or reformist? Was there a class struggle in the industrial revolution? The questions remain unresolved. Yet surely it is the history of English working peoples that has suffered from this burden of praising or burying Marxism through competing interpretations of their early stories.

The burden has been made heavier, moreover, by the weight of continual excoriation from all sides of the ideological terrain for the "refusal" of English workers to precisely fit either of the categories of proper revolutionary or reformist behavior. Indeed "why the peculiarities of the

This chapter is a modified and significantly revised version of Somers, "Narrativity, Narrative Identity, and Social Action: Rethinking English Working-Class Formation," *Social Science History* 16 (winter 1992): 591–630. © by the Social Science History Association. Reprinted with permission. Modifications are by Jennifer Durrn; the author is responsible for the revisions. Interested readers may wish to consult the complete text, as well as Somers 1993, 1994b, 1995a, 1996a, and forthcoming.

English?" has been an intellectual complaint since the birth of the theory of class.[1] Paradoxically, however, the yardstick used to measure the English working class and find it "peculiar" was constructed by classical sociological conceptions of class formation for which *English working people served as the putative historical model.* Surely something is amiss when the original historical actors whose lives were appropriated for a theoretical schema of class formation are subsequently judged deviant by that same theory.[2]

Both the paradox and the burden point to the need for a fresh agenda. Rather than asking yet again what explains the "peculiarities" of the English (or the "exceptionalism" of this or that national working class) the time has come to call into question the peculiarities of a *theory* that judges as deviant each empirical case it addresses.

This essay aims to do just that by offering a critical evaluation of class formation theory—a theory that seeks to explain how and why the working class comes to act the way it does. In this rethinking I join with and benefit from the critical and historical energies of many other students of class formation and social theory,[3] but my approach has a particular twist. I argue that the means to achieve this revised conception must be through an engagement with the concept of *narrative* and with the constitutive place of *narrativity* in social theory. My overall aim is to demonstrate the theoretical and historical significance of narrative and narrativity not only for studies of working-class formation but for social science research more generally.[4]

The relationship between narrative and the core problems of class formation theory is twofold. First, I argue that one particular *story*—the classical story of England's transition from traditional to modern society—is at the center of the problems of class formation theory. This single *metanarrative* was the substantive vessel which carried the theoretical innovations of those we now recognize as founders of the social sciences—Adam Smith, Ricardo, Marx, Mill, Durkheim, Weber, Freud. Ultimately this storied dimension of modern social science was lost from sight, but it did not lose its significance. In a curious inversion, the metanarrative of classical

1. This was E. P. Thompson's (1965) famous response to Perry Anderson and Tom Nairn (Anderson 1964).
2. For the *locus classicus* of the relationship between English working-class history, class formation theory, and capitalist development, see chapter 10 of Marx's *Capital* (1977).
3. Among recent work, see especially Katznelson and Zolberg 1986; Davidoff and Hall 1987; Steinberg 1991; Baron 1991; Rose 1991; and Canning 1992, 1996.
4. For elaboration, see Somers 1994b, 1995c, 1996b, and Somers and Gibson 1994.

modernization became merely a subfield of the social science disciplines ("modernization theory"), while in an utterly fragmented form, key elements of the story were abstracted into the foundations of class formation theory. The conceptual and methodological vocabulary of this theory is built on these abstracted fragments of the classical narrative of English socioeconomic development. For this reason, class formation theory cannot be successfully revised on a theoretical basis alone. Rather, we must recognize, reconsider, and challenge the particular encoded narrative. This being said, however, we cannot and should not attempt to escape altogether the narrative dimension of social explanation more generally (Somers 1994b, 1995c, 1996b); instead, we must rethink, rehistoricize, and ultimately *retell* that foundational story of the English.[5]

This historical deconstruction and reconstruction, however, must be accompanied by a conceptual one, for the classical story of English socioeconomic development was constructed, like all narratives, through a particular conceptual filter. That filter was the social naturalism of the late eighteenth and nineteenth centuries—an attempted epistemological escape from historicity. In social naturalism, temporality, spatiality, relationality, and concrete linkages all give way to the abstract ideals of natural, self-regulating entities (Somers 1995c). But nothing could have been more ironic and paradoxical: A metanarrative of modern English society was produced through the lens of a self-consciously antihistorical, antinarrative, naturalistic conceptual frame.[6] As a result, the foundational story deeply encoded within modern social science has all the formal components of an analytic narrative—a beginning ("traditional" society), a middle (crisis of the industrial revolution), and an end (resolution into "modernity"), as well as leading protagonists in action (classes in struggle) and causal emplotment (the engine of industrialization, proletarianization). The only thing missing is *conceptual narrativity*—social concepts that can embrace time, space, and relationality. The story's conceptual core—classes, society, "tradition," and "modernity"—is comprised of abstractions, denarrativized and atemporal.

The results are the strange hybrid we unconsciously live with today—a social science theory sprung from a vision of escaping the specificities

5. In this essay, I use the term "narrative" to convey the *constructed representation* of history, and the term "history" to convey the actual historical processes believed to be appropriated and rendered into representational form by historians. On my use of the term metanarrative, see below and especially Somers 1995c.
6. See Polanyi 1944; also Block and Somers 1984 and Somers 1990.

of time that is nonetheless constituted on an invisible narrative framework. And in this paradoxical combination can be found the source of many of the problems of class formation theory. In the task of recognizing and rethinking the story of English class formation we must therefore reconstruct historical and relational *concepts*. In this paper I will introduce the two central terms of this revision: *narrative identity* and *relational setting*. Part 1 examines recent theories of English class formation to demonstrate the presence of an encoded metanarrative and the paradoxical problem of this being a "denarrativized" (temporally abstract) narrative. Part 2 addresses the theory of narrative more generally in both its old and its new incarnations, and Part 3 examines the conceptual implications of narrative for social science research. Finally, Part 4 outlines a retold story of English class formation.

The "Denarrativized" Narrative of Class Formation Theory: The Case of The English

Studies of English working-class practices are embedded within and encumbered by the theory of class formation. Yet the paradox is that encoded within the theory is a "denarrativized" metanarrative about the long-term processes of English socioeconomic development. Such a naturalistic rendering of history is abstracted into a general model of the relationship between industrialization, proletarianization, the birth of class society, and the expected behavioral response of the working classes. Whether the concept is "worker," "social actor," "industrialization," "culture," "society," or "class," each element of the theory bears within it the constraints of the metanarrative. And from this obscured but powerful metanarrative comes the problematic that drives all studies of working-class formation: Why the failure (or incoherence, or peculiarity, or deviance) of the "real" working classes?

It is, however, the wrong question, and it rests on a wrongheaded assumption. The incoherences and peculiarities attributed to actual working-class practices are not those of the English or any other historical case. Rather they stem from the incoherences of class formation theory itself— most importantly, from inferring a teleological prediction (a "class in itself" will become a "class in itself" as working people's "objective" interests will eventually translate into revolutionary class consciousness), *not* from an empirical generalization but from a fiction and a metanarrative (Somers 1989, 1996a). New questions need to be asked, and to do so requires new stories being told (e.g. Clark 1995; Frader and Rose 1996; Joyce 1987, 1991; Rose 1991; Steinberg 1996a, 1996b; Tilly 1995). The work of renarrativization, however, also requires careful attention to the ways in which previous studies have been confined and constrained by class formation theory's embedded metanarrative.

The vast literature on English working-class formation in sociology and history can be grouped around three explanatory paradigms. The English working class in the industrial revolution was either (1) reformist (Smelser 1959; Perkin 1969; Thomis 1970; Musson 1976), (2) revolutionary in the 1830s but suppressed by the 1850s (Thompson 1966; Foster 1974; Saville 1988), or (3) "backward looking" and composed of artisans (not factory workers) who were "reactionary radicals" (Calhoun 1981; Bauman 1982). With all injustice duly acknowledged, I am not going to address either the important complexities within these three approaches or the differences among them; it is their common points, instead, that are of interest. Each of these approaches is a different answer to the same question: Why did the English working class in the industrial revolution either conform to or deviate from the revolutionary behavior predicted by class formation theory? That is to say, why did the working class not act in putatively "classlike" ways? And in all three paradigms, this question is addressed not to empirical cases of *variation* but to *deviations* from a prediction: Why, in other words, did the class in itself–class for itself prediction fail? Each approach embodies the same prediction—namely, that under normal conditions there should be a causal link between the societal and economic changes of the industrial revolution (class in itself) and the emergence of a revolutionary class consciousness (class for itself) (Somers 1996a).

The main difficulty with this prediction is that the English working class (and just about all working classes) have resolutely refused to behave properly. Yet when faced with such divergences between observed behavior and theoretical predictions, scholars of class formation have all too rarely asked why workers did what they did compared to *other* working classes. Such a comparative strategy would have led to a healthy multitude of competing empirical explanations to be tested and refined. Instead, the "nonrevolutionary" behavior of working people has been redefined into problems of *deviance* or *anomalousness* of the "real" from the *predicted.* Yet as we know from the philosophy of science, once an empirical finding has been defined as anomalous, *it is rarely used to test or falsify the theory.* Instead, it is the theory and the prediction that remain pristine while countless "alibis" are generated to explain away the deviations.[7] Thus, class formation theory has been reduced to a measuring rod used to chastise the shortcomings of working peoples. The result has been a scholarly preoccupation with what I have elsewhere called an *epistemology of absence* (Somers 1989, 1996a).

Several scholars of working-class formation have criticized just this problem. Ira Katznelson and Aristide Zolberg (1986), in particular, have tried to reframe the theory by jettisoning the constricting teleological expectation built into the concept of class consciousness and converting the explanandum to variations in class formation. Their efforts have been heroic but unsatisfactory. For the problem of failed expectations will not be solved by changing the dependent variable from revolutionary class consciousness to variations in working-class dispositions. The problem lies much deeper: The tenacity of the prediction is inexorably grounded in the tenacity of a single representational narrative. Indeed, all three theories of working-class formation are in essence *three different versions of the same story;* that is, three different "endings" to the same beginning and middle of an encoded metanarrative.

There is, moreover, a ghostly familiarity to this narrative. The story—"The Impact of the Industrial Revolution"—tells of the emergence of an industrial capitalist society from a preindustrial past. It is a story told in many idioms: the transition from feudalism to capitalism, the emergence of market society, the emancipation of civil society from the state, the increasing division of labor, or the rationalization of the modern world. For each version, the societal transformation—whether it is called industrialization, proletarianization, or the division of labor— ushers in the "birth of class society." It is a story that has economic, political, and cultural components. In the economic realm it is a process by which commercialization, an increasing division of labor, and technological development gradually break the bonds of relatively static preindustrial economies into industrial and capitalist growth. Politically, it is the story of the emergence of the liberal state, which provides the framework for and actively supports the new laissez-faire economy and its

7. On sociological alibis for working-class formation see Eley and Nield 1980; Katznelson and Zolberg 1986; and Somers 1989, 1996a.

subsequent class relations. And for social theory, it is a process by which "traditional" relations are transformed into class relations, and communitarian artisanal cultures organized by moral economies are supplanted by new class alignments—from the "bread nexus" to the "wage nexus."

Rather than questioning whether working-class behavior even *should* be explained by the birth of class society, these different versions represent only different views about *how* the working class *responded* to an unquestioned *causal primacy* of modernization. Here, then, is the problem: Each theory takes as given the *same causes*—proletarianization and the impact of capitalist society. This leaves for empirical research only the historical variations of these unquestioned causes. Katznelson's (1986) theory, no less than the prevailing paradigms of English working-class formation, continues to build an a priori causal argument into the research and retains by assertion precisely that which requires questioning and demonstration, namely, the causal primacy proletarianization (or industrialization, or the transition from feudalism to capitalism, or modernization) in explaining the social practices of working peoples.

The different approaches, moreover, do not represent fundamental disagreement over the nature of the transformation. Each version follows the same sequence from traditional preindustrial to modern industrial society to make its case.[8] And when all is said and done about the secondary influences on social action—religious, moral, cultural, political, and community factors—each explicitly makes the same point. First Harold Perkin (1969, 177): "At some point between the French Revolution and the Great Reform Act, the vertical antagonism and horizontal solidarities of class emerged on a national scale from and overlay the vertical bonds and horizontal rivalries of connection and interest. That moment . . . saw the birth of class." Next, E. P. Thompson (1966, 212–13): "When every caution has been made, the outstanding fact of the period between 1790 and 1830 is the formation of the working class. This is revealed, first, in the growth of class consciousness: the consciousness of an identity of interests as between all these diverse groups of working people and as against the interest of other classes. And, second, in the growth of corresponding forms of political industrial organization." Finally, Craig Calhoun (1981, 4): "All were essentially movements of those [nineteenth-century "reactionary radicals"] who would fight against the coming of industrial society, who had traditional communities to preserve."

8. It is a case that is most important for the Durkheimians.

A sequential development from "traditional preindustrial society" to "industrial capitalist society" and a radical rupture between the late eighteenth and the early nineteenth century are thus the essentially uncontested narratives at the heart of theories of class formation. The real linchpin that holds the theory and its prediction together is thus the *story* of the rupture and transformation from a preindustrial to an industrial/capitalist society. Only the *prediction* leads to the problematic of "failure" and "peculiarity" of behavioral outcome. Yet the prediction itself—the expectation of class structure producing class consciousness—is solely predicated on the metanarrative of classical modernity and its conceptual infrastructure. As long as the question of working-class social action is bound a priori to the metanarrative of industrialization and the birth of class society, the research task will be confined to elaborating only different versions of a presumed (but not demonstrated) causal narrative about the transformation to modernity and a predicted working-class consciousness.

What Is Narrativity?

From contesting the metanarrative embedded in theories of class formation, it is only a short leap to suggest that new stories need to be constructed about the long-term history of the English. But new stories cannot merely be the product of one assertion against another. The original metanarrative of modernity was itself constructed from a naturalistic, epistemological attempt to escape from relationality, time, and space. The paradoxical consequence is that the metanarrative at the core of class formation theory is conceptually both antinarrative and ahistorical. If our new stories are not to sound relentlessly like variations on the old, we need more than the deconstruction of the metanarrative of English modernization. We also need to develop a *conceptual narrativity*.

Narrative and the Historians

While narrative has always been the nonexplanatory and nontheoretical "other" for the social sciences, historians themselves have had a conflicting and changing relationship to it (Somers and Gibson 1994). In France in the 1940s, the *Annales* historians rejected both traditional political history and narrative in favor of more anthropological, structural, and quantitative analysis (Stoianovich 1976; Hunt 1986). Meanwhile, a sector of Anglo-American historians led by Carl Hempel (1942, 1962) argued that narrative itself was a science of history and, if done correctly, would produce general laws capable of both explanation and prediction. After two decades of vigorous debate, the Hempelian view of narrative faded (Gardiner 1952; Gallie 1968; Dray 1957; Atkinson 1978), but in the heyday of the social sciences a new movement to reject narrative emerged on both sides of the Atlantic. Historians in North America produced "social science history," while in Britain the revival of Marxist and Weberian theory generated "social history from below" (Kammen 1980; Stearns 1985). Social science methods and theories became favored, and narrative was characterized—and dismissed—as nontheoretical storytelling about elites.

In the late 1970s, however, Lawrence Stone (1979) led a "return to narrative." Stone argued that the overbearing influence of social science historical methods had eliminated any historical concern for meaning. Stone, however, was not really advocating a return to traditional narrative. Influenced by Clifford Geertz (1973) and the emerging "anthropological turn," he was advocating an interpretative approach, and the new "postsocial" history did not return to traditional narrative methods. In the present debates among advocates of poststructuralist, interpretive approaches, and most recently advocates of the linguistic turn, very few defenses can be found of narrative methods (e.g., Megill 1989).

In these various approaches to narrative a common feature can be identified: They all characterized narrative as *a mode of representation*—discursive, rather than quantitative; nonexplanatory, rather than conditionally propositional; and nontheoretical, rather than theoretically driven like the social sciences. The debates among historians were solely over how to *evaluate* that representational form. For "traditional" historians, narrative was ideal because the accurate representation of history was the essence of the historian's craft; while for the social science historians, traditional narrative representational form was inadequate to the task of either explaining or interpreting the past.[9]

Reframing Narrativity

Although historians have debated and increasingly scorned the value of narrative over the past two decades, scholars from a wide spectrum of

9. This view of narrative as representation was shared by philosophers and historiographers.

disciplines (including psychology, medicine, psychoanalytic theory, education, philosophy, political science, gender studies, and anthropology) have quietly appropriated the abandoned concept and often used it to produce major conceptual breakthroughs in their fields.[10] But the concept employed by these disciplines is radically different from the older interpretation of narrative as simply a representational form. The new notion recognizes narrative and narrativity to be concepts of social *epistemology* and social *ontology*. These new views posit that it is through narrativity that we come to know, understand, and make sense of the social world, and through which we constitute our social identities. It matters, therefore, not whether we are social scientists or subjects of historical research, but that we come to *be* (usually unconsciously) who we *are* (however ephemeral, multiple, and changing) by our locations in social narratives and networks that are rarely of our own making.[11]

Common Features of Social Narrativity

It is possible to identify four features of a reframed narrativity particularly relevant for rethinking social theory: relationality of parts; causal emplotment; selective appropriation; and temporality, sequence, and place.[12] Above all, narratives are constellations of *relationships* (connected parts) embedded in *time and space,* and constituted by what I call *causal emplotment.* Unlike the attempt to explain a single event by placing it in a specified category, narrativity demands that we discern the meaning of any single event only in temporal and spatial relationship to other events— hence its fundamental trait of relationality. Narrativity renders understanding only by connecting *parts* (however unstable) to a constructed *configuration* or a *social network* (however incoherent or unrealizable). The connectivity of parts turns "events" into *episodes,* whether or not the sequence of episodes is presented or experienced in anything resembling chronological order. Causal emplotment gives significance to independent instances, and overrides their chronological or categorical order. Without emplotment, events or experiences can be *categorized* only according to taxonomical schemes which are by necessity abstract and out of time—thus lacking deep personal meaning.

10. See Somers and Gibson 1994 for a discussion of these developments.
11. See especially Bertaux and Kohli 1984; Freeman 1984; and L. Polanyi 1985.
12. For a range of discussions of narrative theory, see Ricoeur 1984–86; Danto 1985; Barthes 1974; Scholes and Kellogg 1966; Genette 1980; Jameson 1981; Mitchell 1981; and Brooks 1984.

As a mode of explanation, then, causal emplotment is an accounting (however fantastic or implicit) of why a narrative has the story line
it does (Veyne 1971; Ricoeur 1981, 1984–1986). Causal narrativity allows
us to test a series of "plot hypotheses" against actual events, and then to
examine how—and under what conditions—the events intersect with
the hypothesized plot.[13] To make something understandable in the context of what has happened is to give it historicity and relationality. When
events, however fleeting, are located in a temporal and sequential plot,
we can explain their relationship to other events. Plot can thus be seen
as the logic or syntax of narrative (Veyne 1971; Polkinghorne 1988).
Without attention to emplotment, narrative's explanatory dimension can
easily be overlooked and be misperceived as a nontheoretical representation of events. Emplotment permits us to distinguish between narrative and *chronicle* or *annals* (White 1987). In fact, it is emplotment that
allows us to construct a *significant* network or configuration of relationships. In this respect, narrative becomes an epistemological category
for constructing knowledge.

A third crucial element of narrativity is its *evaluative criteria* (L.
Polanyi 1985; Steinmetz 1992). Evaluation enables us to make qualitative
and lexical distinctions among the infinite variety of events, experiences,
characters, institutional promises, and social factors that impinge on our
lives. Charles Taylor (1989), for example, argues that the capacity to act
depends to a great extent on having an evaluative framework shaped by
what he calls "hypergoods" (a set of fundamental principles and values)
(also see Calhoun 1991). The same discriminatory principle is true of
narrative: In the face of a potentially limitless array of social experiences
deriving from social contact with events, institutions, and people, the
evaluative capacity of emplotment demands and enables *selective appropriation* in constructing narratives (Somers forthcoming). A plot must be
thematic (Bruner 1986; Kermode 1984). The primacy of this narrative
theme or competing themes determines how events are processed and
what criteria will be used to prioritize events and render meaning to
them. Themes such as "husband as breadwinner," "union solidarity," or
"women must be independent" will serve to selectively appropriate the
happenings of the social world, arrange them in some order, and nor-
matively evaluate these arrangements.

13. Donald Polkinghorne (1988) comments on the difference between emplotment and
categorization.

Four Kinds of Narrativity

These relatively abstract concepts can be specified and broken into four different kinds of narrative—ontological, public, conceptual, and meta-narrative.

Ontological narratives are the stories that social actors use to make sense of—indeed, to act in—their lives. We use ontological narratives to define who we *are*, not just to know what to do. Locating ourselves in narratives endows us with identities, however multiple, ambiguous, ephemeral or conflicting they may be (hence the term *narrative identity* [Somers 1992, 1994b; Somers and Gibson 1994]). To have some sense of social being in the world requires that our lives be more than different series of isolated events. Ontological narratives turn events into episodes. People act in part according to how they understand their place in any number of given narratives, however fragmented, contradictory, or partial (cf. Taylor 1989, 51–52).[14]

But identity, like the self, is neither a priori nor fixed. Ontological narratives make identity and the self something that one *becomes*. Narrative embeds identities in time and spatial relationships (place); ontological narratives structure activities, consciousness, and beliefs (Carr 1986). Like all narratives, ontological narratives are structured by emplotment, relationality, connectivity, and selective appropriation. So basic to agency is ontological narrativity that if we want to explain anything about the practices of social and historical actors, their collective actions, their modes and meanings of institution building, and their apparent incoherences—we must first recognize the place of ontological narrative in social life.

But where do ontological narratives come from? How are people's stories constructed? Above all, narratives are social and interpersonal. Even psychologists recognize the degree to which ontological narratives can exist only interpersonally in the course of social and structural interactions over time (Sarbin 1986; Personal Narratives Group 1989). To be sure, agents adjust stories to fit their own identities and, conversely, will tailor "reality" to fit their stories. But the interpersonal webs of relationality sustain and transform narratives over time. Taylor (1989) calls these "webs of interlocution"; others (MacIntyre 1981) call them "traditions"; I will call them "public narratives."

14. For citations to various approaches of what I am calling ontological narratives, see Somers 1992, 619 n. 16.

Public, cultural, and institutional narratives are those narratives attached to "publics," to structural formations larger than the single individual, to intersubjective networks and institutions, local or grand, micro or macro: stories about American social mobility, about the ' freeborn Englishman," about the emancipatory story of socialism, and so on. Public and cultural narratives range from narratives of one's family to those of the workplace, church, government, and "nation."[15] Like all narratives, these stories have drama, plot, explanation, and selective appropriation. Families, for example, selectively appropriate from public narratives to construct stories about their descent into poverty. The media arrange and connect events to fit competing public narratives about the origin of social disorders. The seventeenth-century church uses public narratives to explain the theological reasons for a national famine. Government agencies tell us "expert" stories (public narratives) about unemployment. Taylor (1989, 39) emphasizes the centrality of public to ontological narrative when he states: "We may sharply shift the balance in our definition of identity, dethrone the given, historical community as a pole of identity, and relate only to the community defined by adherence to the good (or the saved, or the true believers, or the wise). But this doesn't sever our dependence on webs of interlocution. It only changes the webs, and the nature of our dependence."

Conceptual/analytic/sociological narrativity refers to the concepts and explanations that we construct as social researchers. Because neither social action nor institution building is solely produced through ontological and public narratives, our concepts and explanations must include the range of factors we call social forces—market patterns, institutional practices, organizational constraints. Herein lies the greatest challenge of analytic and conceptual narrativity: to devise a conceptual vocabulary that we can use to reconstruct ontological narratives, public and cultural narratives, and the crucial intersection of these narratives with other relevant social forces. For the purpose of rethinking social theory, it is the conceptual dimension of analytic narrativity that is most important.[16] To date, few if any of our analytic categories are in themselves temporal and spatial, as modern sociological terms such as "society," "actor," and "culture" were

---

15. Organizational theory has used narrative analysis in particularly creative ways. See Mitroff and Killman 1975; Martin et al. 1983; Meyer and Scott 1983; and Smircich 1983.

16. On narrative methodology in sociology and history, see Brown 1988; Abbott 1990; and Somers 1994, 1995c, 1996b.

intentionally abstracted from their historicity and concrete relationships. The conceptual challenge that narrativity poses is to develop a social analytic vocabulary that can retain its theoretical character yet still accommodate the contention that social life, social organizations, social action, and social identities are narratively constructed.

Metanarrativity, the fourth level of narrativity, refers to the master narratives in which we are embedded as contemporary actors in history and as social scientists (Jameson 1981; Lyotard 1984). Our sociological theories and concepts—Progress, Decadence, Industrialization, Enlightenment—are encoded with aspects of these metanarratives, even though they usually operate at a presuppositional level of social science epistemology or beyond our awareness. These narratives can be the epic dramas of our time: Capitalism vs. Communism, Individual vs. Society, Barbarism/Nature vs. Civility. They may also be progressive narratives of teleological unfolding: Marxism and the Triumph of Class Struggle, Liberalism and the Triumph of Liberty, The Rise of Nationalism, The Rise of Islam. The metanarrative of Industrialization/Modernization out of Feudalism/Traditional Society is only one of many cases in which a presuppositional story gets in the way of historical social science. What is perhaps the most paradoxical aspect of metanarratives is their quality of *denarrativization.* That is, they are built on concepts and explanatory schemes ("social systems," "social entities," "social forces") that are in themselves abstractions. Although metanarratives have all the necessary components of narrativity—transformation, major plot line and causal emplotment, characters, and action—they nonetheless lack a conceptual narrativity.

What Are the New Narrative's Implications for Social Science History?

What, then, are the implications of this new conception of narrative for social and historical research? All four kinds of narrativity are relevant to social science research, but if we are to adequately account for working-class formation and social action, the most important one is the third. Conceptual narrativity demands temporality, attention to place, and emplotment as well as relationality, structure, and historicity. *Narrative identity* and *relational setting* represent concepts that have worked best in my own research.

Narrative identity. I have argued that narrativity is a constitutive condition of social being, social consciousness, social action, institutions, and structures. If so, then our first challenge is to develop concepts that allow us to capture the narrativity through which identities are constructed and social action mediated. The concept of narrative identity is predicated on just this premise: Narrativity is not imputed to social life by scholars, but social life and human lives are themselves "storied" (Carr 1986; Sarbin 1986). Social identities are constituted through narrativity, social action is guided by narrativity, and social processes and interactions—both institutional and interpersonal—are narratively mediated.[17]

Class formation theory, by contrast, explains action with the concept of "interest." Interests are determined from the logic and stages of socioeconomic development, and the social analyst imputes a particular set of interests to people as members of social categories For example, historians commonly argue that the decline of traditional domestic modes of production and the concomitant threat to custom created an "artisanal interest." Although social science historians almost always demonstrate with subtlety how these interests are mediated through intervening factors (culture, gender, religion, residential patterns, etc.), social interests derived from the stage of socioeconomic development remain the foundational explanation for working-class practices and protests. Making sense of social action thus becomes an exercise in identifying social categories from the metanarrative of modernization, deriving putative interests from them, and then doing the empirical work of looking at variations on those interests.

But why should we assume that an individual or a collectivity has any particular set of interests simply because one aspect of their identity fits into one social category? Why should we assume that artisans have "artisanal" interests simply because they are members of the "declining artisanal mode of production" category? To let "class" stand for a determinative experience is to presume that which has not been empirically demonstrated—namely, that identities are *foundationally* constituted by categorization in the division of labor within a socioeconomic metanarrative.

Substituting the concept of identity for that of interest circumvents this problem. An identity approach to action assumes that social action can be intelligible only if we recognize that people are guided to act by

17. This relational approach derives from my interpretation of Karl Polanyi (1944, 1957, 1977), as well as from work in legal history, historical geography, legal anthropology, and anthropology.

the relationships in which they are embedded, rather than by the interests we impute to them. The identity approach focuses on how people characterize themselves in relationships. While a social category such as interest is an internally stable concept—it assumes that under "normal" conditions, entities within that category will demonstrate appropriate "categorical" behaviors—characterization, by contrast, embeds the person within patterns of relationships that continually shift over time and space. These temporally and spatially shifting configurations form the relational coordinates of ontological, public, and cultural narratives. It is within these numerous and multilayered narratives and social networks that identities are formed and challenged.

The narrative dimension of identities thus presumes that action can be intelligible only if we recognize the one or many ontological and public narratives in which actors identify themselves. Rather than deriving from interests, narrative identities are constituted by a person's temporally and spatially specific "place" in culturally constructed stories that comprise (breakable) rules, (variable) practices, binding (and unbinding) institutions, and the multiple stories of family, nation, or economic life. People's experiences as workers, for example, are inextricably interconnected with the larger matrix of relations that shape their lives—their regional location, the practical workings of the legal system, family patterns—and the particular stories (of honor, ethnicity, gender, community, greed, etc.) used to account for the events happening to them.

Although social action is intelligible only through the construction, enactment, and appropriation of public narratives, this does not mean that individuals are free to fabricate idiosyncratic narratives at whim; rather, they selectively appropriate from a repertoire of available stories. Which kinds of narratives will socially predominate is contested politically and will depend in large part on the actual distribution of power (Somers 1993, forthcoming). This is why the kinds of narratives people use to make sense of their situation will always be an empirical question rather than a presupposition. The extent and nature of any given repertoire of narratives available for appropriation is always historically and culturally specific; the particular plots giving meanings to those narratives cannot be determined in advance.

Relational setting. Social action and narrative identities are shaped not only through ontological and public narratives, but also by their environments—from politics to demography. We thus need a conceptual vocabulary that can relate narrative identities to that range of factors we call social forces—market patterns, institutional arrangements and practices, organizational constraints, legal structures and discourses, and so on—that configure together to shape history and social action.

Society is the term that usually performs that work for us in social analysis. When we speak of understanding social action we speak of locating the actors in their *societal* context. For most social science research, a society is a social *system*. As a system, it has a core essence—an essential set of social springs at the heart of the mechanism. This essential core, in turn, is reflected in the broader, covarying societal institutions that the system comprises. Thus when sociologists speak of feudalism, they mean at once "feudal society" as a whole, a particular set of "feudal class relations" at the core of this society, a "feudal manorial economy," and a concomitant set of "feudal institutions" such as feudal political units and feudal peasant communities. Most significantly for historical research, each institution within a society must co-vary with each other. Thus, in "feudal societies," the state by definition must be a feudal state whose feudal character co-varies with all other feudal institutions; feudal workers must all be unfree and extraeconomically exploited peasants. And in "industrial society," a modern industrial/capitalist state must be detached from civil society and the industrial economy, and industrial workers must be individual and free. To be sure, the synchrony is not always perfect. Lags occur during periods of transition from one society to another, and remnants of the old order may persist against the pressures of the new. But despite these qualifications, the systemic metaphor assumes a single entity in which the parts of society co-vary along with the whole.

If understanding working-class formation is to be more than an exercise in extending a unifying core to the assumption of interest, these systemic typologies must be broken apart and their parts disaggregated and reassembled on the basis of empirical relational clusters. The concept of society is rooted in a holistic and totalizing way of thinking about the world. If we want to be able to capture the narrativity of social life, we need a way of thinking that can substitute relational for totalizing metaphors. Here I concur with Michael Mann, who writes, "It may seem an odd position for a sociologist to adopt; but if I could, I would abolish the concept of "society" altogether" (1986, 2).

To make this possible, I am suggesting that we substitute the concept of a *relational setting* for "society." A relational setting is a pattern of relationships among institutions, public narratives, and social practices.

Identity formation takes shape within this relational setting of contested but patterned relations among people and institutions. It is a relational or structural matrix, similar to a social network.[18] One of the most important characteristics of a relational setting is that it has a history and thus must be explored over time and space. Temporally, a relational setting is traced over time by empirically examining if and when the interaction among the institutions of the setting appears to have produced a decisively different outcome from its previous examinations. Social change from this perspective is viewed not as the evolution of one societal type to another but as the outcome of shifting relationships among the institutional arrangements and cultural practices that make up one or more social settings.

Spatially, a relational setting must be conceived with a geometric and morphological rather than a mechanistic metaphor; it is composed of a geometric matrix of institutions linked to each other in variable patterns contingent on the interaction of all points in the matrix.[19] A setting crosses levels of analysis and brings together the effect of, say, the international market, the state's war-making policies, the local political conflicts among elites, and a community's demographic practices. This crosscutting character of a relational setting assumes that the effect of any one level (for example, the protoindustrial textile sector) can be discerned by assessing how it is affected interactively with the other relevant levels. To do so requires that we first *disaggregate* the parts of a setting from any presumed co-varying whole and then reconfigure them in their temporal and geographic relationality. In this way, for example, different regions of England are no longer cast as variants of a single society, but as different relational settings that can be compared (Somers 1993).

Narrative Identity, Relational Analysis, and Class Formation

So far, I have noted two implications of narrativity for engaging in social science: first, that we need to substitute the concept of narrative iden-

18. On networks and relational analysis see White 1992; for historical sociology see Bearman 1993; Mann 1986; Lachman 1987; and Somers 1993.
19. The epistemological implications of recent work in historical geography have been noted in Mann 1986; Aminzade 1992; and Somers 1993, 1995d.

tity for that of interest, and second, that we need to substitute the concept of relational setting for that of society or social system. This new narrative and relational analysis can potentially liberate us as analysts from the overarching metanarratives that have constrained class formation theory. In this final section, I will briefly note how this conceptual apparatus can be used to rethink research on working-class formation and retell the story of English class formation.

One important outcome of making relational settings and narratives the basis of working-class social action is that it eliminates class formation theory's perennial concerns about "inconsistency," "failed predictions," or "deviancy." The identity approach, in contrast, *expects historical contingency* between social practices and the industrial revolution (or any other societal transformation). The *effect* of such historical interactions is what must be explored empirically, as must be the question of whether these interactions will enable or constrain social action. The assumption of contingency thus challenges the assumptions that workers' behaviors that do not conform to categorical assumptions are anomalous, irrational, or "backward looking"; the settings in which identities are constituted have no exogenous directionality or a priori definition of rational action. If the contexts that give meaning, contingency, and historicity to identity have no teleology, no actions can be assessed as more objectively rational than others. All working-class behavior becomes potentially intelligible (Somers 1996a).

Another implication is that our research must begin not from a single category but from the network of relationships and institutions in which actors are embedded; we must then emplot these networks in their varying relationships to each other. Substituting a relational setting for the abstraction of society allows us to induce empirical connections among institutions rather than presupposing covariation among them. The positions and distances within a relational setting help to make sense of what kinds of social practices are possible, both at the level of structural opportunity and of purpose, identity, and meaning. Thus identity reconstitution becomes a two-step process: (1) finding and interpreting the clues left by historical actors regarding the narratives that have guided their actions, and (2) using those clues as well as research on broader social and structural relationships to configure these elements and repertoires into geometric social networks.

My research on the English case can schematically illustrate these points. In the years from 1800 to 1850, English laboring people violently broke machines, and they marched peacefully to Parliament; they mobbed unpopular workhouses, and they petitioned to retain or reinstitute apprenticeship and wage regulations; they demanded new forms of state intervention into the length of the working day, and they tenaciously fought for the right to outdoor poor relief and for local control over its administration; they waged militant strikes, and they formed self-help and community-based educational organizations; families "huddled" and exercised political influence by boycotting selected merchants, and at critical periods they linked these practices to the political demand for working-class participation in Parliament and universal suffrage.[20]

Let us leave aside the question of whether these were revolutionary, reformist, or "backward-looking" goals. Let us note, instead, the central narrative that ran like a thick thread through all the multiple social practices, goals, and movements. Simply, this narrative theme was that working people had inviolable *rights* to particular *political* and *legal* relationships. They claimed these rights as citizens and focused on a particular understanding of the law, a particular understanding of "the people" and their membership in the political community, and a particular conception of the legal relationship between the people and the law. This conception of rights defined independence and autonomy as inexorably linked to the property rights of working people (Jones 1983). But those rights were only in part the fruits of individual labor; they primarily rested on membership in the political community (Somers 1993, 1995a, forthcoming).

The most notable result of this narrative was that in the midst of the worst economic distress of their lives, English industrial families based their protests not on economic demands or those of a "moral economy," but on a broadly conceived claim to legal rights to participation, substantive social justice (poor laws), local government control, cohesive family and community relations, "modern" methods of labor regulation (trade unions), and the right to independence—be it from capitalists, the state, or other workers. They relied on plot lines driven by a conception of justice and *rights in membership* to explain their distress and guide their action (Somers 1994a). Consistently, they aimed their protests toward the law, legal authorities, legal ideals of universality and equity, local political and legal institutions, and toward enhancing the solidarity of the community itself. The relationship between "the people and the law" was thus

20. For the detailed argument and its connection to previous scholarship, see Somers 1995a and forthcoming.

the prevailing public narrative of these working people, and the plot line which configured this narrative was that of a political culture of rights.[21] The narrative of this rights culture was the theme through which events were evaluated, explained, and given meaning. They provided the guides to action, the methods for remedying wrongs and distress.[22]

This characterization does not prioritize either a language of class or of politics. There is no question that a language of class developed from the 1830s on, just as there is no question that there was a language that identified the state as controlling the levers of social power.[23] But most significantly, the language of rights embraced both politics and class; it was the explanatory prism through which class issues and other aspects of social distress were mediated and understood. Rights claims were thus political in the broadest sense: They established the claim to empowerment deriving not only from constitutional and "natural" rights but from community cohesion and autonomy in membership. Because they conjoined artisanal conceptions of property-based citizenship rights, these claims also conjoined our usually separate notions of social and political rights. Rights-bearing identities included class rights as one part of a bundle of rights attached to political membership under law; they combined social power, politics, individual rights, and membership.[24]

To explain these practices through narrative analysis means we must reconstruct the relational settings in which these identities unfolded. But in what did such settings consist? How do we know where to begin the task of reconstitution? This is not the place to summarize such a project of identity reconstitution; I will mention my findings only programmatically.

After first recounting the prevailing narratives, we must follow their themes and plots—about the law, about the communities in which the law operated, and about the local interaction between communities and the

21. On the concept of "the people" see Hill 1981; Rogers 1987; Joyce 1991.
22. On workers' self-narratives and autobiographies see Vincent 1981 and Burnett et al. 1984–89.
23. The classic article on the language of class in the nineteenth century is still Briggs 1967. See also Belchem 1981; Jones 1983; Claeys 1985; Cronin 1986; Epstein 1986; Gray 1986, 1987; Scott 1988; and Steinberg 1991.
24. For the convergence of constitutional and natural rights rhetoric, see Thompson 1965; Belchem 1981; and Epstein 1989. On the link between artisanal skills, property, and political rights, see Sewell 1980; Jones 1983; Hobsbawm 1984; and Rule 1987. See Scott 1988 for a critique of Jones's opposition to political and class claims. For critiques of the opposition of rights claims and community membership identities, see especially Walzer 1982 and Minow 1987. For a sociological view of rights formation, see Tilly 1990, Somers 1994a.

law. And from these we can configure into geometric and temporal form the shifting and varied relational settings in which our actors lived. The identities of nineteenth-century English working peoples can be traced to four roughly different relational settings: (1) pastoral, rural industrial, and later northern industrial communities; (2) agricultural laboring communities; (3) urban artisanal communities; and (4) French pastoral and rural industrial communities. These can be conceived as four different historical and geographical anthropologies (1300–1850) comprised of (1) variations in productive activities and working relations; (2) variations among English and Continental legal institutions, doctrines, statutory claims, ideals, promises, and policies—especially the differing political and legal rights attached to property relations, statutory labor regulations, legal administrative procedures, and discursive ideals of jurisprudence; (3) variations among communities—differing patterns of kinship, demography, inheritance, and migration among England's urban and rural popular communities (both freeholder and laboring); and (4) differences in the practical workings of English law and justice at the local levels of these communities.

Comparing these relational settings involves specifying linkages and constructing networks at two levels. In the setting as a whole, each institution forms a point, or a domain, in a geometric pattern. Connecting lines represent the actual interactive links between the institutions. Rather than imputing an a priori function to a type of production, for example, one asks what kinds of relationships it generated (or gave rise to it in the first place) and what the patterns of these connections were. In the case of eighteenth-century rural domestic industries, for example, I plotted the connections of merchant capitalists to their family "employees" and followed the processes by which work was distributed, wages negotiated, infractions of contract dealt with, and payments organized. This led to plotting the daily treks of a middleman, as well as directly to local administrators of statutory labor law. This in turn led to the participatory mechanisms through which these laws were carried out, which required understanding class power relations in the community. Relational analysis therefore neither dismisses nor reduces production to "the economy" (with all the systematization invoked by that category). Rather it constitutes economic production as one among a multiple network of competing institutions and practices that bear on identity formation.[25]

25. These are, of course, the premises of economic sociology. See K. Polanyi 1954, 1977; Sahlins 1976; Bell 1981; Block and Somers 1984; Hirschman 1984; Block 1989; and Somers 1990.

At a second level, relational analysis transforms each institution from a single entity to a set of relationships. The state, for example, may well be an instrument of coercion, but more important is its actual amalgam of suborganizations and their relationships with one another. Similarly, the historical meaning of law only begins to take shape by charting its numerous institutional and discursive expressions, from the highest courts to the most trivial of local juries to the discourses of social justice and the statutory preambles. This kind of network analysis makes it possible to study the continual shifts in the kinds and consequences of interactive patterns and institutional arrangements. Substituting the term "place" for that of "role" (part of the systemic metaphor) allows us to locate institutions and practices in their relational settings.

The significance for identity formation of each relational setting emerges only by comparing patterns of power, economics, and culture over varying times and places. Thus, it would be a mistake to presume that the lives of seventeenth-century rural industrial families can be understood by simply invoking the category "proletarianized unit of production." Instead, I asked what sorts of family and work ties had to exist, for example, to sustain certain kinds of inheritance practices. Inversely, what sorts of relationships did different inheritance practices produce and support? Similar questions can be addressed to institutional power relations (rather than relying on a priori categories of "strong" or "weak" states). What administrative power did the crown have available for certain policies? How was this power implemented in local communities?

To summarize my alternative story: The meanings of working-class formation are to be found not in the "birth of class society" but rather in the long-term consequences of the legal revolutions of medieval England. Alone among European state builders, only the English created a national public sphere by appropriating from below and extending throughout the land the legal conventions of both the medieval cities and the public villages. In legal practices the state became the city "writ large"; remedies of procedural justice ensuring rights in autonomy and independence coexisted with both national redistributive policies, as well as legal institutions that commanded community participation in the administration of law.[26]

This mandatory participation in legal administration by all freeholders may have been the most crucial factor in English working-class

26. This is further elaborated in Somers 1993, 1994a, and forthcoming.

formation.[27] The most notable result of this participatory system was that which I have dubbed a system of *narrative justice*—the local contextualizing and negotiating of legal processes. This legal narrativity generated different patterns of justice—indeed, different legal cultures in different types of settings. Historically persistent patterns of difference existed in the structure of early labor markets, in the degree of popular participation in political and legal institutions, in the character of corporate village institutions, and above all, in popular conceptions and social narratives of justice and rights. Popular empowerment varied in the degree to which communities were able to appropriate the law into rights. Because local communities administered a formally uniform national law, the multiple narratives of community politics were institutionalized into the heart of the national legal and political apparatus.

Narrative analysis, thus, produces a different picture of English working-class formation. What we recognize as nineteenth-century working-class formation developed from patterns of protest almost exclusively in the northern industrial villages—the inheritors of those strong, popular legal cultures of early pastoral and rural industrial relational settings. Working families carried with them into the nineteenth century a robust narrative identity based on a long culture of practical rights—a culture honed, revised, and adjusted over many centuries, and one they were not likely to dismiss readily at the crossing of a rubicon dubbed by historians only years later as the Industrial Revolution (Somers 1995a).

The aim of this essay has been to explain why class formation theory is so problematic and how it might be reconsidered. My definition of the problem is similar in part to that articulated by Katznelson and Zolberg (1986) in their influential volume on working-class formation. As I see it, class formation theory, with its predictive teleology of class in itself–class for itself, forces an accounting not for actual patterns of variation but for "an epistemology of absence" which in turn had led to a theory that too often has chastised and measured working-class practices against a fictional predictive yardstick (Somers 1989, 1996a). These problems are reflected in the prevailing three approaches to nineteenth-century English class formation, each of which defines working-class

27. For the centrality of legal participation see especially Herrup 1987 and Beattie 1986.

practices ("reformist," "revolutionary," "backward looking") against the presuppositional backdrop of the in itself–for itself theoretical prediction.

But there is a deeper problem, namely, the a priori assumption that the rise of an entity called capitalism must be the foundational causal factor in shaping these practices. Thus, regardless of its ideological persuasion, each of the three paradigms roots the explanation of nineteenth-century working class social action in the "birth of class society"; the *response* to that birth on the part of workers is what distinguishes the approaches. The conceptual limitations of Katznelson's (1986) own revisions show just how intractable a problem this is. Although he avoids teleology through a comparative approach to class dispositions and actions, he stops short of envisioning a theory that escapes from reducing these a priori to the causality of proletarianization and, more generally, to the emergence of capitalism.

The further challenge for theorists of working-class formation is, therefore, not only to liberate the study of class action from the constraints of an a priori teleological outcome, but, more importantly, to free it from the constraints of an a priori causal explanation—the metanarrative of English "modernization," its transition from feudalism to capitalism, and the drama of proletarianization. Freeing the theory from these constraints is no simple matter, however. The underlying problem is the conceptual vocabulary that is the universal parlance of existing discussions of class formation. Contained within this vocabulary is the massively entrenched and conceptually encoded denarrativized story of the making of modern English class society. Such entrenchment and encoding is surprising only if we find it difficult to accept that all theory is not simply theory but also part narrative and part epistemology. Just as we have come to accept the impossibility of setting aside epistemological assumptions, so it is time to accept the impossibility of setting aside the centrality of narrative in theory. The appropriate question we must put to ourselves is not, How can we do away with these distorting metanarratives? but rather, *Which* of many possible narratives are we going to live with for now?

Thus, explaining and recovering the meaning and the making of working-class social action (which is, after all, the goal of class formation theory) demands not only recognizing the centrality of the classical metanarrative; it means also systematically loosening its hold by *renarrativizing* our conceptual language of social action.

References

Abbott, Andrew. 1990. "Conceptions of Time and Events in Social Science Methods: Causal and Narrative Approaches." *Historical Methods* 23 (4): 140–50.

Aminzade, Ron. 1992. "What is Historical about Historical Sociology?" *Sociological Methods and Research* 20 (4): 456–80.

Anderson, Perry. 1964. "Origins of the Present Crisis." *New Left Review* 23: 26–54. Reprinted in P. Anderson and R. Blackburn, eds., *Towards Socialism*. Ithaca, N.Y.: Cornell University Press.

Atkinson, R. F. 1978. *Knowledge and Explanation in History: An Introduction to the Philosophy of History*. Ithaca, N.Y.: Cornell University Press.

Baron, Ava. 1991. "Gender and Labor History: Learning from the Past, Looking to the Future." In Ava Baron, ed., *Work Engendered: Toward a New History of American Labor*. Ithaca, N.Y.: Cornell University Press.

Barthes, Roland. 1974 [1966]. "Introduction to the Structural Analysis of the Narrative." Translated by Richard Miller. Occasional Paper, Centre for Contemporary Cultural Studies, University of Birmingham. New York: Hill and Wang.

Bauman, Zygmunt. 1982. *Memories of Class; The Pre-History and After-Life of Class*. London: Routledge.

Bearman, Peter. 1993. *Relations into Rhetorics*. New Brunswick, N.J.: Rutgers University Press.

Beattie, John. 1986. *Crime and the Courts in England: 1660–1800*. Princeton: Princeton University Press.

Belchem, John. 1981. "Republicanism, Popular Constitutionalism and the Radical Platform in Early Nineteenth-Century England." *Social History* 6: 1–32.

Bell, D. 1981. "Models and Reality in Economic Discourse." In D. Bell and I. Kristol, eds., *The Crisis in Economic Theory*. New York: Basic Books.

Bertaux, Daniel, and Martin Kohli. 1984. "The Life Story Approach: A Continental View." *Annual Review of Sociology* 10: 215–37.

Block, F. 1989. *Post-Industrial Possibilities: A Critique of Economic Discourse*. Berkeley: University of California Press.

Block, F., and M. R. Somers. 1984. "Beyond the Economic Fallacy: The Holistic Social Science of Karl Polanyi." In T. Skocpol, ed., *Vision and Method in Historical Sociology*. Cambridge: Cambridge University Press.

Briggs, A. 1967. "The Language of 'Class' in Early Nineteenth-Century England." In A. Briggs and J. Saville, eds., *Essays in Labour History*. London: Macmillan.

Brooks, Peter. 1984. *Reading for the Plot: Design and Intention in Narrative*. New York: Alfred A. Knopf.

Brown, Richard Harvey. 1988. "Positivism, Relativism, and Narrative in the Logic of the Historical Sciences." *American Historical Review* 92 (4): 908–20.

Bruner, Jerome. 1936. *Actual Minds, Possible Worlds*. Cambridge: Harvard University Press.

Burnett, John, David Vincent, and David Mayall, eds. 1934–89. *The Autobiography of the Working Class: An Annotated, Critical Bibliography*. 3 vols. Hemel Hempstead: Harvester Wheatsheaf.

Calhoun, Craig. 1981. *The Question of Class Struggle*. Chicago: University of Chicago Press.

———. 1991. "Morality, Identity, and Historical Explanation: Charles Taylor on the Sources of the Self." *Sociological Theory* 9 (2): 232–63.

Canning, Kathleen. 1992. "Gender and the Politics of Class Formation: Rethinking German Labor History." *American Historical Review* 97: 736–68.

Carr, David. 1986. "Narrative and the Real World." *History and Theory* 25 (2): 117–31.

Claeys, Gregory. 1985. "Language, Class, and Historical Consciousness in Nineteenth-Century Britain." *Economy and Society* 14: 239–63.

Clark, Anna. 1995. *The Struggle for the Breeches: Gender and the Making of the English Working Class*. Berkeley: University of California Press.

Cronin, James E. 1986. "Language, Politics and the Critique of Social History." *Journal of Social History* 20: 177–83.

Danto, Arthur C. 1985. *Narration and Knowledge: Including the Integral Text of Analytical Philosophy of History*. New York: Columbia University Press.

Davidoff, Lenore, and Catherine Hall. 1987. *Family Fortunes*. Chicago: University of Chicago Press.

Dray, William H. 1957. *Laws and Explanations in History*. London: Oxford University Press.

Eley, Geoff, and K. Nield. 1980. "Why Does Social History Ignore Politics?" *Social History* 5: 249–71.

Epstein, James. 1986. "Rethinking of the Categories of Working-Class History." *Labour / Le Travail* 18: 195–208.

———. 1989. "Understanding the Cap of Liberty: Symbolic Practice and Social Conflict in Early Nineteenth-Century England." *Past and Present* 122: 75–118.

Foster, John. 1974. *Class Struggle and the Industrial Revolution in Three English Towns*. London: Wiedenfeld and Nicholson.

Frader, Laura L., and Sonya O. Rose. 1996. *Gender and Class in Modern Europe*. Ithaca, N.Y.: Cornell University Press.

Freeman, Mark. 1984. "History, Narrative, and Life-Span Developmental Knowledge." Human Development 27: 1–19.

Gallie, W. B. 1968. *Philosophy and the Historical Understanding*. New York: Schocken Books.

Gardiner, Patrick. 1952. *The Nature of Historical Explanation*. Oxford: Clarendon Press.

Geertz, Clifford. 1973. *The Interpretation of Culture*. New York: Basic Books.

Genette, Gerard. 1980. *Narrative Discourse: An Essay in Method*. Translated by Jane E. Lewin. Ithaca, N.Y.: Cornell University Press.

Gray, Robbie. 1986. "Deconstructing the English Working Class." *Social History* 11: 3363–73.

———. 1987. "The Languages of Factory Reform in Britain, c. 1830–1860." In P. Joyce, ed., *The Historical Meaning of Work*. Cambridge: Cambridge University Press.

Hempel, Carl G. 1959 [1942]. "The Function of General Laws in History." In Patrick Gardiner, ed., *Theories of History*. New York: Free Press of Glencoe: 344–56.

———. 1966 [1962]. "Explanation in Science and History." In William H. Dray, ed., *Philosophical Analysis and History*. New York: Harper and Row.

Herrup, Cynthia. 1987. *The Common Peace*. Cambridge: Cambridge University Press.

Hill, C. 1981. "Parliament and People in Seventeenth Century England." *Past and Present* 142: 100–124.

Hirschman, A. 1984. "Against Parsimony." *American Economic Papers and Proceedings,* 74: 89–96.

Hobsbawm, E. J. 1984. "Artisan or Labour Aristocrat?" *Economic History Review* 37: 355–72.

Hunt, Lynn. 1986. "French History in the Last Twenty Years: The Rise and Fall of the *Annales* Paradigm." *Journal of Contemporary History* 21: 209–24.

Jameson, Fredric. 1981. *The Political Unconscious. Narrative as a Socially Symbolic Act*. Ithaca, N.Y.: Cornell University Press.

——. 1984. "Karl Marx and the English Labour Movement." *History Workshop Journal* 18: 124–37.

Jones, Gareth Stedman. 1983. *Languages of Class: Studies in English Working-Class History*. Cambridge: Cambridge University Press.

Joyce, Patrick. 1987. *The Historical Meanings of Work*. Cambridge: Cambridge University Press.

——. 1991. *Visions of the People*. Cambridge: Cambridge University Press.

Kammen, Michael, ed. 1980. *The Past Before Us: Contemporary Historical Writing in the United States*. Ithaca, N.Y.: Cornell University Press.

Katznelson, Ira. 1986. Introduction to Ira Katznelson and Aristide R. Zolberg, eds., *Working-Class Formation: Nineteenth-Century Patterns of Western Europe and the United States*. Princeton: Princeton University Press.

Katznelson, Ira, and Aristide Zolberg, eds. 1986. *Working-Class Formation: Nineteenth-Century patterns in Western Europe and the United States*. Princeton: Princeton University Press.

Kermode, Frank. 1984. "Secrets and Narrative Sequence." In W. J. T. Mitchell, ed., *On Narrative*. Chicago: University of Chicago Press.

Lachman, Richard. 1987. *From Manor to Market*. Madison: University of Wisconsin Press.

Lyotard, Jean-Francois. 1984. *The Postmodern Condition: A Report on Knowledge*. Minneapolis: University of Minnesota Press.

MacIntyre, Alasdair. 1981. *After Virtue: A Study in Moral Theory*. Notre Dame, Ind.: Notre Dame University Press.

Mann, Michael. 1986. *The Origins of Social Power*. Vol. 1, *A History of Power From the Beginning to A.D. 1760*. London: Cambridge University Press.

Martin, Joanne, Martha S. Feldman, Mary Jo Hatch, and Sim B. Sim. 1983. "The Uniqueness Paradox in Organizational Stories." *Administrative Science Quarterly* 28: 438–53.

Marx, Karl. 1977. "The Working Day." In Karl Marx, *Capital*, vol. 1. New York: Vintage Books.

Megill, Allan. 1989. "Recounting the Past: 'Description,' Explanation, and Narrative in Historiography." *American Historical Review* 94 (3): 627–53.

Meyer, John W., and John Scott. 1983. *Organizational Environments: Ritual and Rationality*. Beverly Hills, Calif.: Sage.

Minow, Martha. 1987. "Interpreting Rights: An Essay for Robert Cover."
  Yale Law Review 96: 1860–1915.
Mitchell, W. J. T., ed. 1981. *Recent Theories of Narrative*. Chicago: Chicago
  University Press.
Mitroff, Ian, and R. H. Killman. 1975. "Stories Managers Tell: A New Tool
  for Organizational Problem Solving." *Management Review* 64: 18–28.
Musson, A. E. 1976. "Class Struggle and the Labour Aristocracy
  1830–1860." *Social History* 3: 61–82.
Perkin, H. L. 1969. *The Origins of Modern English Society 1790–1880*. Lon-
  don: Routledge and Kegan Paul.
Personal Narratives Group. 1989. *Interpreting Women's Lives: Feminist The-
  ory and Personal Narratives*. Bloomington: Indiana University Press.
Polanyi, Karl. 1944. *The Great Transformation*. New York: Farrar and
  Rinehart.
———. 1957. "The Economy as Instituted Process." In Karl Polanyi, Con-
  rad M. Arensberg, and Harry W. Pearson, eds., *Trade and Market in the
  Early Empires*. New York: Free Press: 243–69.
———. 1977. *The Livelihood of Man*. Edited by Harry Pearson. New York:
  Academic Press.
Polanyi, Livia. 1985. *Telling the American Story*. Norwood, N.J.: Ablex.
Polkinghorne, Donald. 1988. *Narrative Knowing and the Human Sciences*.
  Albany: SUNY Press.
Ricoeur, Paul. 1984–86. *Time and Narrative*. 2 vols. Translated by Kathleen
  McLaughlin and David Pellauer. Chicago: University of Chicago Press.
Rogers, D. T. 1987. *Contested Truths: Keywords in American Politics Since
  Independence*. New York: Basic Books.
Rose, Sonya. 1991. *Limited Livelihood*. Berkeley: University of California Press.
Rule, J. 1987. "The Property of Skill in the Period of Manufacture." In P.
  Joyce, ed., *The Historical Meanings of Work*. Cambridge: Cambridge
  University Press.
Sahlins, M. 1976. *Culture and Practical Reason*. Chicago: University of
  Chicago Press.
Sarbin, Theodore R., ed. 1986. *Narrative Psychology: The Storied Nature of
  Human Conduct*. New York: Praeger.
Saville, John. 1988. *The British State and the Chartist Movement*. Cambridge:
  Cambridge University Press.
Scholes, Robert, and Robert Kellogg. 1966. *The Nature of Narrative*. Lon-
  don: Oxford University Press.

Scott, Joan. 1988. "On Language, Gender, and Working-Class History." In Joan Scott, ed., *Gender and the Politics of History* (New York: Columbia University Press).

Sewell, William. 1980. *Work and Revolution in France*. New York: Cambridge University Press.

Smelser, Neil. 1959. *Social Change in the Industrial Revolution*. Chicago: University of Chicago Press.

Smircich, Linda. 1983. "Concepts of Culture and Organizational Analysis." *Administrative Science Quarterly* 28: 339–58.

Somers, Margaret R. 1989. "Workers of the World, Compare!" *Contemporary Sociology* 18 (May): 325–29.

———. 1990. "Karl Polanyi's Intellectual Legacy." In Karl Polanyi-Levitt, ed., *The Life and Work of Karl Polanyi*. Montreal: Black Rose Books.

———. 1992. "Narrativity, Narrative Identity, and Social Action: Rethinking English Working-Class Formation." *Social Science History* 16 (4): 591–630.

———. 1993. "Citizenship and the Place of the Public Sphere: Law, Community, and Political Culture in the Transition to Democracy." *American Sociological Review* 58 (5): 587–620.

———. 1994a. "Rights, Relationality, and Membership: Rethinking the Making and Meaning of Citizenship." *Law and Social Inquiry* 19 (1): 1301–50.

———. 1994b. "Narrative and the Constitution of Identity: A Relational and Network Approach." *Theory and Society*: 23 (5): 605–50.

———. 1995a. "The 'Misteries' of Property: Relationality, Rural-Industrialization, and Communities in Chartist Narratives of Political Rights." In John Brewer and Susan Staves, eds., *Early Modern Conceptions of Property*. London: Routledge.

———. 1995b. "What's Political or Cultural about the Political Culture Concept? Toward an Historical Sociology of Concept Formation." *Sociological Theory* 13 (2): 113–44.

———. 1995c. "Renarrating and Remapping Anglo-American Citizenship Theory: The Place of Political Culture and the Public Sphere." *Sociological Theory* 13 (3): 221–65.

———. 1995d. "What's in a Name? Sociological Explanation and the Problem of Place." *American Sociological Review* 60 (5): 797–804.

———. 1996a. "Class Formation and Capitalism." *European Journal of Sociology* 37 (1): 180–202.

———. 1996b. "Where Is Sociology after the Historic Turn? Knowledge Cultures, Narrativity, and Historical Epistemologies." In Terrence J. Mcdonald, ed., *The Historic Turn in the Human Sciences*. Ann Arbor: University of Michigan Press.

———. Forthcoming. *The People and the Law: Civil Society and the Public Sphere in the Making of Citizenship Rights*. Ithaca, N.Y.: Cornell University Press. Published in the University of Chicago Wilder House Series in Politics, History and Culture.

Somers, Margaret R., and Gloria Gibson. 1994. "Reclaiming the 'Epistemological Other': Narrative and the Social Constitution of Identity." In Craig Calhoun, ed., *Social Theory and the Politics of Identity*. Boston: Blackwell.

Stearns, Peter N. 1985. "Social History and History: A Progress Report." *Journal of Social History* 19: 319–34.

Steinberg, Marc. 1991. "Talking Class: Discourse, Ideology, and Their Roles in Class Conflict." In Scott McNall et al., eds., *Bringing Class Back In*. Boulder: Westview.

———. 1996a. "'The Labour of the Country is the Wealth of the Country': Class Identity, Class Consciousness, and the Role of Discourse in the Making of the English Working Class." *International Labor and Working-Class History* 49: 1–25.

———. 1996b. "Culturally Speaking: Finding a Commons between Poststructuralism and the Thompsonian Perspective." *Social History* 21 (2): 193–214.

Steinmetz, George. 1992. "Reflections on the Role of Social Narratives in Working-Class Formation." *Social Science History* 16 (3): 489–516.

Stoianovich, Traian. 1976. *French Historical Method: The Annales Paradigm*. Ithaca, N.Y.: Cornell University Press.

Stone, Lawrence. 1979. "The Revival of Narrative: Reflections on an Old New History." *Past and Present* 85: 3–25.

Taylor, Charles. 1989. *Sources of the Self*. Cambridge: Harvard University Press.

Thomis, M. I. 1970. *The Luddites*. Newton Abbott, England: David and Charles.

Thompson, E. P. 1965. "Peculiarities of the English." *Socialist Register 1965*, 311–62.

———. 1966. *The Making of the English Working Class*. New York: Vintage.

Tilly, Charles. 1990. "Where Do Rights Come From?" Working Paper no. 98, Center for Studies of Social Change. New York: New School for Social Research.

———. 1995. *Popular Contention in Great Britain, 1754–1828*. Cambridge: Harvard University Press.

Veyne, Paul. 1984 [1971]. *Writing History: Essay of Epistemology*. Translated by Mina Moore-Rinvolucri. Middletown, Conn.: Wesleyan University Press.

Vincent, D. 1981. *Bread, Knowledge and Freedom: A Study in Nineteenth-Century Working Class Autobiography*. London: Europa Publications.

Walzer, M. 1982. *Spheres of Justice*. New York: Basic Books.

White, Harrison C. 1992. *Identity and Control: A Structural Theory of Social Action*. Princeton: Princeton University Press.

CHAPTER 3

Statistical Classifications and the Salience of Social Class

Michael Donnelly

"MARX READ THE MINUTIAE OF OFFICIAL STATISTICS, THE REPORTS from the factory inspectorate and the like. One can ask: who had more effect on class consciousness, Marx or the authors of the official reports which created the classifications into which people came to recognize themselves?" Behind this slyly irreverent question, raised by the historian of statistics and philosopher Ian Hacking (1990, 3), lies a serious point. Official statistics have indeed "classed" the population, in varied and sometimes shifting ways, but with the cumulative effect of hardening classifications into enduring and familiar categories—artifacts of the classifiers' decisions. "There is a sense," moreover, as Hacking writes, "in which many of the facts presented by the [new statistical] bureaucracies did not even exist ahead of time. Categories had to be invented into which people could conveniently fall in order to be counted" (1990, 3).

This essay is an exploration into one set of such categories which "had to be invented": the categories used to class or group occupations and thereby represent schematically a given society's occupational struc-

This is a revised version of a paper prepared for the World Congress of Sociology meetings in Bielefeld, Germany, July 1994. I am grateful for suggestions offered by Stephen Turner, John R. Hall, and two anonymous reviewers. The work reported here is an offshoot of a larger project the author is pursuing on the rise of statistical discourse.

ture. The role of these categories in investigations of social class has been fundamental, perhaps because of the apparent ease they allow in gathering data. The parceling out of people according to occupational groups has long provided historians and social scientists with the most serviceable, and the most readily available, indicator of social class.[1] Given the widespread and long-standing use of occupational data in studies of class, it is worthwhile in a phase of stocktaking to reexamine the logic underlying this familiar indicator. If so much of the information used to interpret class has been framed and collected through occupational categories, how were those categories constructed? How have they evolved?

The particular approach outlined here seeks to excavate some of the original rationales that statistical coders used in making decisions about how to classify occupations. The focus accordingly is not on current-day classifications and the specific errors, biases, or ambiguities which they may present to social researchers. There is a large literature on such technical questions, in which both social scientists and government statisticians exchange views.[2] The aim here is rather to place the problem of classifying occupations on a broad historical canvas, and to reexamine the social, political, and intellectual contexts in which certain enduring classifications were developed. Two sets of interpretive questions guide the inquiry: (1) what principles and rationales informed the classification of occupations? and (2) in what way might these classifications have influenced the conceptualization of class? What presumptive bases of class differences did the classifications reflect? Did certain classifications tend to highlight, while others occluded, the salience of class distinctions?

The contribution which such an historical analysis might make to a wide-ranging project of "reworking" class is likewise twofold: First, it may allow a modest but important broadening of our understanding of the conceptual history of "class." Just as social historians have documented the emergence of lay "languages of class" (see Briggs 1960; Sewell 1980; Jones 1983; Corfield 1991), so historians of official statistics might further enrich the picture by reconstructing contrived, bureaucratic "languages" of class—the taxonomies of the statisticians. In fact, there is an intellectual history to be reconstructed of exchanges between government statisticians and social scientists, concerned in their respective ways with strati-

---

1. This is of course not to suggest that occupational data provide a good indicator of "class." That is an issue beyond the confines of the present chapter.
2. See, for example, Scoville 1965; Hodge and Siegel 1965; Crompton 1993.

fication and social differentiation. The exchanges might often resemble a dialogue of the deaf, but the statisticians' discourse is undoubtedly part of the broader conceptual history.[3] Moreover, retracing the history of statisticians' categorizing, and re-embedding the categories in their original contexts, provide a salutary reminder that classification is not merely a technical problem. Official statisticians may do their work in an apparently neutral, technical idiom; but they are also invariably shaped by their sociopolitical environments. Placing official statisticians back into those contexts offers the historian a new and more subtle interpretive key to understanding their activities. What is at issue here is a central instance of the "politics of numbers" (the apposite title of a recent collection edited by W. Alonso and Paul Starr [1987]). The question is how, given a broad mandate to gather information, official statisticians interpret and carry out their brief—to what extent, for instance, they respond or bend to wider political and ideological currents, or themselves carry an ideological agenda; and in turn how social taxonomies foster quasi-official images of social structure, which may ultimately be turned to ideological ends.[4] The answers to those questions require detailed historical reconstruction of the arenas in which this or that statistical bureau operated.

There is also a second, more powerful contribution which such an historical approach may open up, a contribution that turns on the issue tantalizingly highlighted in Hacking's sly question: To what extent might official classifications be seen as an element—both constituent and constitutive—in the very formation of classes? This is a provocative question, and one that may seem to run against the grain of social scientists' normal ways of thinking. Those who work with quantitative social data are inclined to think of statistical aggregates as just that—mere aggregates. There are of course good reasons for the familiar textbook injunctions not to mistake statistical aggregates for real social groups, and not to reify statistical categories as if they manifested latent structures. Historicizing

3. For the case of British sociology, as Philip Abrams demonstrated some time ago, social statistics loomed large over the origins of the field, and continued in a number of ways to blight its independent theoretical development (Abrams 1968).
4. I. Miles and J. Irvine provide an extreme and unduly reductive version of this point of view: "Official statistics form part of the process of maintaining and reproducing the dominant ideologies of capitalist society. . . . [O]fficial statistics are in fact a selection of data typically offering far less of use to the radical critic than the reactionary. . . . [T]he concepts employed serve to reinforce the arguments advanced by political and intellectual representatives of the ruling class" (1979, 126–27).

statistical taxonomies and relocating their origins in time and space may, however, suggest a different way of thinking about the process of category formation and classification, in particular as categories shift and classifications evolve over time. Conventionally, social scientists think of official statistics as gridlike: imposing a grid of categories produces a frozen-frame enumeration of phenomenon X at time Y. But considered over long stretches of time, statistical categories appear less like boxes in an unchanging grid than like evolving elements in a dynamic movement. In one respect, the mutability of statistical categories is obvious and expected: they are updated periodically and self-consciously to correct for, or to accommodate, structural changes in the objects they measure. As Margo Anderson points out, for instance, statisticians in the census offices in both Britain and the United States have periodically rejigged occupational categories in order to maintain over time a certain image of social structure: "The English have maintained their diamond-shaped model [of social class structure] by reordering the occupations comprising the five classes at each census to ensure the same rough distribution of the workforce. For the Americans their original pyramid-like occupational distribution proved discomforting." As a consequence, "the [American] statisticians continually reworked the data to show that, over time at least, the class structure was not rigidifying" (Conk 1983, 96).

Recontextualizing Official Statistics

What needs to be examined, however, is not just the responsiveness of statistical coders to structural changes on the ground around them, but another chain of possible effects and interactions: the consequences over time of the categories themselves on how class is perceived and represented by lay social actors. To explore this possible chain of effects would require thinking of a dynamic interplay carried out over time between classifiers and the uses of classifications, and between taxonomies and the social subjects which they roughly represent or reflect. To give the matter a practical context, one might think of statistical classifications as offering "recognition" to various organized or less organized groups; in this respect it would be possible to speak of a politics of classifying not only among the classifiers but among those struggling or bargaining for recognition in some arena monitored by government.

These problems are complex to broach, elusive to pin down, and perhaps intrinsically difficult to establish. Formulating them in these terms may also seem to reflect a facile variety of social constructionism against which many historians and social scientists would be likely instinctively to react. For analysts of class in particular, accustomed as they tend to be to stressing the heavy weight of economic and social determinants (the materiality of class relations), the decisions of statistical bureaucrats about how to delineate their categories are likely to seem of little moment. Furthermore, the exercise would seem to run the risk of misplaced concreteness, mistaking abstractive categories for the structure of the real, or mistaking mere statistical aggregates for real social groups.

The ambivalence that many social scientists feel about official statistics is likely to present a different sort of obstacle to this inquiry. Social scientists have often harshly criticized government statisticians' work as conceptually muddied or otherwise marred by arbitrary and commonsensical assumptions. Official statisticians and academic social scientists are to some extent professional rivals and competitors; they may both share commitments to wider scientific and policy communities, but they also have separate agendas and serve different masters.[5] In the analysis of class, historians and social scientists have for many practical purposes been forced into an uneasy alliance with government statisticians; they are perforce heavy users of official statistics, but often disgruntled and unhappy ones. Sociologists, for instance, must by and large depend on officially coded data to track changes in class structure or patterns of social mobility; and yet in their efforts to conceptualize class they have shown scant regard indeed for the classificatory work of official statisticians in which much of their data are already encoded. From sociologists' point of view, official statisticians serve too many audiences, with the predictable result that their official classifications tend to muddy distinctions that sociological analysts would keep separate.[6] Where sociologists strive for analytical

---

5. More precisely the conflict suggested here is between official statisticians and *theorists* of class stratification. There has of course been a good deal of movement of experts back and forth between the academy and official statistical bureaus, particularly in the United States since World War II.

6. For a good illustration see Margo Conk's reconstruction of occupational classification in the U.S. Census, 1870–1940 (Conk 1978). She links the periodic changes in classification to demands being placed on the census for new and different kinds of information about the populace. With regard to Alba Edward's comprehensive reworking of categories for the 1940 census, she argues that "the Census served several masters," and the resulting "eclectic ordering"

precision or clarity, official statisticians seem to settle, or are forced to settle, for eclectic or otherwise imprecise categories. There is thus no doubt about who—Marx or the authors of official reports—has had the larger effect on the consciousness of sociologists. Each generation of class analysts has tended to revisit Marx, as well as Weber and a limited number of other "classical" authorities. Indeed much of the theoretical discussion on conceptualizing class is still recognizably shaped by frameworks handed down from the founding fathers. "Reworking" class in this sense has been and remains largely a matter of conceptual retooling, refining or sharpening instruments, or bringing analysis up to date with events breaking on the ground. In this enterprise, sociologists are likely to regard official classifications as in some respects more an obstacle than an aid to their work.

This scant regard for official classifications is often reinforced by the researcher's experience in actually using official statistics. Official statistics are not untypically regarded as something of a necessary evil: they are indispensable, and yet the data available often seem unsatisfactory for the questions which social scientists want to raise. A typical complaint is that the categories of official statistics do not match up with sociological concepts. Government statisticians have not asked the "right" questions. Data may abound, but to the frustration of the historian or social scientist, they are the wrong data, only partially assembled, wrongly classified, or otherwise vitiated by the commonsensical and arbitrary assumptions of the classifiers. As A. H. Halsey puts it, "the problem remains largely that of adapting to social science ends statistics which, from the point of view of the sociologist, are a by-product of administrative and organizational activity" (1988, 3). Mark Granovetter and Charles Tilly have recently made a related, more specific point in far sharper terms. In trying to explain how individuals and groups get sorted out into different, unequal positions in the division of labor, sociologists have typically drawn on sets of occupational statistics. As Granovetter and Tilly acknowledge, "censuses and other surveys make aggregations

---

seems a virtually inevitable outcome (1978, 116). The problem appears to be a quite general one; insofar as statisticians try to make occupation into a kind of all-purpose indicator, they tend to combine an economic fact (levels of skill or branches of industry) with a "social component" (habits, social tastes, culture, moral standards, etc.). The result may jibe with lay perceptions or prejudices, but it makes for an analytical muddle.

of job titles very convenient bases of comparison." And yet "on the whole," they conclude, "that emphasis on occupations has produced an intellectual disaster." It tends to lead to "reifying categories constructed by statisticians, presuming social structure where none exists, inferring that people experience moves from 'service' to 'skilled' occupations as 'social mobility,' facilitating the identification of the person with the category, and diverting attention from the actual processes matching persons with jobs" (1988, 189–90).

The wariness of social scientists about official statistics may thus be perfectly appropriate.[7] There is, however, a wider issue at stake, which Hacking's question obliquely points to. Although official statistics may well be roundly criticized, we need to understand their intended and inadvertent effects, past and present. This requires understanding better how official statistics are produced: not just how the machine of the census, for instance, churns out data, but how statisticians originally codify the social world; how they make decisions about what to count, and how they establish categories in which those counts accumulate. The point is to draw attention to the work of classifying itself, which is a cognitive (and organizational) operation to which social scientists have given too little attention.[8] Much of this work of classifying happens behind the scenes, in venues which are not always easy to observe. But retracing the process historically allows a critical distance, and opens a larger canvas on which to observe developments in progress. Indeed the history of official classification would seem to be an ideal topic for what Otis Dudley Duncan described and urged as a social history of measurement (Duncan 1984). Duncan's point is that technical criticism of measurement instruments in the social sciences may be usefully complemented by understanding the social roots, and political contexts, in which measures were developed. The distancing that historical reconstruction allows may, in other words, be a means of raising welcome but unfamiliar questions about all-too-familiar measures.

7. For a statement of the opposite point of view, see Bulmer 1980. "There is a sufficiently close match between official statisticians'"common sense' understandings of the meaning of occupation, and sociological uses of the concept, for the relation between the two to be relatively unproblematic. . . . [T]hough the theoretical content of 'social class' is far wider, the use of occupation as an empirical indicator of social class has been widely thought to be justified" (1980, 515).
8. Paul Starr's contribution to *The Politics of Numbers* (Alonso and Starr 1987) is an important exception.

In recent years an impressive body of scholarship has in fact begun to document the modern history of census taking and other official information gathering. This is not, in the narrow sense, a technical literature intended mainly for expert practitioners. What characterizes the historical treatments is rather a broad-gauged interest in understanding the census and other official information gathering as phenomena in their own right, not incidentally in terms of their products but as a locus of production to be interpreted within the evolving social, political, and intellectual contexts. As Celia Davies expresses her own strategy in "Making Sense of the Census," she takes the census "more as a 'narrative source' than as a statistical one, [looking] to the character of the classificatory devices employed, not for the ambiguities contained in them and consequent levels of error, but for their substantive character and what they reveal about the contemporary setting" (1980, 582). This is a reasonably typical statement of what has become an increasingly common aspiration. A growing corps of historians and social scientists are pursuing precisely this task, writing in effect the social and intellectual history of official social classification (on Britain, see especially Szreter 1984, 1993; Hakim 1980; Higgs 1988; on France, Desrosières 1977, 1990; Desrosières and Thévenot 1988; on the United States, Conk 1978, 1983; Anderson 1991, 1994). The likely consequence of their work may well be to shift in some respects the way we see official statistics, less as a straightforward source of information about, or as a simple reflection of, the social world than a cultural ordering of it—an imposition on the world which simplifies complexity by categorizing it, and with categories which are not innocent.[9] In sum, social statistics seem to be a distinct order of representation.

Given this body of work, it is an opportune moment in the course of "reworking class" to reconsider the evolution of those statistical taxonomies which serve in one way or another to indicate class. The strategy adopted here narrows a broad problem severely, and offers only an exploratory look forward. The remainder of this essay considers the last century or so of occupational statistics, and takes two cases for comparison, Britain and France. The cases are used somewhat asymmetrically. The general interpretive question, What principles and rationales informed the classification of occupations? is raised principally in the case

9. For a convincing example of such revaluation of a statistical source, see Joan Scott's reading (1986) of a set of occupational statistics produced in the Paris of 1848.

of Britain, with France drawn in largely for purposes of contrast. The second question posed is: How have the respective schemes been bent or revised to take account of changes in the occupational structure over time? This is also an oblique way of raising the issue of the "fit" between statistical categories and active social groups: What consequences might official classifications carry for the consciousness and action of social subjects? Might social groups mobilize to maintain, or to demand, recognition in official classifications? Under what circumstances? In this instance the French case provides an intriguing example. The essay concludes with a comment on the sudden emergence of the new category "cadres" in the French classifications, which might well be taken as a dramatic and suggestive example of a dynamic interplay between statistical categories and the consciousness and action of actual social subjects.

Occupational Classification in Britain

The standard classification in Britain, dating back to 1913, is the Registrar General's fivefold classification, which groups occupations into status grades according to their prestige or social standing in the community. In its origins the classification goes back to the census of 1911 and to discussions in the immediately succeeding years about how to organize and interpret census results (see the careful historical reconstruction in Szreter 1984; see also Leete and Fox 1977). The classification was in fact devised by a medical statistician, Dr. T. H. C. Stevenson, who wanted to answer a fairly specific question: what were the differences in mortality and fertility across the different grades or ranks in British society? To give the question a eugenic inflection, were the lower classes outbreeding the comfortable classes? A rough-and-ready classification of ranks was all that Stevenson required for his task. His fivefold ranking was "designed to represent as far as possible social grades" in British society. Occupations were subsumed under broad categories, designated as

Class I, "the upper- and middle-class";
Class III, "those occupations of which it can be assumed that the majority of men classified to them at the census are skilled workmen"; and
Class V, "occupations including mainly unskilled men."

Two vaguely specified intermediate or buffer classes (II and IV) were inserted to yield the five grades. Some years later, in 1928, Stevenson spelled out his rationales at greater length.[10] He had intended only a straightforward way of dividing society into its top, middle, and bottom. In the event, Stevenson was quite satisfied and felt that the classification had been vindicated when it produced a gradient in both mortality and fertility data: class I experienced the greatest longevity (the lowest mortality) but were also the least fertile, while class V experienced the lowest longevity and the highest fertility; the other classes fit in their rank order accordingly.[11]

Despite the apparently straightforward nature of Stevenson's exercise, the classification involved was more than a simple convenience; what was involved was arguably "a matter of deliberate stratification rather than convenient differentiation" (Davies 1980, 589). How the "top" of society was characterized, for instance, is revealing: "When one speaks," Stevenson wrote, "of the more or less comfortable classes one is thinking largely of the more or less cultured classes." In fact it is "culture," a term which Stevenson did not try to define and which he perhaps used in a somewhat idiosyncratic way, that effectively structured the hierarchy. Since "culture is more easily estimated, as between occupations, than wealth, so the occupational basis of social grading has a wholesome tendency to emphasize it" (1928, 209). The clergy, for example, though relatively poorly remunerated, belonged clearly in Stevenson's view among the more cultured; their relative longevity, moreover, was proof of their good character. Social standing in fact continued to be the central principle behind the Registrar General's social classification, which was and is essentially a status or occupational prestige hierarchy.[12] In the 1951 census, for instance, the expository preface on classification of occupations describes the five class categories as "homogeneous in relation to the basic

---

10. There is some question whether what he wrote in 1928 accurately reports what he was trying to do in 1913 or reflects later developments in his thinking. See Szreter 1984.

11. Two or three generations later, Martin Bulmer points to similar contemporary findings in the course of arguing that sociologists ought to make more use of official statistics: "What is one to make of empirical regularities which regularly turn up in analyses of official statistics done by non-sociologists, for example, the social class gradient in mortality?" (1980, 509).

12. A new occupational classification adopted for the 1981 census replaced reputed "standing within the community" by occupational skill levels as the basis for ordering the classes. The actual consequences of this conceptual change seem thus far to have been relatively minor. See Marshall et al. 1986, 18; Marsh 1986, 126; and Brewer 1986.

criterion of the general standing within the community of the occupations concerned" (General Register Office 1956, vii).

There are two things in particular to note about the origins of the Registrar General's social classes. First, that the classification was the tool of a medical statistician, designed in particular to test empirically the fertility rates of the different "grades" of society. Posing such a question was quite characteristic of the General Register Office; it reflected the prominent role that medical statisticians held there and the higher priority they gave to vital statistics than to a host of economic questions (see Higgs 1991; Szreter 1991). Stevenson was in fact one in a series of medical statisticians who over several generations effectively dominated the GRO, which was the British bureau producing the bulk of social statistics. The orientation of the GRO is significant because the interest of these vital statisticians in class or occupations had little to do with specifically economic questions; their overriding concern was the influence of different occupations on health. These were important and distinctive features in the way that the census had been institutionalized in Britain (in striking contrast, as will become clear, to France; see Desrosières 1991).

The second thing to note is that for Stevenson, as for earlier medical statisticians, the differential life chances across classes evident in their vital statistics appeared to be associated with cultural differences between groups, or as they would more likely have said, with "character." People who lived better, lived longer; and part of living better was knowing how to do it: exercising restraint, acquiring good habits, and so forth. The medical statisticians assumed that different occupations tended to produce or attract people with different degrees of "character," and that as a mediating variable, "character" had a marked effect on life chances. In this sense what structured the original fivefold classification was not skill levels but social standing combined with an implicit *moral* evaluation of better or worse occupations.

In these emphases Stevenson extended faithfully earlier traditions of the General Register Office.[13] But the specific issue of differential fertility of course also evoked the central theme of the contemporary

13. Differences in mortality and morbidity among the social classes have remained to this day a prominent theme in British sociology; see, for example Carter and Peel 1976. Moreover, the existence of such differences is still used as an argument for the validity, or at least the utility, of the Registrar General's social classes; see, in particular, J. Brotherston, "Inequality: Is It Inevitable?" in Carter and Peel 1976.

eugenicists' propaganda. Stevenson was in fact a convinced environmentalist, and like others at the GRO an opponent of the eugenicists; but in order to test (and as he expected, to refute) their claims, he in effect adopted the eugenicists' framework. As Simon Szreter argues, "by participating in this debate, he did, significantly, come to endorse certain of the biometricians' terms of reference" (1984, 527).

Among the precedents for Stevenson's classification was in fact a five-class model presented by Francis Galton in 1900, which became a powerful emblem of eugenicist thinking. Galton divided the population into quintiles—five "ability" classes—which he then simply superimposed on the occupational hierarchy as it had been described by the statistician Charles Booth in his studies on urban life (see MacKenzie 1976; Norton 1981; Szreter 1986, 353–54). Given the basic similarity in Stevenson's and Galton's schemes, it is intriguing to recall the premises underlying Galton's original plan. The plan was based on the idea that the different (hierarchically ranked) occupations recruited individuals according to their different inborn degrees of ability or their (inherited) physique. As a hereditarian, Galton assumed that the resulting social inequality not only depended upon, but could be explained and justified by, differences in the inborn, natural attributes of individuals. Moreover, Galton made an explicit moral evaluation in his classification of occupations. He took the "professional class" to be the desirable standard, those bearing the qualities most valuable to the community at large. He thus tried to equate "genetic worth" (as reflected in the "ability" classes) with "civic worth" (as reflected in the relative prestige of different occupations).

This might seem to be a mere historical curiosity, and yet the irony is that although Stevenson's scheme was produced for rather specific circumstances, and with Galton's framework hovering in the background, it became and has remained the official designation of social classes in Britain. It is important to stress the origins of the classification here because they bring out an unfamiliar feature of what is a very familiar and pervasive schema indeed.[14] As Ivan Reid concluded some years ago

---

14. What makes Stevenson's scheme noteworthy here, to reiterate, is its sheer staying power, not its originality. In its broad outlines and emphases, the scheme faithfully continued the work of two prior generations of British medical statisticians. In many respects, moreover, Stevenson was still heir to the earlier statistical movement which flourished in Victorian Britain, with its characteristic concern for "moral statistics." For treatments of this larger historical context, see Cullen 1975 and Eyler 1979.

in a survey of social class differences in Britain, "the Registrar General's social classes form the basis of all the commonly used social class classifications in Britain" (1981, 39). Even those sociologists who have worked to refine a more discriminating and sociologically informative classification have tried to compare explicitly their new schemes with the Registrar General's standard classification (see, for example, Cole 1955; Marshall et al. 1986). The Registrar General's social classes, moreover, inform the familiar categories used in political polling and market research, and those used in much of opinion surveying and the tracking of social trends. The modern classification has also been adapted by historians as a means of retrospectively reclassifying occupational data from the nineteenth century, in order to produce a much longer times series of apparently comparable occupational statistics (see Armstrong 1972; Banks 1978; Bellamy 1978).[15] As Simon Szreter suggests, the Registrar General's official system of social classification "has, therefore, been projected both forwards and backwards in time, up to seventy years in each direction from its date of inception, 1913." And as Szreter concludes, "it is thereby implicitly claimed to be a tolerably accurate model of a British social structure, apparently essentially unchanging for that century and a half which covers a complete transformation of the countryside, economy and polity" (Szreter 1984, 523).

The significance of Stevenson's schema in fact stretches far wider. There is good evidence that the British classification had considerable influence over U.S. census takers and served as one of the models for the American occupational classification system, adopted by Alba Edwards in the 1930s and used until recently (see Szreter 1993, 295–302). Nor is this prestige-based hierarchy the province only of government statisticians. A number of prominent sociologists have argued that in industrial societies generally there tends to be a graded continuum in the prestige accorded to occupations, running from high-status professionals to low-status unskilled manual trades, a continuum that seems remarkably stable over time and across cultures (see, for example, Inkeles and Rossi 1956). This graded hierarchy has been generally interpreted to result "from a logic imperative in the process of industrialization itself" (Marsh 1986, 129). Hence, the British scheme seems to lay bare the essential structure of industrial society itself. Later studies

15. For a thoughtful reflection on some of the problems involved in interpreting and using occupational statistics in historical research, see Katz 1972.

involving some nonindustrial societies led to even more sweeping claims that such rankings are intrinsic to any social organization involving division of labor (see, for example, Hodge, Treiman, and Rossi 1966 and Treiman 1977a). It follows that this sort of classification—ranking occupations by their social prestige—ought in principle to be universalized, on the grounds that it can be seen working more or less everywhere. This argument has often been presented explicitly in functionalist terms, as an explanation for enduring and apparently stable aspects of social stratification, as if prestige ranking corresponded to some underlying functional logic of stratification. It is hardly surprising that what can be described as the hierarchical "professional model" of social structure (Szreter 1993) seems almost second nature to many social scientists.

The British classification, in sum, constructs social classes from a unidimensional ranking of occupations according to their prestige, descending from the professional classes; and in the background lurks the idea that the top classes are not only top, but morally superior. "Eugenicist assumptions about society as a graded hierarchy of inherited natural abilities reflected in the skill level of occupations, remain embedded in the official, and most commonly used, measure of social class in Britain today" (Marshall et al. 1986, 19).

Occupational Classification in France

The story of occupational classification in France presents a strikingly different pattern. Indeed, it is a useful case to pair with the British, precisely because it runs counter to the putatively universal prestige ranking of occupations (see Szreter 1994).[16] It is not that French public opinion does not rank occupations.[17] But strikingly, their occupational statistics by and large do not do so, and have not in the past. Unlike the hierarchical and linear five-grade British scale (and its somewhat related American counterpart) the French scheme has traditionally lacked status grades. Even the recently (1982) revised classification, in which social scientists had a good deal of input, is structured by no single criterion. In fact, rather than presenting a strictly analytic classification, it is more in the

16. See Szreter 1994 for an extensive comparison of what he calls the Anglo-American "professional model" of stratification with its French counterpart.
17. See Marwick 1980 and Calvert 1982 for concise descriptions of French images of class.

nature of a descriptive inventory, which "displays a complex admixture of . . . diverse historical strata" (Desrosières 1990, 209), survivals as it were from earlier classifications. What best characterizes French occupational statistics from the nineteenth century onwards is the persistence or survival over time of earlier classifications.

The 1982 classification contains about thirty categories grouped into six large classes of occupations:

1. *Agriculteurs exploitants* (agricultural proprietors)

2. *Artisans, commerçants, chefs d'enterprise* (artisans proprietary retailers or dealers, and businessmen)

3. *Cadres, professions intellectuelles supérieures* ("cadres" and other highly qualified public and private sector professional, administrative, and managerial occupations)

4. *Professions intermédiaires* (lower managers and administrators, technicians, and foremen)

5. *Employés* (public and private sector routine nonmanual employees)

6. *Ouvriers* (nonproprietary manual workers) (see Desrosières and Thévenot 1988, 27; Szreter 1993, 288).

What is striking in this list is the lack of any unitary set of rankings. Among the first three classes there is no indication whether any has higher status than the others. There are elements of prestige and skill grading in the finer internal branches of the classification, but interestingly these are not carried over to higher levels of aggregation.

Alain Desrosières has argued that the present mixed system can be traced back historically to a diverse set of origins. On the one hand it grows out of a series of classifications of occupational status. Over the period 1896–1936, for example, distinctions were drawn among employers *(patrons);* manual workers *(ouvriers);* clerical *employés;* those working on their own account or for themselves *(isolés);* and the unemployed *(chomeurs).* The category "isolé" is particularly interesting, and reflects an economy still largely dominated by small enterprises. In 1896, for instance, 23 percent of the active population were classed as isolés; "these could equally be peasant farmers, artisans, traders, or those sub-contractors engaged in industrial home-working" (Desrosières 1991, 526). The size of that category also helps to explain a second important feature in the evolution of French occupational classifications, the remarkable persistence of the vocabulary of guilds and crafts, despite their abolition in 1791 (see Sewell 1980). In fact, even in the census of 1911—"the first to place the emphasis exclusively upon personal occupation as the main taxonomic principle" (Desrosières 1991, 527)—it was the titles of the long-established métiers that were predominant. Only in the 1930s and 1940s, in the context of collective agreements bargained between the unions of salariés and employers (and with the participation of the state) were workers' skill qualifications or the length of their training formally considered in the coding of categories (the so-called Parodi categories). Even then the skill categories "served as a partial substitute for the old vocabulary of trades" (Desrosières 1990, 208).

Comparing the Cases

To sum up this brief comparison: Britain has operated with a unidimensional ranking of occupations by their prestige or social standing, with the professional class at the top. The British system is vertical and hierarchical. The French system, by contrast, can be described as horizontal, dispersed, and descriptive. France has used a number of different classifications, all of them more in the nature of descriptive inventories and generally including a miscellany of categories surviving from earlier periods. The French classifiers introduced skill grading only relatively recently, and have applied that principle only in parts of the larger classification.

What factors might account for such differences? The simple and compelling answer would seem to be the different pattern of economic development and the different political institutions in the two countries. Modern Britain and France have nearly the same population, but France has twice the land mass. The persistence of family-run and other small enterprises in France has been one among several distinctive features of its economic development. On the political side, to cite only one factor, the two countries have quite different traditions of labor law; French droit social, for instance, lays down juridical categories which affect the occupational structure. In the post–World War II period, there has undoubtedly been some measure of convergence in the two economic systems and occupational structures, but past differences obviously are still prominently reflected in the countries' institutions.

Apart from such general structural differences, the ways in which the census was institutionalized in Britain and France may also have come into play. In Britain it was medical statisticians who dominated the General Register Office through the middle part of the nineteenth century, and then again in the early twentieth century. This partly explains Britain's preeminence in vital statistics; it also helps account for the GRO's failures in some respects to gather certain kinds of economic data (see Szreter 1991). In France, by contrast, its own important tradition of medical statistics had relatively little impact on census taking; in fact the Statistique Générale de la France was located within the Ministry of Trade, and it became "an exhaustive machinery of comprehensive investigation tailored primarily to economic, industrial and occupational purposes, rather than those of health or social policy" (Desrosières 1991, 523).

What, finally, might this historical exercise imply about the possible effects of official classifications on the conceptualization of class? What different consequences might have unfolded in the two contrasting cases of Britain and France? Even if the answers must be highly tentative, the issue is worth exploring further. The British system depends on a simple, powerful analytic scale; it divides the community into a hierarchy involving a few gross distinctions. In France, the far more descriptive inventory fails to produce any comparably compact image of social structure; moreover, it narrows dramatically, in a fashion, the gap between popular and official taxonomies. It would not be fanciful to think in the French case of a dynamic interplay over time between classifications and classes. The French classification, one might say, tends to induce a politics of recognition; it offers at least some of the conditions for a open social field on which group identities and prerogatives are competitively worked out, and where one of the contested resources is official recognition in the government's taxonomy. What probably best accounts for the persistence of métiers in the French classifications, for instance, is not an archaic survival, the carryover of dead or empty categories from the past, but a continuity of living categories—of actors who organized themselves in terms of métiers, and who in effect demanded and won recognition from the state as such.

Luc Boltanski's account (1984, 1987) of the emergence of *les cadres* (roughly, salaried workers with skilled qualifications and usually some supervisory responsibilities) provides a recent, dramatic example of such a politics of recognition. "Cadres" is one of the key categories in the current *code socio-professionelle*, and yet it was unknown before the late 1930s. It is a distinctively French term, untranslatable into either English or German. Cadres overlap with certain British and American professional categories, and likewise overlap with certain German *Angestellte*, but the categories are by no means equivalent; indeed they are differently mapped.

The term is in fact somewhat difficult to characterize by objective criteria, with reference, for instance, to its location in the division of labor. As Boltanski presents the problem, "What do the following have in common: a big Parisian businessman, born into the grande bourgeoisie and educated at one of the grandes écoles; an ex-shopfloor worker in a factory who has become workshop manager; a sales representative; and an aerospace research engineer trained in university laboratories?" The answer, simply, is that each could well consider himself or herself a cadre. "Yet they differ in almost every way—in social origin, qualifications, income, type of professional activity, even lifestyle and political opinions" (Boltanski 1984, 469). In the face of such difficulties, Boltanski turns away from trying to map or capture the category in objective, analytical terms, and instead narrates a history of the category, returning to "the historical conjuncture in which the 'cadres' formed themselves into an explicit group, with a name, organizations, spokesmen, systems of representation and values" (1984, 472). The emergence of cadres goes back to the mid-1930s, in particular to the period just after the strike wave of 1936. In a phase of sharpening social tensions and intensifying class conflicts, the so-called "cadres' movement" was one among a variety of attempts to reassert the centrality of the "middle classes," in ideological terms to chart a Third Way between the clashing extremes of collectivism and capitalism. The inspiration for this Third Way was apparently drawn from late-nineteenth-century social Catholicism and from contemporary corporatist theories. On Boltanski's argument, however, what seems to have given it real form were economic changes, "in particular the inflation and crisis which affected large sectors of the bourgeoisie and petite bourgeoisie," in the context of the emergence of new state-sponsored bargaining forums, "where representatives of the State, big business and the working class were already face to face" (1984, 472, 473). The bargaining forums reflected a new involvement of the state in industrial relations, and more broadly, a new relation between the state and civil society. As Boltanski puts it, it was this new institutional pattern "which forced groups and classes whose relative domination had hitherto been secured through the play of practical actions and reactions, to define themselves explicitly, to equip themselves with instruments for political representation and, copying the example of the working class, to conceive of their unity and their boundaries in voluntaristic terms of 'class consciousness'" (1984, 475). The cadres, in other words, organized themselves as a pressure group struggling for official recognition, and thus for the right to be present, to be represented, in the new bargaining arena.

The bearing of this piece of social and political history on a "politics of numbers" becomes quickly apparent. Not surprisingly, the question of the relative weight in society of the "middle classes" was keenly debated. "Far from being a purely 'scientific,' 'sociological' or 'statistical' problem, the counting of the 'middle classes' was in fact a major stake in the ideological struggle between the classes" (Boltanski 1984, 477). If a Third Way were to be a viable direction for French society, the middle classes had to be seen as sufficiently numerous to support and bear the project. The outcome of that struggle was not foreordained and in fact, as Boltanski's patient reconstruction shows, it probably depended upon a long sequence of contingent events. What was key was the group's capacity to accumulate over time what Boltanski refers to as "'objective' evidence of its existence." In the end "the category 'the cadres,' unknown before 1936 and ill-defined even in the immediate postwar years, now occupies a central place within the dominant position in the social world" (1984, 485)— a place visible not least in the official statistics of contemporary France. Indeed, a significant token and emblem of the cadres' success has been to gain a central place in official nomenclature.

The exploratory nature of this essay warrants only limited conclusions. It may nonetheless offer a useful cautionary tale, which carries implications and suggestions for the future plotting of strategies in the analysis of class.

The clearest implication of the exercise bears on the question of national differences in class cultures, or otherwise put, on the possibility and utility of international comparisons. More than a century ago, Marx addressed the German-speaking readers of *Capital,* "De te fabula narratur!" (This story is about you!) (1967, 8). Loosely paraphrased, he was claiming that *Capital* laid bare the laws of motion of capitalism; the analysis, as it happened, focused on England, but only incidentally, since England happened to be the first protagonist of a story that would inevitably be played out elsewhere. Marx's message to the Germans was that hatred of "Manchesterism" and sentimental attachment to their own distinctive national traditions would not save them from the common fate. Whatever Marx's intentions, his old injunction provided early and enduring inspiration for one of the high ambitions of subsequent class analysis—the ambition to work out clear and consistent analytic concepts of class rooted in the mode of production or, to take the later, related social-science variant, in the logic of industrialism. The concepts of class were considered in either case to be ahistorical or transhistorical. Class analysis in this vein has been one of the major enterprises, and one of the accomplishments, in large-scale comparative analysis.

Official statistics are of course one of the main sources of data for such international comparisons; and combining data from different national statistical bureaus is one of the challenges which such research faces.[18] To solve the problem of comparability, what statisticians devise are "equivalency classes" into which information from the different national data streams can be translated, and thus directly compared. In the case of, for instance, occupational data from Britain and France, the procedure would be to disaggregate the respective national totals and reaggregate their information under a new set of common analytic categories, which would then allow the respective figures to be compared. The advantages of such international comparisons are too obvious to need reciting.

There are also, however, limitations necessarily imposed by such comparisons. When national data get prepared for international comparison and translated into international categories, something invariably gets lost in the translation. French "cadres" are not equivalent to British "professional classes," although parts within those categories are probably equivalent. What is lost in the translation are just those distinctive national elements that have been built into the given nation's system of official classification. A higher-order classification cancels out the eugenicist background to the British model of class structure, and equally so the political history of France in the 1930s, when the cadres were constituted.

This essay has argued that a good deal of history remains embedded in official classifications, if only social scientists would look for it. In a sense, the strategy deployed here in a selective comparison of French and British occupational statistics runs directly opposite to the strategy typically involved in preparing official statistics for international comparisons. Where comparative analysis excises or clips off the quirks of

18. Donald Treiman, revealingly, declares that he is willing to downplay "particular features of particular societies," since "our purpose is to understand the general properties of social systems." See his response (1977b, 1053) to criticisms of Burawoy.

national peculiarity in the interests of wider generality, an intentionally historicist and culturally specific reading of occupational statistics tries to find even in apparently neutral categories the traces and residues of past history. Far from being seen necessarily as a limitation on, or flaw in, official statistics, their national specificity might be seen as an opportunity that social scientists can exploit. Official statistics might be read, in other words, as narrative sources that hold interesting keys to understanding class and other fault lines in a nation's life.

References

Abrams, Philip. 1968. *The Origins of British Sociology, 1834–1914.* Chicago: University of Chicago Press.

Alonso, W., and Paul Starr, eds. 1987. *The Politics of Numbers.* New York: Russell Sage.

Anderson [Conk], Margo. 1991. "The U.S. Bureau of the Census in the Nineteenth Century." *Social History of Medicine* 4: 497–513.

———. 1994. "(Only) White Men Have Class: Reflections on Early 19th-Century Occupational Classification Systems." *Work and Occupations* 21: 5–32.

Armstrong, W. A. 1972. "The Use of Information about Occupation." In *Nineteenth-Century Society: Essays in the Use of Quantitative Methods for the Study of Social Data,* edited by E. A. Wrigley. Cambridge: Cambridge Univ. Press.

Banks, J. A. 1978. "The Social Structure of Nineteenth-Century England as seen through the Census." In Richard Lawton, ed., *The Census and Social Structure: An Interpretive Guide to Nineteenth-Century Censuses for England and Wales.* London: Frank Cass.

Bellamy, J. 1978. "Occupation Statistics in the Nineteenth Century Censuses." In Richard Lawton, ed., *The Census and Social Structure: An Interpretive Guide to Nineteenth Century Censuses for England and Wales.* London: Frank Cass.

Boltanski, Luc. 1984. "How a Social Group Objectified Itself: 'Cadres' in France, 1936–45." *Social Science Information* 23: 69–91.

———. 1987. *The Making of a Class: Cadres in French Society.* Translated by A. Goldhammer. Cambridge: Cambridge University Press.

Brewer, Richard. 1986. "A Note on the Changing Status of the Registrar-General's Classification of Occupations." *British Journal of Sociology* 37: 131–40.

Briggs, Asa. 1960. "The Language of 'Class' in Early Nineteenth-Century England." In Asa Briggs, ed., *Essays in Labour History*. London: Macmillan.

Bulmer, Martin. 1980. "Why Don't Sociologists Make More Use of Official Statistics?" *Sociology* 14: 505–23.

Calvert, Peter. 1982. *The Concept of Class: An Historical Introduction*. London: Hutchinson.

Carter, C. O., and J. Peel, eds. 1976. *Equalities and Inequalities in Health*. London: Academic Press.

Coats, R. H. 1925. "The Classification Problem in Statistics." *International Labour Review* 11: 509–21.

Cole, G. D. H. 1955. *Studies in Class Structure*. London: Routledge and Kegan Paul.

Conk, Margo Anderson. 1978. "Occupational Classification in the United States Census: 1870–1940." *Journal of Interdisciplinary History* 9: 111–30.

———. 1983. "Labor Statistics in the American and English Census: Making Some Invidious Comparisons." *Journal of Social History* 16: 83–102.

Corfield, Penelope, ed. 1991. *Language, History and Class*. Oxford: Blackwell.

Crompton, Rosemary. 1993. *Class and Stratification: An Introduction to Current Debates*. Cambridge: Polity Press.

Cullen, Michael. 1975. *The Statistical Movement in Early Victorian Britain: The Foundations of Empirical Social Research*. New York: Barnes and Noble.

Davies, Celia. 1980. "Making Sense of the Census in Britain and the U.S.A.: The Changing Occupational Classification and the Position of Nurses." *Sociological Review* 28: 581–609.

Desrosières, Alain. 1977. "Elements pour l'histoire des nomenclatures socioprofessionelles." In *Pour une histoire de la statistique*, vol. 1. Paris: INSEE.

———. 1990. "How to Make Things Which Hold Together: Social Science, Statistics and the State." In Peter Wagner et al., eds. *Discourses on Society: The Shaping of the Social Science Disciplines*. Dordrecht: Kluwer.

———. 1991. "Official Statistics and Medicine in Nineteenth-Century France: The SGF as a Case Study." *Social History of Medicine* 4: 515–37.

Desrosières, Alain, Alain Goy, and Laurent Thévenot. 1983. "L'identité sociale dans le travail statistique: La nouvelle nomenclature des professions et catégories socioprofessionelles." *Économie et Statistique* 152: 55–81.

Desrosières, Alain, and Laurent Thévenot. 1979. "Les mots et les chiffres: les nomenclatures socioprofessionelles." *Économie et Statistique* 110: 49–65.

———. 1988. *Les categories socioprofessionelles*. Paris: La Découverte.

Duncan, Otis Dudley. 1984. *Notes on Social Measurement: Historical and Critical*. New York: Russell Sage.

Eyler, John. 1979. *Victorian Social Medicine: The Ideas and Methods of William Farr*. Baltimore: Johns Hopkins University Press.

General Register Office (Great Britain). 1956. *Census 1951, Classification of Occupations*. London: H. M. Stationery Office.

Granovetter, Mark, and Charles Tilly. 1988. "Inequality and Labor Processes." In Neil Smelser, ed., *Handbook of Sociology*. Newberry Park, Calif.: Sage.

Hacking, Ian. 1990. *The Taming of Chance*. Cambridge: Cambridge University Press.

Hakim, Catherine. 1980. "Census Reports as Documentary Evidence: The Census Commentaries 1801–1951." *Sociological Review* 28: 551–80.

Halsey, A. H., ed. 1988. *Trends in British Society since 1900*. London: Macmillan.

Higgs, Edward. 1987. "Women, Occupations and Work in the Nineteenth Century Censuses." *History Workshop* 23: 59–80.

———. 1988. "The Struggle for the Occupational Census, 1841–1911." In Roy MacLeod, ed. *Government and Expertise: Specialists, Administrators and Professionals, 1860–1919*. Cambridge: Cambridge Univ. Press.

———. 1991. "Disease, Febrile Poisons, and Statistics: The Census as a Medical Survey, 1841–1911." *Social History of Medicine* 4: 465–478.

Hindess, Barry. 1973. *The Use of Official Statistics in Sociology*. London: Macmillan.

Hodge, Robert W., and Paul M. Siegel. 1965. "The Classification of Occupations: Some Problems of Sociological Interpretation." In *Proceedings*. New York: American Statistical Association, Social Statistics Section.

Hodge, Robert W., David Treiman, and Peter Rossi. 1966. "A Comparative Study of Occupational Prestige." In Reinhard Bendix and Seymour Martin Lipset, eds., *Class, Status, and Power: Social Stratification in Comparative Perspective*, 2d ed. New York: Free Press.

Inkeles, Alex, and Peter Rossi. 1956. "National Comparisons of Occupational Prestige." *American Journal of Sociology* 61: 329–39.

Jones, Gareth Stedman. 1983. *Languages of Class: Studies in English Working-Class History, 1832–1982*. Cambridge: Cambridge University Press.

Katz, Michael. 1972. "Occupational Classification in History." *Journal of Interdisciplinary History* 3: 63–88.

Leete, Richard, and John Fox. 1977. "Registrar General's Social Classes: Origins and Uses." *Population Trends* 8: 1–7.

MacKenzie, Donald. 1976. "Eugenics in Britain." *Social Studies of Science* 6: 499–532.

Marsh, Catherine. 1986. "Social Class and Occupation." In Robert Burgess, ed., *Key Variables in Social Investigation*: Routledge and Kegan Paul.

Marshall, Gordon, et al. 1986. *Social Class in Modern Britain*. London: Unwin Hyman.

Marwick, Arthur. 1980. *Class: Image and Reality in Britain, France and the U.S.A. since 1930*. New York: Oxford University Press.

Marx, Karl. 1967. *Capital*. Vol. 1. New York: International Publishers.

Miles, I., and J. Irvine. 1979. "The Critique of Official Statistics." In J. Irvine, I. Miles, and J. Evans, eds., *Demystifying Social Statistics*. London: Pluto.

Norton, Bernard. 1981. "Psychologists and Class." In Charles Webster, ed., *Biology, Medicine and Society 1840–1940*. Cambridge: Cambridge University Press.

Reid, Ivan. 1981. *Social Class Differences in Britain*. 2d ed. London: Grant McIntyre.

Scott, Joan W. 1986. "Statistical Representations of Work: The Politics of the Chamber of Commerce's Statistique de l'Industrie à Paris, 1847–48." In Steven L. Kaplan and Cynthia Koepp, eds., *Work in France: Representations, Meaning, Organization, and Practice*. Ithaca, N.Y.: Cornell University Press.

Scoville, James. 1965. "The Development and Relevance of U.S. Occupational Data." *Industrial and Labor Relations Review* 19: 71–79.

Sewell, William H., Jr. 1980. *Work and Revolution in France: The Language of Labor from the Old Regime to 1848*. Cambridge: Cambridge University Press.

Stevenson, T. H. C. 1910. "Suggested Lines of Advance in English Vital Statistics." *Journal of the Royal Statistical Society* 73: 685–713.

———. 1928. "The Vital Statistics of Wealth and Poverty." *Journal of the Royal Statistical Society* 91: 207–30.

Szreter, S. R. S. 1984. "The Genesis of the Registrar-General's Social Classification of Occupations." *British Journal of Sociology* 35: 522–46.

———. 1986. "The First Scientific Social Structure of Modern Britain, 1875–1883." In Lloyd Bonfield et al., eds., *The World We Have Gained: Histories of Population and Social Structure*. Oxford: Basil Blackwell.

———. 1993. "The Official Representation of Social Class in Britain, the United States, and France: The Professional Model and 'Les Cadres.'" *Comparative Studies in Society and History* 35: 285–317.

Szreter, Simon. 1991. "The GRO and the Public Health Movement in Britain, 1837–1914." *Social History of Medicine* 4: 435–63.

Treiman, Donald. 1976. "A Standard Occupational Prestige Scale for Use with Historical Data." *Journal of Interdisciplinary History* 7: 283–304.

———. 1977a. *Occupational Prestige in Comparative Perspective*. New York: Academic Press.

———. 1977b. "Toward Methods for a Quantitative Sociology: A Reply to Burawoy." *American Journal of Sociology* 82: 1042–56.

Waites, Bernard. 1976. "The Language and Imagery of 'Class' in Early Twentieth-Century England (circa 1900–1925)." *Language and History* 4: 30–55.

Class Formation and
the Quintessential Worker

Sonya O. Rose

A SENSE OF CRISIS AND UNCERTAINTY SEEMS PERVASIVE AMONG MANY
social historians and historical sociologists who have studied the
relationship between economic disadvantage and protest politics. Within
the last five or so years, edited volumes and special issues of journals have
encouraged scholars to "bring class back in," explore what some worry
is the "end of labor history" or "rethink working-class history" in the wake
of postmodernism, the turn to discursive and cultural analysis, and an ever
accelerating number of scholars who are focusing their substantive interests on issues of race and gender (McNall, Levine, and Fantasia 1991;
Berlanstein 1993).[1] As William Sewell Jr. (1993) has remarked, labor history has lost the intellectual vitality it once had. Even those who celebrate

This essay expands on ideas that developed in Rose 1993b, and with Laura Frader in Frader
and Rose 1996. I thank John R. Hall for his willingness to read and comment on several drafts
of this essay, and Marc W. Steinberg for his helpful comments. Also, I want to thank Julia
Adams, Peggy Somers, Jackie Stevens, and Ann Stoler for their advice on how to make my
argument clearer and stronger. Various student and faculty participants at the following venues
made enormously useful comments on earlier versions of this paper: Workshop on Political
Economy, Department of Sociology, Indiana University; The Institute for the Study of Social
Change at the University of California at Berkeley, and The Center for Comparative Research
on History, Society and Culture at the University of California at Davis.
1. See these special issues on the state of labor history: "The End of Labour History?" *International Review of Social History* 3 (supplement, December 1993); "What Next for Labor and
Working-Class History?" *International Labor and Working-Class History* 46 (1994).

the rich diversity of subject matters explored by labor and working-class historians are worried about scholars jumping ship as "engaged history, in possession at least of the conceit of making a difference, has moved elsewhere, to other subject areas" (Katznelson 1994, 7).

I want to argue for the importance of class analysis and suggest how we might begin to rethink the relationship between economic inequality and the various ways that people respond to it. I will suggest that Jean-Paul Sartre's concept of "seriality" is a helpful heuristic tool for rethinking class formation. It retains the idea that people share economic constraints and opportunities that have the potential of being sites of political mobilization without assuming that what they share defines their identities or dictates the kinds of politics or modes of resistance in which they engage. But before it is possible to rethink class formation, it is crucial to engage in a deconstructive analysis to reveal some of the problems and blind spots that continue to plague the scholarship on class. A central goal of this chapter is to understand the durability of this scholarship's dominant paradigm in the face of both the continuing criticism and the mounting empirical evidence that have cast doubt on its validity and generalizability. Such an understanding is a first but major step in rethinking class formation.

The paradigmatic story of nineteenth-century and much of twentieth-century Western European and U.S. working-class formation centers on the transformation of work and the proletarianization of workers by capitalist development. Those primarily artisanal and skilled workers whose livelihoods were threatened led organized resistance, drawing on their organizational skills and the traditions of solidarity and protest in their trades and communities. In some cases they became active participants in broader social movements that demanded the rights of political citizenship and that may have threatened the stability of the state; in other instances these workers formed political parties. In addition, they often transferred their organizational skills and strategies to semiskilled workers who then became increasingly militant with the advance of industrial capitalism.[2] Finally, scholars have added to the story of why in particular cases workers fail to become politicized or lose their militancy.

2. For an excellent overview of scholarship in labor history that suggests that the central paradigm of the discipline involves "the twin currents of the defense-of-labor-process and defense-of-community," see Fink 1990, esp. 13–15. For a more recent statement of the paradigm see Traugott 1995, 151.

Contributors to this general paradigm in the British case include among others Eric Hobsbawm (1964, 1984), Charles More (1980), John Foster (1974), Jeffrey Haydu (1988), Craig Calhoun (1981, 1983), and E. P. Thompson (1980 [1963]). For France the studies of historians and sociologists from very different theoretical perspectives contribute to the general narrative (see Sewell 1980, 1986; Aminzade 1984, 1993; Hanagan 1980, 1989; Tilly 1978, 1984; Tilly, Tilly, and Tilly 1975; Traugott 1985, 1995). The basic outlines of the story are to be found as well in major works in U.S. labor history (Montgomery 1979; Walkowitz 1978; Dawley 1976), as well as in German history in the scholarship of Jurgen Kocka (1986) and Hartmut Zwahr (1978).[3]

This paradigm—one that centers the study of working-class formation on artisanal and skilled workers engaging in organized political protest—has been subjected to critique by feminist scholars for more than twenty years. Feminists have suggested that such paradigms leave women out of working-class history (see Davin 1981; Alexander 1984; Alexander, Davin, and Hostettler 1979). In addition, feminist scholars have argued that including women as a subject, and gender as an analytical category, would actually challenge accounts of class formation based on male subjects (Kelly 1984; Joan Scott 1988a; Canning 1992; Baron 1991; Kessler-Harris 1990).

Furthermore, empirical research focused on working and working-class women has contributed to a rich body of literature on working-class life and labor activism that does not fit the paradigm. Feminist scholarship has shown that women in unskilled or semiskilled occupations engage in labor activism (Dublin 1980; Cameron 1985; Blewett 1988). Numerous studies have pointed to the significance of families and family life in motivating and fomenting resistance to capitalism (e.g. Bornat 1977, 1986; Joan Scott 1988b). Contrary to what many labor historians have believed, women's family roles do not necessarily dampen militancy or weaken their identities as workers, and family ties may in fact be crucial in generating working-class solidarities (Kaplan 1982; Lamphere 1985; Turbin 1992).

Additionally, there is an ever increasing body of working-class history showing that neither class by itself nor transformations at the point

3. For an important feminist critique of the German historiography of class that uses a "levels" approach, see Canning 1992.

of production are sufficient to account for the various modes of resistance and accommodation that characterize life in working-class communities. Recent studies have pointed to the significance of race and ethnicity in the United States for constructing white male working-class identities (Roediger 1992), for generating class solidarity (Turbin 1992; Frager 1992; Berger 1992), and for fracturing it (Turbin 1992; Janiewski 1985, 1991).

Finally, studies of working-class life have shown the multiple and various ways that people resist their subordination through expressive culture, daily industrial sabotage, and subterranean ways of making do and making out.[4] As Ira Katznelson (1994) has recently noted, working-class history continues to flourish and has become increasingly diverse, having extended its purview from the workplace to issues of consumption, sexuality, race, gender, crime, street life, and the family. Such studies suggest that there are sites outside of workplaces and union halls in which economically disadvantaged people engage in various forms of resistance, and that these various forms of resistance may not conform to the idea of class politics with which many historians and sociologists have been concerned (Gilroy 1987).

This veritable explosion of research and criticism has contributed to the sense of disarray and demoralization that pervades the field of labor and working-class history, but it has not really challenged the basic outlines of the paradigm, nor has it led to its reformulation. This is so, I believe, because the paradigm is based on foundational assumptions that resist or may be impervious to empirical disconfirmation. In the following sections, I will argue that the universal subject of the paradigmatic history of class formation was actually based empirically on particular class actors. This universalizing move was a consequence of assumptions about social life founded in long-established distinctions between public and private in social and political theory; it was elaborated in nineteenth-century ideology and was reinforced by the construction of the nineteenth-century public sphere itself. In effect, my analysis joins critiques made by feminist scholars about liberal political theory and the nature of citizenship (see especially Pateman 1988, 1989a, 1989b) and recent critical assessments of Jurgen Habermas's ideas (1974, 1989) about the bourgeois public sphere (Fraser 1989, 1992; Eley 1992) with a long history of

4. This is a vast literature that defies concise referencing. One important approach is offered by German historians of *Alltagsgeschichte* (e.g., Ludtke 1993, 1995; Eley 1989).

feminist criticisms of working-class history and class analysis (e.g., Kelly 1984; Joan Scott 1988c; Baron 1991; Canning 1992). I attempt to go beyond a mere critique of "essentialism" or "reification" to show the complex intellectual and historical roots of the construction of the "quintessential worker" in the narrative of working-class formation.[5]

It is useful to begin with E. P. Thompson's *The Making of the English Working Class* (1980 [1963]), because Thompson himself was attempting to alter what was then the paradigmatic approach to nineteenth-century class analysis and labor history. In many ways, Thompson's great masterpiece has set the terms of debate ever since its publication. His work has provided much of the inspiration for the florescence of peoples' histories over the last third of a century.

In attempting to rescue agency from the constraints of structural determination and restore it to the historical actors in the drama of industrial and social transformation, E. P. Thompson problematized the link between "class in itself" and "class for itself." In Thompson's magisterial story, working people from diverse walks of life actively created the English working class as they formed themselves into a political community. Drawing on their shared experiences of industrial transformation in the context of a continuing tradition of radical politics, workers conducted struggles in their workplaces and communities that led them to identify common interests "as between themselves, and as against other(s)" (Thompson 1980, 8–9). Thompson introduced his *Making of the English Working Class* by stressing the significance of the productive relations shaping people's experiences, but in much of his historical narrative he emphasized the cultural processes and traditions of political dissent that shape class consciousness. While class experience is a consequence of the relations of production, class consciousness is not. Rather, consciousness of class is the historical process by which those experiences are embodied in "traditions, value-systems, ideas and institutional forms" (Thompson 1980, 9).

5. Recently Anson Rabinbach (1994, 77) has written a provocative critique of poststructuralist analysis, which in his view presents a "unified story of history as a process of essentialization, denial of difference, and discursive suppression." In this essay I am examining the philosophical and empirical bases of such processes of "essentialization, denial of difference, and discursive suppression." I will suggest how a revisioning of class analysis makes it possible both to de-essentialize the subject of working-class history and to transform essentialization and discursive suppression into subjects for investigation. I agree with Rabinbach that although the "ideal of inclusion" is crucial for critical practice, we must remain sensitive to the ways that exclusions and suppressions work even in supposedly inclusionary politics.

In spite of Thompson's attempt to break away from structural determinism, the idea of class formation elaborated by his followers generally presumes that people have common experiences in production relations and that these somehow induce social action. As numerous critics have pointed out, the class formation paradigm continues to be locked into a teleological framework (Katznelson 1986; Somers 1989). As Margaret Somers has argued (1992 and Chapter 2 in this book), the story of class formation, structured around a metanarrative of modernization, continues to undergird scholarship on working-class formation (see also Chakrabarty 1989). How to conceptualize the nature of the relationship between class structure on the one hand and resistance, struggle, and class politics on the other hand remains a significant problem in class analysis (Eley and Nield forthcoming).

The dominant theoretical portrait of working-class formation represents its class subjects as prototypical and portrays their subjectivities as being constituted by work itself. The class subjects are universal characters—raceless and genderless figures in a unidimensional landscape. Yet the subjects upon which sociologists and historians have based their portrait are actually specific historical actors who cannot be seen as representative of the working-class as a whole or as prototypical. These subjects are generally white, male, and skilled workers.

These (mistakenly) universal subjects of working-class history, and the particular activities that are taken to be archetypal indicators of resistance and politics, have been fostered by two overlapping sets of ideas. First, historians of class formation have based their constructions of the subjects and subject matters of class analysis on a gendered binary distinction between public and private. In practice this has meant that historians of class formation have tended not only to situate the genesis and reproduction of class in production relations but also to locate class action in a specific understanding of the public sphere.[6] Second, this focus on particular social actors and particular kinds of activities in the story of class struggle is reinforced by the dominant story line in the paradigm of working-class formation, one that features the process of proletarianization as the historical dynamic leading to class struggle. As a consequence,

6. Elizabeth Faue (1991b, 15–18) also has pointed to the public/private dichotomy as crucial both to social science thinking about social class and to changes in the nature of labor movement organization. She argues that in both instances there was a shift in the primary focus of attention from the community to the point of production.

the bulk of historiography has spotlighted male artisans and skilled workers as the primary class actors. Historians have worked from a model that not only involves an abstract notion of work, as Lenard Berlanstein has noted (1993, 7), but features disembodied workers. What I am calling "the quintessential worker problem" has made incorporating women into class analysis difficult, and has blinded historians from recognizing how both gender and race often have been *constitutive* of class identities. In addition, these foundational assumptions concerning public and private and the centrality of proletarianization have led historians and sociologists to ignore what James C. Scott (1985, 1990) has termed "everyday forms of resistance" (see also see Kelley 1993, 1994; Fox 1994).

Public and Private in the Analysis of Working-Class Formation

Retaining a basically Marxian understanding of class as rooted in workplace relations, Thompson and the scholars who followed him continued to orient their studies around transformations in the nature of work and the impact of these transformations on workers. Crucial to this presumption of the singular importance of production relations for class analysis is the distinction between public and private in Western thought. This distinction, elaborated in particular ways in nineteenth-century theory, ideology, and social practice, ultimately shaped foundational concepts in the emerging social science disciplines.[7] Thoroughly imbricated in the public/private dichotomy are understandings about the different capacities and rights of men and women.

Although the public/private dichotomy has been a relatively continuous feature of western political and social theory since the Greeks, the conceptualization of the spheres and the distinction between them have varied (Weintraub 1995). In liberal political theory the public sphere was conceptualized as being both the realm of the state and the site of public opinion, citizenship, and democratic participation. Participation in the public sphere was governed by "universal, impersonal and conventional criteria of achievement, interests, rights, equality and property— liberal criteria, applicable only to men" (Pateman 1989a, 121). For Locke

---

7. In an important essay, Leonore Davidoff (1990) argues that a series of concepts based on gendered assumptions came to dominate sociology and history influenced by sociological theory.

both the economy and the family were located in the private sphere. In contrast to both the public or political sphere and the economy, the private sphere of the family was governed by the "natural ties of sentiment and blood and on the sexually ascribed status of wife and husband (mother and father)." It was, in other words, the site of emotion governable by the "natural" hierarchies of age and sex, rather than by contract. Furthermore, as Carole Pateman has noted, "the civil body politic is fashioned after the image of the male 'individual' who is constituted through the separation of civil society from women." In liberal political theory, this 'individual' is disembodied" (Pateman 1989b, 46).

While deeply critical of both liberal political theory and the denigration of the private or domestic sphere under capitalism, Marx and Engels also assumed the existence of dichotomous spheres and linked the domestic sphere with women and the public or social sphere with men. Marx identified the forces and relations of production—located in the social sphere—as fundamental to historical transformation. What this meant is that social reproduction, while essential for the development and maintenance of capitalism, responded to social change but did not contribute to it. As Linda Nicholson has written, "When 'productive' activities . . . come to constitute the world of change and dynamism then activities of 'reproduction' become viewed as either the brute, physiological and nonhistorical aspects of human existence or as by-products of changes in the economy" (Nicholson 1987, 25).[8] In addition, Marx and Engels appear to have presumed that the politics of class struggle originated and took place in the public or social sphere. Marx valorized working men's organizations as the active force that would transform society (Benenson 1983, 18). Not only Marx and Engels but also the scholars of class formation who followed them appear to have presumed that both the origins of class struggle and the development of class consciousness were located in the public sphere.[9]

8. Nicholson's essay is a particularly clear examination of the problems in Marxian class theory. See also Harold Benenson's important essay (1983).

9. Most recently discussions of the public sphere have focused on the work that Habermas did in the early 1960s (Habermas 1989, 1974). I draw on and have been inspired by the critiques of Habermas's notion of the bourgeois public sphere, especially by Nancy Fraser (1992, 1989), Mary Ryan (1992, 1990) and Geoff Eley (1992). For an important critique of the apparently male nature of the bourgeois public sphere in the context of post–Civil War African-American communities, see Brown 1994. For an important analysis of the shifting distinctions between public and private in the Revolutionary period in France, see Goodman 1992.

Much Marxist-feminist theorizing in the 1970s attempted to produce a Marxian analysis of capitalism that could incorporate the private sphere of biological and social reproduction. Known as the domestic labor debates, these academic discussions basically retained the idea of separate spheres but attempted to show how the private sphere and women's roles in that sphere were necessary for capitalist accumulation.[10] Yet even in these discussions conducted at the level of abstract theory, the "motor of history" remained in the public sphere. While domestic labor was seen to be functional for capitalism, productive relations and the politics generated as a consequence of them remained the stuff of historical transformation.

It was not just the elaboration of gendered notions of the public and private in formal social and political theory that influenced the development of the social sciences and history. Social and political developments peculiar to the late eighteenth and nineteenth centuries were especially crucial. For it was during this period that the ideology of separate spheres came to be central to the worldviews of both the bourgeoisie and, later, many members of the working class.[11] This ideology identified male activity and masculinity with the public sphere of politics and the market, and female activity and femininity with the private, domestic sphere of the household and reproduction.[12] Indeed, as Harold Benenson has argued (1983), Marx's analysis of capitalism and the historical role of the working class was greatly influenced by this Victorian ideology (see also Joan Scott 1988b).

In England as well as in the United States the doctrine of separate spheres became an organizing principle in the lives of the rising middle classes.[13] Increasingly in the nineteenth century, women and men were seen as having essentially different natures.[14] Because of their different natures, men were believed to be best equipped to deal with the worldly matters of commerce and politics; women were believed especially suited

10. For critical overviews, see Molyneux 1979 and Barrett 1988

11. For an important discussion of the formation of a masculine working class and its relation to the embodiment of separate spheres in radical discourse, see Hall 1990.

12. In the domestic ideology version of the public-private dichotomy, the economy which was considered to be private when contrasted with the state in liberal political theory is understood as part of the public when compared with the domestic realm of family life.

13. For England, see the pathbreaking study by Leonore Davidoff and Catherine Hall (1987). For the United States, see Ryan 1981.

14. For an interesting analysis of changing ideas about the similarities and differences between women and men and their relative status, see Bloch 1978.

to providing moral sustenance as well as physical and emotional nurturance to family members. These ideas about gender difference and the normative ordering of gender relations comprising the middle-class world view were incorporated into the emerging social sciences, as well as into the biological and medical sciences.[15] Mid-twentieth-century sociology and anthropology reworked these ideas, giving them renewed legitimation (Collier, Rosaldo, and Yanagisako 1982).

Working-class and labor historians and sociologists who study class formation have consistently looked only to the so-called "public sphere" as a source of working-class politics. As Carolyn Steedman has remarked (1986, 13), how class consciousness develops in working-class families "as a learned position, learned in childhood, and often through the exigencies of difficult and lonely lives," has been ignored by most class analysts. Several feminist scholars have maintained that class analysts must take into account the relations of reproduction and the dailiness of making ends meet in generating class consciousness (Faue 1990; Kessler-Harris 1991; also Smith 1987, 1990). As Robin Kelley has argued, "the role of families in the formation of class consciousness and in developing strategies of resistance has not been sufficiently explored, in part because most scholarship continues to privilege the workplace and production over the household and reproduction" (Kelley 1994, 36–37).[16] He suggests that the history of the American black working class indicates that black workers had experience with the politics of resistance long before they entered the workplace and joined trade unions.

While feminist scholars since the 1970s have decried the incorporation into social science thinking of the ideology that conceptualizes home, family, and kinship as a feminine sphere separated from the rest of society, only relatively recently have scholars begun to appreciate the significance of nineteenth-century *public* spheres for the development of the concepts used in social analysis—particularly the relevance of who constructed these spheres and how.[17] Recent historical scholarship has docu-

15. There is an enormous literature on how gender, especially as it was worked out in Enlightenment thought, was a constitutive feature of both biology and medicine. For particularly good examples of recent work, see Jordanova 1989 and Wilson 1993.

16. Critics of Neil Smelser (1959) have focused on his reduction of complex historical developments to abstract structural causes; but, interestingly, they have overlooked his empirical observations suggesting that disruption in family lives may be linked to political activism.

17. Barbara Laslett (1992) has argued that the gendered concept of separate spheres strongly influenced theories of human agency by expunging emotion; see also Laslett 1990. See Davidoff's

mented that what social scientists came to identfy as *the* public sphere was actually constructed by historical actors as a masculine domain during the eighteenth and nineteenth centuries. Historically, the oppositional construction of public/private was used to justify excluding women from both politics and the market. In France, for example, Joan Landes's work demonstrates that the bourgeois public sphere became gendered during the revolutionary era, as men purposefully excluded women from politics (Landes 1988). In the United States, the place of white women became identified with the notion of republican motherhood as white men came to define their roles as political actors (Kerber 1980).[18] In England, as Davidoff and Hall have shown (1987), middle-class men dominated the institutions of civil society, while women were actively marginalized. Bourgeois men developed a range of formal associations including employer associations and fraternal orders that brought them together in gender-segregated public spaces. These developments in bourgeois society shaped the assumptions of the emerging disciplines that concerned themselves with the social world generally. They did so despite the fact that white middle-class women engaged in activities that might have challenged the notion of separate spheres but were defined instead, and sometimes by the women themselves, as related to their family roles or as philanthropy rather than politics. Furthermore, as James Vernon (1993) has argued, during the nineteenth century, modern political structures increasingly restricted rather than expanded opportunities for political expression, especially by women.

In addition, there were related developments in the working class that were especially consequential for how sociologists and historians came to understand class politics. Most important, what scholars have identified as the working-class public sphere was created by a distinct *segment* of working-class men. Recent scholarship has stressed that in Europe it was primarily male artisans who organized to defend their trades and to argue for their rights as citizens. Sally Alexander's important work has shown how

exploration (1990) of the influence of separate spheres on the development of the social sciences in the nineteenth century. See also Davidoff and Hall 1987, 29. For an early statement of the link between "representations of gender difference" and "scientific analyses of social and economic life," see Fox-Genovese 1982.

18. See also Linda Kerber's important review essay (1988) on public and private in feminist analysis and Ryan's analysis (1990) of white bourgeois women's challenges to the public/private dichotomy. For the inapplicability of the dichotomy for African-American life in late-nineteenth-century America, see Brown 1994.

in England male artisans stood on speakers' platforms to protest the assault on their livelihoods. She notes how they frequently used masculinist language to depict their plight and claim their rights as those who "held property in their labor" (Alexander 1984). Furthermore, studies of European trade union organizations, especially in England during most of the nineteenth and the early part of the twentieth centuries, have shown that women and unskilled men either were barred from these organizations or were marginalized in them (e.g., Drake 1984; Faue 1991a; Rose 1992. 1993a). For example in England, until the rise of the general trade unions in the 1880s, "respectable men" dominated the working-class public sphere—not all men, and no women (McClelland 1989; Rose 1992, chap. 6; 1993a). In the United States for much of its history, especially after the defeat of the Knights of Labor, the working-class public sphere was dominated by white men. It was not the case that women or nonwhite men were not in the labor force or did not engage in acts of resistance. Rather, they were less visible, either as a consequence of purposeful exclusion or because of the presumptions about work, family headship, and respectability articulated by the white male artisans and skilled workers who led protests and formed associations to protect their interests.

Scholars have developed understandings of class formation using these particular political actors and their activities as prototypes in a universal process. As a foundational assumption of historical analysis, the public/private dichotomy with its deeply gendered associations has had the consequence of limiting scholars' vision of who and what counts as historically interesting and important.

Proletarianization

Working-class historians and historical sociologists reinforced these foundational assumptions by focusing on the process of proletarianization as the "master process" in class formation (Sewell 1993). Influenced by Marxian ideas, analysts of class formation have generally assumed that "class experience" is shaped by events and relations "at the point of production."

In studying proletarianization, scholars have been concerned with both the creation of wageworkers for capitalist industries and the transformation of the labor process that led to the de-skilling of work. Historical studies have detailed the development of technologies and production processes and the reorganization of economic relations that obliterated trades and revolutionized household production in towns and rural areas. Scholars have examined the transformation of urban artisanal occupations, and finally the de-skilling of factory labor. As Sewell (1993) has noted, proletarianization is actually not a single process but several quite different transformations, all of which have been presumed by historians and sociologists to be aspects of a master process formative of class experience.

Interested in examining working-class agency in history, and influenced by the particular construction of the public sphere that developed in the nineteenth century, scholars concentrated their examinations on the impact of industrialization on male workers who were defending their artisanal trades and on skilled workers who were resisting their apparent loss of control over production. The struggles waged by artisans and skilled workers were at the center of historical narratives, and historians probed how these particular workers became politicized and how they expressed their class antagonisms. Scholars debated whether cultural or organizational processes produced working-class politics. Following Thompson's lead, some historians emphasized how workers deployed long-standing traditions of protest in their struggles. Others stressed the organizational resources that enabled artisans and skilled workers to engage in collective action. Regardless of the story they told, however, the subjects of significant class action were generally artisans and skilled workers.

Historians and sociologists took these primarily white, skilled, and male-centered activities and institutions as *constituting* "the social" and "the political" as objects of study (Eley 1997). Indeed, even the concept of "agency" itself has been influenced by these particular conceptions of activism and resistance. At the very least, the story of working-class formation has not only been cast as a heroic "emancipatory narrative," to use Dipesh Chakrabarty's words, it has also generally been the story of a limited number of white males engaging in organized political resistance (Chakrabarty 1989). Scholars of working-class formation have tended to understand other kinds of responses to domination as indicative of "quiescence" or "accommodation". Indeed even when organized political resistance has fought for "bread and butter issues," or has pushed for relatively modest goals rather than revolutionary change, there has been a tendency to understand the working-class as quiescent.

The historiography of mid-Victorian, post-Chartist British labor history has been shaped by exactly that idea.[19] The fact that trade union leaders sought limited gains and often extolled the virtues of a "labor-capital accord" has generally been read as the demise of radicalism, and historians have concentrated their debates on why this occurred. Another outcome of having a uniform or universal story of working-class formation is the frequently criticized view that those working-class experiences that do not fit the prototype are exceptions.[20]

Yet resistance and struggle come in a variety of forms. The literature in the sociology of work is replete with examples of workers who attempt to eke out personal time during the workday, make use of employer-owned material for their own purposes, and express their hostility to their working conditions by absenteeism or quitting. Aihwa Ong's study of Malaysian women working in Japanese-owned factories reveals how these women resisted the dehumanization of their lives through spirit possessions, while Diane Lauren Wolf has shown how Javanese women factory workers engaged in a variety of forms of resistance including "stayouts and spirit visions" (Ong 1987; Wolf 1992, 128). Furthermore, a growing number of studies suggest that members of the working classes have engaged in a variety of forms of expressive culture outside of the workplace, by means of which they both resist capitalist discipline and oftentimes come into conflict with formal working-class institutions (e.g., Willis 1977; Peiss 1986; Kelley 1994). As Kelley has argued with regard to the black working-class in the United States, "The challenge for Southern labor historians is to determine precisely how this rich expressive culture . . . shaped and reflected black working-class opposition" (Kelley 1994, 44). Moreover, as Dorinne Kondo has suggested, resistance is neither unidimensional nor without contradictions. Rather, there are "mobile points of potential resistance moving through any regime of power" (Kondo 1990, 225). Resistance, she insists, is "riven with ironies and contradictions just as coping or consent may have unexpectedly subversive effects" (224). By

19. This is a vast literature. For a representative sample of different positions on why the working class was acquiescent, see Joyce 1980 and Foster 1974. For other arguments concerning a labor aristocracy, see Hobsbawm 1964, chap. 15, 16; 1984, chap. 9, 12, 13; Moorhouse 1978, 1981; Reid 1978; and Kirk 1985. For a rare voice protesting the idea of working-class quiescence, see Price 1975, 1983.

20. For critiques see Wilentz 1984 and responses in Salvatore 1984 and Hanagan 1984. See also Lenger 1991; Zolberg 1986; Chakrabarty 1989, esp. 221–25.

focusing on formal institutions and specific forms of protest in particular public spaces, scholars of working-class formation have sought to understand the rise of identifiably radical political movements with revolutionary potential, but they have often missed the ongoing struggle. As Geoff Eley (1994) has argued, European socialist culture itself failed to reach large numbers of working-class people because it was constructed in opposition to many of the everyday practices and pleasures of working-class life (also see Fox 1994).

Gender, Race, and the Construction of Political Identities

I have been arguing that the paradigm of working-class formation most often employed in historical and sociological scholarship has been based empirically on historical analysis of generally white, male, skilled working-class actors because it has been guided by foundational assumptions privileging work, formal public activities, and organized politics. As a consequence, analysts of class formation have ignored the complexity of working-class people's responses to the exigencies of their lives. They have also missed a crucial piece of the very story that they told. They have ignored the active *exclusions* that were central to the construction of their subjects. While scholars may have been aware that skilled workers built their political *organizations* by excluding unskilled laborers, recent scholarship has emphasized that skill itself was constructed by workers through exclusive apprenticeships (Baron 1989; Somers 1995). Furthermore, as feminist historians and sociologists have been arguing for over a decade, skill was historically constructed as a masculine attribute (Phillips and Taylor 1980; Cockburn 1983; Elson and Pearson 1981; Rose 1992; Baron 1989). Recent work by Laura Tabili (1994) shows that skill was also constructed as a *white* male attribute by the early twenthieth-century British merchant shipping industry, which employed colonial men of color and metropolitan white men. Crucially, then, race and gender were not incidental to the construction of skill, or to the processes by which skilled workers built their organizations, made political alliances, and developed bonds of solidarity. Moreover, recent work on gender, race, and working-class history suggests that these identities were important to the class identities that these working-class subjects developed.

David R. Roediger (1991), for example, has shown that being white was central to the development of white male working-class identities. He argues that whiteness functioned as a "psychological" wage that was significant in the integration of immigrant and native-born white working men into the developing capitalist economy and especially to their accepting the status of wageworkers. Anna Clark, in her important work reexamining the making of the British working class in the early nineteenth century, puts gender at the center of her analysis. She demonstrates that despite alternative possibilities for understanding how the social and political order might be transformed, plebeian radicals combined "the fraternal solidarity of their old artisan culture with the masculine rhetoric of civic humanism to demand radical male citizenship" (Clark 1995, 157). Clark has also shown that in attempting to create a political rhetoric to defend working-class culture from elite attacks, Chartists elaborated a working-class version of the ideology of domesticity that made politics and work the natural province of men. Furthermore, research on male trade unionists' demands in several countries has detailed the prevalence of working men's demands for a "family wage," suggesting that their family lives and the importance of their status as heads of households were significant in shaping their political strategies (Blewett 1988; May 1982; Rose 1992, 1993a; Frader 1996; Hewitt 1991). Gender and race, then, were anything but incidental to class in these accounts.

Such studies suggest, moreover, that class identities are formed, and political solidarities are generated, discursively. They do not spring forth in an unmediated fashion from productive relations to stamp their subjects in a common mold. If, as E. P. Thompson (1980, 8) has written, class is something that "happens in human relationships," then it is important to understand that it is a cultural as well as a social accomplishment. Historically, at least in Western Europe and in America, class identities were forged through discourses of class solidarity that emphasized these racialized and gendered identities.

Rethinking Class Formation: Sartre's Concept of Seriality

To broaden our vision in order to examine the ways that "class happens in human relationships," we need to abandon an exclusive focus on proletarianization and a narrow notion of what constitutes the public sphere and the political. Arenas of contestation exist outside of formal politics. People's everyday worlds—including their efforts to feed families on inadequate financial resources, find affordable housing, and care for the aged and infirm—are potent arenas of struggle. Multiple sites of resistance and contest exist outside of what scholars have considered to be "the public sphere": in families and households, in dance halls, on street corners, at the local bar, and perhaps even in shopping malls, supermarkets, and beauty parlors.[21] As Eley has recently put it, the everyday is "the place where the abstractions of domination and exploitation were directly encountered, processed into manageable meanings, and inscribed as the organizing sense of individual and collective lives. As such, 'everydayness' can be produced in all manner of practical, informal, organized and instituted ways" (Eley 1994).[22]

To rethink class formation, we need to revise our understanding of the binary distinction between public and private that has shaped so much of the scholarship on working-class politics. I want to suggest here that public and private might better be understood relationally and multidimensionally rather than as a unidimensional categorical opposition. Public and private are not fixed categories or spheres of existence. Rather, they are defined in relation to one another, and often they are matters of contest. What counts as a public issue or a matter of common concern, for example, is decided through "discursive contestation" (Fraser 1992, 129). What is defined as public or private, and who defines it and how, are matters for empirical investigation. The empirical referents of these concepts, in other words, need to be *discovered* rather than presumed in an a priori fashion.

The dimensions that might be explored in deploying the relational distinction between public and private include physical sites, concerns, or issues, and collectivities engaged in a variety of activities. One fruitful way of thinking about public collectivities, as Nancy Fraser (1992) has suggested, expands Habermas's (1989) notion of the bourgeois public sphere to include multiple and contesting publics and counterpublics.

But how do we reconnect these physical sites, concerns, issues, and activities to economic inequality? To think about the links between

---

21. Work in cultural studies makes this argument for the arena of popular culture. See, for example, Hebdige 1979, 1988. For a theoretical discussion of the creativity of everyday practice, see de Certeau 1984.
22. The special significance of the "everyday" as a source of understanding for women has been a major theme in the work of Dorothy E. Smith (1987, 1990).

large-scale processes and how they shape everyday worlds, I have found the work of social geographers helpful (Soja 1989; Pred 1990; Pred and Watts 1992). Pred and Watts (1992, xiii), for example, are concerned with the "context-dependent, geographically and historically contingent forms of contestation that develop in response to the inner contradictions" of processes of capital accumulation. How people are economically situated and how these processes are spatially and culturally articulated in their everyday worlds makes a profound difference in how they live. This does not mean that capitalism and its resulting economic inequalities are constituted in the world without regard to gender, race, and other hierarchical divisions. Nor does it mean that these economic relations form in the absence of politics and culture. Rather, as Mark Granovetter (1985) suggests, and as Karl Polanyi (1957) so masterfully argues, economic relations are embedded in social, cultural, and political relations. Economic inequalities, in other words, are generated by complex cultural, social, and political processes that organize the constraints and opportunities shaping people's everyday worlds. We need a way of thinking about class that captures these linkages, and the practices that develop along with them in "geographically and historically specific circumstances," that does not depend on or generate a universal working-class subject. What I suggest below is Sartre's concept of seriality, which I see as a "sensitizing concept" (Blumer 1969) to orient and guide research rather than a theory that provides a universal account of class formation. It is a way of thinking that attempts to avoid the problems of false universalizing that I have discussed above.

A helpful way to think about the problem of class formation that avoids equating inequality and class identity is to follow the lead offered by R. W. Connell (1983) and by Iris Marion Young (1994) to use Sartre's metaphor of seriality (Sartre 1976, esp. bk. 1, chap. 4, and bk. 2; see also Fantasia 1988, 16–17). For Sartre, a series exists when people share a common situation by a logic that is outside of them. To use Young's rephrasing, seriality is a structure "arising from people's historically congealed institutionalized actions and expectations that position and limit individuals in determinate ways that they must deal with" (Young 1994, 732). Class, in this sense, refers to those people who share particular constraints and opportunities stemming from how they are economically situated. This is class conceptualized as "effects," as the consequences of the structuring of inequality by racialized and gendered capitalisms. Pierre Bourdieu (1989) has conceptualized this locational understanding of class as "social space." Class is not a unified group, and people similarly situated in this social space will not necessarily form specific groups or organizations. Yet the complex historical workings of capitalism create changing conditions, physical spaces, and opportunities for people to engage in a range of possibilities of resistance in a variety of different kinds of collectivities (Pred and Watts 1992). Class as a serial structure constrains and enables action, but does not determine it (Young 1994).

There is more to class, however, than these locales and potential sites of contest. Class consists of "constant ebbs and flows of groupings out of series; some groups remain and grow into institutions that produce new serialities, others disperse soon after they are born" (Young 1994, 735). Furthermore, as Adam Przeworski (1985) has suggested, and Fantasia (1988) has demonstrated, class is an effect of struggle. Equally important, I believe, is that class is formed discursively by cultural or symbolic processes that define a common project and create for the participants the sense of having a group identity (Eley and Nield forthcoming). Political identities are formed from a series, in other words, as a consequence of political mobilization that involves discourses. These discourses always entail processes of inclusion and exclusion and inevitably are boundary-making endeavors (Wacquant 1991).[23]

Let me give a brief example from my own work to illustrate what I mean. In my research on gender and class in nineteenth-century Britain, I have examined how trade union solidarity was discursively constructed—specifically, how the category "worker" was created rhetorically by trade union leaders (Rose 1993a). By examining the language used by these leaders in a major strike and lockout in the cotton textile districts in 1878, I show that they attempted to build solidarity and maintain the loyalty of their followers by deploying images of workers as respectable family men. But since the striking workers were a diverse group made up of single and married women as well as young single men and male laborers, the rhetoric had the consequence of marginalizing numerous workers whose loyalty was crucial. These workers, who were identified by the leadership in language that portrayed them as traitors to the union's cause, took to the streets and engaged in disruptive behavior challenging both

23. The idea that political mobilization depends on discourse has become central to sociologists of social movements who have developed the concept of "collective action frames." See, for example, Gamson 1992 Snow and Benford 1988; Tarrow 1994, esp. chap. 7).

the union leadership and the employers, who had threatened the workers with drastic reductions in their wages. In this study, I argue that the articulation of an "identity of interests" was constructed around a set of inclusions and exclusions. The image of "respectable manhood" constructed only particular men as working-class stalwarts, unifying them by accentuating their differences not only from their employers but from those working-class others who did not fit the mold.

One can think of the Lancashire workers and community residents who were participants in this complex struggle as initially being in a series. They were a series of workers who varied by the kinds of jobs that they did, by whether or not they had joined the union, by whether they were union officials or rank-and-file workers, by whether they were male or female, married or single, old or young, Protestant or Catholic, and so forth. They formed a series insofar as they all worked for the textile industry and their employers had decided to reduce their wages. Or they belonged to families of textile workers. This was a series demarcated spatially, such that the streets, the mill yard, the factory floor, and the moors high above the town all were potential sites of public meeting and contest. It was marked as well by the fact that trade unions existed, although only 60 percent of the factory workforce were members (Rose 1992). The weavers' union was the dominant collectivity that mobilized the workers to protest the cut in their wages. But the political class grouping that formed in the course of the struggle did not include all those who were members of either the union or the series. Instead, the process of political mobilization involved including some and excluding others.

To think of the processes of group formation arising out of a series encourages an awareness that class actors are always a subset of the series and are not necessarily representative of the whole. Furthermore, as Connell emphasizes, groups do not arise out of what people have in common by the addition of "consciousness." Rather, they arise as a consequence of processes of negation and transcendence. What this means is that in the creation of common political identities, the process of mobilization involves *suppressing* difference—creating allegiances and uniformities out of disunity (Connell 1983, 68–69). Thus political identities are always unstable.

As people interact around particular issues or events, they may engage in collective action of the sort that Sartre identifies as a 'fused group'—the kind of collectivity involved in bread riots, mass protests, and impromptu street demonstrations. Such collective actions involve people in overcoming the dispersal characteristic of the series. To move to a more institutional level, further negations are necessary. So also, I would argue, is it necessary that group boundaries become forged, demarcating the "we" who are acting in concert from both those against whom the struggle is being waged and those who are not incorporated into the new political identity.

In addition, I think it is important not to prejudge what counts as resistance or political contestation. In the example described above, I focus on what labor and working-class historians generally have taken as oppositional action, that is, strikes and street demonstrations. But what I want to emphasize here is that it is important to rethink what we mean by resistance, and not limit it to relatively organized counterhegemonic activities. Rather, I am advocating that the concept of resistance be broadened to include a host of activities that may not, in themselves, be overtly oppositional, but that may heighten people's sense of disadvantage and lead them into collectivities that could be the basis of more formal contestation. Moreover, as Kelley (1993, 111) suggests, the relationship between such oppositional activities and "collective, open engagement with power is dialectical, not a teleological transformation from unconscious accommodation to conscious resistance." Furthermore, along with Fox (1994), I think it is important to create an understanding of resistance that is not limited to activities that reject dominant cultural values or that are overtly counterhegemonic. Rather, important insights into working-class formation can be gained by examining how people struggle for conditions that provide them with a modicum of self-worth, without judging such struggles by theoretically or politically derived standards.

Moreover, recent studies of black working-class communities, especially by Paul Gilroy (1987) in Britain and Kelley (1994) in the United States, suggest that expressive popular culture may be a form of resistance; it may provide the context and the occasions for collective struggle, and it may supply the discursive politics necessary for the formation of group identities. Kelley and George Lipsitz both suggest, for example, that black and Chicano men wearing zoot suits in the 1940s conveyed a sense of self-assertion "and provided a means of creating a community out of a disdain for traditional 'community' standards" (Lipsitz 1994, 84). Rather than being simply a fashion fad, zoot-suiters were engaging in "the politics of a spontaneous youth movement with a sophisticated understanding of the transitions and transformations of America instigated by the war" (86). Similarly, Gilroy (1991, 210) argues that nighttime leisure activities of black

Britons are both sources of pleasure and expressions of resistance to the "temporal and spatial order of the dominant culture." Periodically, dance halls and clubs have become sites of hostile surveillance and intervention by police that provoke more formal collective protests by community members (93). This is not to say that all of the collective activities in which disadvantaged people engage are necessarily "hidden forms of resistance" to be uncovered by the sociologist or historian. People create their lives by intimacies and pleasures as well as through the daily struggle to make ends meet. Yet, we cannot in advance rule out those intimacies and pleasures as possible sites of contestation that form the seedbeds of organized forms of resistance (Morris 1992).

Finally, Sartre's ideas about the social, and about class, do not presume that one level of practice leads to another in any simple way or in any predefined narrative of class development. Rather, as Sartre puts it: "The working class is neither pure combativity, nor pure passive dispersal nor a pure institutionalized apparatus. It is a complex, moving relation between different practical forms" (Sartre 1976, 690). Class formation, then, may be considered to involve this "complex, moving relation between different practical forms," in which class identities may come and go, and class actors may engage in a variety of social actions. Our job as historians and sociologists is to understand the variety of forms of resistance and existence involved in seriality as well as in the processes and conjunctures that result in "negation and transcendence," and in inclusion and exclusion when groups are formed and political identities are created. What I am advocating is an open-ended analysis that explores how the practices by which people make do, make out, and gain pleasure are shaped by their location in a series or in social space—an analysis that traces the particular paths by means of which varieties of organized groupings emerge from and also inform these activities.

These are preliminary thoughts on how to reconceptualize working-class formation that divest the concept of the foundational assumption of a quintessential working-class subject. They encompass both the idea that economic relations have consequences for people's lives and the notion that class identities, groups, and organizations are the outcome of an active political mobilization that involves the discursive making of solidarity and identity. They also allow for incorporating within class analysis people's acts of resistance, negotiation, and accommodation—indeed the entire range of expressive activities of the everyday world.

References

Alexander, Sally. 1984. "Women, Class and Sexual Differences in the 1830s and 1840s: Some Reflections on the Writing of a Feminist History." *History Workshop* 17: 125–49.

Alexander, Sally, Anna Davin, and Eve Hostettler. 1979. "Labouring Women: A Reply to Eric Hobsbawm." *History Workshop* 8: 174–81.

Aminzade, Ronald. 1982. *Class, Politics, and Early Industrial Capitalism: A Study of Mid-Nineteenth-Century Tolouse, France.* Albany: SUNY Press.

———. 1993. *Ballots and Barricades: Class Formation and Republican Politics, in France, 1830–1871.* Princeton: Princeton University Press.

Baron, Ava. 1989. "Questions of Gender: Deskilling and Demasculinization in the U.S. Printing Trade, 1830–1915." *Gender & History* 1: 178–99.

———. 1991. "Gender and Labor History: Learning from the Past, Looking to the Future." In Ava Baron, ed., *Work Engendered: Toward a New History of American Labor.* Ithaca, N.Y.: Cornell University Press.

Barrett, Michele. 1988. *Women's Oppression Today: The Marxist/Feminist Encounter.* Rev. ed. London: Verso.

Benenson, Harold. 1983. "Victorian Sexual Ideology and Marx's Theory of the Working Class." *International Labor and Working Class History* 25: 1–23.

Berger, Iris. 1992. *Threads of Solidarity: Women in South African Industry, 1900–1980.* Bloomington: Indiana University Press.

Berlanstein, Lenard. 1993. Introduction to Lenard Berlanstein, ed., *Rethinking Labor History.* Urbana: University of Illinois Press.

Blewett, Mary H. 1988. *Men, Women, and Work: Class, Gender, and Protest in the New England Shoe Industry, 1780–1910.* Urbana: University of Illinois Press.

Bloch, Ruth H. 1978. "Untangling the Roots of Modern Sex Roles: A Survey of Four Centuries of Change." *Signs* 4 (winter): 237–52.

Blumer, Herbert. 1969. *Symbolic Interactionism.* Englewood Cliffs, N.J.: Transaction.

Bornat, Joanna. 1977. "Home and Work: A New Context for Trade Union History." *Oral History* 5: 101–23.

———. 1986. "'What about That Lass of Yours Being in the Union?' Textile Workers and Their Union in Yorkshire, 1888–1922." In Leonore Davidoff and Belinda Westover, eds., *Our Work, Our Lives, Our Words.* Totowa, N.J.: Barnes & Noble.

Bourdieu, Pierre. 1989. "Social Space and Symbolic Power." *Sociological Theory* 7 (spring): 14–25.

Brown, Elsa Barkley. 1994. "Negotiating and Transforming the Public Sphere: African American Political Life in the Transition from Slavery to Freedom." *Public Culture* 7 (1): 107–46.

Calhoun, Craig. 1981. *The Question of Class Struggle*. Chicago: University of Chicago Press.

———. 1983. "The Radicalism of Tradition: Community Strength or Venerable Disguise and Borrowed Language?" *American Journal of Sociology* 88: 886–914.

Cameron, Ardis. 1985. "Bread and Roses Revisited: Women's Culture and Working-Class Activism in the Lawrence Strike of 1912." In Ruth Milkman, ed., *Women, Work and Protest: A Century of U.S. Women's Labor History*. Boston: Routledge and Kegan Paul.

Canning, Kathleen. 1992. "Gender and the Politics of Class Formation: Rethinking German Labor History." *American Historical Review* 97: 736–68.

Chakrabarty, Dipesh. 1989. *Rethinking Working-Class History: Bengal 1890–1940*. Princeton: Princeton University Press.

Clark, Anna. 1995. *The Struggle for the Breetches: Gender and the Making of the British Working Class*. Berkeley: University of California Press.

Cockburn, Cynthia. 1983. *Brothers: Male Dominance and Technological Change*. London: Pluto.

Collier, Jane, Michelle Z. Rosaldo, and Sylvia Yanagisako. 1982. "Is There a Family? New Anthropological Views." In Barrie Thorne and Marilyn Yalom, eds., *Rethinking the Family: Some Feminist Questions*. New York: Longman.

Collins, Patricia Hill. 1990. *Black Feminist Thought: Knowledge, Consciousness, and the Politics of Empowerment*. Boston: Unwin Hyman.

Connell, R. W. 1983. *Which Way is Up? Essays on Class, Sex and Culture*. Sydney: George Allen & Unwin.

Davidoff, Leonore. 1990. "'Adam Spoke First and Named the Orders of the World': Masculine and Feminine Domains in History and Sociology." In Helen Corr and Lynn Jamieson, eds., *The Politics of Everyday Life: Continuity and Change in Work, Labour and the Family*. New York: St. Martin's Press.

Davidoff, Leonore, and Catherine Hall. 1987. *Family Fortunes: Man and Women of the English Middle Class, 1780–1850*. London: Hutchinson.

Davin, Anna. 1981. "Feminism and Labour History." In Raphael Samuel, ed., *People's History and Socialist Theory*. London: Routledge and Kegan Paul.

Dawley, Alan. 1976. *Class and Community: The Industrial Revolution in Lynn*. Cambridge: Harvard University Press.

de Certeau, Michel. 1984. *The Practice of Everyday Life*. Translated by Steven Rendall. Berkeley: University of California Press.

Drake, Barbara. 1984 [1920]. *Women in Trade Unions*. London: Virago Press.

Dublin, Thomas. 1980. *Women at Work: The Transformation of Work and Community in Lowell, Massachusetts, 1826–1860*. New York: Columbia University Press.

Eley, Geoff. 1989. "Labor History, Social History, *Alltagsgeschichte*: Experience, Culture, and the Politics of the Everyday—a New Direction for German Social History?" *Journal of Modern History* 61 (June): 297–343.

——. 1992. "Nations, Publics, and Political Cultures: Placing Habermas in the Nineteenth Century." In Craig Calhoun, ed., *Habermas and the Public Sphere*. Cambridge: MIT Press.

——. 1994. "Cultural Socialism, the Public Sphere, and the Mass Form: Popular Culture and the Democratic Project, 1900–1924." Paper presented at a conference, "Past and Present: The Challenge of E. P. Thompson," Princeton University, April 22–23.

——. 1997. "Is All the World a Text? From Social History to the History of Society Two Decades Later." In Terrence MacDonald, ed., *The Historic Turn in the Human Sciences*. Ann Arbor: University of Michigan Press.

Eley, Geoff, and Keith Nield. Forthcoming. *Classes as Historical Subjects? Some Reflections*. Ann Arbor: University of Michigan Press.

Elson, Diane, and Ruth Pearson. 1981. "Nimble Fingers Make Cheap Workers: An Analysis of Women's Employment in Third World Manufacturing." *Feminist Review* 7: 87–107.

Fantasia, Rick. 1938. *Cultures of Solidarity*. Berkeley: University of California Press.

Faue, Elizabeth. 1990. "Reproducing the Class Struggle: Perspectives on the Writing of Working Class History." Unpublished paper presented to the meeting of the Social Science History Association, Minneapolis, October.

——. 1991a. *Community of Suffering and Struggle: Women, Men, and the Labor Movement in Minneapolis, 1915–1945*. Chapel Hill: University of North Carolina Press.

———. 1991b. "Paths of Unionization: Community, Bureaucracy, and Gender in the Minneapolis Labor Movement of the 1930s." In Ava Baron, ed., *Work Engendered; Toward a New History of American Labor*. Ithaca, N.Y.: Cornell University Press.

Fink, Leon. 1990. "Looking Backward: Reflections on Workers' Culture and Certain Conceptual Dilemmas within Labor History." In J. Carroll Moody and Alice Kessler-Harris, eds., *Perspectives on American Labor History: The Problems of Synthesis*. DeKalb: Northern Illinois University Press.

Foster, John. 1974. *Class Struggle and the Industrial Revolution*. London: Weidenfeld and Nicolson.

Fox, Pamela. 1994. *Class Fictions: Shame and Resistance in the British Working-Class Novel, 1890–1945*. Durham, N.C.: Duke University Press.

Fox-Genovese, Elizabeth. 1982. "Placing Women's History in History." *New Left Review* 133 (May/June): 5–30.

Frader, Laura Levine. 1996. "Engendering Work and Wages: The French Labor Movement and the Family Wage." In Laura Levine Frader and Sonya O. Rose, eds., *Gender and Class in Modern Europe*. Ithaca, N.Y.: Cornell University Press.

Frader, Laura Levine, and Sonya O. Rose. 1996. "Gender and the Reconstruction of Working-Class History in Modern Europe." In Laura Levine Frader and Sonya O. Rose, eds., *Gender and Class in Modern Europe*. Ithaca, N.Y.: Cornell University Press.

Frager, Ruth. 1992. *Sweatshop Strife: Class, Ethnicity, and Gender in the Jewish Labour Movement of Toronto, 1900–1939*. Toronto: University of Toronto Press.

Fraser, Nancy. 1989. "What's Critical about Critical Theory? The Case of Habermas and Gender." In Nancy Fraser, ed., *Unruly Practices: Power, Discourse, and Gender in Contemporary Social Theory*. Minneapolis: University of Minnesota Press.

———. 1992. "Rethinking the Public Sphere: A Contribution to the Critique of Actually Existing Democracy." In Craig Calhoun, ed., *Habermas and the Public Sphere*. Cambridge: MIT Press.

Gamson, William A. 1992. "The Social Psychology of Collective Action." In Aldon D. Morris and Carol McClurg Mueller, eds., *Frontiers in Social Movement Theory*. New Haven: Yale University Press.

Gilroy, Paul. 1987. *"There Ain't No Black in the Union Jack": The Cultural Politics of Race and Nation*. Chicago: University of Chicago Press.

Goodman, Dena. 1992. "Public Sphere and Private Life: Toward a Synthesis of Current Historiographical Approaches to the Old Regime." *History and Theory* 31: 1–20.

Granovetter, Mark. 1985. "Economic Action and Social Structure: The Problem of Embeddedness." *American Journal of Sociology* 91 (November): 481–510.

Habermas, Jurgen. 1974. "The Public Sphere: An Encyclopedia Article (1964)." *New German Critique* 1 (fall): 49–55.

———. 1989. *The Structural Transformation of the Public Sphere: An Inquiry into a Category of Bourgeois Society*. Translated by Thomas Burger. Cambridge: MIT Press.

Hall, Catherine. 1990. "The Tale of Samuel and Jemima: Gender and Working-Class Culture in Nineteenth-century England." In Harvey J. Kaye and Keith McClelland, eds., *E. P. Thompson: Critical Perspectives*. Cambridge: Polity Press.

Hanagan, Michael. 1980. *The Logic of Solidarity: Artisans and Industrial Workers in Three French Towns, 1871–1914*. Urbana: University of Illinois Press.

———. 1984. "Reply to Wilentz." *International Labor and Working Class History* 26 (fall): 31–36.

———. 1989. *Nascent Proletarians: Class Formation in Post-Revolutionary France*. Oxford: B. Blackwell.

Haydu, Jeffrey. 1988. *Between Craft and Class*. Berkeley: University of California Press.

Hebdige, Dick. 1979. *Subculture: The Meaning of Style*. London: Routledge.

———. 1988. *Hiding in the Light: On Images and Things*. London: Routledge.

Hewitt, Nancy A. 1991. "'The Voice of Virile Labor': Labor Militancy, Community Solidarity, and Gender Identity among Tampa's Latin Workers, 1880–1921." In Ava Baron, ed., *Work Engendered: Toward a New History of American Labor*. Ithaca, N.Y.: Cornell University Press.

Hobsbawm, Eric J., ed. 1964. *Labouring Men*. London: Weidenfeld and Nicolson.

———. 1984. *Worlds of Labour*. London: Weidenfeld and Nicolson.

Janiewski, Dolores. 1985. *Sisterhood Denied: Race, Gender and Class in a New South Community*. Philadelphia: Temple University Press.

———. 1991. "Southern Honor, Southern Dishonor: Managerial Ideology and the Construction of Gender, Race, and Class Relations in Southern Industry." In Ava Baron, ed., *Work Engendered: Toward a New History of American Labor*. Ithaca, N.Y.: Cornell University Press.

Jordanova, Ludmilla. 1989. *Sexual Visions: Images of Gender in Science and Medicine between the Eighteenth and Twentieth Centuries*. Hemel Hempstead, Herts.: Harvester Press.

Joyce, Patrick. 1980. *Work, Society and Politics*. Brighton, Sussex: Harvester Press.

Kaplan, Jemma. 1982. "Female Consciousness and Collective Action: The Case of Barcelona, 1910–1918." *Signs* 7: 546–66.

Katznelson, Ira. 1986. "Working-Class Formation: Constructing Cases and Comparisons." In Ira Katznelson and Aristide Zolberg, eds., *Working-Class Formation: Nineteenth-Century Patterns in Western Europe and the United States*. Princeton: Princeton University Press.

——. 1994. "The 'Bourgeois' Dimension: A Provocation about Institutions, Politics, and the Future of Labor History." *International Labor and Working-Class History* 46 (fall): 7–32.

Kelley, Robin D. G. 1993. "We Are Not What We Seem." *Journal of American History* 80: 75–112.

——. 1994. *Race Rebels: Culture, Politics, and the Black Working Class*. New York: The Free Press.

Kelly, Joan. 1984. "The Doubled Vision of Feminist Theory: A Postscript to the 'Women and Power' Conference." In *Women, History and Theory: The Essays of Joan Kelly*. Chicago: University of Chicago Press.

Kerber, Linda. 1980. *Women of the Republic: Intellect and Ideology in Revolutionary America*. Chapel Hill: University of North Carolina Press.

——. 1988. "Separate Spheres, Female Worlds, Woman's Place: The Rhetoric of Women's History." *Journal of American History* 75: 5–39.

Kessler-Harris, Alice. 1990. "A New Agenda for American Labor History: A Gendered Analysis and the Question of Class." In J. Carroll Moody and Alice Kessler-Harris, eds., *Perspectives on American Labor History: The Problems of Synthesis*. DeKalb: Northern Illinois University Press.

——. 1991. Keynote address presented at the conference on North American Labor History, Detroit, October.

Kirk, Neville. 1985. *The Growth of Working Class Reformism in Mid-Victorian England*. Urbana: University of Illinois Press.

Kocka, Jurgen. 1986. "Problems of Working-Class Formation: The Early Years, 1800–1875." In Ira Katznelson and Aristide Zolberg, eds., *Working-Class Formation: Nineteenth-Century Patterns in Western Europe and the United States*. Princeton: Princeton University Press.

Kondo, Dorinne K. 1990. *Crafting Selves: Power, Gender, and Discourses of Identity in Japanese Workplace.* Chicago: University of Chicago Press.

Lamphere, Louise. 1985. "Bringing the Family to Work: Women's Culture on the Shop Floor." *Feminist Studies* 11: 519–40.

Landes, Joan B. 1988. *Women and the Public Sphere in the Age of the French Revolution.* Ithaca, N.Y.: Cornell University Press.

Laslett, Barbara. 1990. "Unfeeling Knowledge: Emotion and Objectivity in the History of Sociology." *Sociological Forum* 5: 413–33.

———. 1992. "Gender in/and Social Science History" *Social Science History* 16 (summer): 177–95.

Lenger, Friedrich. 1991. "Beyond Exceptionalism: Notes on the Artisanal Phase of the Labour Movement in France, England, Germany and the United States." *International Review of Social History* 36: 1–23.

Lipsitz, George. 1994. *Rainbow at Midnight: Labor and Culture in the 1940s.* Urbana: University of Illinois Press.

Ludtke, Alf. 1993. "Polymorphous Synchrony: German Industrial Workers and the Politics of Everyday Life." *International Review of Social History* 38 (supplement): 39–84.

———, ed. 1995. *The History of Everyday Life: Reconstructing Historical Experiences and Ways of Life*, Translated. by William Templer. Princeton: Princeton University Press.

May, Martha. 1982. "The Historical Problem of the Family Wage." *Feminist Studies* 8: 399–424.

McClelland, Keith. 1989. "Some Thoughts on Masculinity and the 'Representative Artisan' in Britain, 1850–1880." *Gender and History* 1 (summer): 164–77

McNall, Scott, Rhonda Levine, and Rick Fantasia, eds. 1991. *Bringing Class Back In: Contemporary and Historical Perspectives.* Boulder: Westview Press.

Molyneux, Maxine. 1979. "Beyond the Domestic Labour Debate." *New Left Review* 116: 7–35.

Montgomery, David. 1979 *Workers' Control in America: Studies in the History of Work, Technology and Labor Struggles.* Cambridge, England: Cambridge University Press.

Moorhouse, H. F. 1978. "The Marxist Theory of the Labour Aristocracy." *Social History* 3: 71–90.

———. 1981. "The Significance of the Labour Aristocracy." *Social History* 6: 71–81.

More, Charles. 1980. *Skill and the English Working Class, 1870–1914*. London: Croom Helm.

Morris, Aldon D. 1992. "Political Consciousness and Collective Action." In Aldon D. Morris and Carol McClurg Mueller, eds., *Frontiers in Social Movement Theory*. New Haven: Yale University Press.

Morris, Aldon D., and Carol McClurg Mueller, eds., *Frontiers in Social Movement Theory*. New Haven: Yale University Press.

Nicholson, Linda. 1987. "Feminism and Marx: Integrating Kinship with the Economic." In Seyla Benhabib and Drucilla Cornell, eds., *Feminism as Critique*. Minneapolis: University of Minnesota Press.

Ong, Aihwa. 1987. *Spirits of Resistance and Capitalist Discipline: Factory Women in Malaysia*. Albany: SUNY Press.

Pateman, Carole. 1988. *The Sexual Contract*. Cambridge: Polity.

———. 1989a. "Feminist Critiques of the Public/Private Dichotomy." In *The Disorder of Women: Democracy, Feminism and Political Theory*. Stanford: Stanford University Press.

———. 1989b. "The Fraternal Contract." In *The Disorder of Women: Democracy, Feminism and Political Theory*. Stanford: Stanford University Press.

Peiss, Kathy. 1986. *Cheap Amusements: Working Women and Leisure in Turn-of-the-Century New York*. Philadelphia: Temple University Press.

Phillips, Anne, and Barbara Taylor. 1980. "Sex and Skill: Notes towards a Feminist Economics." *Feminist Review* 6: 57–79.

Polanyi, Karl. 1957 [1944]. *The Great Transformation: The Political and Economic Transformation of Our Times*. Boston: Beacon Press.

Pred, Allan. 1990. *Making Histories and Constructing Human Geographies: The Local Transformation of Practice, Power Relations, and Consciousness*. Boulder: Westview.

Pred, Allan, and Michael John Watts. 1992. *Reworking Modernity: Capitalisms and Symbolic Discontent*. New Brunswick, N.J.: Rutgers University Press.

Price, Richard. 1975. "The Other Face of Respectability: Violence in the Manchester Brickmaking Trade, 1859–1870." *Past and Present* 69: 110–32.

———. 1983. "The Labour Process and Labour History." *Social History* 8: 57–85.

Przeworski, Adam. 1985. *Capitalism and Social Democracy*. Cambridge: Cambridge University Press.

Rabinbach, Anson. 1994. "Intellectual Crisis or Paradigm Shift." *International Labor and Working-Class History* 46: 73–80.

Reid, Alistair. 1978. "Politics and Economies in the Formation of the British Working Class: A Response to H. F. Moorhouse." *Social History* 3: 347–61.

Roediger, David R. 1991. *The Wages of Whiteness: Race and the Making of the American Working Class*. London: Verso.

Rose, Sonya O. 1992. *Limited Livelihoods: Gender and Class in Nineteenth-Century England*. Berkeley: University of California Press.

———. 1993a. "Respectable Men, Disorderly Others: The Language of Gender and the Lancashire Weavers' Strike of 1878 in Britain." *Gender & History* 5 (autumn): 382–97.

———. 1993b. "Gender and Labor History: The Nineteenth-Century Legacy." *International Review of Social History* 38 (supplement): 145–62.

Ryan, Mary. 1981. *Cradle of the Middle Class: The Family in Oneida County New York, 1790–1865*. New York: Cambridge University Press.

———. 1990. *Women in Public: Between Banners and Ballots, 1825–1880*. Baltimore: Johns Hopkins University Press.

———. 1992. "Gender and Public Access: Women's Politics in Nineteenth-Century America." In Craig Calhoun, ed., *Habermas and the Public Sphere*. Cambridge: MIT Press.

Salvatore, Nick. 1984. "Reply to Wilentz." *International Labor and Working Class History* 26 (fall): 25–30.

Sartre, Jean-Paul. 1976. *Critique of Dialectical Reason*. Vol 1. Translated by Alan Sheridan-Smith. London: New Left Books.

Scott, James C. 1985. *Weapons of the Weak, Everyday Forms of Peasant Resistance*. New Haven: Yale University Press.

———. 1990. *Domination and the Arts of Resistance: Hidden Transcripts*. New Haven: Yale University Press.

Scott, Joan Wallach. 1988a. "Women in *The Making of the English Working Class*." In *Gender and the Politics of History*. New York: Columbia University Press.

———. 1988b. "Work Identities for Men and Women: The Politics of Work and Family in the Parisian Garment Trades in 1848." In *Gender and the Politics of History*. New York: Columbia University Press.

———. 1988c. *Gender and the Politics of History*. New York: Columbia University Press.

Seccombe, Wally. 1986. "Patriarchy Stabilized: The Construction of the Male Breadwinner Wage Norm in Nineteenth-Century Britain." *Social History* 11: 53–76.

Sewell, William H., Jr. 1980. *Work and Revolution in France: The Language of Labor from the Old Regime to 1848*. Cambridge: Cambridge University Press.

———. 1986. "Artisans, Factory Workers, and the Formation of the French Working Class, 1789–1848." In Ira Katznelson and Aristide Zolberg, eds., *Working-Class Formation: Nineteenth-Century Patterns in Western Europe and the United States*. Princeton: Princeton University Press.

———. 1993. "Toward a Post-Materialist Rhetoric for Labor History." In Lenard Berlanstein, ed., *Rethinking Labor History*. Urbana: University of Illinois Press.

Smelser, Neil. 1959. *Social Change in the Industrial Revolution*. Chicago: University of Chicago Press.

Smith, Dorothy E. 1987. *The Everyday World As Problematic: A Feminist Sociology*. Boston: Northeastern University Press.

———. 1990. *The Conceptual Practices of Power: A Feminist Sociology of Knowledge*. Boston: Northeastern University Press.

Snow, David E., and Robert Benford. 1988. "Ideology, Frame Resonance, and Participant Mobilization." In Bert Klandermans, Hanspeter Kriesi, and Sidney Tarrow, eds., *International Social Movement Research*, vol. 1. Greenwich, Conn.: JAI Press.

Soja, Edward W. 1989. *Postmodern Geographies: The Reassertion of Space in Critical Social Theory*. London: Verso.

Somers, Margaret. 1989. "Workers of the World, Compare!" *Contemporary Sociology* 18: 325–29.

———. 1992. "Narrativity, Narrative Identity, and Social Action: Rethinking English Working-Class Formation." *Social Science History* 16 (4): 591–630.

———. 1995. "The 'Misteries' of Property: Relationality, Rural-Industrialization, and Community in Chartist Narratives of Political Rights." In John Brewer and Susan Staves, eds., *Early Modern Conceptions of Property*. London: Routledge.

Steedman, Carolyn. 1986. *Landscape for a Good Woman, A Story of Two Lives*. London: Virago.

Tabili, Laura. 1994. *"We Ask for British Justice": Workers and Racial Difference in Late Imperial Britain*. Ithaca, N.Y.: Cornell University Press.

Tarrow, Sidney. 1994. *Power in Movement: Social Movements, Collective Action and Politics*. Cambridge: Cambridge University Press.

Thompson, E. P. 1980 [1963]. *The Making of the English Working Class.* Harmondsworth, England: Penguin Books.

Tilly, Charles. 1978. *From Mobilization to Revolution.* Reading, Mass.: Addison-Wesley.

———. 1984. "Demographic Origins of the European Proletariat: A Proletarian World." In David Levine, ed., *Proletarianization and Family History.* Orlando, Fla.: Academic Press.

Tilly, Charles, Louise Tilly, and Richard Tilly. 1975. *The Rebellious Century, 1830–1930.* Cambridge: Harvard University Press.

Tilly, Louise, and Joan Scott. 1978. *Women, Work and Family.* New York: Holt, Rinehart & Winston.

Traugott, Mark. 1985. *Armies of the Poor.* Princeton: Princeton University Press.

———. 1995. "Capital Cities and Revolutions." *Social Science History* 19 (spring): 147–68.

Turbin, Carole. 1992. *Working Women of Collar City.* Urbana: University of Illinois Press.

Vernon, James. 1993. *Politics and the People: A Study in English Political Culture, c. 1815–1867.* Cambridge: Cambridge University Press.

Wacquant, Loic J. D. 1991 "Making Class: The Middle Class(es) in Social Theory and Social Structure." In Scott McNall, Rhonda Levine, and Rick Fantasia, eds., *Bringing Class Back In: Contemporary and Historical Perspectives.* Boulder: Westview Press.

Walkowitz, Daniel. 1978 *Worker City, Company Town: Iron and Cotton-Worker Protest in Troy and Cohoes, New York, 1855–84.* Urbana: University of Illinois Press.

Weintraub, Jeffrey. 1995. "Varieties and Vicissitudes of Public Space." In Philip Kasinitz, ed., *Metropolis: Center and Symbol of Our Times.* New York: New York University Press.

Wilentz, Sean. 1984. "Against Exceptionalism: Class Consciousness and the American Labor Movement, 1790–1928." *International Labor and Working Class History* 25 (fall): 1–24.

Willis, Paul. 1977. *Learning to Labor: How Working Class Kids Get Working Class Jobs.* New York: Cambridge University Press.

Wilson, Lindsay. 1993. *Women and Medicine in the French Enlightenment: The Debate over Maladies des Femmes.* Baltimore: Johns Hopkins University Press.

Wolf, Diane Lauren. 1992. *Factory Daughters: Gender, Household Dynamics, and Rural Industrialization in Java.* Berkeley: University of California Press.

Young, Iris Marion. 1994. "Gender as Seriality: Thinking about Women as a Social Collective." *Signs* 19 (spring): 713–38.

Zolberg, Aristide. 1986. "How Many Exceptionalisms?" In Ira Katznelson and Aristide Zolberg, eds., *Working-Class Formation: Nineteenth-Century Patterns in Western Europe and the United States.* Princeton: Princeton University Press.

Zwahr, Hartmut. 1978. *Zur Konstituierung des Proletariats als Klasse.* Berlin: Akademie-Verlag.

PART 2

Cultural Structurings
of Class Identities

CHAPTER 5

Work and Culture in the Reception of Class Ideologies

Richard Biernacki

THE CURRENT PREOCCUPATION OF LABOR HISTORIANS WITH THE explanatory significance of culture represents in large measure a response to a theoretic challenge which Marx set for himself but did not meet: that of explaining how workers' experience of the labor process guides the formation of their collective movements for social change. In the research agendas of the 1960s to the 1980s, most historians and sociologists of labor qualified the effects of work relations upon workers' allegiance to oppositional movements by highlighting the mediating influences of communal and occupational traditions (Thompson 1963; Sewell 1980; Wilentz 1984). At the close of the 1980s, the course of critique reached its current end point: many now reject out of hand attempts to make inferences about the influence of workplace structures upon workers' ideologies of resistance (Judt 1986; Laclau and Mouffe 1985). Analysts underscore instead the constitution of workers' experience through discursive traditions that are maintained in the community and public sphere (Scott 1988; Sonenscher 1989; Somers 1992).

Historical investigators have brought about this change of perspective by conceiving of culture as a discursive framework. They do so when they make culture the focal point of empirical inquiry and when they delineate its formation and influence in concrete settings. It is surprising to say, but the use of this notion of culture in concrete research has misled investigators (even those who are in principle dedicated to cultural explanations) into embracing economically reductionist accounts whenever they attempt to *explain*—not just describe and retell—the formation and adoption of oppositional ideologies. I will illustrate this paradox and offer an alternative model of culture's role in the crystallization of workers' movements, a model centered on the signifying practices of manufacture in the workplace. For a case example of my approach, I present a controlled comparison of shop-floor procedures in nineteenth-century British and German textile mills. The symbolic arrangement of manufacturing techniques in textiles, as in other industries, lent German and British workers divergent and nationally distinctive understandings of the transfer of labor as a commodity before the First World War, and these understandings were carried into the union movements of each country. These specifications of labor as a commodity lent British and German workers correspondingly different notions of exploitation and of the nature of the class boundaries between workers and employers. Disclosing the cultural constitution of manufacture makes it feasible to draw determinate but nonreductionist linkages between techniques at the point of production and public ideologies of class resistance.

Explanatory Dilemmas

Although debate on culture's influence has outdistanced E. P. Thompson's *The Making of the English Working Class*, this opus reveals the enduring dilemmas which have arisen from portraying culture principally as a discursive framework and, correlatively, from incompletely appraising culture's constitution of the labor process. In Thompson's work, processes of economic change frame the narration of workers' evolving responses. Culture—in this instance, primarily the current of political and moral discourses (Thompson 1963, 711)—supplies the material of workers' responses: "They suffered the experience of the Industrial Revolution as articulate, freeborn Englishmen" (831). Thompson describes the workplace as a site for this personal experience, but he does not set out to show that the practices of manufacture themselves—the rules for putting machines to work, for defining tasks, for distributing workers, for methods of remuneration, and for using the space of the shop or mill—were systematically patterned by culture. In a word, he highlights the workers' development of discursive traditions to interpret productive relations, not the cultural structure *of* production. With this perspective, Thompson depicts the articulation and endorsement of radical ideas in two incompatible ways. First, he presents it as a process of intellectual "self-making," for which the life practice of workers cannot account (726–27). This stance may trace an intelligible progression in ideologies, but it does not attempt to distinguish the precise causes of their change and persistence. Second, when Thompson enters the field of genuine determinations, he attributes the form and circulation of insurgent ideas to the technological setting, to the degradation of labor, and to economic distress.

This second, reductionist choice, as incompatible as it is with the tenor of Thompson's work, often commands the argument of *The Making of the English Working Class* (Thompson 1963, 9; Joyce 1995, 78 n. 18). Thompson attaches the sequence of ideological innovation among workers to that of industrial advance: "artisan culture had grown more complex with each phase of technical and social change" (Thompson 1963, 830–31). He uncovers the logic of John Thelwall's vision by referring it to the economic position of the petty artisans (156–160). He mechanically correlates fluctuations in the propagation of radical ideas with cycles of "rising prices and of hardship" (185). Most explicitly of all, Thompson's account of the Luddite movement employs images of involuntary human response to deprivation. "People were so hungry," he reasons, "that they were willing to risk their lives upsetting a barrow of potatoes. In these conditions, it might appear more surprising if men had *not* plotted revolutionary uprisings than if they *had*" (592). Thompson is hardly a thoroughgoing reductionist, but these gestures toward economic determinism recur because he did not find a satisfactory method for integrating his insights into the development of discourses with his accounts of "real" productive relations (Anderson 1980, 39, 47–48; Scott 1994, 375).

Thompson is not alone among cultural historians in surreptitiously embracing reductionist explanation. In parallel fashion the agenda-setting historian Patrick Joyce has drawn correspondences between workers' political visions and the crudest economic features of work. In *Work, Society and Politics* Joyce explains the decline of political radicalism in the British textile districts after mid-century as the result of "the power of mechanization to recast the social experience of the worker" (Joyce 1980, 80). The decline of workers' independent political movements, he asserts, mirrored the veritable erosion of workers' autonomy in the labor process.[1] The supposition that the formulation and acceptance of political ideologies reflects the conditions of production, rejected in his theory, is embraced in his history.

Of course Thompson and Joyce always include vignettes of culture's unavoidable influence upon manufacture. Precisely in so doing, they assign culture a superficial role. Joyce coined the term the "culture of the factory," yet he sees it exemplified in expressive activities such as company parties and teas or in family loyalties that accommodate workers to their lives of labor—not in the procedures of manufacture proper. Indeed, Joyce underscores the ways culture grows out of the factory when people are disengaged from production, when they sing ("as and when the tasks to hand permitted"), or when they gossip during breaks (Joyce 1991, 131–32). Analogously, Thompson restricts his methodological illustrations of culture's influence on production to the socialization of agents *outside* of work and to outdated customs of mutuality in the "moral economy" which industrialization eroded or used to its own ends (Thompson 1978, 292, 294).

Thompson's rich vignettes of work life show that cultural traditions were a necessary ingredient of economic practice, not necessarily that they were initiatory or formative in their own right. With Thompson's demonstrations, culture might serve as an indispensable reservoir of meanings for the construction of practices, while the forces of market and technological development might on their own configure the survival, reshaping, and use of these symbolic resources—and thus the form and development of practice. In fact, Thompson himself offers such evidence. He shows how the common people's invocation of the moral economy survived only so long as it facilitated rank price bargaining among the common people, the gentry, traders, and local authorities (Thompson 1971, 126, 129). The lofty corporate traditions of artisans, in Thompson's view, were degraded in the end by a crude, earthly logic: "The form and

1. Joyce 1980, 81–82; 1991, 88. Small wonder that theorists experimenting with forms of socioeconomic determinism welcome Joyce's thesis (Burawoy 1985). Richard Price has focused on the same transition from the "formal" to the "real" subsumption of labor in the workplace to explain precisely the opposite outcome from Joyce's: the rise of labor militancy in the late 1880s (Price 1985). By Price's account, workers inserted into subordinate positions in the factory embraced the maverick visions of the burgeoning socialist movement in the quarter century before the First World War. The divergent outcomes in the accounts of Price and Joyce make evident the inadequacy of explanations focused exclusively on the technological and organizational (rather than the cultural) structure of work.

extent of deterioration relates directly to the material conditions of the industry—the cost of raw materials—tools—the skill involved—conditions favouring or discouraging trade union organisation—the nature of the market" (Thompson 1963, 258). Finally, in the uneven transition to the factory system, Thompson shows how the differences among British workers in the sense and valuation of time depended on "work situations" and "technological conditioning" (Thompson 1967, 76, 80; similarly, 70, 85). He correlates the epochal shift in the culture of time with "changes in manufacturing technique which demand greater synchronization of labour and a greater exactitude in time-routines in *any* society" (Thompson 1967, 80; cf. Biernacki 1995, chap. 8).

Thompson's and Joyce's unwitting reductionism, so contrary to their rhetorical intent, results from their investigating culture as a discursive framework, so that it appears exterior to the execution of work in the capitalist production process. To be sure, discourse in this perspective may influence work by sponsoring interpretations of the work environment. But the notion that culture functions through "representations"—the premise actually guiding the research and its presentation—establishes a culture *for* or *around* practice, not one subsiding in the execution of its techniques. It thereby leaves in place an unreconstructed, implicitly "economic" view of manufacture. It permits Thompson and Joyce to link the reception of insurgent ideas to the most essential features of manufacture only by requiring ideas to conform to the "economic" aspects of work.

As Joyce has grown increasingly self-critical of unwitting forms of reductionism (Joyce 1991), he, like other historical analysts, has sought to avoid them by emphasizing that discourse is constitutive of—and in this sense "prior to"—social experience, including the experience of work. Yet this axiom does not disclose new solutions for the original puzzle, that of concisely explaining variation in the formulation and adoption of oppositional ideas across historical settings. Gareth Stedman Jones inadvertently demonstrated this more than a decade ago in his landmark analysis of popular radical discourse, "Rethinking Chartism." In his portrayal, the diagnoses of the Chartists followed autonomous traditions of political analysis, not movements of the economy or the designs of work. How to explain the persistence of a particular framework of radical ideas in the first half of the century and its eclipse in the second? The radicals' cry that government bore responsibility for economic oppression began to ring untrue as parliament introduced new regulatory legislation in the 1840s (Jones 1983, 177). In sum, when Jones offers causal clarification, he merely shifts the arena of reduction. The form and the appeal of the culture of insurgency copies the real state of affairs—in government, not in the economy per se. Jones illustrates the logic by which analysts who seek the determinant causes of change in culture, yet who continue to model culture primarily as a discursive framework, end up reducing culture to a primitive correlate of institutional structures. Similarly, in his most recent historical research on narrative conventions in Victorian Britain, *Democratic Subjects*, Joyce asserts that the wide circulation of models of factory relations that drew upon an idealized rural past was a natural concomitant of the objective fact that many employers came from the countryside (Joyce 1994, 125). The social reductionism which appears here, even though Joyce affirms in his introduction "the 'prefigurative' role of discourse" (Joyce 1994, 12), confirms that a new means is required for linking the discursive practices to institutional ones and that it must be invented not in general prolegomena but in concrete explanations.

One response to the dilemma of explanation is to suspend the moment of social linkage. In a penetrating critique of Jones, Joan Scott situates Chartist programs in their historical setting without collapsing them into a replica of institutions (Scott 1988). She expands the field in which they acquired their meaning and shows how they interlocked with parallel as well as discrepant discourses for marking relations of gender and power. But this enlargement of perspective also delays resolution of the problem which motivated inquiry in the first place, that of specifying the causes of change and persistence in an oppositional ideology— or, now, more profoundly, in the terrain of discourses as a whole. Scott accepts this as her challenge (Scott 1988, 66), and she suggests that Chartism acquired its resonance by "evolving the notion of property in labor for disenfranchised and otherwise propertyless working men" (62). But if we suppose that the workers' self-ascribed lack of "property" is itself a discursive construction, how do we explain in turn the emergence and dominance of discourses about "property"? Scott does not address this puzzle, but obviously a change of perspective is required to avoid economically reductionist or ahistorical readings of a term such as "property," whose form and resonance so easily appear as natural, inevitable accompaniments to commercial society.

To address these fundamental challenges, it is necessary to reconceive the operation of culture and to do so by returning to the point of production. The shop floor is a starting place because it serves as a model for the endurance of concise and peremptory concepts in the ongoing execution of practices rather than in verbal representations. Treating culture as a set of schemata realized in the life of practice, not as mere representations of or for practice, reaches two goals at once. First, it discloses how the procedures of production are composed by a cultural logic. This is preparatory to offering, second, a nonreductionist explanation of how practices at the point of production configure the development and reception of ideologies of class resistance.

The Cultural Structure of the Workplace

Cross-national comparison of factory procedures reveals that the techniques of manufacture were organized and executed as signifying practices, not as simple means of output. The cultural schemata that composed the most essential industrial procedures were independent of the immediate technical and economic circumstances for production. A comparison of wool textile mills in Germany and Britain during the nineteenth century demonstrates culture's structural effects. In this important branch of industry, German and British enterprises developed under compellingly similar economic circumstances. Britain's reputation as a textile pioneer rests on the precocious mechanization of cotton production in Lancashire. In Yorkshire, however, the center of Britain's wool weaving trade, power looms did not prevail until after the middle of the nineteenth century—by which time the wool and cotton mills in Germany had also begun to mechanize. A comparison of weaving mills in Yorkshire with those in regions of Germany such as the Wupper Valley and the lower Rhine not only controls for the timing of development, it also juxtaposes firms that employed the same equipment in each country, were of comparable size, were as a rule family owned, and competed against each other on an equal footing in the world market (Biernacki 1995, 4–12). The fundamental similarities in the immediate economic settings highlights the separate, contrasting influence of national differences in cultural specifications of labor as a commodity. To demonstrate that these cultural contrasts prevailed at the national level, supplementary evidence can be drawn from other textile regions and branches of manufacture in Germany and Britain.

The test comparison of wool industries reveals that when German employers and workers enacted the conveyance of labor as an abstract substance, they founded the transaction on the sale of the disposition over the workers' labor activity and on the appropriation of labor power, or as they termed it, over *Arbeitskraft*. British employers and workers enacted the principle that the capitalist employment relation rested on the appropriation of abstract labor as it was carried in tangible products. This difference in the definition of the conveyance of abstract labor structured the most fundamental aspects of industrial relations, including methods of remuneration, calculation of output and costs, disciplinary techniques, rights to employment, articulation of grievances, mill architecture, and even the apperception of time and space (Biernacki 1995). Here I offer but three examples.

Terms of Employment

By the most accurate measures, the occupation of weaving during the second half of the nineteenth century comprised the single largest job category in the manufacturing sector of the British and German economies (Germany 1900, 27–32; United Kingdom 1891). In Britain weavers were required to deliver products at a regular pace to their employers, but not necessarily their personal labor time. Weavers in the wool trade who occasionally preferred to stay at home to attend to domestic chores could often send substitutes to operate their looms, so long as the employer continued to receive the expected fabric. Accordingly, managers in Britain usually did not keep track of the earnings of individual weavers, only the output of each loom by number, even when the number of looms operated by each weaver varied within the mill. They credited pay to looms, not to weavers. In Germany, by contrast, bookkeepers credited pay directly to weavers. German weavers contracted for the disposal over their personal labor time itself and had to show up in person. The language of the factory workers reflects this national difference. German weavers seeking employment asked for a "position." British weavers only asked if the employer "had any looms to let"—as if the weavers were independent renters of the machine for whose product they were paid (Biernacki 1995, 78–84; 358–59).

Piece Rate Scales

The construction of the weavers' piece rate scales in each country parallels this difference between the transfer of 'embodied labor' in Britain versus the transfer of the disposition over the labor activity in Germany. The weaver's job was to ensure that the weft thread in the loom's shuttles moved horizontally across the vertical threads of the warp. As the shuttles laid their threads, a beam underneath or alongside the loom unfolded the warp. The speed at which this beam let out the warp largely determined how tightly the weft threads would be woven next to one another in the cloth. The slower the warp moved forward, the denser the weave. From almost the earliest days of power loom weaving, mill owners in both Germany and Britain preferred to pay weavers by piece rates. They maintained that this method gave weavers an incentive to work without close supervision and thereby reduced management costs (Pollard 1963; German 1878, 251, 404–5, 664). Piece rates prevailed in almost all branches of weaving, but the construction of the systems followed fundamentally different principles in Britain than in Germany.

In Britain the piece rate scales applied distinctive cultural precepts to appropriate workers' labor as it was materialized in cloth. A representative British scale, issued in 1883 in Huddersfield and the Colne Valley (Kirklees Archives), appears in Figure 5.1. As its vertical axis indicates, the length of fabric woven comprised the basic unit of measurement, with rates cited per 180 feet of the woven warp. If more weft threads were woven into each inch of this standard length of warp, the payment rose. The chart's horizontal axis specifies the requisite weft threads inserted per inch, which in the trade were called the "picks" or, more precisely, the "picks per inch." For basic weaving, with one shuttle and one beam, remuneration for a fixed length of cloth rose linearly as picks per inch rose. For more complicated weaves, with bonuses for extra shuttles, remuneration for a fixed length always rose with increases in density, but not at a constant rate (Figure 5.2).[2]

The pay system of a wool firm in Euskirchen on the lower Rhine, issued in 1911, appears in Figure 5.3 (Deutscher Textilarbeiterverband 1912, 75). Compared to practices in Britain, the German system did not

2. For a truly encyclopedic collection of piece rate scales founded on this principle, see British Association for the Advancement of Science, Manchester Meeting of 1887, *On the Regulation of Wages by Means of Lists in the Cotton Industry* (Manchester: John Heywood).

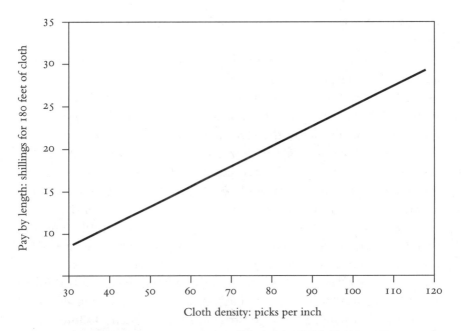

FIGURE 5.1   British Data on British Axes, Huddersfield, Simpler Weaves, *1883*

use an indirect correlate of the weaver's activity—length of cloth—as the criterion of pay. The German method centered its categories directly on the weaver's primary activity of having the shuttle move back and forth. The weavers earned a sum for every thousand times their shuttle shot across the warp—that is, per one thousand weft threads woven. The Germans called this remuneration by the number of *Schüsse*, literally, pay by the number of "shots" of the shuttle. German managers said they preferred pay by shot over pay by length because it offered the most immediate measure of the execution of labor (Biernacki 1995, 69–71) As indicated in Figure 5.3, the remuneration per one thousand shots rose linearly with decreases in the shots woven per centimeter. This feature of the scales compensated weavers for more frequent changes of the warp when producing low-density fabrics.[3]

3. Reports in Germany indicate that about four-fifths of German wool firms paid weavers directly by the shot. Many of the remaining firms (in some regions, almost all) who paid by length of cloth, however, used the system of the shot to calculate how much to pay per length (Biernacki 1995, 63, 62 n. 62).

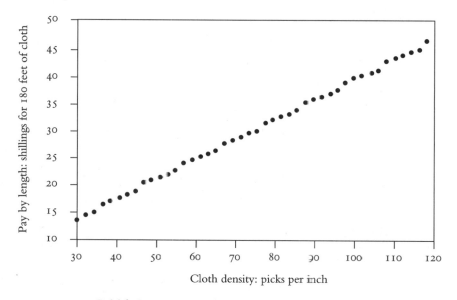

FIGURE 5.2   British Data on British Axes, Huddersfield, Fancy Weaves, Two
Beams, Four Shuttles, *1883*

The dimensions of linearity on the British and German tables reveal
the core axes of thought inscribed in (and reproduced through) the techniques of remuneration. It is impossible to translate the data from British
weaving price lists onto the German dimensions of thought without
altering the intelligibility of the distribution. To demonstrate this, Figure
5.4 displays the values for three types of English cloth on the Huddersfield scale but plots them on the German axes of thought, in pennies per
one thousand "picks" or *Schüsse*. (Table 5.1 presents the equation for the
transfer of data). Locating the British information on the German dimensions of thought leads to two discoveries. The British data lose the shape
of a line, in contrast with the German table in Figure 5.3; instead, as picks
per inch decline, the points arrange themselves in a kind of curve. The
deformed series of points obtained by the transfer confirm that the
British system of measurement embodied a concept of remuneration
which was inseparable from the length of the product.

The transfer of the British data onto the German dimensions of
thought also shows that implicit assumptions of material practice guided
the weavers' independent reflections upon the appropriation of labor
by capitalists. When British weavers had more than one shuttle or one
warp beam in operation, which often was the case, their payment per shot

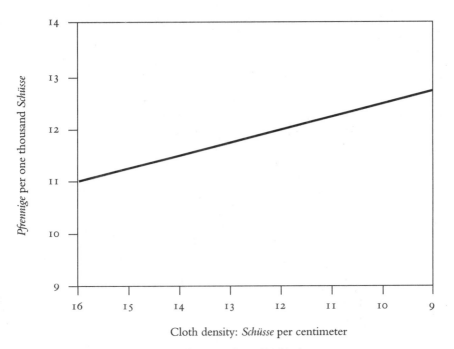

FIGURE **5.3**   German Data on German Axes, Euskirchen *1911*

did not necessarily drop as the number of shots per inch rose on various weaving jobs. Given a fixed length of cloth, the net pay rose as the number of shots per inch rose, to be sure. Yet the pay *per shot* inserted—the measure of the weavers' effective motion—followed an irregular pattern. As Figure 5.4 indicates, the more complex the weave, the more irregular and "irrational" the British method appears from a "German" point of view; that is, the more complex the weave, the more the table deviates from the expected pattern of higher earnings per shot when the number of shots per inch declines. For example, on some types of cloth, the British weaver earned less for weaving fifty-six weft threads per inch than for sixty-two, even though fifty-six would certainly take longer *per thread* to weave, because the warp would have to be changed more often. The irregularities are not derivable from the requirement to calculate in terms of pence or half-pence. Were this their cause, the weaves in which pay were highest would show the most regular curve, whereas Figure 5.4 reveals the reverse.

Would not the British weavers have noticed this apparent source of inequitable earnings for different densities of cloth? At least until the First

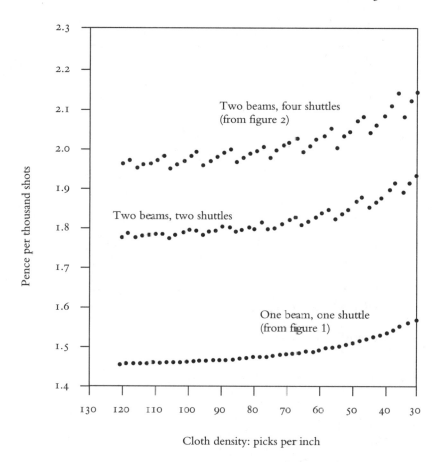

FIGURE 5.4 British Data on German Axes, Huddersfield Scale, Woolens

World War, they could not. For instance, weavers in the Colne Valley alleged that the 1883 pay table lowered their wages, especially on the loosely woven cloth. They composed meticulous analyses of its rates, based on the English axes of thought, to formulate their criticisms of the slope and intercept of the straight line.[4] But since they did not conceive the system in terms of pay per weft thread, they could not identify the embedded inequities. They looked straight at the problem, but did not recognize it as such, a telling demonstration of how their perception of output took the length of the cloth as the standard of pay. Truly, they identified and compared human labor only as it appeared in the misleading guise of the product itself (Marx 1967, 72). Through the scale's

4. *Northern Pioneer*, 14 April 1883; *Huddersfield Examiner*, March and April 1883.

TABLE 5.1   Equations for transferring English data to German axes, simplest weave

---

Let $x = \dfrac{\text{picks}}{\text{inch}} = \text{density}$

$y = \dfrac{\text{pay}}{\text{inch}}$

English axes mean:

$y = mx + b$

$\dfrac{\text{pay}}{\text{inch}} = m\left(\dfrac{\text{picks}}{\text{inch}}\right) + b$

To convert to German axes, find $\dfrac{\text{pay}}{\text{pick}} = y$

Continuing from last equation,

$\text{pay} = m(\text{picks}) + b(\text{inch})$

$\dfrac{\text{pay}}{\text{pick}} = m + b\left(\dfrac{\text{inch}}{\text{pick}}\right)$

$\dfrac{\text{pay}}{\text{pick}} = m + \dfrac{b}{\text{density}}$ ← English data on German axes

---

quotidian use, definitions of labor as a commodity were reproduced without deliberate reflection.

In Germany, by contrast, the cloth comprised merely the unit of observation; the insertion of the shots was the actual subject of analysis. As industrial sociologists from Germany have long taken care to emphasize, a piece-rate scale can use the product as a convenient surrogate for measuring the workers' action and need not accept the product as the object of payment (Maucher 1965, 62). Or, as one student of wage forms in the German textile industry expressed it in 1924, the visible output could be adopted for the sake of making an "empirical" reading, as distinguished from the actual execution of the shots for which the worker was in truth remunerated (Müller 1924, 65). Unlike the British, the Germans used the product as a convenient token, not as the object of remuneration. German workers often complained about the intensification of work in terms of thousands of shots executed, not inches of cloth delivered. In doing so they measured changes in exploitation by the use of labor power, not merely by the product requisitioned (Biernacki 1995, 69, 383).

The weaving branch shows how German employers and workers understood the conveyance of abstract labor as the transfer of labor power with a piece-rate index. Conversely, British employers who paid time wages in some textile occupations, as well as in branches of industry such as metalwork, used time wages as a token of the fundamental labor the workers conveyed in their products. The industrial steward George Wood declared in Yorkshire in 1910 that "we may define Time-Work as 'A Contract to sell all the produce of labour in a certain time'" (Biernacki 1995, 88, 59 n. 51). In other words, just as the German workers could sell their labor power by piece rates, so the British workers could sell their labor products by time. Marx had perspicuously separated the social construction of the new substance of "labor" in capitalism from the histories of wage forms that had operated even in antiquity (Marx 1976, 675–700; Biernacki 1995, 58, 336–37). But the pivotal distinction between wage forms and the essence of abstract "labor" that Marx tested in the shadows of theory, capitalist producers affirmed in the clear day of practice.

Time Discipline

The measurement and enforcement of attendance at the factory illustrates this recurring difference between the conveyance of labor embodied in a product in Britain versus the delivery of labor power itself in Germany. British managers marked the beginning and close of the daily cycle of production by subjecting their workers to exceedingly rigid controls on entry into and exit from the factory. The most common expedient at mills in Yorkshire and Lancashire, though not the universal custom, was to latch the doors at the start of the workday, compelling latecomers to return home. Workers who dashed to enter exactly at starting time had the mill door slammed on their feet. A winder in Preston, Lancashire, reported to her union in 1915 that the manager caught her entering the mill exactly when the door began to close. He "mangled and bruised" her arms: "On Monday morning when I went to work I had just got my foot on the threshold of the door when the door was slammed to and my foot was caught between the door and the door jamb. I pushed the door open with my hand and as I entered the manager was standing there who said to me 'Outside—*you are not coming through.*'"[5] To be sure, some textile mills, especially in Lancashire, imposed fines for tardiness, generally standard amounts that served as a disciplinary tool rather than as a carefully graduated form of recompense for the employer. Yet oral testimony and workers' newspapers show that locking out represented the expected and predominant routine. Mills also combined fines with locking out; workers less than, say, fifteen minutes overdue could pay a penny for admittance, whereas those arriving later were barred for the day or week (Biernacki 1995, chap. 3).

When British employers excluded workers from the premises, they failed to treat the workers' time itself as a form of property for whose loss they claimed restitution (United Kingdom 1854–55, 149). Shutting workers out did not lay claim to the labor power lodged in the person of the offenders, but it suspended the contract with them as if they were contractors who had not taken due care to meet delivery deadlines. The struggle was over the acquisition of the product: "Discipline," an early employer declared, "was to produce the goods on time" (Pollard 1963, 258). In complementary fashion, British workers asserted that employers had no right to fine for lost time, but agreed that employers could sack workers who failed to furnish a reasonable output (Biernacki 1995, 112).

German employers by contrast treated unpunctual attendance as a denial of labor power, whose loss could be calibrated and precisely counterbalanced. Many textile factories applied a sliding scale of fines which adjusted the penalty to the worker's average earnings or specified percentages of average earnings to be levied as a fine for various periods of tardiness. Rather than fixing the penalty at nominal amounts for gross intervals of tardiness—that is, rather than using the fine as a simple tool of discipline—German employers monetized the lost labor capacity itself and froze it with a metric (Biernacki 1995, chap. 3). In a corresponding manner, German workers distinguished themselves by demanding compensation for commitment of minutes, however inappreciable, to tasks after the official close of work, such as waiting in line at the exit to punch time cards (375–76).

For the analyst, the parallels in each country between the typical rules of employment, the design of piece rate scales, and time discipline—three of many other concurrences—merely clarify the theory that cultural

5. Lancashire Record Office, DDX 1089/8/3, Preston, 19 June 1915.

schemata shaped a relatively consistent province of practice. For the workers who executed these procedures, however, they comprised an experienced whole. The national differences in the concept of the transmittal of labor as a commodity, received silently by workers in the everyday enactment of manufacture, shaped workers' development and reception of ideologies of class exploitation.

From the Workplace to Ideologies of Class Exploitation

At the end of the nineteenth century the textile towns of Yorkshire served as the home for new British movements dedicated to socialist ideals, especially the Independent Labour Party (Hinton 1983, 50–75; Reynold and Laybourn 1975). Many of these labor movements claimed an allegiance to Marxist economic theory, but interpreted Marx in keeping with the British specification of labor. All assumed that capitalists extract a profit only by manipulating the relations of exchange through which they secured and disposed of products, the workers' materialized labor. The cultural constitution of factory practices in Britain discouraged members of the labor movement there from adopting faithfully Marx's analysis of exploitation at the point of production based on the conveyance of living labor power (Marx 1976).

Accordingly, British workers throughout the nineteenth century considered the marketplace the locus of exploitation. The *Bradford Labour Echo*, the organ of the Independent Labour Party in the textile factory district of Bradford, claimed in 1898 that workers were exploited because "all sorts of middle-men" cut workers out of the full value of the product.[6] In the widely distributed tract *Merrie England*, published in 1894, Robert Blatchford sought to revive the theoretic analysis of labor's exploitation. He identified the extraction of profit with precision: "As a rule, profit is not made by the producer of an article, but by some other person commonly called 'the middleman' because he goes between the producer and the consumer; that is to say, he, the middleman, buys the article from the maker, and sells it to the user at a profit" (Blatchford 1894, 82–83). In parallel fashion Blatchford defined class differences between employers and workers by their points of access to the market (84).

6. *Bradford Labour Echo*, 9 April 1893.

The socialist press outlined in detail how the capitalist's purchase of labor resembled that of the home consumer's purchase of a finished product. The only point of contrast was that the capitalist used his ownership of the implements of production and his position in the market to devise an unfair exchange. "Every child who buys a pennyworth of nuts or toffee in a tuck-shop is, in one and a true sense, an employer of labour," the *Bradford Labour Echo* claimed in 1898. "But, though every buyer, as such is, like this child, an employer of labor, he is not an interceptor of part of his employees' earnings, nor therefore an earner of 'employers' profits.'"[7] Based on this image of workers' transmittal of labor in goods and of their exploitation in the sphere of exchange, Ben Turner, the leading spokesperson for the Yorkshire textile union before the First World War, emphasized that profit was made on cloth, not labor (Biernacki 1995, 410). The employer exploited workers by purchasing their fabric at unfairly depressed prices.

Targeting the seizure of profits through the mechanism of exchange also guided workers' assessment of the remedies for exploitation. Abolition of the employer's immediate domination over the use of labor power did not serve as a focal point of visions for change. Ben Turner emphasized that he did not condemn employers, "only the system under which employers in the district *traded*."[8] British workers sought to assure fair returns in the realm of exchange not just as a means of achieving socialism but as socialism's final goal (Biernacki 1995, 193, 410).

In Germany, by contrast, the workers' everyday experience of the sale and transmission of labor as a commodity provided the foundation for the sympathetic reception of Marx's analysis of the extraction of profit from living labor power. During the period of union expansion in the two decades before the First World War, the socialist-aligned, so-called "free" textile unions in Germany adopted the Marxist theory of the extraction of surplus at the point of production, based on the difference between the use value and the exchange value of "labor power."[9] The assumption that the worker transferred abstract "labor" to the employer in the form of labor power shaped the literate workers' descriptions of conflict with employers. The German newspaper *The Textile Worker* treated "labor power" as a detached, reified *thing* that the capitalist tries

7. *Bradford Labor Echo*, 26 November 1898.
8. *Yorkshire Factory Times*, 11 December 1903, emphasis added.
9. *Der Textil-Arbeiter*, 1 August 1902.

to seize. For example, the newspaper warned its readers in 1901 that "above all their labor power and their very selves must be protected from exploitation."[10] This typical phrasing treated labor power as an entity apart from the concrete person and identified its use as the cause of exploitation. At the conference of workers from the jute textile industry in 1906, a representative complained that "the piece rates are arranged so that to achieve the pay of 1.6 marks, the labor power is fully absorbed [by the capitalist]."[11] Labor power comprised a real substance which the employer "consumed." This expression shows that even when textile workers did not engage in abstract discussions of political economy, they supposed that their struggles pivoted around the calibrated exploitation of "labor power" at the point of production. They believed that the employers' exercise of authority at the point of production formed the essence of exploitation and of class division (Biernacki, 193, 460).

Of course, not all workers in unions were in those aligned with the socialists. On the eve of the First World War, about one-quarter of the unionized textile workers in Germany were in the Christian, Catholic-based union.[12] The Christian union, too, adopted the prevailing German notion of the sale of "labor power" to portray the workers' insertion into the capitalist economy. In an article entitled "Is Labor a Commodity?," their *Textile Worker's Newspaper* made explicit in 1900 the telling but characteristic German distinction: employers, it explained, "regard labor *or, rather, labor power* as a commodity."[13] This journal also identified labor power as an entity "alienated" by the worker: "Conceiving of labor as merely a commodity, which the owner of the *labor power* sells," it explained, "makes the worker dependent on the purchase offer that the employer makes to him."[14] In view of the pervasive differences between the experiences of Catholic and Protestant workers *outside* the workplace in the period before the First World War and between the intellectual roots of their leaders (Brose 1985; Sperber 1984), the convergence in the underlying view of labor in the competing Catholic-based and socialist labor movements suggests the influence of something else which their

10. *Der Textil-Arbeiter,* 5 April 1901.
11. *Die Sklaven des Jute-Kapitals*, Protokoll, Jutearbeiter-Konferenz Braunschweig, 7 October 1906.
12. *Jahresbericht des Deutschen Textilarbeiterverbandes* for 1910; *Geschäftsbericht*, 1908 to 1910, Zentralverband Christlicher Textilarbeiter.
13. *Textilarbeiter Zeitung,* 30 June 1900, emphasis added.
14. Ibid., emphasis added.

members shared in common: namely, the workers' everyday experience of the conveyance of "labor power" at the point of production.

An Agenda for Theory and Research

The striking correspondence between the definitions of exploitation in workers' collective movements and the symbolic form of German and British factory techniques shows that the workers' experience of the execution of these techniques configured their reception of formal ideologies. This finding underscores the importance of the labor process for the formation and adoption of workers' discourses of exploitation and class, but it does not compel a return to the naive view that this discourse mirrors the economic structure of production. The practices of production, such as the piece rate systems, were constituted by culture and installed by a cultural logic, not by natural adaptation to technical circumstances. Otherwise we would not observe the contrast in the constellation of factory techniques between German and British factories, which developed in locally similar environments; nor would we observe the similarity in the constellations within each country, in Britain across late-developing Yorkshire as across early-developing Lancashire, or in Germany across both the progressive Wupper Valley and the more slowly developing Silesia.

Marx's distinction between "labor power" and "embodied labor," applied respectively to the German and British contexts, offers a theoretic key for carrying on his task of connecting workers' experience of the labor process to their understanding of the nature of class boundaries and exploitation. But Marx's terms fulfill this task for reasons he never imagined. As elemental components of bourgeois culture and political economy, the concepts of "labor" as a commodity and of "capital" are usually applied, in Marx's fashion, as purely analytic constructs with the same definition across all capitalist societies. But in point of fact these categories function for historical agents as everyday tools of practice; they can take on different definitions and refer to different operations in each society; and their varying cultural incarnations impart critically different logics to economic functions that appear deceptively similar to analysts applying crude economic paradigms. Restoring these elemental forms to their birthplace in the life experience of production shows that the contrasting German and British notions of class boundaries and exploitation were fixed by the cultural particularities of manufacture in the two countries.

This understanding of culture in production not only furnishes new tools for theorizing history, it also historicizes theory. If the revelation Marx himself considered his most pivotal for political economy, the delineation of the concept of *Arbeitskraft*, illuminates the history of German manufacture, so must the history of German manufacture illuminate Marx. It appears that Marx's elaboration of the concept of *Arbeitskraft*, though disguised as a deduction, owed its genesis to contemporary German schemata of practice (Biernacki 1995, chap. 6).

The workplace served as a source and anchor of workers' outlooks because the symbolic shape of its practices incarnated most vividly and durably the cultural model of labor's transfer between class agents. In Germany and Britain the contrasting specifications of labor as a commodity acquired an uncanny stability in nineteenth-century debate, despite overwhelming change in other aspects of public discourse concerning the nation, the family, and the sacred (Biernacki 1995, chap. 9). The distinctive German and British understandings of the conveyance of labor surfaced so invariably in the discourse of the public sphere because they were reproduced invisibly in the hidden abode of production. Manufacture did not, thereby, represent another, more genuine order of reality than that of discourse and ideological debate. The techniques of production, too, were constructed and arranged by a cultural logic. Decisive national differences in workers' experience and conceptual assumptions arose immediately from the execution of manufacture, a symbolically constituted order of reality distinct from the mere "representation" of the world via the ambiguous and insecure divisions of purely verbal language.

This brief sketch of the material installation of cultural concepts of labor and of their reemergence in socialist movements necessarily leaves several pressing issues undiscussed. Among the important historical issues raised by this program of research is that of the origin of the contrasting concepts of the transmission of labor. The long record of popular and elite discourses about labor shows that the cultural divergence is traceable to conjunctural differences in each country's momentous transition from the corporate and feudal organization of work to a formally free market in labor. In Britain the prolonged statutory regulation of the sale of labor power during the seventeenth and eighteenth centuries encouraged a cultural focus on the independent craftspeople as the idealized vendors of labor in a formally free market. These workers disposed of their labor only as it was concretized in products. In Germany the extraordinary endurance of the guilds into the nineteenth century excluded urban crafts from the practices that were culturally formative of labor as a commodity. Instead, the survival of feudal templates for labor relations in German agriculture offered the guiding models for the delivery of labor as a service capacity in German factories. The outcomes in Britain and Germany represent merely two branches on the full tree of possibilities realized in Europe (Biernacki 1995, pt. 2).

Finally, the consequences for industrial conflict demand consideration. Did the divergent German and British analyses of exploitation configure the conduct of strikes and other tactics of resistance? There are many exemplars of such linkage. German weavers, calling on the notion they sold their *Arbeitskraft*, demanded indemnities for time lost waiting on work materials. British weavers, in keeping with the sale of materialized labor, supposed they should receive compensation for such lost time through raises in the price scale for cloth delivered (Biernacki 1995, 362–82). How did the understanding of the conveyance of labor structure the possibilities for compromise between employers and workers? What were the implications for workers' alliances with professional employees, supervisors, and petty entrepreneurs? By contrast with their British counterparts, German textile workers in the decades before the First World War meticulously contested signs of the employers' domination over the person of the worker and broadened points of contention to debate the employers' administration of the mill. In collective actions they were less inclined to seek alliances with supervisors (Biernacki 1995, chap. 10). Recasting the commodification of labor as a culturally variable process establishes an agenda for comparative research which extends from the dawning of markets in labor at the inception of the liberal capitalist order to the cresting and ultimate decline of labor insurgency in the present century.

References

[works with full citations in endnotes are not included here]

Anderson, Perry. 1980. *Arguments within English Marxism*. London: Verso.

Biernacki, Richard. 1995. *The Fabrication of Labor: Germany and Britain, 1640–1914* (Berkeley: University of California Press.

Blatchford, Robert. 1966 [1894]. *Merrie England. A Series of Letters to John Smith of Oldham—a Practical Working Man*. New York: Monthly Review Press.

Burawoy, Michael. 1985. *The Politics of Production*. London: Verso.

Deutscher Textilarbeiterverband. 1912. *Jahrbuch des deutschen Textilarbeiterverbandes, 1911*. Berlin: Karl Hübsch.

Germany. 1878. Enquete-Kommission, *Reichs-Enquete für die Baumwollen- und Leinen-Industrie Stenographische Protokolle über die mündliche Vernehmung der Sachverständigen*. Berlin: Julius Sittenfeld.

Germany. 1900. *Die deutsche Volkswirtschaft am Schlusse des 19. Jahrhunderts*. Berlin: Puttkammer und Mühlbrecht.

Hinton, James. 1983. *Labour and Socialism*. Amherst: University of Massachusetts Press.

Jones, Gareth Stedman. 1983. *Languages of Class: Studies in English Working-Class History, 1832–1982*. Cambridge: Cambridge University Press.

Joyce, Patrick. 1980. *Work, Society and Politics*. London: Methuen.

———. 1991. *Visions of the People*. Cambridge: Cambridge University Press.

———. 1994. *Democratic Subjects*. Cambridge; Cambridge University Press.

———. 1995. "The End of Social History?" *Social History* 20 (1): 73–91.

Judt, Tony. 1986. *Marxism and the French Left*. Oxford: Clarendon Press.

Laclau, Ernesto, and Chantal Mouffe. 1985. *Hegemony and Socialist Strategy*. London: Verso.

Marx, Karl. 1976. *Capital*. Vol. 1. London: Penguin.

Maucher, Herbert. 1965. *Zeitlohn Akkordlohn Prämienlohn*. Darmstadt: Darmstadt Druck- und Verlags-Gesellschaft.

Müller, Alfred. 1924. "Die Lohnbemessungsmethoden in der Chemnitzer Textilindustrie." Marburg: Dissertation.

Pollard, Sidney. 1963. "Factory Discipline in the Industrial Revolution," *The Economic History Review*, 2d ser., 16 (2): 254–71.

Price, Richard. 1985. "The New Unionism and the Labour Process." In *The Development of Trade Unionism in Great Britain and Germany, 1880–1914*. London: George Allen & Unwin.

Reynold, J., and K. Laybourn. 1975. "The Emergence of the Independent Labour Party in Bradford." *International Review of Social History* 20, pt. 3: 313–46.

Scott, Joan W. 1988. *Gender and the Politics of History*. New York: Columbia University Press.

———. 1994. "The Evidence of Experience." In James Chandler, Arnold I. Davidson, and Harry Harootunian, eds., *Questions of Evidence*. Chicago: University of Chicago Press.

Sewell, William H., Jr. 1980. *Work and Revolution in France*. Cambridge: Cambridge University Press.

Somers, Margaret R. 1992. "Narrativity, Narrative Identity, and Social Action: Rethinking English Working-Class Formation." *Social Science History* 16 (4): 591–630.

Sonenscher, Michael. 1989. *Work and Wages. Natural Law, Politics and the Eighteenth-Century French Trades*. Cambridge: Cambridge University Press.

Thompson, E. P. 1963. *The Making of the English Working Class*. New York: Vintage Books.

———. 1967. "Time, Work-Discipline, and Industrial Capitalism." *Past and Present,* no. 38: 56–97.

———. 1971. "The Moral Economy of the English Crowd in the Eighteenth Century." *Past and Pressent,* no. 50: 76–136.

———. 1978. *The Poverty of Theory and Other Essays*. New York: Monthy Review Press.

United Kingdom. 1854–55. Parliamentary Papers (421). Vol. 14.

United Kingdom. 1893. *Census of England and Wales, 1891*. H.M.S.O. Vol. 3.

Wilentz, Sean. 1984. *Chants Democratic: New York City and the Rise of the American Working Class, 1788–1850*. New York.

CHAPTER 6

The Meaning of Class and Race: French and American Workers Discuss Differences

Michèle Lamont

*I*N THIS CHAPTER, I ANALYZE HOW FRENCH AND AMERICAN WHITE-COLLAR workers conceptualize differences between themselves and others, drawing on in-depth interviews conducted with members of both groups. More specifically, I consider how workers talk about individuals who are positioned above and below themselves in the class structure and about attributes and cultural orientations that are often associated with the upper middle class, namely upward mobility, ambition, success, money, power, knowledge, and education. I also analyze how race is used in discussions of class differences. Instead of taking as a point of departure a universalized notion of class (or an essentialized construct of race), I document which dimensions of class and race are most important for these workers and how they frame them. The discourse of these workers is shaped by their experience of class and race at work, in their families, in their communities—in the public and private sphere. It is also shaped by economic globalization and restructuring, macro changes in systems of production, political transformations, working class mobilization, and so forth. Here, however, the causes of these changes are

This research is supported by the National Science Foundation (grant no. 92-13363), the German Marshall Funds of the United States, the Russell Sage Foundation, and the John Simon Guggenheim Foundation. I gratefully acknowledge the research assistance provided by Jacky Gordon.

bracketed in order to focus on the definitions of reality produced by these workers at the discursive level.

A French-American comparison promises to be particularly fruitful because important differences have been noted in the cultures of French and American workers. Richard Hamilton (1967) and Duncan Gallie (1983) have documented the strong support of French blue-collar workers and low-status white-collar workers for the Left in the 1950s and 1970s. Michael Mann (1973) showed that France's revolutionary tradition still had an important impact on French workers in the 1960s and early 1970s. In contrast, Seymour Martin Lipset (1977) and others have described American workers as more identified with the middle class than their French counterparts. American workers, it was argued, believe in the American dream and their attitudes toward the business class are more positive than that of their French counterparts because they do not carry the weight of a feudal past that would sustain a tradition of class struggle. In addition, the racial diversity of American workers and the organization of urban politics around ethnic groups have had negative effects on class mobilization (Katznelson 1981). Also, the American working class is rapidly losing its cultural specificity as working-class men increasingly define their identity not through work but through their middle-class consumption patterns and lifestyle (Halle 1984). Although the unique qualities of French working class culture are also rapidly declining due to the effect of the mass media and the educational system (Terrail 1990) and a decrease in income inequality (Morrison 1988), we need to ask whether this culture might maintain elements of a revolutionary tradition fueled by communist unions such as the Confédération Générale du Travail. In 1975, 24 percent of French workers were unionized and this figure had fallen to 10 percent by 1992 (Trade Unions and Employers' Organizations of the World 1994, p. G-20). Nevertheless, a cultural repertoire emphasizing antagonism toward higher classes might still be shaping their perception of class differences in a significant way. Furthermore, because this revolutionary tradition stresses solidarity with the exploited, French workers might be more inclusive toward the poor and the lower class than their American counterpart. This tradition of solidarity might also push French workers to be more inclusive of racial minorities than American workers are.

In this chapter I empirically assess these hypotheses, drawing on in-depth interviews conducted with low-status white-collar workers living in the suburbs of New York and Paris. I also compare their discourse with that of professionals and managers, drawing on earlier work on the upper middle class in France and the United States (Lamont 1992). Like their upper-middle-class counterparts, I expect American workers to put more weight than the French on ambition, success, and money when discussing the differences between themselves and others. I expect French workers, however, to attach more importance to being cultured, a quality highly valued by the French upper middle class.

A reconsideration of cultural orientations among French and American workers is particularly timely because available comparative studies of these groups were written in earlier decades and could well be outdated. Furthermore, social scientists need to rethink the place of class in French and American society. Past studies have argued that class is more important in France than in the United States and that the French are more elitist than Americans. In contrast, I propose that class is important in the way French and American workers evaluate others, but that these two groups emphasize different dimensions of class. Furthermore, although class differences shape the discourse of American workers on race significantly, the effects are less in the French case, in part because a republican tradition inherited from the 1789 Revolution remains very influential among French workers. This tradition downplays differentiation based on ascribed characteristics, instead emphasizing citizenship as a universal criteria of inclusion independently of race.

This chapter draws on interviews that I conducted with thirty stable white-collar workers—fifteen French and fifteen Americans. These men have high-school degrees but not college degrees.[1] When possible, I matched them by occupation and age.[2] I selected them at random from phone books of working-class towns located in the New York suburbs such as Elizabeth and Linden, New Jersey, and Hempstead and Uniondale on Long Island, and in the suburbs of Paris such as Nanterre, Aubervilliers, and Ivry. In this random selection, I aim not to build a representative sample but to tap a wide range of perspectives within a community of workers, thereby going beyond the unavoidable limitations

1. These workers have been working full-time and steadily for at least five years. They do not supervise more than ten workers.

2. Hundreds of letters were sent to potential respondents living in working-class suburbs in the New York and Paris areas. I chose interviewees who categorized themselves as whites and who met other criteria of selection pertaining to occupation, age, nationality, and level of education.

of site-specific research.[3] Although the growing presence of women and immigrants has dramatically altered the character of the French and American working classes,[4] in order to minimize cultural variations unrelated to occupation I talked to nonimmigrant men only. This choice is justified in part because the larger study within which this particular project takes place is concerned with cultural differentiation between college and non-college-educated men and not with the character of the working class *per se*. The interviewees include bank clerks, salesmen, postal workers, and other service workers. Each interview lasted approximately two hours, long enough for me to develop a complex view of the ways in which these men understood the similarities and differences between themselves and others. I conducted all the interviews myself at a place chosen by the men. In future research I will compare the trends that emerged from the interviews with national survey data and other secondary sources.[5]

I compare first how low-status white workers perceive groups that are below and above themselves. I also consider their attitudes toward social mobility, success, and ambition. Second, I consider the place of money and power in their discussions of the differences between themselves and others. Third, I consider their definition and assessment of the place of intelligence, knowledge, education, and culture in evaluating others. Fourth, I discuss how race interacts with class in the way interviewees discuss differences and similarities between themselves and others.

3. By using in-depth interviews instead of ethnographic observation, I sacrifice depth for breadth. However, by choosing respondents in twelve different communities, I maximize the likelihood of tapping internal differences within both populations. Furthermore, while interviews cannot tap class consciousness "in action," they can provide information on broader cultural frameworks that are transportable from one context of action to another. For a study of working-class consciousness that is more context dependent, see Fantasia 1988.

4. Space limitations prevent me from dealing with the complexity of the changing social, occupational, and economic characteristic of the working class. On these issues, see Stacey 1991; Dudley 1994; and Rubin 1994.

5. At times, I compare the interviews I conducted with working-class men with interviews conducted with college-educated professionals and managers residing Paris, New York, Clermont-Ferrand, and Indianapolis. As is the case for the working-class project, all respondents were asked to describe people with whom they preferred not to associate, those to whom they felt superior or inferior, and those who evoked hostility, indifference, and sympathy. They were also asked to describe negative and positive traits in their coworkers and acquaintances, as well as their child-rearing values. The criteria of evaluation behind their responses were systematically compared to recreate a template of their mental map of their grammar of evaluation.

Class, Success, and Ambition

When comparing the discourse of French and American low-status white-collar workers, one is struck with the fact that the French rarely draw boundaries against the poor, the lazy, and the deviant. These individuals are simply more absent from their descriptions. Like their American counterparts, however, they do draw boundaries against blue-collar workers, stressing both moral and cultural differences. For instance, a former blue-collar worker says that becoming a photographer in a major cosmetic firm has allowed him to be in contact with more interesting people. Others express their repulsion of stereotypical blue-collar traits, such as dirty hands. Many, however, view blue-collar workers as equal to themselves, mentioning that "we are all salaried, we are all exploited" and that one should not distinguish between blue- and white-collar workers.

In contrast, American workers promptly admit to having more negative attitudes toward blue-collar workers. A young paper-goods salesman from New Jersey who also had done manual work expresses commonly found attitudes. I interviewed him in a Sheraton Hotel situated next to the Newark Airport. Trying to speak English correctly, he says:

> I went to one of my wholesale distributors yesterday. I was inside the building with my jacket, tie, and everything, and I heard that they were interviewing for a warehouse job, and I saw all these guys coming in, wearing jeans and sneakers, and I just thought that I used to be in that position. I used to be there and look at who I am now.... When I used to do autobody work in Elizabeth Port, I hate to say this, but [the workers] seemed they were low class, and they didn't have a direction in life. They lived from week to week, and they did not really have an idea or a clue about what they wanted to do in life.... I was just miserable around those types of people because they weren't doing anything for me.... So getting into my type of field, you know, [where] the people you deal with on an everyday basis is more professional, have a direction and a lifestyle, goals, and they have things that we all like to have. And it's just better, good to hang around with people who are successful rather than not successful. That's what I want.

The middle class also often comes up in French descriptions of feelings of superiority and inferiority, and again differences are described in moral or cultural terms. Like several American interviewees, a fine-produce salesman says that he dislikes interacting with professionals. He says: "These people are very comfortable . . . they talk about things that I don't know. . . . I have not studied for very long, but I consider myself a *français moyen*. If they want to talk to me about children, things like this, OK. But if they want to talk about politics, I would not feel at ease because I don't want to go very deep." Several French and American workers say they feel inferior to many professionals and managers because of their knowledge and education. Overall, however, the language of class struggle is much more present in French interviews than in American interviews. The French often express their dislike for the middle class as a group, viewing middle-class culture as incompatible with their own. For instance, a photographer declares:

> I cannot stand the petit-bourgeois. . . . They are social climbers, and I am disgusted that by the sole fact of being born, they have made it. Good for them; they were lucky, but they are imbeciles. In short, I don't like them. . . . I think that they are not interesting. They only think about money. They are all dressed the same. . . . They live in a system where they are unable to make things improve. They have received an education where they learned that they had to think like this, this, and this [hits the table]. They are prisoners, and their field of vision is very narrow.

Several men I talked to are equally critical of the bourgeoisie in general, stressing its lack of morality and conformism in particular.

In contrast, American white-collar workers identify more with the middle class. After mentioning that his former neighbor was a pharmacist, an electronics technician compares him with other neighbors:

> He was very pleasant and interesting. . . . You could pretty much talk to him about anything. He had a very good background as far as school, which is nice, because I find, especially with a lot of people in my neighborhood, there are very few things I can talk to them about, because there are a lot of the local populace who end up as assistant contractors, and educationally it's very hard to communicate because they're so preoccupied with sports. . . . They can just sit there with their friends and talk about [sports] all day, and they look at each other as equal because of that. . . . They feel good about that because they know what year, who hit what, when, and where.

A notion of class struggle is also present in the way French workers talk about exploitation, a notion more absent in the American interviews.

Some describe their environments as having a strong working-class tradition. A train ticket salesman says that in his town, Ivry, which elected a Communist mayor for ninety years, people mobilize easily: "When there is something, the closing of plant, there is always a big fight; . . . an old tradition like this does not disappear easily." Working-class militancy clearly remains part of the discourse of these workers. Yet a few argue that there is no working class anymore. According to one draftsman, the working class no longer exists "the way it did during my father's time. It was another time. There are no workers anymore. I don't know any." Along these lines, several describe themselves as part of the middle class because of their levels of income. They define their class status by their market capacities, "being able to do and get some things but not others, for instance, buy a house." I interviewed an electronics technician in his small apartment, where his four children between the ages of one and six were eating. He describes the situation thus: "I am middle class because I have enough resources to have some choice, but I still have constraints, in that I am not able to invest." Still others, borrowing the rhetoric of the Left, describe themselves as working class because they are salaried, and bosses try to get all they can from them. Taken together, these interviews suggest that the traditional concept of class struggle is being eroded but is still present in the way French individuals perceive the class structure and that, overall, French workers are less middle-class-identified than their American counterparts and less disparaging of blue-collar workers.

Along these lines, French low-status white-collar workers very often criticize people who evaluate the worth of people on the basis of their social position. The labels "pretentious" and "snob" are constantly used when these men are asked to describe the types of people they do not like. These labels are associated with that of the "social climbers who are able to do anything to succeed," "who are too ambitious, who are friends with you only to gain something," "who exaggerate small differences," "who drive nice cars and believe that they are above others while in fact they are not better," "who take expensive vacations when they cannot afford it," and "who [are] always trying to sell themselves and are not sincere." A draftsman, whom I interviewed in the studio where he works on the town's newsletter, describes people who are social climbers as "small." "We only live once, there are so many things to discover on earth, things to do. Why spend one's life consulting one's career, trying to have a nice car, a social status above others? Really, I don't see the point."

Unlike American white-collar workers, very few French workers view themselves as ambitious. This rejection is justified because "the end of the world could happen anytime" (according to a phone technician) and "the world will continue to exist for many billion years after us. We have time. These people are unable to see beyond their deaths, as if we were the end of it all." Time-consuming social climbing is seen as incompatible with a strong family life. This popular view is expressed by a dynamic bank clerk whom I interviewed on the stone terrace he built behind his small house in Stains—we could hear planes taking off from the nearby Charles de Gaulle Airport. In his early thirties, he is among the most upwardly mobile Frenchmen I talked to. He says: "I have two lives, my professional life and my family life. I have a main one, my family life, and the role of my professional life is to feed my family life." Social climbing is also opposed to egalitarianism, symbolized for some by their dislike of people who wear ties or who abide by middle-class formalities. The fine-produce salesman, who is in his late fifties, proudly describes the ambiance of his bicycling club in the following terms: "I have nothing to do with last names, all I want to learn is first names. All these people in this picture, I can only tell you their first names. When we meet on Sunday, I get there and I go: 'Bonjour Lucien, bonjour Pierre.'"

Many link their rejection of ambition to their awareness of the limits that their class background puts on their own mobility. A phone technician, for instance, says: "I know that our children will be approximately what we are. I don't have any illusion socially. The sons of low-level civil servants will become middle-level civil servants. . . . The children of primary school teachers will become professors; those of professors will become doctors. . . . I am lower than my father. He was a mathematics teacher in a lycée." Similarly, a draftsman says of the engineers that he works with: "It is logical that they became polytechnicians [high-status engineers]. It was not accidental . . . it is not about to change. . . . They were raised for that." The airplane technician explains how his parents limited his ambition "because of my origins" by teaching him modesty, "not to put yourself forward." Definitions of success reflect this awareness of structural limitations to mobility. Some define success as being able to keep a job "because there are four millions of unemployed people right now" (postal worker). Others define it in terms of helping their children, "making the apartment soundproof, doing a little repair."

We have some indication that success is more admired in the United States than in France: four of the American respondents chose "ambitious" and three chose "successful" as the qualities they most value from a list presented to them. In contrast, two of the French interviewees chose "ambitious" and none chose "successful." American workers often define success in economic terms, as when a civil servant says that his daughter is successful because she is making fifty thousand dollars a year. The economic level that one should reach to be considered successful varies greatly. For instance, a civil servant says that he is successful because "I can support myself, which is hard to do these days. I bought a brand new car in June, and I'm paying for that. It's not paid for, but I am enjoying the new car and everything." Often, material success is described as important, but American workers, like the French, believe that it should be associated with a good family life. The way this draftsman combines material success and family in defining success is fairly typical of American interviewees: "I'm more successful, I'm making more money now than I ever have before. I have two great kids, a great wife. We own this place, we own two cars. I think we're a lot more successful than a lot of other people [who] are our age." Similarly, an electronics technician says he is successful because "materialistically, I do all right. I have a decent house, I make decent money. I have three cars, two motorcycles. . . . I am [also] successful in that I can love very easily. I have a happy marriage, so I fell, right off the bat there. . . . I think I will have a lot of love to give when my child comes."

Success, however, is also more defined in terms of occupation and mobility in the United States than it is in France. For instance, the manager of a dry-cleaning business says that he feels superior to others because he is supervising several people. An insurance salesman describes his brother in admiring terms because "he now holds the highest position in the company next to a college engineer. What I like about him is that he just didn't sit back and say, 'Well, I just want a job' and show up every day and get paid. I look up to people who try to be the best they can be. I don't like people who don't try to continue to improve themselves. I don't think very highly of them." As this quote suggests, one finds drastic differences in the value that French and American workers give to ambition and upward mobility. This contrast also translates into frequent expressions of dislike for the poor and people on welfare among American workers, which are almost absent among the French I talked to. American descriptions of disliked people often also revolve around ambition and morality. Here again, one of the most despised categories comprises arrogant, snobbish people: Arrogant people are viewed as "so self-assured, so self-intense that they don't really care about anyone else" (electronics technician). Snobbish people "put up a front. If people don't like you for yourself, obviously those aren't the type of people you should be around. . . . If you have to become snobby for them to want to be around you, well then screw this person!"

As some French white-collar workers do, several American workers talk about their blocked mobility at work. They say that their investment in success is limited because they are in dead-end jobs. This trend, however, is less pronounced in the United States than it is in France. There is a certain pessimism about whether children will be able to follow the American dream: "If that's your dream, follow your dream, but I just hope it does not fall through for you."

The picture that emerges is one of nuanced contrasts. French and American workers share a definition of success that stresses a good family life. They equally dislike people who are snobbish and overly ambitious and both groups are aware of the limits of their mobility. Overall, however, the French draw weaker boundaries against the poor and blue-collar workers and are less middle-class-identified than their American counterparts. The French also value success and ambition less than the Americans and use the language of class struggle to describe their feelings toward the petite bourgeoisie and the bourgeoisie.

Money and Power

The attitudes of French workers toward money reflect their attitudes toward success and ambition. Many strongly condemn overly materialist attitudes. For instance, a bank clerk says: "I don't like people who only talk about money. . . . People who always ask you how much you have paid for this or that drive me crazy. . . . I don't spend my time trying to find ways to have more money. I don't recognize myself in this. It is really not me." Like their upper-middle-class counterparts (Lamont 1992, chap. 3), many French low-status white-collar workers view money as inherently corrupting. They view the bourgeoisie as dishonest because making a profit requires stealing, that is, selling something for more than one paid for it. As is the case for French professionals and managers, these workers' attitudes toward money are nuanced. Although many say that money is not important, they spend considerable time and energy maintaining and improving their financial situations and are attached to the goods they own. In part because French workers have more of a security blanket than do American workers—French society still offers generous social benefits, including universal health care coverage (Baldwin 1993; Kouchner 1989)—their attitudes toward money are often less conservative than those of their American counterparts. For instance, a bank clerk says: "What we share, my wife and I, is that we have a very short-term view of things. As long as the children are clothed, we are mostly concerned with having fun, with eating well. On the other hand, we decided not to buy an apartment, because we did not want to borrow money for fifteen or twenty years, while we can die tomorrow.... We prefer going on vacation, rather than spending our vacations in our own apartment."

Money is not downplayed by American workers the way it is by French workers. Like their upper-middle-class counterparts, many see it as a positive asset that gives freedom. Several also define their goal in life as getting rich, as does this electronics technician: "I'm always trying to figure out a way [to get rich]. If I could figure out a way, I would definitely pursue it. I would love to have more money, enough money to say I can get anything I want. I'm materialistic; I'm not going to deny that. ... I would love to have a Porsche or a Ferrari. That would make me extremely happy." Like this man, most New York interviewees believe in the American dream and many view self-employment as the key to this dream (see also Sennett and Cobb 1973). Unlike the French, they explicitly perceive the ability to make money as a reflection of one's intelligence and work ethic. For instance, the receiving clerk says: "I don't believe that people who are wealthy did something unscrupulous or deceiving or deceptive to get their wealth. There's a lot of people out there who are wealthy, and I'm sure they have worked darn hard for every cent they have." Like this insurance salesman, several insist that money is the legitimate reward of hard work. He says of his former job: "I saw that everybody got paid the same amount of money regardless of their ability. If you were better than somebody, it didn't matter, you know. Why should I try to better myself and educate myself and do a better job if somebody else is getting paid the same or might even be getting paid more because they're with the company longer? If I do a better job than somebody else, I want to get paid more."

Security is also much more valued by American workers than it is by the French. A few stress the importance of having several skills to bring to the market. As a bank clerk puts it: "What you need today is not only one job, whatever you're doing. You need a second line to fall back on. Whether you have a bus license or whether you are a bartender at a friend's place ... that's the way it is today." Finally, many discuss the violence that surrounds them daily, murders being committed for no other reason than "he was just in my face." They describe physical fights with neighbors; a 240-pound individual slammed a draftsman on the head because he was upset when the individual yelled at his daughter. All this makes high income more crucial to the lives of American workers: it allows them to move away from undesirable neighborhoods and buy peace. In contrast, in France, relatively high quality public housing is more widely available, even for the lower middle class, and income plays a lesser role in determining access to peace and security (Paugam 1993).

The attitudes of French workers toward power parallels their attitudes toward money: it is both valued and rejected. Several interviewees have highly internalized the organizational hierarchy they live in, and they recognize the legitimacy of authority based on competence and knowledge. Unlike their upper-middle-class counterparts, however, they often say that they do not appreciate power as such and that they value collaboration. It is more important to be "the one to whom others come when they need information. It is nice to know what answer to give. It is much more valorizing than having to tell someone 'first you fill this form and then this one'" (phone technician). These workers often say that they downplay differences between themselves and the people they supervise, in part because they identify themselves more with them than with their own bosses because they have had similar trajectories and "read the same newspaper." Again, the emphasis is on class solidarity. Others mention little struggles for control that are part of daily office life, in which being the first to open the mail signals one's position in a pecking order. Most, however, are quite critical of power in general, as if they experienced it negatively as coercive and repressive instead of empowering. Drawing again on a language of class struggle, they stress the importance of maximizing the autonomy of workers. A draftsman who has been involved in the Parti Communiste since 1980 and has actively opposed the European Union because it threatens French social benefits, describes the kinds of people he likes as "the rebels, those who in relation to institutions do not accept established rules, like marriage. . . . People who fight, who do not accept society as it is, who refuse a number of things, like watching television." This position often extends to a more articulate critique of the class structure. For instance, the photographer who dismisses the petite bourgeoisie says: "I come from a working class milieu, and I cannot stand people, the bourgeois, who dominate. It is disgusting what they do. They succeed in creating conditions that make people hungry, while they make a fortune. . . . Social injustice is something that I find enormously disturbing. The top boss of my firm makes what someone on minimum wages takes his whole life to make. Is it necessary that he makes so much money? Could the minimum-wage guy make a little more, so that he can take vacations once in a while, buy books for his kids?" Others are critical of power without borrowing from the rhetoric of the Left. Such people greatly value autonomy, the ability to make decisions independently from others, particularly educated professionals and technicians "who take away degrees of freedom in my action." They criticize those who use their influence to get their friends hired. They see the quest for power as a never ending and meaningless race.

In contrast, American workers have a more positive view of power, which they see as the main reward that comes with mobility. As a sales agent puts it, "There are certain things which I just cannot do in my position that I would like to do. There are certain improvements that I think are necessary and I don't have the power to do it. Actually, that probably has quite a lot to do with it. It's the level of power one has in the work environment. Working class people have the least of power; people in my position don't have too much, but there is a degree of autonomy and creativity, and professionals have much, much more." In addition, like the French, Americans often legitimize authority by knowledge, expressing anger against incompetent supervisors. The receiving clerk says of his boss: "I definitely recognize Jim as the boss. What he says goes. . . . You can see when you ask him a question, he is thinking about the options, the contingencies that are involved. He thinks before he comes to a conclusion." Often they describe people who are promoted as "the best individual, the one who is the best at his job, the one who can express his ideas, who can communicate better. The one that they think will make them look good. The one that they feel safe putting into the job. So really a lot of it depends on the individual, sidestepping politics." A civil servant feels that those who are promoted deserve it because "they fought for where they are today and everything by hook or by crook, by talking faster or saying the right thing or being at the right place at the right time to get the job or something like that." When asked if he deserves to be a boss, this civil servant says that he does not, but that he could be as good as they are if he had a better education. Like their upper-middle-class counterparts (Lamont 1992, chap. 3), these workers clearly do not associate the authority that bosses exercise on them with domination. For instance, the broadcast worker says: "I don't think that for me to show up five days a week and do certain things all the time in turn for them paying me to do this job is controlling me. I mean I think it's a contract that we have. . . . We have no goddamn right to treat [people] like slaves or to be rude to them or anything else just because they're employees." Again, the dream of becoming a small businessman is the answer that many have to satisfy their yearning for greater autonomy and creativity. This dream is rarely if ever mentioned by French workers.

Attitudes of French and American workers toward money and power parallel their attitudes toward success, ambition, and the middle class more generally: the French dislike materialism although they acknowledge that money shapes their lives. They also view power as repressive but recognize the legitimacy of competent supervisors. American workers are less critical of materialistic attitudes, more concerned with security, and have a fairly positive view of power, dissociating it from domination. A closer examination of French and American attitudes toward knowledge, intelligence, and education also reveals notable national differences.

Intelligence, Knowledge, and Education

Both French and American workers greatly emphasize intelligence, knowledge, and education when discussing their feelings of superiority and inferiority. These traits are often referred to in descriptions of blue-collar workers lives as if these attributes acted as the main marker between the two groups. Indeed, American and French low-status white-collar workers perceive their work to be more varied and complex than that of blue-collar workers, who have "a monotonous job, or a button pusher . . . like a factory worker where you do the same routine, day after day." Education and knowledge are also mentioned in descriptions of their relationships with professionals as if the boundary with this group was also primarily marked by these traits, reflecting objective criteria of access to upper-middle-class occupations. For instance, a French draftsman describes how he feels when he interacts with engineers at work: "They are very brilliant, they talk very fast, they have very little time to give us, and we have to be extremely concentrated for a short period of time. If I don't understand, I don't dare ask a question and seem completely stupid. I feel very small next to them." Again, both French and American workers often view the authority of their bosses as legitimate because of their knowledge and education. For instance, when asked if he would like to become a manager, the French photographer says, "Yes, but one needs to be competent. You cannot just become a boss. I have a technical degree, and many engineers and others have a Ph.D. in physics. I cannot compete with someone like that." He adds, "I have a tendency to have an inferiority complex. . . . I have a lot of *lacuna* in mathematics, physics. . . . My boss does not underestimate me. He appreciates me, but is aware of my limits."

Both French and American workers value formal education, but many had negative experiences with the education system. Most stress that their parents did not encourage them at school. The French are formally tracked for nonprofessional jobs after they complete the equivalent of elementary school, whereas Americans who are high-school graduates can, and some have, attended college. In this context, the French are often resentful that "being workers," their parents forced them to go to a technical school "because they were afraid that I would fail elsewhere" (phone salesman) Like Americans, several explain that their parents had very little time to give them. For instance, an electronics technician says, "I want to teach my children some things. My parents did not teach me much, all things considered. They only taught me things that I was asking them about, when I needed it. But they never initiated anything or provoked my curiosity." Others remember that their parents were constantly putting them down, comparing them with neighbors, telling them they would never do anything and that they were stupid. As the photographer puts it, "My mother is someone who has never, never trusted her kids." Descriptions suggest that the parents of these French workers did not believe in class mobility and often resented the passage of their children to the white-collar world, reflecting stronger class boundaries and a stronger working-class culture. Americans also stress the role of the family in limiting their educational experience, but they more often attribute this to specific incidents, such as their father leaving home when they were young, instead of to parental reproduction of class cultures. In other words, their descriptions are not framed in terms of structural class limitations as much as in terms of parental availability, which contrasts with French descriptions.

The boundary between the world of workers and that of educated people appears to be more permeable for American interviewees. Several still aspire to obtain a college degree, a dream that is inaccessible to French workers. This is expressed by the American receiving clerk who, although he is in his fifties, says, "I'd like to have a college degree for the pure satisfaction of having it and being considered an educated man . . . because I think that is what I am. I think I want that certification. I want the label. I want that recognition . . . to be on that plane of educated people. Not that I am uneducated. I mean, you can educate yourself to a great extent by reading, but I'd like it done formally . . . to be able to say I've got a bachelor's, or I've got a master's. To have it in writing. People recognize you and there's respect."

Because they do not have a college degree, the primary condition for access to high status occupations, many American interviewees are battling to acquire knowledge on their own. The insurance salesman who strongly identifies with the upper-middle-class world says that he has been obsessively trying to make up for the time he lost as a young man. He has great respect for expert knowledge. For instance, he envies "someone who's in some totally unrelated field of something that I have no knowledge of whatsoever. Not inferior to the person, but I would feel lower or intimidated. I would put that person ahead of me; say, like a doctor, maybe the president of General Motors. . . . I do feel inferior to somebody who knows so much more than I do in some kind of related field like business. That bothers me, and I feel that I should know more. That's what drives me. . . . I am trying to catch up." Earlier he said:

> I'm very knowledgeable in my field. People—agents, my peers—are constantly calling me for advice and information on a product. Sometimes I enjoy that, sometimes I resent it, because I'm the one that spent hours at night reading the stuff. . . . I don't like not knowing something. . . . I have my clients, my relatives, my friends, they call me up for all these kinds of information. . . . Even after they see a lawyer or an accountant, they ask me before they see them or after they see them, just to double-check to see if it's right. About leas-

ing a car, buying a car. I have a reputation among my peers. . . .
If they ask me something and I say it, that's the truth, that's it, and
that's gospel. . . . I don't go out learning and doing and preaching
that and telling everybody I know everything, but that's the reputation I got because when people ask me, they find out.

This man's emphasis on knowledge of facts is reflected in his descriptions
of the people he admires and in his reading habits ("mostly the finance
section, to see how my investments are doing . . . strategy books to find
better ways of thinking"). Similarly, the paper-goods salesman says about
his boss, "If you ask him about taxes, if you ask him about the stock market, whatever has to do with business, in a nutshell, he knows about it
because he has knowledge. He has education, as opposed to me." American professionals and managers particularly value expertise, "knowing the
facts," compared to their French counterparts who put more emphasis on
humanistic knowledge and general education (Lamont 1992, chap. 4). The
concern with expertise that American workers express might suggest their
relative cultural proximity to upper-middle-class culture.

Another difference between French and American workers is that
Americans value education more for the proper economic benefits it provides. Again, "making it" is viewed as a reflection of one's intelligence,
and feelings of inferiority and superiority are shaped by this belief. An
intricate relationship between education, intelligence, and success is
described by the electronics technician who says of professionals: "I feel
envious of them, but if they're rich, well, hey! They were smart enough
to get rich. I wish I could be it, but I don't necessarily feel inferior to
them. Not even intellectually. They may be smarter than me because they
had the smarts to get it. But that doesn't instill the feeling of inferiority
in me. But like I said, the engineer that's talking circles around me, for
some unknown reason . . . that gives me the inferior feeling."

Another electronics technician says that if he had to draw a line to distinguish superior from inferior people, "then I would say intelligence probably ranks high [in making] that distinction. The fact that there are some
people out there I think [who] could do better and don't try. . . . There's
nothing wrong even if you don't want to become something, but don't
blame somebody else for it." Again, intelligence is associated with success,
and on this basis boundaries are drawn against individuals who lack ambition and implicitly, against the poor. The same electronics technician says:
"If I talk to someone who has fourteen degrees, and I realize that I'm not

their caliber, I would feel inferior, but it wouldn't bother me. I want to make that distinction. I don't think that you can say that there's people who just because they know something are better than you. I don't believe that. I don't believe financially that makes somebody better than you. And I think that because I feel I'm in a middle-class, fairly comfortable position." He defines "being better" in terms of "being better off financially" and dissociates this from intelligence, stressing that workers often make a better living than college graduates. He also dissociates education from moral virtues when he says, "You don't have to be well educated to be likable. Education doesn't instill your values and your morals, and education doesn't make your personality. So whether you're highly educated or not, your personality is your personality, and your values and morals stay the same." This worker puts socioeconomic criteria of evaluation above cultural ones and below moral ones, stressing that what counts is whether or not you are a good person and how much money you make.

The distance of these French and American workers from the middle class is reflected in their criticisms of the educational system and of mainstream definitions of intelligence that this system promotes. To this, they contrast the practical knowledge that they have acquired while working. As an American draftsman explains, "I have twelve, thirteen years worth of concrete knowledge. . . . I would try to teach [kids] that, more than book-learning type of stuff . . . there's no reason to teach a kid something that he is not going to use." An American electronics technician says, "Anybody can read a lot. . . . Knowing a lot about politics has nothing to do with intelligence. That is just what you're interested in. Opinions, interests, keeping up with current events or not keeping up with current events has nothing to do with intelligence." Some define intelligence as being street wise "in a person-to-person sense." For instance, an American bank clerk says that he thinks he is of average intelligence because "I know when trouble is coming." You can recognize it on the street," he says, "or you can recognize it at your job. I know when to keep my mouth shut, and I know when to speak up. I know basically what's going on." These alternative definitions of intelligence are more present among American workers than they are among the French, reflecting a certain populism and anti-intellectualism that is present in American upper-middle-class culture (Lamont 1992, chap. 4).

French workers more often express admiration for people who are cultured than Americans do. Like this bank clerk, several say that they feel inferior to people who are very cultivated "on everything, on many top-ics. . . . It is particularly the ability to remember everything. For instance, on the games on TV where people are asked general questions, you have people who can answer in one second questions on all kinds of topics." Or some, like this French draftsman, describe people they feel inferior to as people "who are continuously working on themselves, permanently, to cultivate themselves, who know a lot of things, who are conscious of a lot of things. It is a permanent effort. Me, I sometimes give up because I need to relax. People like that, when we meet them, make us feel very small." Here again, class cultures leave their imprint on the relationship with culture that these French workers have. The photographer explains that "my parents were people with whom we discussed very little, in fact . . . we never went to the movies together, we never went out together. My parents only watch TV. . . . Sometimes when I have friends who tell me that they are going to see a movie or go to the theater with their par-ents, I think it would never happen to me." A few link their interest in culture to their involvement in communist cells that encouraged politi-cal discussions and the diffusion of high culture among workers. An inter-viewee who has been a member of a cell for several years describes his experience thus: "They want to discuss everything all the time. . . . They have very logical minds when it comes to politics, whereas me, I don't always see all the details, and they destroy me. I cannot defend my argu-ments." These workers also associate refinement with class privilege: "Can someone who is born in a working-class family and who lives in a build-ing in Sarcelles be refined? It is something that is passed on by the fam-ily. Therefore I don't want to judge people on this basis because that could lead us to ignoring wonderful people who are not refined, don't have good manners" (bank clerk). Nevertheless, teaching politeness and good manners to children is seen as important by many, who say that above all they want their children to be "polite, work at school, and don't get in trouble."

In the picture that emerges, French and American workers are sim-ilar in their respect for intelligence, knowledge, and education. The French, however, value culture more than their American counterparts do, whereas Americans are more concerned with "knowing the facts." Furthermore, Americans seem to place more value on practical defini-tions of intelligence, and they equate intelligence with economic success. Finally, the relationship that French workers have with the educational system seems to be shaped by their parents' unwillingness to assist them in social mobility projects.

The Rhetoric of Racial Differences

A last dimension of class to be discussed here is that of race. Implicitly, both in France and the United States, nonwhites are assumed to make up a relatively large fraction of the lower classes. Thus, boundaries that are drawn against racial minorities are often simultaneously boundaries drawn against the non–middle-class world. It is in this context that I examine briefly the racist rhetoric produced by low-status white-collar workers in both countries (for a more detailed analysis, see Lamont 1995a).

Although references to racial differences are almost totally absent from upper-middle-class interviews in France and the United States, they are quite salient in interviews with American low-status white-collar workers. These interviewees often explicitly draw strong boundaries against African-Americans, defining them in opposition to middle class values they cherish. They often associate blacks with the underclass, describing them as parasites who live off the work of others and have not entirely internalized American standards of hard work and success. Blacks are depicted as "having a tendency to try to get off by doing less, the least possible as long as they still maintain being able to keep the job, where whites will put in that extra oomph" (electronics technician). They are also "getting away with murder . . . with things that I wouldn't even think of doing" (civil servant). One respondent summarizes the way many perceive the situation: "What is a nice way to say it? . . . I know this is a generality and it does not go for all, it goes for a portion. It's this whole unemployment and welfare gig. What you see mostly on there is blacks. . . . A lot of the blacks on welfare have no desire to get off it. Why should they? It's free money. And I can't stand seeing my taxes go to that. I can't stand to see my hard-earned money going to pay for someone who wants to sit on their ass all day long and get free money." Again, these workers strongly condemn those who are not self-sufficient and they perceive African-Americans as being overrepresented in this category. Although they often distinguish between people they know and black people in general, they also make moral distinctions, distinguishing between "blacks and niggers . . . whites and white trash . . . Spanish people and Spiks. Do you get my point? It has to do with being an undesirable whatever your ethnic background is, whatever your religious background is. . . . If you are a scuzzball, then I want nothing to do with you no matter where you come from. . . . I like nice people, period" (receiving clerk). The lines that are drawn against blacks are simultaneously based on morality and race and indirectly on class because blacks and "scuzzball behavior" (delinquency and vandalism) are concentrated in lower social groups (for a full development of this argument, see Lamont 1995b). This bundle of meaning is expressed by an interviewee who says, "Blacks see how fast and easy it is to make a buck selling drugs. Go out and buy an Uzi machine gun, and now they have some protection. [Yet] I think you can instill some morals in them because a few of them come out of the system OK."

Some racial prejudices are extended to nonwhite groups other than blacks. A civil servant describes East Indians as cheap and another resents Latino immigrants who come to the United States and collect social security when they turn sixty-five even if they have worked in this country for only a few years. A few American white-collar men I talked to, however, openly adopted antiracist positions. One talks about the importance of "exposing our children to a diversity of people, so that when they hear slurs, they can ward off these preconceptions [with] their experience with people of different backgrounds" (clerical worker). But such reactions were exceptional in the small group of American white-collar respondents to whom I talked.

By contrast, white race was not salient in the interviews that I conducted with the French upper middle class. French low-status white-collar workers most often adopt an explicitly antiracist discourse. They do so in the name of republican principles that have shaped the political culture in France since the Revolution of 1789. These ideals include the Jacobin notions of equality, universalism, and national unity, which negate particularism based on locality, corporate membership, and birth and therefore discourage people from drawing boundaries based on ascribed characteristics. The state is viewed as the exclusive representative of common interests; and citizens are units totally substitutable for one another, constituting an equal and undifferentiated mass. Thereby, French nationality draws a clear line between an in-group and an out-group and downplays internal stratifications within the population that could act as alternative identity bases. Consequently, racism is expressed more often on the basis of citizenship than on skin color (Lamont forthcoming).

Interviewees do express concern about the decline of their neighbor-hoods, resulting from the growing immigrant population that refuses to assimilate culturally, despite taking advantage of the benefits that French society offers. French workers are worried about the consequences of these changes for their children and remember nostalgically the more car-ing and integrated communities in which they grew up, where traditional African clothing was never seen on the street.

It is interesting to note that the few Parisian white-collar workers who are racists appear to justify their attitudes in universalistic terms, to have a sociological understanding of the reasons for differences in behav-ior, or to distance themselves toward their racism. For instance, an air-plane technician confesses:

> Whether we want it or not, we always have behaviors that are more or less racist. When I go to a shopping center where you have young North Africans who are hanging out, sometimes I have negative feelings toward them. It is always at the level of the stereotype, the typical reaction toward foreigners, or some foreigners. You will tell me racism is not nice, people repeat this to us all the time, and it is true that it is not nice to have these stupid reactions, but sometimes it is stronger than us because they are very deep inside of us. . . . I ask myself what are they doing here? My reaction is almost at the aesthetic level. Some have *sales gueules* . . . but there are Arabs with whom I work, and we get along very well.

A wood salesman explains that everyone is a little bit racist in France because there is not enough room for all the newcomers and so much of the new delinquency is initiated by young Arab men.

The rhetoric of racism here is similar to that used by American workers in that specific groups are identified with the lower class and defined in opposition to the values of mainstream society. In France more than in the United States, however, in the name of solidarity and egalitarianism, interviewees oppose racism and other forms of segrega-tion: they view racism as an extension of the type of hierarchical think-ing that led some to believe that wearing a tie makes one a better human being. Thus, I found several denunciations of racism, sexism, and ageism among the white-collar interviewees. For instance, a draftsman says, "Wherever I go, the secretaries I see are always pretty and young. I ask myself where are the old ones now? It is a form of racism. There is not only the racism of color."

Much of the racist discourse addressed to racial minorities in France and the United States is shaped by class attributes that are associated with specific racial groups. More specifically, racial minorities are rejected because they are assimilated with the lower class and are defined against values that are key to American society. These attitudes are important to white racial consciousness (Kluegel and Bobo 1993). In the French case, the rejection appears to be less violent, at least among white-collar workers, in part because it is attenuated by republicanism and by the discourse of solidarity that is part of working class culture.

In this chapter, I have documented the ways in which French and American workers understand differences of class and race in the way they talk about what matters in life, who deserves respect, and how to assess jobs. Descriptions of how intergroup boundaries are channeled by these representations challenge the more mechanistic views of class relations; they embed these boundaries in concrete discussions of what matters to workers' sense of self. In this respect, this chapter contributes to the important literature on working class culture that builds on the work of E. P. Thompson and includes the work of the Birmingham School and recent cultural historians. It also traces interclass relationships from the perspective of how workers draw boundaries, instead of positing a universal logic of identity construction by opposition that would function in an undifferentiated manner across settings. Clearly, the men I talked to define who they are relationally: they oppose their concepts of a good life and a good person with those of other groups. But they do so differently across contexts, for instance by stressing different aspects of class behavior and attitudes given the cultural repertoires that are present in each country (for example, the rhetoric of the Left in France) and the resources to which they have access in the context of unequally developed welfare states.

Of course, the boundaries that these men draw do not capture the entire reality of class in contemporary societies, but they do point at often neglected dimensions. They do not capture cultures of solidarity "in the making"—that is, how workers come to gain awareness of belonging to a group sharing common interests and mobilize to defend these interests. Ethnographic and historical research is better suited for the study of such processes. However, these boundaries inform us about the class experience of white workers in general—not only union organizers or activists. This experience of class is tapped by comparing salient class attributes in the descriptions that white-collar workers provide of others and in their abstract evaluations of class. This is a fruitful approach because for most workers, class is often experienced and expressed at this very level, that is, in the way they react to poor people and to people with money, power, education, and "success." This approach reveals that although some studies suggest that American workers deny the existence of class, they constantly affirm it in their evaluations of others.[6]

The worldviews of the French and American workers I interviewed reveal that some of the national differences noted in earlier comparative studies of French and American workers might still hold to some extent today. For example, the language of class struggle is still present in the way French workers describe their relationship with other classes. Furthermore, French workers express more solidarity toward blue-collar workers and the poor than do their American counterparts, and they value ambition, money, and success less as criteria to evaluate people's worth. They also, however, often define themselves as middle class because of their income level, and they value culture, expertise, and other middle-class traits, suggesting nuanced patterns of cultural similarities and differences between middle- and working-class people in France. In the United States, low-status white-collar workers appear to be more middle-class-identified than their French counterparts, at least in relation to their attitudes toward money, power, ambition, and success, and in the way they draw boundaries against the poor and against blue-collar workers. Although these cross-national differences could be explained by objective differences in levels of inequality and mobility in France and the United States, recent comparative work has shown that between 1983 and 1990 interclass inequality has increased more in the United

6. It should be noted that here—as in Lamont 1992, chap. 7, and Coleman and Rainwater 1978—I do not predefine class, whether in terms of income, relations of production, or collective mobilization. Instead, I analyze whether interviewees privilege socioeconomic characteristics that are generally understood to be class related: income, power, education, knowledge, and so forth. I take prestige, or status, to be one such dimension. This approach does not privilege class consciousness as an a priori attribute of class, but considers its relative salience among other attributes.

Although I analyze the individual opinions expressed by randomly sampled workers, as do studies of the subjective dimension of class, I consider these opinions to reflect mental maps shared by the lower middle class. This does not mean that workers' evaluations of other classes and class attributes do not vary across settings, but it does suggest that by comparing the worldviews expressed by a number of workers, it is possible to identify important and possibly relatively stable characteristics of the worldviews that predominate in this group.

States than in France (Wolfe 1995). Furthermore, studies of intragenerational mobility conducted in the 1980s show slightly more upward mobility in France than in the United States when all classes are considered (Haller et al. 1985).

These interviews need to be compared with national surveys to assess whether the trends identified here are generalizable to the working class at large across genders and races. Mary Jackman's recent work (1994) suggests important parallels between the men I interviewed and a national sample: she finds that working-class people subscribe to principles of income inequality much as do members of other classes (236–37). She also finds that morality plays an important role in justifying inequality in the American context and that workers associate higher classes with higher intelligence. She suggests that to reach a better understanding of the moral bases of unequal relationships, one needs to document how certain traits—those that are popularly selected as salient comparison points between groups—are used to delimit the place of each group in society. Despite its limitations, the analysis presented here provides an important step in this direction because, unlike survey research, it proceeds inductively to identify characteristics that are most salient to workers.

The trends I have identified relate in interesting ways to macrocultural patterns characteristic of French and American societies. Indeed, high culture is more highly valued by French professionals and managers than by their American counterparts (Lamont 1992), and this appears to shape how French workers understand the importance of culture. It also suggests, on the one hand, that the French upper middle class has been relatively successful in institutionalizing criteria of evaluation other than purely economic ones, thereby reinforcing the place of culture and education in shaping the way people assess self-worth. On the other hand, American low-status white-collar workers do not appear to have a great deal of autonomy toward an upper-middle-class culture that stresses economic success and upward mobility as normative, despite an important economic recession and a dramatic restructuring of the labor market for workers with few or no skills. This resonates with findings by Carl Nightingale (1992), Jennifer Hoschshild (1995), and others that even African-American workers who are positioned at the bottom of the labor market still strongly invest in the American dream and engage in the cult of consumerism that characterizes American society as a whole. This trend is particularly surprising given that spatial segregation between races and classes has increased in recent years (Massey and Denton 1993).

The interviews discussed here suggest that the language of class remains very present in the way both French and American workers talk about differences between themselves and others. Again, whereas American workers might de-emphasize boundaries between classes when discussing, for instance, their relationship with the middle class, they draw very strong boundaries between their own class or racial group and those they locate below them. In contrast, the French appear to draw weaker boundaries between themselves and people below them, but stronger ones with regard to people above. Therefore, class is a very important principle of segmentation of reality in both countries, but it operates differently, suggesting the importance of considering the multidimensionality of class relations when comparing class cultures cross-nationally. A breaking down of caricatural representations of class is essential to a more complex understanding of the uneven changes that French and American society are undergoing today.

References

Baldwin, Peter. 1992. *The Politics of Social Solidarity: Class Bases of European Welfare State, 1875–1975*. New York: Cambridge University Press.

Coleman, Richard P., and Lee Rainwater, with Kent A. McClelland. 1978. *Social Standing in America: New Dimensions of Class*. New York: Basic.

Dudley, Kathryn Marie. 1994. *The End of the Line: Lost Jobs, New Lives in Postindustrial America*. Chicago: University of Chicago Press.

Fantasia, Rick. 1988. *Cultures of Solidarity: Consciousness, Action and Contemporary American Workers*. Berkeley: University of California Press.

Gallie, Duncan. 1983. *Social Inequality and Class Radicalism in France and Britain*. Cambridge: Cambridge University Press.

Halle David. 1984. *America's Working Man: Work, Home and Politics among Blue-Collar Property Owners*. Chicago: University of Chicago Press.

Haller, Max, Wolfgang Konig, Peter Krause, and Karin Hurz. 1985. "Patterns of Career Mobility and Structural Positions in Advanced Capitalist Societies: A Comparison of Men in Austria, France, and the United States." *American Sociological Review* 50 (5): 579–603.

Hamilton, Richard. 1967. *Affluence and the French Worker in the Fourth Republic*. Princeton: Princeton University Press.

Hochschild, Jennifer. 1995. *Facing Up to the American Dream: Race, Class, and the Soul of the Nation*. Princeton: Princeton University Press.

Jackman, Mary. 1994. *The Velvet Glove: Paternalism and Conflict in Gender, Class, and Race Relations*. Berkeley: University of California Press.

Katznelson, Ira. 1981. *City Trenches: Urban Politics and the Patterning of Class in the United States*. Chicago: University of Chicago Press.

Kluegel, James R., and Lawrence Bobo. 1993. "Opposition to Race-Targeting: Self-Interest, Stratification Ideology, or Racial Attitudes." *American Sociological Review* 58: 443–65.

Kouchner, Bernard. 1989. *Les nouvelles solidarités: Actes des assises internationales de 1989*. Paris: Presses Universitaires de France.

Lamont, Michèle. 1992. *Money, Morals, and Manners: The Culture of the French and American Upper-Middle Class*. Chicago: University of Chicago Press.

———. 1995a. "The Rhetoric of Racism and Anti-racism in France and the United States." Paper presented at the conference on Culture and Hatred in France, Dartmouth College, October.

———. 1995b. "National Identity and National Boundary Patterns in France and the United States." *French Historical Studies* 19 (2): 349–65.

———. Forthcoming. "The Frontiers of Our Dream Are No Longer the Same: Cultural Dynamics of Exclusion and Community in France, the United States, and Quebec." In Wolfgang Danspeckgruber with Sir Arthur Watts, eds., *Self-Determination and Self-Administration: A Sourcebook*. Boulder: Lynn Rienner.

Lash, Scott. 1984. *The Militant Worker*. Cranbury, N.J.: Associated University Press.

Lipset, Seymour Martin. 1977. "Why No Socialism in the United States." In S. Bialer and S. Sluzar, eds., *Sources of Contemporary Radicalism*. Boulder: Westview Press.

Mann, Michael. 1973. *Consciousness and Action among the Western Working Class*. London: Macmillan.

Massey, Douglas, and Nancy A. Denton. 1993. *American Apartheid: Segregation and the Making of the Underclass*. Cambridge: Cambridge University Press.

Morrison, Christian. 1988. "Une révolution tranquille: L'égalisation des revenus en France depuis 20 ans." *Commentaire* 11 (41): 203–12.

Nightingale, Carl Mullhauser, 1992. *On the Edge: Poor Black Children and the American Dream*. New York: Basic.

Paugam, Serge. 1993. *La société française et ses pauvres*. Paris: Presses Universitaires de France.

Rubin, Lillian B. 1994. *Families on the Faultline. America's Working Class Speaks about the Family, the Economy, Race, and Ethnicity*. New York: Harper Collins.

Sennett, Richard, and Jonathan Cobb. 1973. *The Hidden Injuries of Class*. New York: Random House.

Stacey, Judith. 1991. *Brave New Families: Stories of Domestic Upheaval in Late Twentieth Century America*. New York: Basic Books.

Terrail, Jean Pierre. 1990. *Destins ouvriers, la fin d'une classe?* Paris: Presses Universitaires de France.

Trade Unions and Employers' Organizations of the World. 1992. London: Longman Group, Ltd.

Wolfe, Edward N. 1995. *Top Heavy. A Study of the Increasing Inequality of Wealth in America*. New York: Twentieth Century Fund Press.

 CHAPTER 7

Rethinking Cultural and Economic Capital

Jan C. C. Rupp

SOCIAL SPACE MAY BE DEFINED AS THE STRUCTURED CONGLOMERATE OF domains or fields (in French, *champs*) of human action. Many social theories conceptualize social space as one-dimensional, structured by economic differentiation in social classes and their relationships. Despite their differences, stratification and market theories, as well as Marxist and neo-Marxist formulations, share this conception. The social theory of Pierre Bourdieu develops an alternative approach by drawing on Max Weber's distinction between socioeconomic class, status, and power. Bourdieu and Jean-Claude Passeron (1969) introduced a fundamental distinction between cultural and economic capital (cf. Brubaker 1985), thus breaking from both the one-sided economist and culturalist approaches long dominant in social theory. For these theorists, the cultural domain should be seen neither as an epiphenomenon of the economic sphere nor as a domain where charismatic individuals operate, free from the play of interest and power. Rather, culture is an arena sui generis, with its own forms of power, its own social logic, and its own "market" of symbolic goods.

The English version of this essay has been edited by Jennifer Dunn. Previous versions were presented at the Tenth Anniversary Theory, Culture & Society Conference, Pittsburgh, August 16–19, 1992, at the ISS Conference The Sorbonne, Paris, June 21–25, 1993, and at a Seminar conducted by Pierre Bourdieu at the Amsterdam School for Social Science Research, June 7, 1994. A different version of this essay was published in *Actes de la Recherche en Sciences Sociales*, September, 1995.

Once culture is added as a basis of theorization, social space becomes two-dimensional.

In Bourdieu's (1990, 218–29) view, social space and its dimensions are real. Groups such as social classes exist only on paper (cf. Lukacs 1923; Gramsci 1971; Lash 1990); classes are constructions that do not operate in a social vacuum but are subject to the structural constraints of social geography. Objective relations—located within the social universe—are relations between positions occupied within the distribution of resources that are or may become active and effective, "like trumps in a game of cards," in competition for the appropriation of scarce goods. Agents are distributed in the overall social space according to the volume and structure of their capital. These can change over time. They are also gender and ethnicity dependent, and manifested by the past and potential trajectories of individual agents and groups in social space. Agents who occupy similar positions find themselves in similar conditions, subjected to similar conditionings, and they have every chance of developing similar dispositions and interests. But groups are not given in social reality; they have to be made.

In Bourdieu's *Distinction* (1984), social space is structured by the global *volume* of economic and cultural capital in play within its bounds. The possession and use of economic and cultural capital organizes actors into social classes, whereas the predominance of economic or cultural resources differentiates cultural versus economic fractions within a social class. Within the dominant elite and the middle classes, the *structure* of capital—the proportion of each type of capital relative to the total volume of capital—determines whether a fraction will be predominantly culturally or economically oriented. Bourdieu's conceptual schema is represented in Table 7.1. If the lower class is defined in terms of its lack of either cultural or economic capital, and the dimensions of social space are conceptualized in terms of the forms of capital, the lower class will necessarily be theorized as undifferentiated and homogeneous.

TABLE 7.1 Position, habitus and lifestyle

Position in social space	Habitus	Lifestyle
Position in the structure of living conditions: volume, composition, and reproduction of cultural and economic capital	Disposition and value orientation	A whole ensemble of preferences and tastes

The object of the present study is to explore theoretically and empirically the possibility of distinguishing between culturally and economically oriented fractions within the lower class, in the same way scholars identify such orientations within other social classes. There is already some empirical evidence for this possibility, but it needs to be developed, and its theoretical implications need to be pursued. Indications for differentiations among the lower classes already can be found in *Un art moyen* (Bourdieu et al. 1965) and in Bourdieu's work on education. In *Distinction* Bourdieu says: "For the working classes, who are strongly ranked by overall capital volume, the data available do not enable one to grasp differences in the second dimension (composition of capital). However, differences such as those between semiskilled, educationally unqualified, provincial factory workers of rural origin, living in an inherited farmhouse, and skilled workers in the Paris region who have been in the working class for generations, must be the source of differences in lifestyle and religious and political opinions" (1984, 115). At the time, Bourdieu did not realize that in order to be able to grasp such differences, it would have been necessary to reformulate the theory.

By rethinking Bourdieu's concept of habitus as a concept of *value orientation*, I consider habitus rather than capital to be the basic variable structuring the social space. Moreover, by reconceptualizing capital as a concept of *investment*, in which actors within social classes devote differential time and energy to *materializing* their value orientation into culturally or economically valued goods, I redefine the volume of economic and cultural capital as the volume of economic and cultural investment, and I redefine the structure of capital as based upon the proportion of cultural versus economic investment. In this way, investment is a more general concept than capital. Upper-class investments take the specific form of capital investment, in the double meaning of (re)production of resources and of power, whereas in the middle and lower classes the form of investment is the (re)production of cultural and economic values. Finally, I reconceptualize lifestyle as *symbolizing* the basic value orientation.

Empirically, the present study is based on an investigation carried out in a Dutch "Middletown." I identified two elementary schools in working-class neighborhoods—one predominantly cultural in emphasis, the other, economic. In turn, I interviewed parents of students attending those schools to determine whether the value orientations of parents differed along economic and cultural dimensions. My basic questions concerned whether members of culturally oriented fractions of the lower class can be distinguished from more economically oriented ones on the basis of patterns of investments that have symbolic cultural value as opposed to symbolic economic value. If the valuations of cultural and economic investment vary, this variation would indicate that the social space for the lower class is two-dimensional in the same way as the domains of the middle and upper classes, which would support my contention that the two dimensions of capital have to be redefined in ways that work across the entire social space.

Theoretical Framework

In Bourdieu's (1984) analysis, the lower class appears as an undifferentiated, homogeneous social class. Bourdieu represents social space in the form of a funnel, in which there is a greater degree of differentiation at higher class levels (1984, 128–29). This representation is necessarily the consequence of defining dimensions of social space in terms of capital. It is further contingent upon the use of survey instruments exclusively oriented toward legitimate "high" culture. Both theoretically and methodologically, the position of the lower class in social space and the objective life conditions of actors in this class are defined by the lack of either cultural or economic capital. The lower class does not attend the schools of the middle and upper classes, which (re)produce economic and cultural capital. This exclusion from access to capital works similarly, and more fundamentally, in relation to what Bourdieu's calls habitus. As a hypothetical construct, habitus amounts to the conceptualization of a disposition that explains the coherence among lifestyle elements, and relates this coherence as mediated through one or another position in social space, reflected by observable capital and investments. For the lower class, habitus is negatively defined in this theoretical formulation; it amounts to a structuration of life from the position of nonpossession. The lifestyles of the lower class are the negation of the lifestyles of the upper classes. Consonant with this theory, most research on working-class culture has failed to ask whether and how it is differentiated.[1] This approach risks

1. See Thompson 1966; Horkheimer and Adorno 1972; Clark, Critzer, and Johnson 1979; De Witte 1990; Gartman 1991; and Mukerji and Schudson 1991. For a different opinion see Williams 1958. Cultural historians, such as M. M. Bakhtin (1968) and Peter Burke (1978), make no distinctions within popular culture except for national origin.

regarding the culture of lower classes as a negatively defined, homogeneous mass culture.

In this formulation, those in cultural power determine which goods on the cultural market represent legitimate "high" art and which do not; that is, they establish which forms of art have cultural value and which forms are excluded from this category. Forms of "low" art typically have no cultural capital value, unless they are transformed into high art by being placed within a context of legitimate art. Similarly, those in economic power—economic capitalists—decide which financial investments on the economic market are good ones and which are not. There are ongoing debates about the criteria for distinguishing high from low art (Peterson 1983; Gans 1985; DiMaggio 1987; Levine 1988; Zolberg 1990), and good from bad economic investments. The point here does not concern the criteria. It is, rather, that such distinctions are made, and that they have an organizing, constructing effect.

Forms of low art may have no value as cultural capital. This does not imply, however, that low art has no cultural value for the lower class, in particular, for the fraction within the lower class with cultural dominance. It is only in specific situations that a disposition for low art is annihilated through the imposition of standards of high art. Cultural power prefers the use of the mechanism of exclusion (Lamont and Lareau 1988; Rupp and de Lange 1989). When forms of exclusion fail to work properly, the response is symbolic violence. This happens when working-class children try to enter institutions of the cultural elite. In the *lycées*, Bourdieu and Passeron (1969) emphasize, those from the lower class are forced to assimilate preferences for high culture when they try to climb the social ladder, and they are expected to unlearn and abjure their original preferences and tastes, including their manner of speaking. Mutatis mutandis, by extending the analysis to the economic dimension, we can specify a thesis about lower-class economic "investments" and "properties." Although lower-class economic goods may have little or no economic capital value, they can hold symbolic economic value for fractions within the lower class characterized by a predominantly economic orientation.

In sum, I am arguing that the relevant dimensions of social space are not the volume and structure of cultural and economic capital, but the volume and structure of cultural and economic investment. These investments take the form of capital only in the upper classes. Thus, forms of high art have symbolic capital value. Forms of low art are a cultural value resource for a culturally oriented fraction within the working class. Some prefer investing in economic resources; others invest in cultural goods—either highbrow art or lowbrow, depending on their class position. It is not capital that constitutes the disposition of a social class, but rather the basic (predominantly economic or cultural) value orientation. Value orientations are materialized in economically and culturally valued goods.

Research Strategy

The main object of this study is to learn whether the lower class is structured in terms of two dimensions—economic and cultural investment. Such a finding could have implications for revising Bourdieu's (1984) social theory of differentiation among classes. Specifically, my interest is in determining what forms of "low" art hold symbolic cultural value for a predominantly culturally oriented fraction of the working classes, and what forms of economic investments hold symbolic economic value for the other, predominantly economically oriented, fraction of the working class. Meaningful differences have to be not only statistically significant but structurally significant as well. This implies that the differences ought to make distinctions between fractions of the lower class, not just between the lower and upper classes. Moreover, it must be recognized that differences in lifestyle may be relatively easy to find in the working classes. The structural requirement implies that such differences in lifestyle must be produced by differences in habitus, and that these different dispositions must be structured by different positions in social space. Table 7.2 presents the research program resulting from these considerations in diagrammatic form. Position in social space is indicated by cul-

TABLE 7.2   Position, habitus and lifestyle

Position in social space	Habitus	Lifestyle
Cultural investments (participation in forms of "low" art), economic investments (economic property), and reproduction of value orientation (educational philosophy of the school)	Disposition	Preferences with respect to view of children's prospects, holiday spending, recreation, presentation of wife, home furnishings

tural investments, economic investments, and the reproduction of value orientations in schools. The basic value orientation is materialized in cultural and economic investments, which determine market position in the social space, and is symbolized in lifestyle, which determines status position in the social space.

My basic argument is that fractions of the working class, like fractions within the upper classes, can be differentiated according to cultural and economic value orientation, investment, and lifestyle. In Bourdieu's view, the school is the key institution for (re)producing capital.[2] This view suggests a relevant venue for examining the thesis of the two-dimensional working class. My assumption is that on the schooling market—that is, when parents have a choice in schools—differences in positions and dispositions lead working-class parents to choose schools for their children that reflect their own predominantly cultural or economic value orientations. I define schools with an economic value orientation as those that reflect a pragmatic attitude toward learning, an achievement orientation,

2. Bourdieu's theory of two-dimensional social space has primarily directed his research into the investments of the upper classes in education. He mapped segments of French secondary and higher education designed for the reproduction of the various economic and cultural elites. He discovered not only that success at school, intermarriage, and the like are greatly dependent on the cultural and economic capital of the parents, but also that the various economic or cultural fractions of the upper class in France have institutionalized different routes in and segments of the higher educational system (Bourdieu 1984; see also Bourdieu 1989).

This view of education, as diversified and tracked along economic and cultural preferences, is fundamentally different from Bourdieu's earlier view, which made reference to *the* dominant culture inculcated in schools (Bourdieu and Passeron 1977). For this shift in interpretation, see Bourdieu and Wacquant 1992. Various studies have demonstrated national and historical differences in manifestations of these investment strategies. M. Kalmijn and R. Batenburg (1986) demonstrated that in the case of the secondary schools market for the Dutch elites, both economically and culturally oriented schools can be found; and each type attracts its own public—predominantly economic or cultural. Jan Rupp and others (1990) found the same effect on the elementary schools market for upper-class children. These schools form national networks. Research by G. Beekenkamp (1984) indicates that a significant proportion of the Dutch industrial elite, unlike the French, still prefers in-service training in an industrial enterprise above university education for their offspring, in contrast to cultural, political, and banking elites, who prefer academic education. These results indicate significant national differences in social distance between business classes and cultural classes and between cultural dispositions and economic dispositions. In the Netherlands, this distance is structurally different from France, where each elite has its own Haute École, and also from the United States, where business schools, humanities departments, and art schools are situated on the same campus—although business schools are always separate from colleges of arts and sciences—and where quite a few universities and other cultural institutions have been founded and sponsored by the business class. Moreover, in the United States, sons and daughters from the business class and the cultural elite are educated at the same boarding schools (Cookson and Hodges Persell 1985).

a "no-nonsense" teaching policy, an emphasis on cognitive subjects, and use of traditional teaching methods. Schools with cultural value orientations are those that emphasize the child and his or her social and emotional development, self-expression, independence, and creativity, and that offer a balance of cognitive and noncognitive subjects, art, and culture. In order to locate parents who might be identified with one or the other fraction hypothesized for the working class, I asked school administrators in a medium-size industrialized Dutch city to select a culturally oriented elementary school and an economically oriented one, based on the criteria described above. In order to control for demographic variation, I requested that each school have a high percentage of lower-class children enrolled, and that both schools be located in the same working-class neighborhood of uniform single-family terraced houses, near the old center of the town (see Haarmans 1992). Curriculum plans outlining the educational philosophy of the school are required in Dutch elementary schools, and a content analysis of the curriculum plans of the two schools as well as talks with teachers confirmed that the administrators' selections met my criteria.

I then needed to determine if the culturally oriented school was attended by children with culturally oriented parents and if the economically oriented school was attended by children with economically oriented parents. I used a standardized questionnaire to interview about twenty-five couples from each school. All working-class parents of children in the last two grades of the elementary schools were interviewed. Couples from the two schools did not differ with respect to age, gender, number of children, civil status, level of income, or education. They were all working-class parents: graduates or dropouts from lower vocational training schools. Thus, possible differences in positions in social space, dispositions, and lifestyle cannot be ascribed to these variables. The interviews with the couples were based on a standardized questionnaire that focused on the educational philosophy of the school, the parents' participation in cultural activities, their possessions, the prospects of their children, their leisure activities, and the wife's appearance. We also discussed lifestyle elements such as meals, parties, and home furnishings.

In order to determine whether the parents attending the predominantly cultural school had a cultural value orientation, and the parents of children in the predominantly economic school an economic orientation, I asked both groups about the educational philosophy of the school their children attended. I did this to verify the selection made by local administrators and my own analysis of the schools' curriculum plans. Parents of children attending the school identified by administrators as culturally oriented indeed described the school's educational philosophy as emphasizing emotional development, creativity, cooperation, critical thinking, and responsibility for self—terms indicating a "cultural educational philosophy" according to my criteria for measuring this variable. Similarly, parents from the school that administrators identified as economically oriented described the curriculum as attentive to good manners, politeness, and high achievement—indicating an "economic educational philosophy."

On other issues, the questionnaire needed to be constructed differently from previous instruments designed to measure the volume of cultural and economic capital (Rupp and de Lange 1989). I now had to form ideas about what might be elements of lower class cultural taste and what might be typical working-class economic investments. Interview questions concerning cultural and economic investments were developed on the basis of extensive participant observation in typically lower-class areas in Dutch cities.[3] Using items from the interview questionnaires, I constructed variables to measure respondents' art participation, ownership of economic property, evaluation of their children's school educational style, perception of their children's economic prospects, manner of spending leisure time and holidays, attention paid to the wife's appearance, and home furnishings.[4]

The following variables were constructed to measure parental value orientations. *Participation in "lowbrow" art*, an indicator of a cultural value orientation, was defined on the basis of questionnaire items concerned with playing a musical instrument (guitar, accordion, piano, flute, trumpet, or the voice), reading (modern) books, watching TV art programs, and paying visits to an exchange mart. *Economic property*, an indicator of a working class economic value orientation, was represented by the age

3. It is plausible to assume that manifestations of lower-class cultural and economic value orientations and investments depend on national traditions that change over time, whereas standards for cultural and economic capital are more likely international.

4. The variables were constructed using Cronbach's Alpha as a criterion. Cronbach's Alpha is a statistical measure for determining whether the internal consistency and coherence of particular items is great enough to form a variable. In the present study, only Alphas of more than .50 are considered significant enough for the researcher to assume beyond a reasonable doubt that the items really constitute a variable.

of the respondent's secondhand car. An *economic educational philosophy* variable was formed from interview items concerned with the learning of politeness or other good manners, and on achievements; on the other hand, emphases on emotional development, creativity, cooperation, critical thinking, social relations, responsibility, and dealing with computers were taken as indicators of a *cultural educational philosophy*.

The following variables tapped differences in lifestyles. The variable measuring respondent's ideas about the *economic prospects for their children*—manifesting an economic value orientation—was indicated by emphases on earning a good salary and getting a good job. The way in which holidays were spent and the preference for the kind of holiday formed the variable *spending holidays*. I reasoned that a taste for camping or vacationing in a trailer or recreational vehicle on a fixed site manifested a cultural value orientation, whereas a predominantly economic value orientation would likely express itself in a preference for hotels and summer cottages. The variable *leisure activities* reflected walking and cycling—the anticipated practices of culturally oriented parents, whereas I expected participation in sports to be more common in economically oriented parents. Finally, I chose the variable *presentation of the wife*, indicated by an emphasis on conspicuously expensive clothing and a preference for trousers rather than blue jeans, as a measure of the manifestation of a predominantly economically oriented lifestyle; and I used *cultural furnishings*, indicated by the presence of a timber ceiling and pure brickwork on the walls of the respondent's home, as a measure of the manifestation of a predominantly culturally oriented lifestyle.

Working Class Cultural and Economic Investment

Separate measurements for the parents of children attending the culturally oriented or economically oriented schools were carried out for each of the study's variables, as defined above. For each variable, the difference in means between the two groups of parents was tested with a two-tailed t-test. As shown in Table 7.3, the results suggest significant differences for the two groups of parents. I found that parents of children attending the culturally oriented school invest more time and energy participating in forms of "low" art. These cultural investments include singing, playing musical instruments such as the guitar, accordion, piano, flute and trum-

TABLE 7.3   Overview of the tested variables

	Cronbach's Alpha	t-test difference between cultural vs. economic lower class (probability values)
Art participation	.54	.020
Economic property		.050
Economic educational style	.67	.000
Cultural educational style	.60	.000
Economic prospects	.64	.000
Holidays		.051
Leisure time		
a. Walking and cycling		.004
b. Sports		.009
Presentation of the wife	.51	.000
Furnishings	.49	.023

pet (string instruments, typically associated with elite groups, are not mentioned), and reading a book every month. Culturally oriented working-class parents read more often, and they prefer "modern" novels and family/regional novels. In contrast, economically oriented working class parents are more likely to read medical novels—the fantasies of romances between nurses and doctors, available in every supermarket next to the chewing gum assortment. Culturally oriented parents report among their favorite television programs "art programs" on natural museums, in which old villages are reconstructed and old crafts revitalized. These parents are also more likely to visit exchange marts, where collectors exchange stamps, coins, postcards, beer mats, international train tickets, matchboxes. Virtually anything can be transformed into a collectible. This is one of the most important ways lower-class people produce cultural values.

I expected economically oriented parents to invest more time and energy in economic goods than their culturally oriented counterparts, and the findings support this hypothesis. Parents from the two schools do not differ in monthly net income (between Dfl. 2,000 and Dfl. 3,000); they live in the same working-class neighborhood consisting of uniform single-family terraced houses (worth Dfl. 75,000 at the time of purchase and Dfl. 110,000 at the time of the interviews). Thus, it is impossible for families to distinguish themselves by the type of house they occupy, and the modest income of these people considerably restricts the range of 'economic property" available for investment. For these reasons, it seems likely that lower class economic orientation would be expressed in the possession of newer model secondhand cars (working-class families cannot afford the purchase of new cars). Cars are parked on the street in working-class neighborhoods. Since in the Netherlands the registration plate is a precise indication of the age of a car, it was easy to determine that the cars of economically oriented parents are, indeed, newer than the cars of parents of children attending the culturally oriented school. Although there are no differences in the make of the cars, the economically oriented parents' cars are an average of two and a half years newer than those of culturally oriented parents. Moreover, the disposition of the economic fraction is well expressed by the knowledge that members have of legal, shady, and other means of acquiring "almost new" cars at very low cost.

Lifestyles

After establishing the significance of differences in cultural and economic investments between parents of children attending culturally oriented schools and economically oriented schools, my next step in the investigation was to see if these differences were reflected in different lifestyles. I chose the following aspects of lifestyle to investigate: the parents' vision of their children's future, the family's holiday and recreation patterns, the attention the couple paid to the wife's appearance, and furnishings in the home.

Economically oriented parents have different expectations for their children's future, placing more value on "holding down a good job" and "earning a good salary" than do culturally oriented parents. I found significant differences in holiday and recreation patterns as well. When asked how they had spent their holiday in the previous year and what kind of holiday they prefer, culturally oriented parents report preferring relatively simple holidays, such as camping or a permanent caravan. Economically oriented parents, on the other hand, favor staying in a hotel or summer cottage.

I expected that culturally oriented parents would prefer walking and cycling during recreation periods. Walking and cycling are seen by culturally oriented people as activities by which one can come "close to nature," in contrast with touring by car, which makes it impossible to see things other than cars and landscapes flashing by. Economically oriented parents were expected to choose to participate in competitive sports. Both these hypotheses were confirmed. As for sports, the lower class as a whole does not engage in those perceived in the Netherlands to be elitist, such as field hockey, tennis, and golf. Economically oriented parents are more likely than culturally oriented parents to be involved in popular sports such as swimming, gymnastics, and soccer.

Appearance is an important way in which people try to distinguish themselves from others, and therefore I investigated differences in the attention wives paid to their appearance. I expected economically oriented women to attach more value to their outward appearance, and according to the indicators I established for this variable, they do. The economically oriented women I interviewed attach a great deal of importance to conspicuously expensive clothing, and they prefer clothing other than blue jeans, displaying what some call "working-class chic." And finally, I looked at aspects of home furnishings, and found that culturally oriented parents appear to have a taste for "natural" environments, including timbered ceilings and pure brickwork on the walls of their homes.

The question remained whether the variables that I constructed were consistently related to structures of cultural and economic investments, that is, whether they differentiated between a predominantly cultural fraction and a predominantly economic fraction within the lower classes. In order to resolve this question, I carried out a factor analysis.[5] In the first factor solution, four factors were found, but in the case of the third of these factors, only the "furnishing" variable was highly loaded, and in the case of the fourth factor, only the "sports" variable. For this reason, I opted for a two-factor solution. In this solution, only the variables "sports in leisure time" and "furnishing" appear to be less differentiating than I expected. Otherwise, the results, presented in Table 4, largely support my theory.

Habitus and Capital versus Investment

To complete the circuit of this analysis, we must ask, which differences in habitus, constituted by different patterns of investment, produce the

5. I reassessed the data by means of discrimination function analysis, which some colleagues might prefer to my and Bourdieu's use of the t-test and factor analysis, but the results were not significantly different from those presented here.

TABLE 7.4   Factor weighting of the variables on the two dimensions of the investigation

	Factor 1 Economic orientation	Factor 2 Cultural orientation
Art participation	−.120	.896
Economic property	.501	−.325
Economic educational style	−.346	.506
Cultural educational style	.830	−.095
Economic prospects	.683	−.276
Holidays	−.286	.560
Leisure time		
a. Walking and cycling	−.100	.120
b. Sports	.439	.243
Presentation of the wife	.649	−.135
Furnishings	.149	.254

differences in lifestyles between culturally oriented parents and economically oriented ones? My answer, at this point, can be only suggestive. Economically oriented workers, by their way of life, seem to express a claim about the financial ability to afford economic property, and within the margins of their modest incomes, they manifest a kind of working-class chic. Culturally oriented workers, in contrast, emphasize the development of a taste for simple art forms and the currently prevailing Dutch working-class notion of a healthy, natural, and uncomplicated lifestyle. These emphases reflect the idea that it is unwise to have an excessive interest in the material aspects of human existence. Instead, when one's financial conditions are limited, a cultural orientation emphasizes that there are more important things in life.

This differentiation is reminiscent of descriptions of working-class lifestyles found in the work of social historians, such as Ger Harmsen (1961) and H. C. M. Michielse (1980), who have studied the Dutch youth movement. Harmsen (1961, 36) concludes that "the youth movement has not done any creative cultural work." Nevertheless, it is evident that the AJC (the socialist youth movement) has made its mark on cultural work as a whole, including home furnishings. In the artistic domain, Symbolism and *Jugendstil* (also known as "modern style," "art nouveau," "Stil von 1900") were of great importance, as was the NIVON (association of nature friends) movement in leisure activities. Similarly, the two fractions of the working class have manifested themselves on many occasions in the history of Dutch trade unions. Harbor workers appear to be the most economically oriented occupation, whereas workers in the graphic industry seem to be the most culturally oriented. What are we to make of these differences?

Were I to examine cultural capital theory reflexively, I would describe it as an attempt to contribute to the emancipation of the cultural field from the domination of the economic and political arenas. It is the revenge of the superstructure on the structure (Lash 1990). However, the use of concepts such as "capital," "market," "entrepreneur," "investment," "goods," and "resources" (which are borrowed from and strongly intertwined with the economic realm) indicates the continuing superordination of the economic terrain over the cultural. Historically, the theory of two-dimensional space emerged in France, where culture, in the form of the arts and sciences, is held in high esteem (Fumaroli 1992) and where, consequently, lower-class "art" has little merit among the elites. The most critical commentary on cultural capital theory originated in the United States, widely perceived as the most business-oriented nation in the world, and in which as many cultural centers appear to be established by business organizations as by churches and governments. Perhaps it is no coincidence that I make my argument from the Netherlands, the country with the greatest social distance and a delicate power balance between business and the arts and sciences.

In my theoretical and empirical inquiry, I sought to determine whether social space is two-dimensional for the working classes, in ways that parallel the organization of social space inhabited by the middle and upper classes. My research suggests that fractions exist within the lower class just as they do within the middle and upper classes. The differences that I found according to elementary school type indicate a differentiation between predominantly culturally oriented fractions and predominantly economically oriented fractions within the working classes. These differences are paralleled by differences in lifestyles. They cannot be interpreted as simply a consequence of the so-called embourgeoisement of the working classes. The culturally oriented fraction of the lower class participates in art, but the participation is in lowbrow art. Working-class economic goods, such as newer secondhand cars, continue to have little or no economic capital value. Nor can the differentiation be ascribed to a general rise in the importance attached to the field of culture;

I found similar differences among fractions of the working classes in the late 1960s (Rupp 1969).

These results are seemingly opposed to Bourdieu's analysis. Bourdieu and Passeron (1970) claim that cultural standards destroy any preference for lowbrow art, and in *Distinction* (1984) Bourdieu asserts that the lower class becomes a virtual zero point in the depiction of lifestyles in social space. This theorization is the logical consequence of conceptualizing the position of the lower class within a social space that is defined by the volume, composition, and seniority of economic and cultural *capital* rather than by economic and cultural *investment*. My results can, however, be interpreted within the general context of Bourdieu's social theory when this theory is redefined. If the two dimensions of social space are conceptualized in terms of the volume and structure of cultural and economic value orientations and investments, the research reported in this chapter can be seen as complementary to Bourdieu's work.

Bourdieu characterized the cultural middle class, whose members are oriented toward social climbing, as practicing an ascetic lifestyle. This habitus reflects a willingness to make considerable sacrifices in order to promote upward mobility for one's children. By contrast, the cultural elite demonstrates its disregard for the material aspects of eating and drinking: it embraces the formal, aesthetic aspects exemplified in, for instance, *la nouvelle cuisine*, with its emphasis on an exquisite but rather insubstantial dish. This attitude manifests the ability to afford a feeling of superiority. The terms employed by Bourdieu for the habitus of the cultural elites and the middle classes return, in a different form, for the cultural working classes. The preference I found among culturally oriented working-class parents is for a simple life, uncluttered by excess possessions, ostentatious dress, and other forms of conspicuous consumption. There seems to be, then, both a powerful correspondence and a set of important shifts between the cultural fractions of the various social classes.

In the lower class, an economically oriented lifestyle tends toward material and outward display—showing off—and toward working-class chic. Class location does make for an important difference. An economically oriented working-class person can be a genius at "finding a way," and tends to be generous because his or her circumstances are modest (the poorer, the more generous). By contrast, the economic elite is oriented toward display because there is no longer any need to count pennies. Overall, however, the correspondence between the habitus of the economic lower class and Bourdieu's (1984) descriptions of the economic elites and the bourgeoisie is striking. Indeed, it is possible that under certain conditions, differences between predominantly culturally oriented groups or between predominantly economically oriented groups of *different* social classes might be smaller than differences among culturally and economically oriented groups *within* a social class. Be that as it may, social space is fundamentally two-dimensional, and the divisions within each social class are as important as the division between the social classes.

The Production of Values

Bourdieu's class concept is Weberian rather than Marxist, which implies that it misses any emancipatory potential (for the same reason it does not imply the unfortunate idea of "historical necessity"). Jay MacLeod (1987), Paul Willis (1977), Henry Giroux (1983), and other neo-Marxist authors define cultural capital among working-class families in terms of "resistance" against what is pleonastically called "dominant cultural capital." These authors do not follow Bourdieu in conceptualizing working-class culture as the zero reference point for dominant culture; rather, they regard lower-class culture "more optimistically" (as they put it) as the dialectic negation of upper-class cultural capital. But neither Bourdieu nor MacLeod see working-class families as producers of cultural or economic value.

Within the domain of human valuations cultural and economic values are universal and eternal rivals. Social space is structured along these two dimensions. The core concept of a revised theory of the two-dimensional social space is the habitus, to be defined as the predominant value orientation, cultural or economic. On the one hand, the habitus produces and reproduces "material" cultural and economic values, which are stratified following permanently contested criteria. On the other hand, the habitus expresses itself symbolically in lifestyles, ranked along social status differences. Value orientations are real, (market) position and status are constructions (see Table 7.5). Cultural and economic values are produced by each social class. The specific value production (investment) of the upper classes is capital production, that is to say, the (re)production both of resources giving rise to privilege and of the power to dominate value distinctions. It is the doubtful prerogative of the upper classes to develop,

TABLE 7.5   Relations of value to arena of operation

"Market position"	Habitus	"Status" lifestyle
"Material" value	Value orientation	"Symbolic" value
Cultural and economic investments (Production and reproduction of values)	Cultural and economic	Cultural and economic

justify, and reproduce criteria for distinguishing high art from low art, high cultural value from low cultural value, as well as big economy from small economy, high economic value from low economic value. It is an upper-class sociopolitical construction that only what is scarce has value, and that what has value is scarce.

Compared with upper-class culture, little is known about the actual economic and cultural value production of the lower classes (what is known are the costs of labor). In our research project, we attempted to trace some cultural and economic values, material as well as symbolic, produced by predominantly culturally and predominantly economically oriented working-class families.

Society and social progress depend upon production of cultural as well as economic values. Without the production of low art (an infinite variety of collections) there would be no high art; without a small economy of massive scale (an endless diversity of local marketplaces) there would be no big economy. It was Alexis de Tocqueville who in *Democracy in America* (1835–40) formulated the law governing the relationship between quantity and quality: the more productive a democratic society is on a mass scale, culturally as well as economically, the greater the chance of excellence.

References

Bakhtin, M. M. 1968. *Rabelais and His World*. Cambridge: M.I.T. Press.

Beekenkamp, G. G. 1984. De plaats van het onderwijs in de recrutering van president-directeuren. In F. N. Stokman, ed., *Nederlandse elites in beeld: Recrutering, samenhang en verandering.* Van Loghum Slaterus: Deventer.

Bourdieu, Pierre. 1984 (1979). *Distinction.*Cambridge: Harvard University Press.

———. 1989. *La noblesse d'état: Grandes écoles et esprit de corps.* Paris: Minuit.

———. 1990. *In Other Words.* Stanford: Stanford University Press.

Bourdieu, Pierre, Luc Boltansky, Robert Castel, and Jean-Claude Chamboredon. 1965. *Un art moyen.* Paris: Minuit.

———. 1990. *Photography: A Middle-Brow Art* Cambridge: Polity Press.

Bourdieu, Pierre, and Jean-Claude Passeron. 1970. *La reproduction: Elements pour une theorie du systeme d'enseignemen.* Paris: Minuit.

———. 1977. *Reproduction in Education, Society and Culture.* Beverly Hills: Sage.

Bourdieu, Pierre, and Loic J. D. Wacquant. 1992. *Réponses.* Paris: Seuil.

Brubaker, Roger. 1985. "Rethinking Classical theory: The Sociological Vision of Pierre Bourdieu." *Theory and Society* 14: 745–75.

Burke, Peter. 1978. *Popular Culture in Early Modern Europe.* London: Temple Smith.

Clarke, John, Chas Critzer, and Richard Johnson, eds. 1979. *Working Class Culture. Studies in History and Theory.* London: Hutchinson.

Cookson, Peter W., and Caroline Hodges Persell. 1985. *Preparing for Power. America's Elite Boarding Schools.* New York: Basic.

De Witte, Hans. 1990. *Conformisme, radicalisme en machteloosheid.* Leuven: Hoger Instituut voor de Arbeid.

DiMaggio, Paul J. 1987. "Classification in Art." *American Sociological Review* 52: 440–55.

Fumaroli, Michel. 1992. *L'Etat culturel, essa sur la religion moderne.* Paris: Fallois.

Gans, Herbert J. 1985. "American Popular Culture and High Culture in a Changing Class Structure." *Prospects* 10: 17–37.

Ganzeboom, H. 1988. *Leefstijlen in Nederland.* Rijswijk: SCP.

Gartman, David. 1991. "Culture as Class Symbolization or Mass Reification? A Critique of Bourdieu's *Distinction." American Journal of Sociology* 97: 421–47.

Geertz, Clifford. 1983. *Local Knowledge.* New York: Basic Books.

Giroux, Henry A. 1983. *Theory and Resistance in Education.* London: Heinemann.

Goldthorpe, John, David Lockwood, Frank Bechhofer, and Jennifer Platt, eds. 1969. *The Affluent Worker and the Class Structure*. Cambridge: Cambridge University Press.

Gramsci, Antonio. 1971. *Selections from the Prison Notebooks*. New York: International Publishers.

Haarmans, Loes. 1992. *School-keuze, een kwestie van smaak. Een onderzoek naar kultureel versus economisch gerichte arbeidersscholen en hun publiek*. Utrecht: Vakgroep ETS.

Harmsen, Ger. 1961. *Blauwe en rode jeugd*. Assen: Van Gorcum.

Horkheimer, M., and T. Adorno. 1972. *Dialectic of Enlightenment*. New York: Herder and Herder.

Kalmijn, M., and R. Batenburg. 1986. "Reproductie van cultureel en economisch kapitaal op een traditioneel en een Montessori-lyceum." *Tijdschrift voor Onderwijsresearch* 11: 149–63.

Lamont, Michel, and Annette Lareau. 1988. "Cultural Capital: Allusions, Gaps and Glissandos in Recent Theoretical Developments." *Sociological Theory* 6: 153–68.

Lash, Scott. 1990. *Sociology of Postmodernism*. London: Routledge.

Levine, Lawrence W. 1988. *Highbrow Lowbrow. The Emergence of Cultural Hierarchy in America*. Cambridge: Harvard University Press.

Lukacs, G. 1923. *History and Class Consciousness*. London: Merlin.

MacLeod, Jay. 1987. *Ain't No Makin' It: Leveled Aspirations in a Low-Income Neighborhood*. Boulder: Westview Press.

Michielse, H. C. M. 1980. *Socialistische vorming*. Nijmegen: SUN.

Mukerji, Chandra, and Michael Schudson, eds. 1991. *Rethinking Popular Culture. Contemporary Perspectives in Cultural Studies*. Berkeley: University of California Press.

Peterson, Richard A. 1983. "Patterns of Cultural Choice: A Prolegomenon." *American Behavioral Scientist* 26: 422–38.

Rupp, Jan C. C. 1969. *Opvoeding tot Schoolweerbaarheid*. Groningen: Wolters-Noordhoff.

Rupp, Jan C. C., and Rob de Lange. 1989. "Social Order, Cultural Capital and Citizenship." *Sociological Review* 37: 658–705.

Rupp, Jan C. C., Marieke Walet, and Bibi van Wolput. 1990. "Cultureel versus economisch georienteerde basisscholen en hun publiek." *Sociologische Gids* 37: 333–50.

Thompson, E. P. 1966. *The Making of the English Working Class*. Harmondsworth, England: Penguin.

Tocqueville, Alexis de. 1990 [1835–40]. *Democracy in America*. New York: Vintage.

White, Harrison 1992. *A Structural Theory of Social Action*. Princeton: Princeton University Press.

Williams, Raymond. 1958. *Culture and Society, 1780–1950*. Hammondsworth, England: Penguin.

Willis, Paul E. 1977. *Learning to Labor*. Aldershot, England: Gower.

Zolberg, Vera. 1990. *Constructing a Sociology of the Arts*. Cambridge: Cambridge University Press.

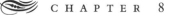

CHAPTER 8

Cannery Row: Class, Community, and the Social Construction of History

John Walton

D URING THE FIRST HALF OF THE TWENTIETH CENTURY, MONTEREY, California, became the most important fishing port in the United States, and the world's third largest, by tonnage of industrially processed fish.[1] Although several kinds of fish were both canned and "reduced" to fish oil and meal, the California sardine was emblematic of Monterey's Cannery Row. More than two dozen canneries and reduction plants lined Cannery Row in the peak years of the industry around 1940, each with its own brand name and colorful sardine label, which decorated cans, quarter-pound tins, pound ovals, packing boxes, and cannery buildings. The October to February sardine season experienced wide monthly and yearly fluctuations in volume of the catch, but at its zenith it employed three to four thousand people directly in fishing, canning,

The author gratefully acknowledges the assistance of the following persons, organizations, and institutions: Rosalie Ferrante and the Monterey Fishermen's Historical Association; Pat Hathaway, California Views; Michael Hemp, Cannery Row Company; Joseph Johnson and the Monterey Public Library; Susan Klusmire, Dorothea Sallee, and the Colton Hall Museum; Maryanne Teed, Monterey Peninsula College; Tim Thomas and the Monterey Bay Cultural History Project. The work is supported modestly but faithfully by Faculty Research grants, University of California–Davis. Valuable comments on an earlier draft were provided by Arnold Bauer, Fred Block, William Hagen, James O'Connor, and Tim Thomas.

1. Hull, England, and Stavanger, Norway, ranked ahead of Monterey in tonnage of processed (canned or reduced) fish. Estimates based on the value of the total product would lead to a different ranking (*Monterey Peninsula Herald*, 25 March 1938).

and reduction at a time when Monterey's total population numbered ten thousand.[2]

> The chief industry in Monterey since the turn of the century has been large-scale commercial fishing, canning, processing, and distribution of sardines. So dependent is Monterey upon the sardine for its livelihood that the industry's seasonal fluctuations now affect the local economy with the precision of a seismograph recording earthquake tremors. Merchants solemnly claim that they observe "a falling off of trade even during full moon periods and in rough weather when the boats do not go out" (*WPA Guide* 1941, 69).

The *WPA Guide* notes that "Monterey has never been a Yankee town" (67), an observation all the more true of the local fishing industry. From its beginnings at the hands of Portuguese whalers and Chinese marketers, commercial fishing was a multiethnic undertaking, dominated in the 1920s and 1930s by Sicilian boat owners and crews with minority participation of Japanese, Spanish, and North Americans—virtually all of them men.[3] Not so in the canneries, where women, children, people of motley national origins, and many an Okie migrant worked at specialized ethnic niches along the production line. Women, including many wives, sisters, and daughters of fishermen, packed sardine cans. Until their skills were automated, Asian and Spanish men and women were fish cutters. White males dominated skilled mechanical tasks such as tending boilers that cooked the canned fish and, until electrification, powered the line. One of the larger canneries boasted of its "all [female] white packers" and hardy Spanish warehousemen (*History of Portola* n.d.). Foremen, superintendents, and cannery owners were men of Anglo-European extraction, with the notable exception of several Sicilians who rose from fishing to cannery ownership and management.

Diverse in gender, nationality, language, and heritage, cannery workers and fishermen nevertheless formed a working-class community with its own emergent culture. Wedged together in ethnic slices along Monterey's waterfront, Sicilians, Chinese, Portuguese, Japanese, Spanish, and

2. The U.S. Census indicates the City of Monterey had a population of 9,141 in 1930 and 10,084 in 1940. If at peak season in November nearly 40 percent of the population was employed directly in the fishing and canning industry, and perhaps 30 percent as a seasonal average, a good many more enjoyed employment indirectly supported by the industry (e.g., rooming houses, restaurants and bars, equipment and repair businesses, the railroad, and trucking).

3. A few Asian women and at least one African-American male worked as commercial fishers.

Anglo families pursued socially segregated lives in full awareness of one another. On important occasions they came together in churches, labor unions, and community festivals. Cannery Row took shape during the First World War when business boomed and enough new plants were built side by side along the beach in New Monterey to form a row. In local parlance, the term "Cannery Row" dates from this period, but the name enjoyed no broader recognition until John Steinbeck's 1945 novel. Appearing almost at the close of the sardine era, the opening pages of *Cannery Row* momentarily looked back on the period of industrial movement and community sentiment.

> Cannery Row in Monterey in California is a poem, a stink, a grating noise, a quality of light, a tone, a habit, a nostalgia, a dream. . . . In the morning the sardine fleet has made a catch, the purse-seiners waddle heavily into the bay blowing their whistles. The deep-laden boats pull in against the coast where the canneries dip their tails into the bay. . . . Then cannery whistles scream all over the town men and women scramble into their clothes and come running down to the row to go to work. Then shining cars bring upper classes down: superintendents, accountants, owners who disappear into offices. Then from the town pour Wops and Chinamen and Polaks, men and women in trousers and rubber coats and oilcloth aprons. They come running to clean and pack and cook and can the fish. The whole street rumbles and groans and screams and rattles while the silver rivers of fish pour in out of the boats and the boats rise higher and higher in the water until they are empty. The canneries rumble and rattle and squeak until the last fish is cleaned and cut and cooked and canned and then the whistles scream again and the dripping, smelly, tired Wops and Chinamen and Polaks, men and women, straggle out and droop their ways up the hill into town and Cannery Row becomes itself again—quiet and magical (Steinbeck 1945, 1–2).

Here, however, any resemblance between Steinbeck's *Cannery Row* and the working-class community on Monterey Bay ends. For artistic purposes, Steinbeck designed his story to work at several thematic "levels" (Steinbeck and Wallsten 1975, 273), expressed in friendship and society among a humble lot of bums, prostitutes, Chinese, and an exemplary marine biologist who lived along the eponymous street. Although Steinbeck's characters were based on real persons, his quixotic tale makes no mentioned of the industrial surround—Sicilian fishermen, cannery

women, and their labor unions, meeting halls, churches, workdays, entertainments, virtues, or iniquities—which, of course, is the novelist's privilege. No one on Steinbeck's Cannery Row has a regular job, save perhaps
the Chinese storekeeper whose labors are ridiculed. Cannery Row is a
tumbledown redoubt of lovable rascals, far from the world of industrial
production and working-class family reproduction. Social history must
not confuse these two different stories. As we shall see, however, cultural history profitably may explore how and why the two stories have
been confounded in popular memory.

Memory and Social Class

Social class was one of the central organizing principles of society on
Cannery Row, a force that interacted with gender, race, and ethnicity but
also one that on many occasions rose above other determinants of group
formation and decisively shaped collective experience. So, at least, is the
interpretive claim of this chapter and the evidentiary purpose of much
that follows.

A perennial debate among social scientists concerns the importance
of social class. Does class matter? Do social classes exist in America? Have
the confining class positions of industrial society dissolved in a socially
mobile, postindustrial world where status groups, lifestyles, and concerns
of personal identity have become the central features of experience? Such
questions have shaped the pitched battles that typically pit classical,
including Marxist, European theorists and social historians against progressive North American social scientists who study social mobility, race,
gender, and ethnicity. Over the past forty years, the debate has developed
along three fronts. First, class theorists have acknowledged fundamental
historical changes in the socioeconomic order requiring, as Marx himself urged, a reformulation of class categories, which in their modern
form continue to shape group identities, inequalities, and actions (Mills
1951; Dahrendorf 1959; Giddens 1973; Wright 1985). Second, social historians have argued that class is not a "structure" or societal accounting
scheme but a conscious experience of group life which assumes greater
or lesser coherence to the extent that people recognize themselves as subjects of a common socioeconomic fate, organize to change it, and develop
a culture in the process (Thompson 1963; Sewell 1980; Calhoun 1982;

Jones 1983; Reddy 1987). Third, other social scientists have stressed the importance of alternative bases of group formation in race, gender, nationality, religion, ethnicity, or "status groups," which generally coexist with class but often assume greater importance as determinants of collective experience (Gans 1962; Bendix 1974; Wilson 1978; Tilly and Scott 1978; Baron 1991). Despite these conceptual refinements and empirical advances in the theory of social classes, the "death of class debate" (Waters 1994) rages on, with some observers insisting that social classes have no palpable presence or consequential effect in postindustrial society (Bell 1973; Clark and Lipset 1991).

I shall argue, in support of modern class theorists, that social class usually matters, sometimes decisively, and routinely in combination with status groups. *Social class* refers to the condition in which a number of people share common life chances insofar as those are determined by their power to attain goods, services, and income in the market place—specifically in labor, credit, and commodity markets. Class requires that people recognize this common situation and develop an awareness of themselves as a collectivity (Weber 1946; Giddens 1973). I subscribe to E. P. Thompson's (1963, 9–10) proposition that class is "an historical phenomenon, unifying a number of disparate and seemingly unconnected events both in the raw material of experience and in consciousness . . . something which in fact happens (and can be shown to have happened) in human relationships . . . [and] class-consciousness is the way these experiences are handled in cultural terms: embodied in traditions, value-systems, ideas, and institutional forms." As Thompson observes about a common misunderstanding of class experience, because the crude notion of class attributed to Marx may be faulted with ease, *"it is denied that class has happened at all."* Pursuing this point, I hope to plant something new in the well-plowed field of class analysis. I want to demonstrate that social class may be *written out* of history, deleted from collective memory in the social construction of history as a process that obeys its own dictates somewhat independent of actual events. Class is denied when the historical record and collective memory, for whatever reasons, minimize the extent to which class has "happened" as an experience and agent of social life.

Much has been written about collective memory and the growing realization that history is less a single factual narrative than a socially constructed ensemble of multiple and competing renditions of the past (Berger and Luckmann 1966; Cohen 1994; Kuhn 1962; Lowenthal 1985;

Trouillot 1995). Although the existence of an alternative "revisionist history" has long been recognized, only recently have analysts attempted to examine the social construction of history as an empirical phenomenon in its own right. As a result, we now have a more sophisticated appreciation of how seemingly primordial traditions actually may be recent "inventions" designed to legitimize the state, how museums may sanitize the national past, festivals romanticize a bygone era, and history texts ignore women, minorities, and the daily life of the common person.

Much less attention has been devoted to explaining why history is socially constructed and how different manifestations of the process stem from different circumstances. Two schools of thought may be identified on this question, although the differences between these complementary analyses should not be overemphasized. One position, deriving from the works of Antonio Gramsci (1971) and elaborated by critical theory and British cultural studies, stresses the purposes of *cultural hegemony* served by conventional history. Powerful interests in bourgeois society and the state control the means of intellectual production and symbolic reproduction just as firmly and for the same ends as they control the means of material production (Horkheimer and Adorno 1972; Samuel 1981; Johnson et al. 1982). In contrast to blunt ideological domination, the Gramscian notion of hegemony suggests a negotiated consensus about political and cultural leadership in which oppositional views are heard, absorbed, and rearticluated in the overarching interests of the hegemonic group (Williams 1977; Turner 1990; Maddox 1993). At bottom, however, the theory of cultural hegemony gets its bite from the presumed power of dominant groups to construct history their own way despite resistance (Trouillot 1995). The second position derived from Emile Durkheim and his student Maurice Halbwachs (1980) stresses *social memory*, the distinctive ways in which differently situated groups understand and commemorate their own past (Connerton 1980; Fentress and Wickham 1992). Memory is primarily a social rather than an individual phenomenon, and history is far from consensual but understood in very different ways by circumstantially rooted groups, classes, communities, and nations. In monuments and rituals, groups commemorate their past just as they recreate it under present conditions in ways that may repress or romanticize memory (Wagner-Pacifici and Schwartz 1991; Zerubavel 1995). The two theories differ more in emphasis than in any strictly opposed claims. Each captures an important aspect of the social construction of history, although I shall argue in the end that neither fully explains the process as it changes over time.

The story that follows endeavors, first, to demonstrate the central role of social classes in Monterey history and society and, second, to provide a theoretically informed account of how local history and collective memory have dealt with that experience.

Class and Community in Monterey

Monterey's industrial era began at the turn of the century and lasted into the 1950s, when the sardines precipitously vanished. Commercial fishing on the bay dated from the mid-nineteenth century, and by 1896, when the first cannery was attempted, small communities of Chinese, Portuguese, Japanese, and Genoese Italians made a living at market fishing and supplying San Francisco packers. The initial canneries, including one founded by Frank Booth, began packing salmon but encountered financial difficulties made worse by the reluctance of Monterey fishers to sell their catch to local upstarts rather than their San Francisco patrons. Booth, who ran a successful salmon cannery at Black Diamond (later Pittsburg) in the Sacramento River delta, returned in 1902, purchased a struggling plant next to Fisherman's Wharf, and began experimenting with the bay's overabundant sardines. Booth succeeded, owing to his own perseverance and the critical contributions of two immigrant men. Knut Hovden was a Norwegian fisheries expert and engineer who designed a modern assembly line operation and much of the machinery for mass production of tinned sardines. Pietro Ferrante was a Sicilian fisherman whose early success on the Sacramento delta led to conflicts with bay area Genoese and to his interest in relocating in Monterey, where Booth needed a loyal fleet. Ferrante and his brother-in-law, Orazio Enea, arrived in 1905, quickly attracted members of their extended families from a group of fishing villages in the immediate vicinity of Palermo, and steadily assumed control of the Monterey fleet by displacing Genoese and Asian competitors.

With a growing labor monopsony of Sicilian fishermen, mechanized production facilities, a ready cannery labor force including the families of fishermen and displaced ethnic fishers, and bountiful sardine runs, Booth's cannery led Monterey into the industrial age. World War I created brisk demand for the once specialized sardine market and led to an actual row of eight canneries and reduction plants along the beach in New Monterey about a mile from Booth's original Fisherman's Wharf site (see Map 8.1 below). Hovden left Booth's employ in 1916 and built a large modern plant at the far end of a street soon christened Cannery Row. The industry expanded in the 1920s as larger boats and nets were introduced and an increasing proportion of the catch was reduced to fish oil, meal, and fertilizer, where profits were far greater. Early warnings of depletion by overfishing from California's Fish and Game Division met disbelief and resistance in Monterey. Legislative limitations on the profligate reduction process, which set a quota or ratio on the volume of canned to reduced product, were persistently attacked: in the courts as unconstitutional, in political arenas as a restraint of free enterprise, and in public as a hardship on workers who needed jobs during the economic depressions of the period. Indeed, ecological jeremiads of "the fish and game" seemed to be refuted by periodic upsurges in the catch after several years of decline. But in the long run the state's biologists were right (Rosenberg 1961; Mangelsdorf 1986; McEvoy 1986).

Whether a result of overfishing, changes in ocean tides and temperatures, long-term species life cycles, or some combination of all, the annual sardine catch—often in excess of two hundred thousand tons during the boom years of the 1930s—had fallen to two thousand tons by 1960. The industry collapsed during the 1950s with exiguous yields, massive plant closings, and property sales to real estate and salvage firms. Industrial, working-class, ethnic Cannery Row came to an end; and Steinbeck's Cannery Row, with its property development, service industry, and tourism, eclipsed the original. Old Cannery Row had no more virtue or character than new Cannery Row, but they are very different historical constructions. Key to the difference is how a multiethnic community of men and women organized and experienced life in class ways—how class happened, and how that story took shape in collective memory.

Labor

The characteristic feature of Monterey's fish industry is a level of social complexity that defies conventional labor/management, worker/owner dichotomies. In the first instance, the industry consisted of four groups, each with its own organization[1] : cannery owners, cannery workers, fishermen who owned boats, and fishermen who comprised the boat crews. Hierarchies of skill and occupational prestige governed each of the four sectors, from prosperous cannery owners (including a few absentee corporations) to migratory cannery workers. Individuals and firms crossed sectoral lines. Some boats were owned by several fishermen, others by families (brothers, sons, and nephews) who constituted the crew, and yet others by crew-member collectives. Canneries owned some of the boats and leased them to fishermen, who thus became *de facto* cannery workers. Similarly, some boat owners compromised their independence by contracting regularly to sell fish to a given cannery. In one case, fishermen owned a cannery, the San Carlos Cannery, founded in 1926 as a cooperative for Sicilian boat owners. Finally, cannery workers were often former fishers or members of fishing families.

Who were these workers? No simple answer suffices here either. The labor force in fishing had a profile very different from that of cannery workers, and both changed over time. The year 1920 provides a convenient baseline for examining the labor force. The industry had just stabilized after its explosive growth during World War I, but it had not yet taken off—technological advances and generous reduction permits came only in the 1930s. Moreover, 1920 is the year of the most recent manuscript census open to public view at this writing.

In the 1920 census, 357 people (all men) identified themselves as fishermen, and among them only a very small number said that they were also boat owners (see Table 8.1).[5] The number of boat owners or part-owners may be underestimated because that information was volunteered to census takers who may not have probed the simple response "fisherman." Half

---

4. Boat owners, who were usually fishermen, were the first to organize in 1914, followed by cannery owners in 1918, crew fishermen in 1925, and cannery workers in 1937. Although documentation is scant, this pattern is supported by the early creation of a Japanese Fishermen's Association, which was noted in 1909 (*Monterey Daily Cypress*, 11 August 1909).

5. The census was based on a household survey and was taken in early January, after the peak months of the sardine season in the fall. Both factors privilege local residents and undercount seasonal-migrant boat owners, crews, and cannery workers. Another study estimated that there were 1900 cannery workers in 1924 and, in the two seasons of 1920 and 1922, an average of "about 260 fishermen employed in supplying the canneries. In addition 20 to 40 men were fishing sardines for other markets" (Scofield 1929, 17). These numbers are not inconsistent with the manuscript census, assuming that (a) the cannery worker count, four years later, refers to peak season and (b) the number of fishermen is an underestimation based only on the sardine fleet. Some Japanese fishermen, for example, specialized in abalone.

TABLE 8.1 Monterey fisherman, 1920

	Number	Percent
Position		
Owner	9	2
Captain	3	1
Fisherman	345	97
Total	357	100
National origin		
Italy	172	49
Japan	79	23
Spain	40	12
United States	37	11
Portugal	9	2
Other (UK, Yugoslavia)	11	3
Total	348	100
Citizenship		
United States	39	11
Naturalized	19	6
Alien	285	83
Total	343	100
Immigration year		
(naturalized & alien)		
1915–19	26	9
1910–14	77	26
1905–09	69	24
1900–04	83	28
Before 1900	39	13
Total	294	100
English speaking		
Yes	203	58
No	147	42
Total	350	100

Compiled by the author from the 1920 Federal Manuscript Census. Total numbers in each panel vary due to incomplete information, illegible entries, or restricted categories.

the fishermen are Italian (Sicilian), but in 1920 there are still significant numbers of Japanese and Spanish. Ethnic concentration is even greater if one includes a number of second-generation immigrants: American-born young men who fish with their fathers and uncles. The fact that this is largely an immigrant labor force is highlighted by the data on citizenship. Few are citizens by U.S. birth and fewer yet have become naturalized; fully 83 percent are resident aliens. Some may not have lived in the country long enough to qualify for citizenship, but data on year of immigration indicate that in fact 65 percent have resided in the United States for ten years or more. This is consistent with oral histories of families which indicate that most immigrants did not bother to become citizens. Cultural insularity was especially characteristic of fishermen: 42 percent did not speak English, even after a significant length of residence. In summary, the fishermen are mainly Sicilian, Japanese, and Spanish workers (crew) who, although they immigrated to the United States before World War I, continue to form close-knit family and ethnic groups.

Cannery workers are a larger and more diverse lot (Table 8.2). Thirty percent are women, a number that increases in canneries as opposed to reduction plants. Although nearly half of all workers describe themselves as general "laborers," many others performed specialized tasks on the production line. Canneries had a wage-and-status hierarchy running from casual labor to assembly line work and to specialized equipment operation (Friday 1994). In 1920, before machines eliminated their jobs, fish cutters were a skilled group of men and women, heavily Asian (Chinese and Japanese) and Spanish. Packers were exclusively women, who placed the filleted fish in tins which were then sealed and steam cooked in a boiler or "retort" (Fig. 8.1). Beyond a handful of office workers and laborers, most women were either cutters or packers. White men dominated the high-status jobs (engineer, mechanic, cook/fryer) and year-round employment (maintenance, warehouseman), although they were also the largest contingent among the ethnically varied laborers. In sharp contrast to fishermen, the majority of cannery workers are U.S.-born citizens. Although many were aliens, shoreside workers were more enculturated (English speaking) and longer resident than fishermen. During the sardine season, migratory workers who followed the summer fruit canning circuit would move into rooming houses and rental shacks on the waterfront, remaining as long as the canneries provided steady work.

TABLE 8.2 Monterey cannery workers, 1920

	Number	Percent
Position		
Owner, manager, foreman	30	4
Clerical	14	2
Engineer/inspector	14	2
Mechanic/craftsman	36	5
Cutter	136	20
Packer	102	15
Fryer	19	3
Labeler	13	2
Warehouse/maintenance	13	2
Laborer	308	45
Total	685	100
Gender		
Male	494	70
Female	211	30
Total	705	100
National Origin		
United States	351	52
China	94	14
Japan	57	9
Spain	66	10
Italy	28	4
Mexico	13	2
United Kingdom and Canada	27	4
Other (Port., Aus./Yug., Swe., Ger., Den.)	33	5
Total	677	100
Immigration year (naturalized & alien)		
1915–19	29	12
1910–14	41	18
1905–09	49	21
1900–04	26	11
Before 1900	88	38
Total	233	100
English speaking		
Yes	544	81
No	124	19
Total	668	100

Compiled by the author from the 1920 Federal Manuscript Census. Total numbers in each panel vary due to incomplete information, illegible entries, or restricted categories.

Photographic evidence supports this portrait. A typical group of cannery workers posed outside the Bayside Fish Company in 1919. Dressed specially for the occasion, the group of eighteen women and twenty-eight men includes nine Asians, perhaps one African American, and no doubt a number of Italian and Spanish descent. Most of the women are white, some quite young. Two appear affectionate—they are married, perhaps, or anticipating its pleasures. 'The average worker is one of a four member family in which both parents work as they can and sometimes one of the children if old enough" (*Monterey Peninsula Herald*, 23 February 1940).

The labor force experienced a number of changes over the next several decades. Most important, it increased fourfold to embrace as many as four thousand workers in record seasons like 1941–42. Automation of ethnic specializations such as fish cutting lessened diversity, a trend that paralleled the industry's growing dependence on the reduction of fish oil and meal, which mainly relied on male laborers. Japanese fishermen, whose numbers remained constant, became a proportionately smaller segment of the expanding fleet, falling from 23 to 6 percent in their last season (1940–41) before wartime internment. Sicilians came to dominate the fleet (86 percent in 1930), but they were increasingly second-generation Monterey men, who combined with Anglos from various home ports to produce a majority of U.S.-born fishermen by 1940 (*Fish Bulletin* 1946).

Sardine fishing in Monterey underwent a series of changes in its fifty-year history, but none was more decisive than the shift from the Italian *lampara* launch and net to the larger and more efficient purse seiners. Sicilians at the turn of the century revolutionized sardine fishing in California with the lampara "outfit" (a launch with a lighter in tow for the catch) and large nets (1200 feet long by 200 feet deep) which encircled schools of fish. The early lampara boats were small at 20 feet in length and were manually operated by three fishermen—but in the 1930s they grew to 45 feet, were equipped with gasoline engines, had a capacity of 40 to 50 tons, and carried a crew of 11 to 14. In 1926, cannery owners introduced purse seiners from southern California in an effort to avoid local labor demands and land more fish in menacing competition with offshore reduction ships (which were eventually outlawed). Seiners of the late 1920s ran 55 to 85 feet in length, carried 80 to 100 tons, used diesel engines (allowing week-long trips over a much wider area), were safer and more stable in rough seas and, with their power winches for hauling the nets, required a crew of only 7 to 9 men (Scofield 1929; Phillips 1930;

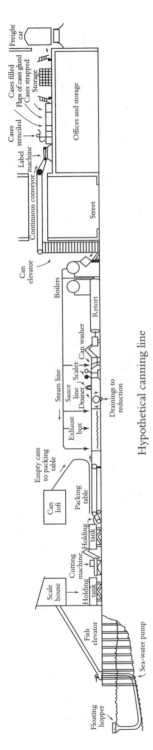

Hypothetical canning line

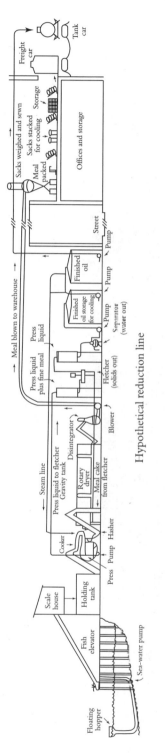

FIGURE 8.1 The production processes in canning and reduction differed somewhat. These two "hypothetical" or typical sketches of the production lines show the steps from intake of fish from boats to warehouse storage of cans or containers of fish oil and sacks of fish meal. Production lines are connected to the warehouses by elevators or tramways that pass above the street. (Drawings from the *Monterey Peninsula Herald*.)

Cannery workers of the Bayside Fish Company, 1919. Dressed up for the occasion, the group demonstrates ethnic and gender diversity in the workforce. The group of eighteen women and twenty-eight men includes nine Asians, one African American, and several individuals of Italian and Spanish descent, many quite young. Bayside Fish Company was owned by a group of Asian investors. Photo courtesy of Pat Hathaway, California Views.

Rosenberg 1961). By 1930, purse seiners comprised one-third of the fleet; before long they took over completely, with even larger boats that averaged 80 to 100 feet and 150 tons by 1940 (*Monterey Peninsula Herald*, 28 February 1941).

Initially, local fishermen opposed the new boats, which required a much larger capital investment, reduced labor demand, and worried those already alert to the prospects of depletion (Rosenberg 1961, 141). But as reduction quotas were eased during the depression, the more efficient seiners rewarded those who borrowed money to purchase or lease larger boats.[6] Purse seiners clearly had their virtues. Sardine fishing took place on moonless nights when schools of fish revealed themselves by a luminescent glow on the water. Fish hunting on dark, cold, and treacherous seas was not only safer and more comfortable aboard the hefty seiners, but fewer hands and larger yields meant greater profits divided among the crew. In addition to many uneventful hours and days spent looking for the glowing schools, the hardest work in fishing involves rapidly setting and hauling the nets. Winches and motorized turntables that played out the enormous nets improved significantly on the lampara method, in which the nets were set by hand from a lighter rowed around the swarming fish. Riding deep in the water when the catch was good, the seiners were less likely to capsize in rough seas on the way home.

Cannery work followed the rhythms of the sardine catch. During full moons, storms, poor runs, and the five spring and summer months there was little work.[7] But when the boats came in loaded, whether in the middle of the night or midday, the whistles that distinguished each plant sounded across waterfront neighborhoods summoning workers immediately to the production line. Former workers recall the "clomp-clomp" of women walking down the gentle hills to the New Monterey shoreline in their (self-provided) rubber boots, aprons, and hair nets. The line ran until every fish was canned or reduced and twelve- to fifteen-hour days were not uncommon when the catch was good. The work was repetitive. Cutters and packers who stood in one place for the entire shift suffered from the cold and the damp. Yet they also found the irregular

6. Some others retained the older boats but replaced the lampara net with a larger ring net that operated in a fashion similar to the purse seine, which had finer mesh and closed at the bottom like a drawstring purse.
7. Small amounts of squid, albacore and tuna were packed in the off-season. In the early years the season lasted ten months, but it was later limited to between August and February, roughly.

tempo and changing fortune an exciting atmosphere. Esther Compoy recalls, "I was awful shy, but in the canneries it was one big family. . . . It was exciting" (McKibben 1991, 16). On the shop floor women developed a work culture which offered identity and collective solutions to daily problems (Ruiz 1987). Women welcomed the independence that came with an income, and they experienced a spirit of camaraderie, particularly when the union was organized (Monterey Fishermen's Historical Association 1995). Mavis Lautaret was working in the office at Sea Pride Cannery when she discovered that "the take-home pay of the cutters and canners was quadruple what I earned"; so she asked for a tryout on the cutting line. A few nights later she was called to the plant at 1 A.M.—the night's catch was coming in.

> The workers all knew me, but I cannot say I received a warm welcome. What was an office worker doing dressed in their mode? Most couldn't (or wouldn't) speak English in those days, and I was getting the message—without understanding what they said—that I was trespassing on their territory. . . . the foreman placed me in back of a rapidly moving conveyor belt, which had many deep slots for the fish. Sardines were pouring out from the hopper onto a platform by the conveyor so fast that they were spilling all over the floor. . . . And cold? It was freezing! I never knew before why the workers wore boots, now I did. The floor was almost knee-high with excess icy ocean water that came in along with the sardines. . . . I started slapping the fish in the right way so they could be canned in a relatively gutless fashion. I slapped sardines for hours, I thought, and my back was breaking and I was freezing. I looked at the clock and only 20 minutes had passed. I slapped, slapped, and slapped pilchards, looked up again and five minutes had slipped by. . . . When the sardines finally stopped coming and the whistles blew again, it was 7:15 A.M. I could barely walk. My fingers were stiff and blue, my back was breaking, my head was splitting, and I was fishy from my hair to the toes of my boots. Dragging myself outside, a funny thing happened. All the workers (who now miraculously spoke English) crowded around me and some pounded me on the back and we all sat down on the curb and drank coffee from a thermos someone had brought. . . . I had hung in and I had become "one of the group" (Lautaret 1990, 15).

Like most things on Cannery Row, wages were varied and complex. Fishermen were paid on the basis of shares in the catch. Boats had a fixed number of shares, often twelve, into which the receipts of the catch were divided after expenses such as gas, oil, and food were deducted. A boat owner-captain would receive, say, four shares (more or less depending on the period and how much of the operating expenses he assumed), the cook and each of the fishing crew one share (a cook who also fished got two). A fisherman who captained a cannery-owned boat and also fished might receive one and one-half shares. Apprentices less than sixteen years old earned half shares. The general principle was varied in application. The larger purse seiners, for example, calculated on the basis of nineteen shares, with seven going to the boat. A fisherman's seasonal income could vary from nothing up to several thousand dollars,[8] and wages rose over the years. Data for selected years indicate that fishermen were the local labor aristocracy. In the 1930s, $1,000–2,000 was typical. With wartime prices in effect, the average for 1942 was $3,100. In a bad year like 1947, the range was $100–3,000 and the mean $800. Fortunes reversed in 1948 with a range of $1,500–4,600 and an average of $3,600. In the best years, crews on the top boats earned $4,000–5,000, although that was rare and ephemeral (*Monterey Peninsula Herald*, 27 February 1942, 7 March 1947, 2 April 1948).

Cannery workers were paid in piece-rate and hourly wages. Piece rates were computed for cutters by the bucket of fish and packers by the dozen tins. Experienced hands made what they considered good money as long as the line was running and the job secure—often it was not. Most jobs lacked such an obvious metric and received hourly wages. Wages of men and women differed, but not by much. A survey conducted by the Women's Bureau of the U.S. Department of Labor in 1939 found hourly rates of 63¢ and 58¢ for men and women respectively (Sutherland 1941). In 1942, wartime restraint held rates to 70¢ and 65¢ respectively. By 1948 the unions had achieved a substantial increase: $1.21 for women, $1.28 men, and $1.36 in the reduction plants employing men (*Monterey Peninsula Herald*, 2 April 1948).

The key to gender differences and seasonal income generally lay in the number of hours worked, however. The 1939 study showed that two-thirds of the women worked less than forty hours per week but only 41 per cent of the men did so, resulting in a weekly pay difference of $20.55

---

8. Some fished in Alaska during the off season, whereas others took shoreside jobs or just maintained their boats and equipment. Their earnings from sardine fishing comprised a big chunk of their annual income.

for women and $30.85 for men.[9] This was the result, once again, of the relative concentration of women on the production line and men in full-time jobs such as maintenance and warehousing. Those who managed to put in a sixteen- to twenty-week season were doing well, and within that group men earned $260 but women only $181. Most were employed for twelve weeks or less, and the average seasonal income for all workers, short and long term, was $189 for men and $71 for women. Seasonal incomes less than a couple of hundred dollars dramatically demonstrate the humble lot of cannery workers, particularly those men and women who headed households.

Community

Monterey working families experienced class as poignantly in their communities as on the job. Social class is not simply an occupational phenomenon but also a way of being and acting, shaped by institutions ranging from the local neighborhood to the state (Dawley 1976; Katznelson 1981; Harvey 1985). Added complexity is introduced by the fact that Monterey's working-class communities were simultaneously organized along ethnic lines—national origin, culture, associated lifestyles, and an emergent sense of group identity that stemmed from being ethnic minorities in America (Yancey et al. 1976). They were an alloyed compound of working-class and ethnic communities. In real societies, class does not operate alone in shaping experience, although I shall argue below that on some occasions people from segmented ethnic groups united in overarching class awareness and action.

Well defined ethnic neighborhoods ringed Cannery Row and the harbor. The social order was reproduced spatially in ways that affected group life and interaction. The *WPA Guide* (1941, 67) observes,

> the medley of nationalities, each confined to its own neighborhood, includes Greeks and Italians, Chinese and Japanese, Spanish and Portuguese and Mexicans. Even more isolated are Monterey's few Negroes and Filipinos. In the town's various foreign quarters English is the language least heard. Home of the Italians is Oak Grove,

9. Note that 1939 was a fair year in terms of the sardine catch, and the recently established cannery workers union was in full operation.

between El Estero and Del Monte; of the Chinese in downtown
Old Monterey and behind Cannery Row; of the Spanish, Mexi-
cans, and Portuguese, New Monterey.

There were status differences between neighborhoods. Beginning
with Pietro Ferrante, Sicilian fishing families concentrated on the
promontory across from Booth's cannery and the boat harbor. In time,
a number of captains and boat owners built view-lot homes on
"Spaghetti [some say Garlic] Hill." On the flat between downtown and
the elegant Del Monte Hotel, Oak Grove housed diverse working-class
folk including Italians, Anglos, and at least one Black family. Between Oak
Grove and downtown were distinct Chinese and Japanese "towns."

As the canneries were established along the beach at New Monterey,
an intricate residential and social pattern developed. Sicilian fishermen
and cannery workers were of lower status than their "in town" relatives.
The wives and daughters of boat owners and captains did not work in
canneries. Hispanic families were common in New Monterey, and a small
Japanese neighborhood developed near the dividing line with Pacific
Grove. Another Chinatown existed right in the middle of Cannery Row.
Recently arrived from China, Won Yee settled in New Monterey around
1918 and built the well known Wing Chong ("glorious and successful")
store and a squid export business.[10] "Wing Chong was a general store
geared to serving the cannery workers living and working nearby; Won
Yee stocked not only food but also the equipment the cannery workers
needed—gloves, rubber boots, and fishing tackle" (Lydon 1985, 381).

Monterey's ethnic communities were populated with urban villagers.
The Sicilians came from close-knit kinship networks based in four villages
near Palermo. Like the Genoese community at San Francisco's North
Beach, local Italians were highly provincial. Dino Cinel (1982, 197) observes
that these communities were governed not only by generalized notions of
nationalism and regionalism but by a fine-grained *campanilismo*—"the sense
of loyalty and attachment to the traditions of one's commune (literally to
the local bell tower) rather than to the entire region." Cultural solidarity was all the more intense among fishermen who followed their traditional calling according to the old ways, worked and socialized mainly

10. Local legend maintains that Won Yee grew rich and loaned money to Knut Hovden during periodic crises in the cannery business. Steinbeck's character Lee Chong is based on Won
Yee, but Lee Chong is something of a simpleton without Won Yee's financial accomplishments.

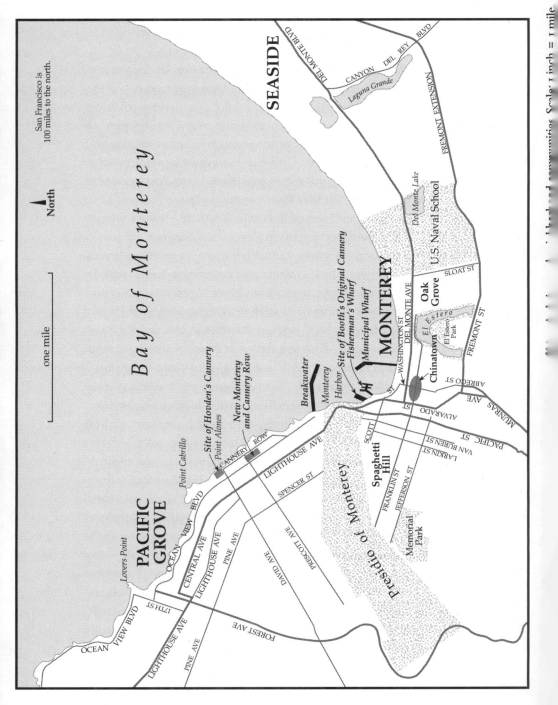

San Francisco is
100 miles to the north.

North

Bay of Monterey

one mile

SEASIDE

DEL MONTE BLVD

CANYON DEL REY BLVD

Laguna Grande

FREMONT EXTENSION

Del Monte Lake

U.S. Naval School

SLOAT ST

Oak
Grove

El Estero
Park

El Estero

FREMONT ST

Chinatown

ABREGO ST

MUNRAS AVE

DEL MONTE AVE

WASHINGTON ST

MONTEREY

Municipal Wharf

Fisherman's Wharf

Site of Booth's Original Cannery

Harbor

ALVARADO ST

PACIFIC ST

VAN BUREN ST

LARKIN ST

Monterey

Breakwater

Monterey

ST

SCOTT

FRANKLIN ST

JEFFERSON ST

Spaghetti
Hill

Memorial
Park

Presidio of Monterey

Site of Hovden's Cannery
Point Alones

New Monterey
and Cannery Row

Point Cabrillo

CANNERY ROW

LIGHTHOUSE AVE

OCEAN VIEW BLVD

SPENCER ST

PRESCOTT AVE

DAVID AVE

PINE AVE

LIGHTHOUSE AVE

CENTRAL AVE

PACIFIC
GROVE

Lovers Point

OCEAN VIEW BLVD

17TH ST

LIGHTHOUSE AVE

PINE AVE

FOREST AVE

OCEAN

with one another in the native tongue, married women from kindred village families, and brought up their sons in the trade. "Fishermen proved that . . . a group could isolate itself almost totally from the larger society, recreating patterns of economic and social organization almost entirely from the Old World" (Cinel 1982, 221). Supporting evidence for this pattern comes from local women who presided over a strong family-centered tradition yet traveled in wider circles of the town and canneries, leading to their greater proficiency in English. Peter Cutino describes the Sicilian neighborhood in the 1940s.

> Life on Garlic Hill was rather structured. During the day, the men slept to prepare themselves for the night fishing or when awake sewed nets. . . . For many years some of the Old World's ways remained with the residents of Garlic Hill. A good example is the roving vendors who plied their trade through the neighborhoods of Monterey until the late 1950s. In the evenings, if the men were out fishing, the family would sit around the upright, most-up-to-date radio console invented, listening to the "news." Over the short wave band, the boats would broadcast their positions, the fish they were catching, when they expected to unload, and when they would be home. A good catch meant the proverbial "bread on the table." [My] mother [was] the emotional "fire" in our family . . . because Dad spoke practically no English, she carried the load of disciplining the children. (Cutino 1995, 100)

Asians maintained their own cultural enclaves for different reasons. Nativism raged in California dating from the nineteenth century, when Chinese were imported for mining and railroad labor (Saxton 1971). In 1906 residents of early Chinese fishing villages along the Monterey coast were evicted, perhaps burned out, and forced from commercial fishing. Anti-Japanese sentiment in the 1920s threatened their property and right to hold fishing licenses. In self-defense and cultural solidarity, the Chinese organized against opposition to resettle on Cannery Row, aligned with the San Francisco–based Chinese Consolidated Benevolent Association (or Six Companies), and contributed to a new Chinese American Citizens Alliance (Lydon 1985). Somewhat later the Japanese Association organized its constituents, built a meeting hall downtown in 1925, and took public positions in labor disputes (Yamada 1995).

In other arenas, associational life mitigated ethnic separation. A Spanish Hall existed in New Monterey, but its patrons joined Italians,

Portuguese, and others in a lively round of Catholic Church activities. The local trade union movement grew from 1920 to 1950, uniting classes of workers from all ethnic groups.

Beyond work and family, Monterey enjoyed its public life and entertainments. The fishing season began in the fall with the blessing of the fleet during the Santa Rosalia festival, which honored Palermo's patron saint of fishermen and attracted the entire town to a waterfront parade, a flotilla of decorated boats, and a picnic. Later years saw the development of a season's-end festival which, in 1940, announced a "gargantuan banquet to feed 4,000 people [with] music, games, and dancing . . . a celebration [which] promises to surpass any of the historic old world carnivals in color, excitement, and lusty rejoicing" (*Monterey Peninsula Herald*, 23 February 1940). Indeed, no less a chronicler, not to say a lusty rejoicer, than John Steinbeck (1941, 24–25) testifies that the extravagant promise was met.

> At the end of the sardine season, canneries and boat owners provide a celebration. There is a huge barbecue on the end of the pier with free beef and beer and salad for all comers. The sardine fleet is decorated with streamers and bunting and serpentine, and the boat with the biggest season catch is queen of a strange nautical parade of boats; and every boat is an open house, receiving friends of owners and of crew. Wine flows beautifully, and the parade of boats that starts with dignity and precision sometimes ends in turmoil. . . . With five thousand other people we crowded on the pier and ate great chunks of meat and drank beer and heard speeches. It was the biggest barbecue the sardine men had ever given . . . the speeches rose to a crescendo of patriotism and good feeling beyond anything Monterey had ever heard.

Class, State, and Collective Action

With four parties to any action affecting the enterprise of fishing and canning, potential conflicts and alliances were already plentiful before the state became increasingly involved in efforts to regulate the industry. Boat owners struck the canneries almost annually over the price of fish and closed-shop demands. Although heterogeneous cannery workers were hardest to organize, the effort succeeded in 1937 after a long struggle. Occasionally, crew fishermen struck their fellow ethnic boat owners and

demonstrated solidarity with cannery workers. As the state endeavored
to conserve sardines through limits on reduction, fishermen and cannery
owners joined forces with civic boosters and agribusiness to bring political pressure on the legislature. Yet even here there were divisions. A few
farsighted canners (including the pioneer Booth) and fishermen believed
the warnings about depletion issued by Fish and Game scientists and
argued with professional pride that their business was to provide food for
human consumption, not fertilizer.

In 1915, the new Monterey Fishermen's Association, in cooperation
with an older union of Japanese fishermen, refused to fish for salmon until
Booth increased the cannery price from three to four cents per pound.
Then a 1917 price dispute divided the fishermen: Japanese boats continued delivering to Booth while Sicilians repudiated their price contract—
citing wartime inflation—and won some satisfaction in a court settlement.
With nine canneries operating by 1918, owners had reason to form the
Monterey Bay Canners Association, although competition and personal
rivalries militated against industry solidarity. A postwar cycle of national
(and international) labor insurgency boosted local fishermen into an ethnically integrated, industry-specific Sardine Fishermen's Association,
which struck the canners unsuccessfully in 1919 and 1920 for fifteen dollars a ton and exclusive (closed shop) contracts (Rosenberg 1961).

More dramatic was the 1920 fish cutters strike, led by the more Amer-
icanized Japanese within this ethnically diverse specialization (*Monterey
Daily Cypress*, 26 July 1920). Workers sought a closed shop, uniform conditions across canneries, and wage guarantees. In a published statement of
their aims, the Japanese Fish Cutters of New Monterey cited only restoration of the previous year's piece rate of ten cents a bucket (as opposed to
reduction to eight cents) and uniform rates across canneries.

> The Japanese fish cutters ask the for fair treatment only. They do
> not ask for an increase in pay, but only ask for the same working
> conditions and the same pay that they received last year, which was
> 10¢ a bucket. They DO ask, however, that all canners pay the same
> wages. As it is now, one Canner pays one price and one another.
> Each seems to want to outdo the other and be the favorite one. This
> makes dissension among the cutters. . . . The Japanese people also
> would like to state that they were not the only ones responsible
> for the dissension between Cutters and the Canners. The Chinese,
> Mexicans, Italians, and Spanish, as well as the Americans, who are

cutting fish, are dissatisfied with present conditions (*Monterey Daily Cypress,* 30 July 1920).

Canners and the local press reacted in angry racial tones. "Japs Stir Up Strife" headlined the *Monterey Daily Cypress* (27 July 1920): "brown men accused of creating dissension among laborers along Cannery Row." K. Hovden, Bayside Fish, and Monterey Canning companies threatened to import Filipino replacement workers and advertised "permanent positions for men and women" paying as much as $15–18 per day and $50 per week for "light work [requiring] only the skills of the ordinary housewife." Cutters acknowledged that the pay was good, yielding the equivalent of something more like $1.00–1.25 per hour, but irregular and not uniform—even the size of ten-cent buckets varied across plants, they said. Tacitly conceding their need of skilled workers, the cannery owners gave in after a month and unilaterally announced ten cents a bucket where scaling the fish was required, eight cents without scaling, and uniform wages in the plants of the nine signatory members of the Monterey Canners Association (except Booth). At the same time, however, they threatened to replace all Japanese workers, not only cutters, and continued hiring docile replacements. The fish cutters were not satisfied and resumed their walkout. This provoked a special meeting of the community-wide Monterey Japanese Association, which published a statement lamenting the strike, "the deplorable conditions caused by the Fish Cutters," and the wholesale dismissals of Japanese workers. "The Japanese Fishermen . . . will remain faithful to the Canners" (*Monterey Daily Cypress*, 2 September 1920).

This dramatic vertical class division within the Japanese community was neatly complemented by a horizontal alliance across ethnic working-class groups. In sympathy with the strike, Chinese fish cutters staged a "small riot" at the Carmel Canning Company, "throwing rocks at the cannery building, firing revolvers, and [causing] other disturbances" to protest fellow Chinese entering the plant to work (*Monterey Daily Cypress*, 1 September 1920). In the end, the Canners Association stuck by their concessionary wage offer; they replaced workers and, before long, eliminated the skilled and feisty cutters altogether. But 1920 marked the beginning of working-class struggle on Cannery Row, a style of conflict that would soon visit the fishing fleet and return again to the canneries in the 1930s.

Class action expressed in strikes and public broadsides routinely shaded into political violence, sabotage, and sullen resistance. Italian fishermen traditionally employed force when necessary to establish and maintain control of fishing grounds. Cinel (1982, 219) notes that in San Francisco's Genoese-dominated industry "violence and intimidation . . . helped establish a quasi-monopoly, in a city where anti-Chinese sentiment made these tactics safe and useful ways to achieve economic success." The same methods were used less successfully by Genoese against Sicilians on San Francisco Bay in the 1890s. "Boats were sunk, nets have been cut, and sometimes owners too have been cut," in a pattern of intimidation that led some Sicilians to resettle at the Sacramento Delta town of Pittsburg. Indeed, taking the process another step, a family history suggests that Pietro Ferrante left Pittsburg for Monterey owing in part to "envy and jealousy," followed by a fire that destroyed the wharf—arson, one might conjecture (Ferrante family history n.d.). Property owners and fishermen were united in their wish to eradicate the original Chinese fishing village near the present site of Cannery Row, and although arson was never proven in the 1906 fire that destroyed the community, it was suspected; the blaze was cheered by onlookers, firefighting equipment was held up, and the ruins were looted (Lydon 1985). Hovden claimed that two destructive fires in his plants were the work of incendiaries (Mangelsdorf 1986, 55), a credible charge given the systematic arson in fruit canneries such as swept nearby Watsonville at the time (*Monterey Peninsula Herald*, 8 July 1926). Bombs were planted (but failed to explode) on one of the boats and at the home of Angelo Lucido, whose San Carlos Cannery was accused of undercutting the fishermen's contract price during a 1931 strike (Mangelsdorf 1986, 88). Threats of violence and sabotage attended every major conflict of Monterey's industrial period.

The mid-1920s saw all the intricacies of class struggle in operation at once. Important strikes took place in each year from 1923 to 1926 as the canneries recovered from a postwar slump and began expanding again—good fortune entailing new labor needs. As an indicator that labor's moment had arrived, the canners agreed in 1925 to the long-standing demand that they employ only union boats (Rosenberg 1961, 127). The agreement did not last, and it was a bit symbolic in any event because unionized Sicilians dominated the fleet. Yet it was a significant symbol.

But success brought new worries. With a growing capacity to can and reduce fish, cannery owners began to consider adoption of the larger and more efficient purse seiners. A favorable climate for labor rights in 1925—as well as threats posed by the big boats, which used mechanized

equipment and needed fewer hands—led to formation of the Monterey
Fishermen's Protective Union, an organization of crew members separate from fellow Sicilian boat owners. Ironically, the boat owners retali-
ated by dismissing their crews and threatening to import fishermen from
southern California experienced in the use of purse seine nets. The dispute was settled in time for the 1926 season opening, when both organizations of boat owners and fishermen struck for a 25 percent increase
in the cannery price for sardines (from $10.00 to $12.50 a ton). Now the
canners resisted. To keep his cannery in operation, Hovden brought two
purse seiners and their crews from San Pedro, the *Admiral* and the *Mari-
posa,* "larger than any sardine fishing boat ever seen in the bay" (*Monterey
Peninsula Herald,* 19 July 1926). Booth brought in strikebreakers, too, but
in the form of lampara crews from San Francisco, who worked boats
Booth had recently repossessed from members of the boat owners' association (*Monterey Peninsula Herald,* 7 August 1926). Those boats were mys-
teriously scuttled at anchor while the formidable purse seiners chugged
on to victory for the canners in the long strike.

Increasingly, the conflicts on Cannery Row between fishermen, boat
owners, and canners were orchestrated, even superseded, by state efforts
to regulate the industry. As Monterey's sardine harvest burgeoned,[11] close
observers such as the Scofield brothers of the Fish and Game Division
began to think that the fishery would be destroyed without state-enforced
conservation. The "fisherman's problem" rested on a resource that was
common property: "No one of them owns the resource so as to keep others away from it. As a result, everyone has an incentive to keep fishing so
long as there is any money to be made in the effort, whereas no one has
an individual incentive to refrain from fishing to so as to conserve the
stock. Every harvester knows that if he or she leaves a fish in the water
someone else will get it and the profit, instead" (McEvoy 1986, 10).

Progressive in the early years of the century (Mowry 1951), the state
legislature passed the California Fish Conservation Act of 1919, amend-
ing it two years later to require that reduction use no more than 25 percent of the total sardine catch (a quota also expressed as fifteen cases of
packed tins for each ton of processed fish). The law and its enforcement
agents, however, soon found themselves on the weak side of economic

11. In the first decade after World War I, sardine landings increased from about thirty thousand to one hundred thousand tons just as the industry was preparing for the next technological revolution dominated by purse seiners and reduction (Heimann and Carlisle 1970).

logic and political influence. Sardines were never a favorite of American consumers, Europeans preferred the smaller Norwegian species of pilchard, and recent sales increases had depended on wartime conditions (U.S. government purchases for sea rations and exports aided by threats to North Sea fishing). At the same time, however, fish by-products enjoyed growing demand: fish meal for animal feed and fertilizer; fish oil for soap, paint, medicine, salad oil, leather tanning, glycerin, precision machine oil. Although manufacturers touted the nutritional wonders of sardines, devised new recipes, advertised creatively, and actually developed new markets,[12] it was apparent before long that industry profits lay in reduction. Where at one time only the offal was reduced, whole fish were now being used, and later canners would be accused of (and vigorously deny) "putting up a low-quality pack" by saving the best fish for reduction. A more plausible rumor held that fish were canned and sold for human consumption below cost in order to increase the quota for reduction.

The reduction dispute was complicated in the 1930s by the advent of offshore, shipboard reduction factories, or "floaters," which anchored beyond the three-mile limit and the reach of California law. Canners and civic boosters argued effectively to the legislature for liberalized reduction quotas in order to lift the "handicap" borne by the shore-based, tax-paying, job-providing canneries. In 1929, the 25 percent limit on the catch subject to reduction was increased to 32.5 per cent (and so the ratio of packed tins *reduced* from 15 to 13.5 cases per ton). More liberalization followed in 1932 and 1933 with appeals for depression jobs in a state legislature "vulnerable to . . . well-organized processers and their allies in agribusiness" (McEvoy 1986, 181). A popular referendum banning offshore reduction was promoted by conservation groups and endorsed by the voters in 1938, but by then compromises of the original conservation law favoring the canneries had rendered the floaters uneconomical. As the several groups that constituted the fishing industry joined forces in support of greater reduction, class conflict gave way to concerted, even prodigious action, but action headed for ecological ruin.[13]

12. Essay contests were held in Monterey public schools on the value of the California sardine, and the colorful labels that decorated cans and packing cartons rivaled the famous pop art of California fruit canners and citrus packers.

13. In some years during the late 1930s and early 1940s, as many as twenty-six plants processed catches from 230,000 to 250,000 tons, six times the volume of the great season 1919–20, for example.

A new level of working-class organization was attained in 1937 when cannery workers formed their first real union and struck for recognition. In the fall of 1936 the American Federation of Labor (AFL), which represented cannery workers in San Pedro, sent an organizer to Monterey, who opened an office on Cannery Row, held mass meetings, and launched the Cannery Workers Union Local no. 20305. By January, however, Monterey workers, noted for their independence from the national labor movement and their communal ties to local canneries, rejected AFL control. Retaining formal links to the AFL, the union insisted upon autonomy in negotiations with canners and elected their own slate of officers headed by Mrs. Garnet Sture, president, and James Mattingly, business agent.

Meanwhile, fishermen became embroiled in a national struggle over control of the union movement. The Monterey Sardine Fishermen's Protective Union, dating from 1925, had no national affiliation, but local men who worked off-season on the coast from Oregon to Alaska necessarily held dual membership in the dominant Deep Sea and Purse Seine Fishermen's Union– AFL. When the Deep Sea Union began its Monterey organizing efforts in 1936, a potent dilemma was posed for local fishermen. On one hand, many of them valued off-season employment opportunities contingent on AFL solidarity. On the other hand, they preferred local union autonomy, a condition endorsed by all the canners—except Booth, the individualist, who had contracts with the AFL union. When the AFL challenged Monterey canners with a strike call in September 1936, the large majority of local fishermen and canneries announced their opposition and pursued their strikebreaking labors—and Booth's cannery suffered a serious fire of unknown origin. It became clear that the AFL could not break local traditions of autonomy and cannery loyalty. Rival unions made peace in January 1937, agreeing on de facto local autonomy with formal AFL links, and called a strike mainly as a show of strength celebrating their newfound unity.

But the Cannery Workers Union sprung a surprise by electing to strike in solidarity with the fishermen. In this job action, their first, cannery workers above all wanted recognition and a closed shop, but they also bargained for a minimum wage (fifty cents per hour for men and forty-five cents for women), overtime (an additional five cents per hour), time-and-a-half for Sundays, a shop grievance committee, and preferential hiring of union members (*Monterey Peninsula Herald*, 18 January

1937). The fishermen's dispute posed no obstacle for prompt settlement with canners, but resumption of fishing and processing was stalled by the awkward honeymoon of the two virgin unions. "It is refusal of the fishermen to work for plants which have not signed up with the cannery workers union that makes the latter strike effective." Under the circumstances, the strike was settled within the week and formalized in a twenty-seven-point document which began: "Wage demands of the cannery workers union are granted. . . . The union is recognized" (*Monterey Peninsula Herald*, 22, 28 January 1937). Although the closed-shop provision did not win agreement, workers got most of what they wanted and in the process set a new standard of cooperative class action, one that rose above craft, ethnic, gender, and communal divisions in the labor force.

Sarah Sousa, who was a cutter, joined the union organizers. "A small group of us could see that we weren't getting ahead," she recalled. "We wanted to better ourselves. It was a powerful feeling, but I was scared too. We went to a lot of meetings, and the men led, of course. But there were a few women who spoke their piece" (McKibben 1991, 16). Charlie Nonella, who packed cans into cases, recalls "in 1929–1930 we were makin' 38 cents an hour. In 1936 the unions came in and we were jacked up to $1.08 an hour. When I quit in 1946, we were makin $1.35" (Kinney and Lonero 1987, 12).

For a time, class happened in Monterey. The "old Spanish capital" of California grew up with the twentieth century to become an industrial and union town, an identity on which it prided itself.

> There is a population here of hundreds of families supported by the industry of the men who man these vessels. There are thousands of people who make their hard living by packing and reducing tens of thousands of tons of sardines. The old town of Monterey shared with the rest of the country the long and difficult years of the depression. But it was during that period that the town woke up to the fact that it wasn't such a bad idea to be called a "fishing village" after all. Tradesmen and bankers realized to a greater degree than ever before how fundamentally basic to the economic welfare of this region the fishing industry was. . . . This Peninsula is one of the rare places on earth, but it is the reality of labor and productivity that saves this place from being one of those baubles whose beauty [is] at the service of those that neither reap nor sow. . . . The fishing fleet and cannery row remind those that live here and those

that come to look and see, that there is something more than scenery, recreation and conversation to the Monterey Peninsula. Monterey's fishermen saved this beautiful area from being damned to be only a "resort" (*Monterey Peninsula Herald*, 24 February 1939).

Class happened in segmented ethnic communities, across self-conscious groups of workers, at the wellsprings of spirited collective action, and as a defining principle of how they thought about themselves as a town, who they were.

Social Construction of History

Monterey's sardine fishery gave out in the late 1940s; canneries were closing left and right by the early 1950s. A group called Cannery Row Properties—some of whom were former cannery managers; others, San Francisco investors—began buying the dormant plants and by 1957 owned fifteen parcels comprising 50 per cent of waterfront footage. In that year, there were just five functional canneries left, not packing sardines but operating intermittently on tuna, anchovies, mackerel, and other sea products. When Cannery Row Properties began buying up the plants in 1953, its principal business was machine salvage, converting cannery boilers and dryers to other industrial uses or selling them to new fisheries in South America. No plan existed to rejuvenate the street as a restaurant row or tourist attraction. On the contrary, the desultory property market took its own course as a series of small local businesses gradually moved in (*Monterey Peninsula Herald*, 26 February 1957). In 1964 a San Francisco firm calling itself Cannery Row Development Company purchased its predecessor and came forward with a plan for building a tourist Mecca, but its efforts became entangled with restorationist aims of the city's general plan and the new California Coastal Commission. The San Francisco firm slowly ceded its properties to the Foursome Development Company, composed of local restaurateurs and realtors.

John Steinbeck's popular novel, of course, made the idea of Cannery Row an American commonplace, and long-term residents of the street (Ocean View Avenue, until renamed Cannery Row by the city in 1953) reported a steady stream of visitors in search of Mack and the boys, the Bear Flag restaurant and bordello, or Doc's lab. Nor did Steinbeck's contribution to local publicity end there: with *Sweet Thursday* the author provided a popular sequel in 1954; Richard Rodgers and Oscar Hammerstein used this work as the basis for their lesser-known 1955 musical, *Pipe Dream*; and the two novels were merged in a subsequent stage play and film, both called *Cannery Row*. Curious visitors to the Monterey waterfront encountered small businesses, restaurants, and gift shops, as well as the imposing hulks of vacant canneries and covered plant-to-warehouse conveyors bridging the street in a well-defined, twenty-block area, which the city hoped to redevelop as a historical business and office center. These surroundings of course included Steinbeck's landmarks, since the familiar story was bound to figure in any description of the area and its picaresque past. But those circumstances certainly did not dictate a particular version of history or require that the industrial and working-class experience be excluded and "Steinbeck's Cannery Row" privileged. Steinbeck's work scarcely exhausted the history and character of Monterey's waterfront, nor did it celebrate all those features that were apt to interest visitors, from the imposing industrial architecture to lingering bands of workers and the brilliant bay itself. Potentially, there was a rich history waiting to be developed for tourists, residents, students, Steinbeck buffs, Asian and Italian heritage groups, sea-farers, scientists, laborites, and environmentalists. The possibilities were abundant. Nothing determined that one version would predominate.

In fact, however, shortly after the takeover by property developers, "Steinbeck's Cannery Row" began to monopolize popular memory. Class, ethnicity, gender, the fishermen themselves, resident working women and men, the industrial engine of town prosperity—all these were neglected or treated as props in another play. As Martha Norkunas (1993) shows in her study of Monterey's "public texts," property owners recreated Steinbeck memorabilia in sidewalk murals, a wax museum, and a statue of the author. A series of guidebooks and local histories written over a period of years effectively assimilated the complex history of Can-nery Row to the simple story of Steinbeck's savvy nonconformists and the novelist himself (March 1962; Person 1972; Reinstedt 1978; Man-gelsdorf 1986; Hemp 1986; Larsh 1995).[14] In some cases these were good histories and excellent photographic essays, but they merged two differ-ent realities and increasingly foregrounded the novel to stand for the larger experience.

---

14. Steinbeck was from Salinas, about twenty miles inland, and wrote what many consider his best works, *Grapes of Wrath* and *East of Eden,* about the settlers and workers of California's agricultural valleys.

This was not Steinbeck's doing. By 1957 he had fallen out with his Monterey friends and contributed a sarcastic critique of California's "pseudo-old/new-old" architectural and redevelopment schemes for the local newspaper addressed to "Cannery Row purchasers" (*Monterey Peninsula Herald*, 8 March 1957). In fact, no one was singularly responsible. Norkunas (1993, 63, 93) accurately describes what happened, although in my view she misjudges the reasons.

> Steinbeck and his fictional characters, rather than the canneries themselves or the actual cannery workers, have become the referents to Cannery Row. With Steinbeck as focal point of the Row, there is no longer a need to refer to the city's industrial legacy. Rather than anchoring the past in the physical remains of the canneries, it is Steinbeck who is used as the implement of authentication, the anchor to specificity of place, the organizing imagery for tourism on the Row. . . . These texts [historical restorations and monuments] had not been marshalled out of the reality of the city, but had been selectively constructed to affirm a particular ideology. Certain groups in the city claimed their power was based on social evolutionary superiority and substantiated that claim through distortions in historical and touristic texts. History, literature, ethnicity, class, nature, and even industrialism were brought under control and integrated into the ideology of dominance.

There were, to be sure, "certain groups" with agendas concerning the historical record—local historical societies, commercial chambers, city government, ethnic heritage societies—some of them even relatively powerful on the local scene, but typically they had different historical visions and none was capable of establishing a dominant ideology.

These observations recall schools of thought on the social construction of history presented at the outset, particularly the theory of *cultural hegemony,* which argues that powerful interests in society and the state orchestrate a consensual meaning of the past. In a general way, the eclipse of Monterey's working-class history might be interpreted as an achievement of bourgeois domination. Yet there is no evidence that any group or class actively sought to suppress that history or co-opt its popular themes in some negotiated bourgeois consensus. Indeed, "Steinbeck's Cannery Row" is less a dominant or hegemonic story than one account that enjoyed undisputed popularity for a time and may now be on the decline as social conditions change. That interpretation, of course, sounds like the processual, group-based theory of social memory. And there is merit in the notion that distinctively situated groups—from the WPA Writers' Project to the property developers of a deindustrialized Cannery Row to today's ethnics organized in Italian heritage societies—would produce competing accounts of local history. But neither theory tells us much that is not already commonplace. We know that groups construct their own histories and powerful groups command more attention. But we do not know much that is generalizable about how given collective memories are constructed in the first place, how they achieve popularity or consensus, when they are challenged, and how they change over time. We need an alternative theory of *collective invention* which explains public history in modern societies as a construction of civic, governmental, and professional groups with diverse (consensual and conflictual) entrepreneurial aims. The public history of popular consumption—in museums, monuments, commemorative performances, and textbooks and guidebooks—is typically a product of invention rather than scholarship, although inventors may draw selectively on respected sources (Hobsbawm and Ranger 1983). Groups engaged in inventing their past under constraining social conditions must deal with one another and with audiences; credibility requires cooperation and negotiation. The past is continually reinvented for collective purposes in the present, dramatically so when the social conditions underpinning earlier constructions collapse: an industry dies, the environment declines, the economy restructures, families move geographically or socially, or a community discovers symbols fit for a new day.

In Monterey, popular memory of "Steinbeck's Cannery Row" has held center stage until recently, but its hold is less than hegemonic. Local history is constructed by individuals and groups with civic aims, which may be either commercial agendas or nonprofit purposes such as promoting legacies that are endangered, deserve recollection, or express something essential about local culture. Local history is often the work of volunteers organized in decentralized interest groups—entrepreneurs, of a sort, on behalf of civic ends. These public historians and civic entrepreneurs work through voluntary associations of modest scale, publish their material locally in specialized (tourist, educational) markets, endeavor to impress their message on city and state agencies in charge of museums and restoration works, and blandish private patrons such as the late David Packard, who funded the highly successful Monterey Bay

Aquarium, built on the converted site of Hovden's cannery. These voluntary associations often compete for resources and the public's attention. Where a cultural critic may see certain groups purveying a dominant ideology, participants in the history construction process experience a continuous struggle of getting their message out. Lately both "Steinbeck people" and heritage groups have lamented the aquarium's lack of interest in social history and its preponderate attention to the natural history of Monterey Bay.

The social construction of "Steinbeck's Cannery Row" must be understood in a more nuanced interpretation of collective invention, one that includes *its own historical analysis* and anticipates change. In the first instance, association of the fishing industry and tourism dates from the late nineteenth century, when visitors to the exclusive Del Monte Hotel were given tours of the beach to take in colorful Chinese fishing villages and buy seashell souvenirs. During the height of commercial fishing, the waterfront was promoted as a colorful site of "old world charm" of interest to artists and visitors. The Steinbeck-centered account was one in a time-honored series of romanticized portraits designed to develop the local service economy. Second, when the fishery collapsed, neither fishers nor canners wanted to accept responsibility (which led to numerous and fanciful explanations, including the fishermen's belief that the sardines were out there but swimming much deeper, and Hovden's charge that the U.S. Navy's dumping of munitions had killed the fish). Fishermen and canners alike may therefore have welcomed an innocuous alternative history of the Row. If property developers benefited from the area's romanticized appeal, no one else was putting forth an alternative version in the early 1950s. Third, before long other constituencies began to organize in the interest of different, purposeful visions of the essential past for present action. Local history today is being recast by the same kinds of civic entrepreneurs, around themes of cultural heritage and environmentalism (Lydon 1985; Yamada 1995; Gordon 1977; Gilliam 1992; Henson and Usner 1993; O'Connor 1995).

Class, industrialism, and their gendered and cultural foundations were all neglected in the available histories of Cannery Row. A particular historical construction reigned for a time, one that romanticized the industrial past and served those who helped destroy the fishery as well as those who hoped to foster a new service economy—not because an ideology achieved cultural domination at the behest of certain groups, but because the historical construction provided a serviceable myth in the absence of competing versions with their own constituency. A past was invented in the crisis of industrial collapse, a past based on selective perception and willing delusion. A limiting myth about Cannery Row arose and even enjoyed temporary hegemony before eventual contestation with changing times and new cultural, ethnic, and environmental constituencies. History is a contentious process. Interpretations shift with material conditions, world views, competing group interests, and inventive storytellers. Late capitalism and multiculturalism encourage us to view events differently than we did during confident industrial revolutions or nostalgic postwar transformations. Class is suppressed in popular memory, along with other things, making it easy for social theorists also to forget that class happened. That said, it is the job of class theorists to join the struggle of historical interpretation along with insurgent ethnics and environmentalists, and engaged local historians.

References

Baron, Ava. 1991. *Work Engendered: Toward a New History of American Labor.* Ithaca, N.Y.: Cornell University Press.

Bell, Daniel. 1973. *The Coming of Postindustrial Society.* New York: Basic Books.

Bendix, Reinhard. 1974. "Inequality and Social Structure in the Theories of Marx and Weber." *American Sociological Review* 39: 149–61.

Berger, Peter L., and Thomas Luckmann. 1966. *The Social Construction of Reality: A Treatise in the Sociology of Knowledge.* New York: Anchor.

Calhoun, Craig. 1982. *The Question of Class Struggle: Social Foundations of Popular Radicalism During the Industrial Revolution.* Chicago: University of Chicago Press.

Cinel, Dino. 1982. *From Italy to San Francisco: The Immigrant Experience.* Stanford: Stanford University Press.

Clark, Terry N., and Seymour Martin Lipset. 1991. "Are Social Classes Dying?" *International Sociology* 6 (November): 397–410.

Cohen, David William. 1994 *The Combing of History.* Chicago: University of Chicago Press.

Connerton, Paul. 1989. *How Societies Remember*. Cambridge: Cambridge University Press.

Cutino, Peter J. 1995. *Monterey—A View from Garlic Hill*. Pacific Grove, Calif.: Boxwood Press.

Dahrendorf, Ralf. 1959. *Class and Class Conflict in Industrial Society*. Stanford: Stanford University Press.

Dawley, Alan. 1976. *Class and Community: The Industrial Revolution in Lynn*. Cambridge: Harvard University Press.

Fentress, James, and Chris Wickham. 1992. *Social Memory*. Oxford: Blackwell.

Ferrante family history. n.d. Monterey Fishermen's Historical Association.

Fish Bulletin. 1946. "The Commercial Fish Catch of California for the Years 1943 and 1944." No. 63, State of California, Division of Fish and Game.

Friday, Chris. 1992. *Organizing Asian American Labor: The Pacific Coast Canned-Salmon Industry, 1870–1942*. Philadelphia: Temple University Press.

Gans, Herbert J. 1962. *The Urban Villagers: Group and Class in the Life of Italian Americans*. New York: The Free Press.

Giddens, Anthony. 1973. *The Class Structures of the Advanced Societies*. New York: Barnes and Noble.

Gilliam, Harold, and Ann Gilliam. 1992. *Creating Carmel: The Enduring Vision*. Salt Lake City: Peregrine Smith Books.

Gordon, Burton L. 1977. *Monterey Bay Area: Natural History and Cultural Imprints*. Pacific Grove, CA: The Boxwood Press.

Gramsci, Antonio. 1971. *Selections from the Prison Notebooks of Antonio Gramsci*. Translated and edited by Quintin Hoare and Geoffrey Nowell Smith. New York: International Publishers.

Halbwachs, Maurice. 1980. *The Collective Memory*. New York: Harper.

Harvey, David. 1985. *Consciousness and the Urban Experience*. Baltimore: Johns Hopkins University Press.

Heimann, Richard F.G., and John G. Carlisle, Jr. 1970. "The California Marine Fish Catch for 1968 and Historical Review 1916–1968," *Fish Bulletin*, no. 149. State of California, Department of Fish and Game.

Hemp, Michael Kenneth. 1986. *Cannery Row: The History of Old Ocean Avenue*. Pacific Grove, Calif.: The History Company.

Henson, Paul, and Donald J. Usner. 1993. *The Natural History of Big Sur*. Berkeley: University of California Press.

History of Portola. n.d. Monterey: K. Hovden.

Hobsbawn, Eric, and Terrance Ranger. 1983. *The Invention of Tradition*. Cambridge: Cambridge University Press.

Horkheimer, Max, and Theodor Adorno. 1972 [1944]. "The Culture Industry: Enlightenment as Mass Deception." In *Dialectic of Enlightenment*. New York: Continuum Books.

Johnson, Richard, et al. 1982. *Making Histories: Studies in History-Writing and Politics*. London: Hutchinson.

Jones, Gareth Stedman. 1983. *Languages of Class: Studies in English Working-Class History, 1832–1982*. Cambridge: Cambridge University Press.

Katznelson, Ira. 1981. *City Trenches: Urban Politics and the Patterning of Class in the United States*. New York: Pantheon.

Kinney, James, and Kathy Lonero. 1987. "Down on the Row," *Weekly Herald Magazine*, 26 April. 26, 12.

Kuhn, Thomas. 1962. *The Structure of Scientific Revolutions*. Chicago: University of Chicago Press.

Larsh, Ed B. 1995. *Doc's Lab: Myth and Legends From Cannery Row*. Monterey: PBL Press.

Lautaret, Mavis. 1990. "Out of the Office, into the Muck," *Monterey Peninsula Herald, Alta Vista Magazine*, 10 February. 15.

Lowenthal, David. 1985. *The Past is a Foreign Country*. Cambridge: Cambridge University Press.

Lydon, Sandy. 1985. *Chinese Gold: The Chinese in the Monterey Bay Region*. Capitola, Calif.: Capitola Book Co.

Maddox, Richard. 1993. *El Castillo: The Politics of Tradition in an Andalusian Town*. Urbana: University of Illinois Press.

Mangelsdorf, Tom. 1986. *A History of Steinbeck's Cannery Row*. Santa Cruz, Calif.: Western Tanager Press.

March, Ray A. 1962. *A Guide to Cannery Row*. Monterey: Ray A. March.

McEvoy, Arthur F. 1986. *The Fisherman's Problem: Ecology and Law in the California Fisheries, 1850–1980*. Cambridge: Cambridge University Press.

McKibben, Carol. 1991. "Women of the Canneries," *Monterey Peninsula Herald, Alta Vista Magazine*, 10 February, 12–16.

Mills, C. Wright. 1951. *White Collar: The American Middle Classes*. New York: Oxford University Press.

Monterey Fishermen's Historical Association. 1995. Oral history videotapes.

Mowry, George E. 1951. *The California Progressives*. Berkeley: University of California Press.

Norkunas, Martha K. 1993. *The Politics of Public Memory: Tourism, History, and Ethnicity in Monterey, California*. Albany: State University of New York Press.

O'Connor, James. 1995. "Three Ways to Think about the Ecological History of Monterey Bay." *Capitalism, Nature, Socialism: A Journal of Socialist Ecology* 6 (June): 21–47.

Person, Richard. 1972. *History of Cannery Row*. Monterey: Department of City Planning, City of Monterey.

Phillips, J. B. 1930. "Success of the Purse Seine Boat in the Fishery at Monterey, California," *Fish Bulletin* 23 (April). State of California, Division of Fish and Game.

Reddy, William M. 1987. *Money and Liberty in Modern Europe: A Critique of Historical Understanding*. Cambridge: Cambridge University Press.

Reinstedt, Randall A. 1978. *Where Have All the Sardines Gone: A Pictorial History of Steinbeck's Cannery Row*. Carmel, Calif.: Ghost Town Publications.

Rosenberg, Earl H. 1961. *A History of the Fishing and Canning Industries in Monterey, California*. Master's thesis, University of Nevada.

Ruiz, Vicki L. 1987. *Cannery Women, Cannery Lives: Mexican Women, Unionization, and the California Food Processing Industry, 1930–1950*. Albuquerque: University of New Mexico Press.

Samuel, Raphael. 1981. *People's History and Socialist Theory*. London: Routledge.

Saxton, Alexander. 1971. *The Indispensable Enemy: Labor and the Anti-Chinese Movement in California*. Berkeley: University of California Press.

Scofield, W. L. 1929. "Sardine Fishing Methods at Monterey, California," *Fish Bulletin* 19 (March). State of California, Division of Fish and Game.

Sewell, William H., Jr. 1980. *Work and Revolution in France: The Language of Labor from the Old Regime to 1848*. Cambridge: Cambridge University Press.

Steinbeck, Elaine, and Robert Wallsten. 1975. *Steinbeck: A Life in Letters*. New York: Viking/Penguin.

Steinbeck, John. 1941. *The Log from the Sea of Cortez*. New York: Penguin/Viking.

———. 1945. *Cannery Row*. New York: Bantam/Viking.

Sutherland, Arthur T. 1941. "Earnings and Hours in Pacific Coast Fish Canneries." *Bulletin of the Women's Bureau*, no. 186. Department of Labor. Washington, D.C.: Government Printing Office.

Tilly, Louise, and Joan Scott. 1978. *Women, Work, and Family*. New York: Holt, Rinehart, and Winston.

Thompson, E. P. 1963. *The Making of the English Working Class*. New York: Vintage.

Trouillot, Michel-Rolph. 1995. *Silencing the Past· Power and the Production of History*. Boston: Beacon Press.

Turner, Graeme. 1990. *British Cultural Studies: An Introduction*. London: Routledge.

Wagner-Pacifici, Robin, and Barry Schwartz. 1991. "The Vietnam Veterans Momorial: Commemorating a Difficult Past." *American Journal of Sociology* 97 (2): 376–420.

Waters, Malcolm. 1994. "Succession in the Stratification System: A Contribution to the 'Death of Class Debate.'" *International Sociology* 9 (September): 295–312.

Weber, Max. 1946. *From Max Weber: Essays in Sociology*. Edited by Hans Gerth and C. Wright Mills. New York: Oxford University Press.

Williams, Raymond. 1973. *The Country and The City*. New York: Oxford University Press.

———. 1977. *Marxism and Literature*. Oxford: Oxford University Press.

Wilson, William Julius. 1978. *The Declining Significance of Race: Blacks and Changing American Institutions*. Chicago: University of Chicago Press.

WPA Guide to the Monterey Peninsula. 1989. Tucson: University of Arizona Press. Originally published in 1941 by the Writers' Program of the Works Progress Administration of Northern California.

Wright, Erik Olin. 1985. *Classes*. London: Verso.

Yamada, David. 1995. *The Japanese of Monterey Peninsula: The History and Legacy, 1895–1995*. Monterey: Japanese American Citizens League.

Yancey, William L., Eugene P. Erickson, and Richard N. Juliani. 1976. "Emergent Ethnicity: A Review and Reformulation." *American Journal of Sociology* 41 (3): 391–403.

Zerubavel, Yael. 1995. *Recovered Roots: Collective Memory and the Making of Israeli National Tradition*. Chicago: University of Chicago Press.

PART 3

The Economic, the Social, and the Political Agencies of Class

CHAPTER 9

World of Capital / Worlds of Labor: A Global Perspective

Dale Tomich

S INCE THE LATE 1940S, A SERIES OF DEBATES OVER THE ORIGINS, SCOPE, and character of modern capitalism and the historical processes of development and underdevelopment have broadly influenced our understanding of social class, both as an analytical construct and as a historical phenomenon. The contributors to these debates have included, among others, Maurice Dobb, Paul Sweezy, Andre Gunder Frank, Ernesto Laclau, Immanuel Wallerstein, and Robert Brenner. The subject matter, purpose, and approach of each of these authors have varied. The cornerstone of these controversies has been Dobb's studies of the historical development of capitalism from the decline of feudalism through the Second World War, focusing on England as the classic case (Dobb 1947).

In particular, Dobb's treatment of the transition from feudalism to capitalism attracted the attention of scholars. He was concerned to demonstrate that the disintegration of feudalism was the result of struggles between lord and serf over rents. While the decline of feudalism created the conditions for the emergence of capitalism (that is, the dominance of the capital–wage labor relation), it was not caused by the rise of the capitalist mode of production. Among the critics, Paul Sweezy was most influential in shaping the terms of the debate, particularly through his emphasis on the role of long-distance trade in dissolving European feudalism (Sweezy 1976a, 33–56; 1976b, 108). In Sweezy's view, it was not not the internal struggle between lord and serf but the external influence of commerce and the rise of towns that was necessary to break down the system of serfdom. A system of production for the market emerged alongside feudal production for use, and eroded the feudal system. In Sweezy's view, these processes were not equivalent to the rise of capitalism, which he believes to have taken place two hundred years later and identifies with the emergence of the capital–wage labor relation.

During the 1960s, the theoretical issues raised in this debate were revisited in a new context. Andre Gunder Frank challenged the identification of capitalism with the capital–wage labor relation. Instead, he emphasized the appropriation of surplus through the relation between metropolis and satellite in determining the capitalist character of Latin American and Third World underdevelopment, despite the prevalence there of nonwage relations of production (Frank 1967). In response, Ernesto Laclau, writing from a more conventional Marxist position, reasserted the identification of capitalism with the relation between capital and wage labor. He emphasized the autonomy of distinct modes of production understood as national phenomena and distinguished between capitalism as a mode of production (wage labor and capital) subject to its own autonomous "laws of development" and capitalism as a system resulting from the "articulation" of capitalist and noncapitalist modes (Laclau 1971).

Beginning in the 1970s, Immanuel Wallerstein transformed the dependency position by conceptualizing capitalism as a world system—a historical whole—rather than as a series of dyadic metropolis-satellite relations. He conceived of capitalism as a global division of labor organized through a singular world market and a system of multiple states. In his view, this world system emerged in the sixteenth century and remains the organizing structure of economic, political, and cultural life (Wallerstein 1974). Robert Brenner sharply criticized Wallerstein, along with Frank and Sweezy, as "circulationists" who overestimated the role of the market in capitalist development and, as a result, misapprehended the nature of capitalism and the processes of change within it. Brenner, in contrast, called attention to contingent class struggles in determining the transition to capitalism (Brenner 1977). For Brenner, too, this transition was achieved with the establishment of the capital–wage labor relation as the exclusively capitalist form of production.

Undeniably, these controversies have stimulated important historical research on a variety of topics and generated increasingly sophisticated theoretical approaches by several generations of scholars. Nonetheless, from today's vantage point, perhaps the most striking feature of the debate is that over the course of fifty years, its terms have been reasserted ever more forcefully despite dramatic shifts in purpose, subject matter, and intellectual context. In general terms, the debates have crystallized around two broad perspectives. The first emphasizes the importance of the market in the historical development of capitalism. In this perspective, capitalism is identified with production for the market, and diverse forms of waged and unwaged labor are regarded as capitalist. The second is a more conventional Marxist approach which emphasizes the specificity of social relations of production and identifies capitalism strictly with the social organization of production by means of wage labor. At each juncture, these positions and the theoretical premises associated with them have shaped discussion independently of the ostensible subject matter. Indeed, it is arguable that the persistent contraposition of market and production relations has provided the essential continuity of these controversies.

This chapter argues that these basic positions have been continually repeated because the terms of debate do not permit their resolution. The logic of each position impedes comprehension of historical processes, while the choices offered within the debate pose a false set of alternatives for conceptualizing capitalist development and class formation. The chapter examines Wallerstein's and Brenner's methodological assumptions and procedures, and it reconceptualizes class relations within the global processes of capitalist development in ways that go beyond the simple dichotomies—production for the market vs. wage labor production; capitalist vs. precapitalist—that have characterized these controversies.

Immanuel Wallerstein: Class in the Modern World System

During the 1970s Immanuel Wallerstein posited a theoretical conception of capitalism as a world system that emphasizes the importance of unwaged labor and the sociohistorical complexity of modern capitalism. He argues that capitalist modernity is defined precisely by the coexistence and systematic interdependence of a multiplicity of forms labor, both waged and unwaged, that comprise the modern world system. All these labor forms are integral to the system and the production of surplus value.

The character of the system derives from the relation among them, and the processes of class formation occur on a world scale.

Social class is conceptualized within the framework of Wallerstein's capitalist world system. This is regarded as a historically distinct system comprised of a singular world market and multiple state structures. The market is the structure "within which calculations of maximum profitability are made and which therefore determine over the long run the amount of productive activity, the degree of specialization, the modes of payment for labor, goods, and services, and the utility of technological innovation." The state structures, on the other hand, "serve primarily to distort the 'free' workings of the capitalist market so as to increase the prospects of one or several groups for profit within it" (Wallerstein 1979, 222–23). From this perspective, the market defines the capitalist character of production. The interaction of market and states here shape the axial division of labor (core, semiperiphery, and periphery) that integrates diverse forms of production into the unified and unifying structure of the world economy and provides the conditions for class and class formation.

Within this framework, classes are defined on the basis of whether or not they appropriate surplus value. Wallerstein views class relations as a structural polarity between bourgeois (those who receive surplus value that they do not themselves create and use some of it to accumulate capital) and proletarians (those who yield to others part of the value they have created) on a world scale (Wallerstein 1979, 285–86). Wallerstein uses the proportion of surplus value appropriated or retained and the form of remuneration to labor in order to distinguish further between different "modes of labor control" in the capitalist world economy. In his view, the producer may keep all, part, or none of the surplus. If some portion of it is transferred to (appropriated by) someone else, the producer may receive no remuneration or be remunerated in goods, money, or some combination of the two. On the basis of these *logical possibilities* he constructs a typology of modes of labor control to which various historical forms of production relations—wage labor, petty production, peasant production, tenant farming, sharecropping, slavery, peonage—are assigned (289). Thus, Wallerstein at once accounts for the multiple forms of class relations that characterize the capitalist world economy and maintains the essential polarity between bourgeois and proletarian.

The market structure maximizes the production of surplus value and creates conditions of exploitation and class structure that characterize *the*

world economy as a whole. The structural polarity between bourgeois and
proletarian is mediated and given its particular forms by the workings on
a world scale of the antinomies economy/polity and supply/demand
(Wallerstein 1979, 275–76). World class structure emerges from the contradictory need of capital(ists) to at once maximize the appropriation of
surplus and realize profit through the sale of the product (277). Wallerstein argues that although wage labor is suitable for tasks requiring a high
degree of supervision, it is a relatively expensive form of labor organization for labor processes that can be supervised simply. Consequently,
it is not the desired option for those who appropriate surplus value, and
it has never been the exclusive or even the predominant form of labor
organization in the world economy. Indeed, Wallerstein attributes the
expansion of wage labor in the world economy not to its productive efficiency but to the system's need to increase effective demand over the long
run by returning a portion of the surplus to the producer in the form
of wages. In contrast, he contends that coercive forms of labor control
maximize the expropriation of surplus value by pushing toward zero the
share going to labor. The ideal arrangement for this, in his view, is one of
the many varieties of so-called "quasi-feudal" relations in which the cash-
crop sector or industry is controlled by an enterprise (277).

The contradictory need of the system at once to maintain effective
demand and maximize surplus appropriation works through market and
state structures to differentiate and unevenly distribute the various forms
of labor control through space (core, semiperiphery, periphery) and time
(cycles of expansion and contraction) (Wallerstein 1979, 278–79, 290–91).
There are systemic differences in kinds of bourgeois and proletarian in
the core and the periphery. Core states contain a higher percentage
nationally of the bourgeoisie than peripheral states. Skilled, waged labor
is concentrated in the core, while in the periphery forms of coerced labor
predominate. Through processes of unequal exchange, surplus flows from
the periphery to the core, as strong states of the core are able to divert a
disproportionate share of the surplus to the bourgeois located within their
borders (292–93).

Thus, this conception treats the capitalist world economy as a historical and geographical whole and attempts to identify the mechanisms that
integrate it into a single system. While insisting on the historical uniqueness of the world market and therefore the capitalist world system, Wallerstein offers a comprehensive account of capitalism and of class relations

within the world economy. His approach eliminates wage labor as the defining condition of the proletariat and of capitalism. The bourgeois-proletarian relation (capitalism) is not identified exclusively with wage labor nor is it confined to national societies. Rather, it encompasses a variety of modes of labor control—wage labor and self-employment, tenancy and sharecropping, slavery and other forms of coerced cash-crop production—unevenly distributed among core, semiperiphery, periphery, and integrated through the world market. The persistence of nonwage relations is not seen simply as "resistance" by feudal (semifeudal, or quasi-feudal) groups to the advance of capitalism, but instead is regarded as a defining structural feature of the system. In this view, the world economy is regarded as capitalist, at least from the sixteenth century onward, as are the nonwage labor relations that characterize peripheral and semiperipheral social formations. *Relations of production are the relations of the whole system* (Wallerstein 1979, 127). The expansion of the system entails the differential incorporation of various forms of "labor control" and not the generalization of wage labor.

Robert Brenner: Class Struggle and the Transition to Capitalism

In an influential article published in 1977, Robert Brenner sharply criticized Wallerstein's conception of capitalist development and social class. For purposes of exposition, I shall focus not on Brenner's historical essays (Aston and Philpin 1985) but rather on the 1977 essay, which continues and constructs the debate about the transition to capitalism and makes his methodological and theoretical assumptions more explicit. In this essay, Brenner contends that Wallerstein, like Sweezy and Frank before him, displaces class relations from their proper position in the analysis of economic development and underdevelopment. By equating capitalism with a trade-based division of labor, such "neo-Smithian" approaches fail to account for either the way in which specific class structures determine the course of economic development or the way in which class structures themselves emerge. Instead, classes are treated as technical adaptations to market requirements. Differences between forms of class relations are de-emphasized, and diverse forms of class relations are treated as uniformly capitalist. Consequently, Brenner contends, Wallerstein is unable to analyze the qualitatively distinct processes of capitalist development and class formation.

In contrast, Brenner emphasizes the primacy of the social relations of production in determining both the character of a given mode of production and the contingent outcomes of class struggles in determining the transition from one mode to another. Instead of presuming a universal response by producers to the pressures of the capitalist market, Brenner's perspective draws attention to the "differential limitations and potentialities imposed by different class structures on differentially placed exploiters and producers responding to such market forces—and, further, the different sorts of interests or goals to which such exploiters and producers might attempt to subordinate exchange" (Brenner 1977, 38). From this perspective, capitalism is identified exclusively with the capital–wage labor relation. This economic relationship is constituted through the free laborer's sale of her or his labor power. It requires as its necessary preconditions the separation of the direct producer from possession of means of production and the emancipation of laborers from any direct relation of domination (such as slavery or serfdom). On the other hand, if the social relations of production are not characterized by free wage labor, then the mode of production is not capitalist, even if its products are destined for the world market.

By emphasizing the specificity of particular forms of class relations Brenner calls attention to the qualitative difference between capitalist (wage labor) and pre- or noncapitalist (nonwage) modes of production and the distinctive processes of capitalist development. He argues that only the capital–wage labor relation generalizes commodity production. The commodification of labor power alone allows systematic development of productive forces through technological innovation and increasing productivity of labor (relative surplus product), which, for Brenner, is the decisive characteristic of capitalism. Thus, in his view, the class structure of the economy as a whole determines the character of capitalist economic development by compelling individual component "units" to increase their production, develop their forces of production, and increase the productivity of labor in order to secure their reproduction. In contrast, he contends that even where trade is widespread, precapitalist (nonwage) economies can develop only within definite limits because the class structure of production neither requires nor permits systematic increases in productive forces and labor productivity as the condition of their reproduction (Brenner 1977, 32–33).

This emphasis on the specificity of the capital–wage labor relation leads Brenner to dissociate capitalist development from underdevelopment as separate and distinguishable processes (Brenner 1977, 60–61). According to this view, the market is regarded as external to the prevailing relations of direct production. Surplus transfer (unequal exchange) accounts for neither development in the core nor underdevelopment in the periphery. Rather, economic development is a qualitative process, which requires not merely the accumulation of wealth in general but the development of the productivity of labor of the direct producers of the means of production and means of subsistence. The capital–wage labor relation is privileged as both the source and the site of capitalist economic development. On the other hand, peripheral social formations characterized by nonwage labor are regarded as distinct precapitalist (or noncapitalist) modes of production that coexist with capitalist modes in the world capitalist system. But they are outside the decisive capital–wage labor relation and are externally "articulated" to it. The particular pattern of their development is determined by the internal structure of class relations.

Furthermore, Brenner's emphasis on the specificity of the capital–wage labor relation raises the question of the historical origins of capitalism. From his perspective, the origins of capitalism are to be found not with the expansion of the world market and the rise of a world division of labor in the sixteenth century, but rather with the emergence "of the property/surplus extraction (class system) of free wage labor—the historical process by which labor power and the means of production become commodities" (33). In contrast to more economistic conceptions, Brenner stresses that the historical formation of class relations of capitalist production cannot be understood as the product of ruling-class selection of optimal methods of labor control under the pressures of a competitive world market. Rather, he contends that capitalist class relations result from the "process of 'self-transformation' of class relations in Europe from serfdom to free wage labor—that is, of course, the class struggles by which this transformation took place" (38). In his analysis, the contingent outcomes of these struggles, above all in agriculture, created the uniquely successful conditions for the development of capitalism in Western Europe: "a class system, a property system, a system of surplus extraction, in which the methods the extractors were obliged to use to increase their surplus corresponded to an unprecedented, though enormously imperfect, degree to the needs of development of the productive forces" (68).

Brenner's approach emphasizes the specific character of social relations of production in determining economic development and underdevelopment. Class relations are either characterized by nonwage labor and are regarded as precapitalist, or identified with wage labor and are viewed as capitalist. In this interpretation, the market is of secondary importance. It is regarded as external to the prevailing relations of direct production. One the one hand, thus, we can speak of the historic emergence of the capitalist mode of production only with the triumph of the wage labor relation (within a given national arena); on the other hand, we should regard peripheral social formations as distinct precapitalist modes of production that coexist with capitalist modes of production in the world capitalist system.

Critique: Theoretical Dualism

The perspectives under consideration here appear to present two distinct and generally opposed conceptions of class, capital, and world economy. There is an underlying unity beneath these apparent differences, however. Common to both views is the independence of their concepts from historical process. Each approach presented here takes a single feature seen in isolation, the market or the wage form, and treats it as if it were the sole defining characteristic of capitalism. These key theoretical concepts thereby assume a universal validity independent of the historical relations that they are intended to represent. In each case, these abstracted and partial concepts form a priori models through which the respective historical narratives of capitalist development, underdevelopment, and class formation are reconstructed. Each reconstruction creates a privileged realm of systemic necessity that is at once the source and arena of the "laws of motion" of the system, while relations and processes outside this realm are treated as contingent and secondary. Thus, the theory and the history of capitalist development and class formation are collapsed into each other. The privileged concept becomes identical with the "real history" of the system. The complexities of capitalist development are thereby reduced to a single dimension, which comes to define its essence as a historical system. These two theoretical perspectives are thus opposed to one another within a shared set of assumptions: their respective interpretations are mirror images of one another.

In its attempt to understand capitalism as a unified historical whole, Wallerstein's world system theory emphasizes the market as the connecting link between geographically bounded categories of core, semiperiphery, and periphery. Through integration into the market and division of labor, diverse forms of class relations—wage laborers, petty commodity producers, tenant farmers, sharecroppers, peons, slaves—are subsumed under the heading "proletarian" and subjected to a universal logic of profit calculation. In this perspective, what classes have in common takes precedence over what differentiates them. Each form of class relation is equated with every other as production for the market. Production for the market becomes the lowest common denominator to which all forms of social labor are reduced.

This perspective offers no theory of social relations, and we are unable to theoretically reconstitute historical class relations. The category "proletarian" is reduced to the most general and therefore the most abstract determinant of class—the appropriation of surplus product—and is imposed from without upon the most diverse social relations. Classes are defined in relation to the products of labor rather than by their relation to one another in the processes of social production and reproduction. It is as if people's relations to things rather than to one another were decisive. We are left with concepts that apply to the products of human social relations rather than to these relations themselves; or conversely, social relations themselves appear as things. The structural polarity of bourgeois and proletarian overrides the specific character of particular forms of class relations. Class is treated as an essential relation independent of the specific forms which particular relations may take: differences that distinguish one form of class relation from another are regarded as secondary and contingent. Instead, historical class relations are classified into a series of logical types which are functionally related to the universal requirements of a static and unchanging market structure. The specific development of distinct forms of social labor and class relations is eliminated as subject matter, as are the historical relationships among these forms; moreover, the differences between distinct forms of class relations—and, indeed, change itself—are reduced to a merely quantitative dimension.

This failure to come to grips with the historical specificity of class relations undermines the insights of the world economy perspective . As presently constituted, it is unable either to distinguish between different forms of class relations or to comprehend the relations between these different forms in the historical development of the capitalist world economy. The fundamental categories of class (as well as those of core, semiperiphery, periphery, etc.) are taken as given rather than theoretically reconstructed from the elements that constitute them in specific historical circumstances. Both market and production are understood independently from the global web of relations that sustain and support them. The relation between them is functional, not historical. Specific forms of class relations and particular local histories are reduced to their positions within a predetermined whole. The result is a historical system without a history, a choreography of events within a static and immutable framework. It is as if the capitalist world economy had existed virtually full-blown from the sixteenth century onward. In consequence, not only does the market appear as the dynamic force of historical development, but it simultaneously remains an ahistorical abstraction—"not only the teleological outcome of history . . . [but] also its starting point" (Merrington 1976, 174)—which is itself not explained.

On the other hand, Brenner's approach, identifying itself with Marxism, emphasizes the autonomy of separate, geographically bounded modes of production. It is based upon Marx's theoretical claims of the primacy of production over exchange, a perception of the historical specificity of different forms of social relations of production, and the importance of the internal development of each form of class relations as the source of fundamental change. However, although scholars writing from this perspective regard production as determinant, they fail to distinguish adequately between the concept of production and the historical forms in which production manifests itself, or, to put it otherwise, between the conditions for and the results of theoretical reflection. Treating particular local forms of production as if they were empirically or conceptually equivalent with the general category "production" requires theoretical justification. Failing such demonstration, it cannot be presumed that social relations of production (above all capitalist relations) are exclusively the attribute of a given local or national "society," or that such local or national class relations are to be regarded as invariably prior to market relations (and to the state, ideology, etc.) and as universally determinant.

Thus, approaches such as Brenner's that stress the primacy of production relations confuse the general and the particular. They treat empirically given production relations as if they coincided with and directly expressed the general theoretical category 'production." From this perspective, production is understood simply as the combination of human labor with the instruments and materials of production. These elements are regarded as attributes of each independent form of class or production relations; that is, each such form possesses or contains its own integral "production" processes. What distinguishes one form from another is the manner in which these elements are socially organized. These "primary" relations of production form the necessary starting point of analysis, and all understandings of the development of the "society" in question derive from them.

This conception of class relations thus operates on a distinction, taken to be analytically decisive, between what is internal and what is external. It treats each form of production relations as a closed entity, possessing a stable and self-contained internal structure subject to autonomous laws, and having a fixed and singular external boundary demarcating it from other such units. It regards each form as discrete and analytically independent and considers it in terms of its own "internal" characteristics. One such form is related to another as if to an external object.

This conception loses sight of the global dimensions and systemic character of such relations. Each immediate local form of production is examined in its particularity, in isolation from the wider range of relations constituting it (Corrigan 1977, 437). Commodity production is artificially separated from commodity circulation. Geopolitical spaces and temporalities are taken as given or are derived directly from the conception of production. The wage labor form alone is regarded as authentically capitalist, and capitalism is identified exclusively with its empirical presence. In contrast, nonwage forms of labor are treated as inherently noncapitalist, while market relations are at best derivative and secondary, at worst inconsequential.

This approach remains abstract and fails to adequately conceptualize the interrelation between various forms of production and reproduction of social labor in the world economy. By granting analytical priority to what it construes as primary production relations, this approach necessarily constructs the world economy as a fragmented and heterogeneous ensemble with no systemic unity. It conjoins isolated and autonomous individual forms of production and class relations with one another to create a pluralistic conception. Capitalist and pre- or noncapitalist class relations coexist within a composite of linear historical spaces and temporalities: modern, not yet modern, never to become modern (Corrigan

1977, 441). Emphasis on the apparently distinctive "internal" characteristics of these relations privileges the peculiarity of prevailing local forms and contingent local outcomes. The world economy appears here as no more than the sum of its parts and serves merely as the general backdrop against which the "primary" individual units play their roles.

Thus, within the premises of this perspective, world-scale processes of class formation are distorted or excluded from consideration altogether. Production relations are fragmented. Ostensibly "primary" class relations, the justification for the approach, remain abstract and partial in the sense that some aspects of class formation are emphasized but not others. Markets are viewed in isolation from production relations and seen as simply the realm of abstract exchange. The historical interrelation and interdependence of diverse forms of class relations on a world scale is eliminated as theoretical subject matter.

Consequently, both approaches fail to develop an adequate methodology for reconstituting capitalist development and class formation in their historical complexity *as world process*. Instead, the theoretical strategy pursued by each generates the continual (and unresolvable within the theoretical claims and methodological conditions of each argument) juxtaposition of production and exchange, wage and nonwage labor, capitalist and precapitalist production, world and national/local system, which have shaped their respective understandings of the character and role of class relations in modern capitalism.

Theoretical Reconstruction: World Economy and Class

An alternative to this dualism, and a more productive theoretical approach, would emphasize the nonidentity of theoretical categories with historical narratives of capitalist development and class formation. The approaches discussed above treat concepts of production and exchange as if they coincided with social processes and thereby exhausted historical reality. I suggest that such concepts be seen as points of departure in the process of cognition of a reality yet to be known. From this perspective, neither production nor exchange may be privileged as the singular authentic domain of social historical development. Rather, if we treat both categories as analytical abstractions, that is, as the means of comprehending historical phenomena, it becomes possible—and necessary—

to reconstruct theoretically their changing historical interrelation and interaction. Here, the concept at once serves as the means to describe, evaluate, order, and interpret particular phenomena more adequately and to explicate the complex, differentiated historical structure and coherence of the politico-economic whole. It thereby enables us to disclose the dense historical interconnectedness of specific relations and processes of capitalist development through multiple temporal and spatial frameworks. Such an approach broadens the range of interpretive possibilities and indicates new dimensions of the organization of labor and class formation on a world scale.

In contrast to the conventional Marxist conception of production as simply the socially organized combination of human labor, instruments, and materials, production may be theoretically constructed as a general historical relation that presupposes distribution, exchange, and consumption. (Although this line of thought in Marx's work has been less influential, it opens rich possibilities for historical reconstruction and interpretation.) Taken together, these relations form an interrelated and mutually dependent theoretical whole, "distinctions within a unity." Each of these terms requires the others and is defined through its relation to them. Their interrelation delineates the processes of social economy (Marx 1973, 83–100). As analytical abstractions, these broad categories are intended to isolate the common features of all social production. Taken by themselves, they yield no "general laws" and tell us little about specific historical conditions of production (83–88). Nonetheless, this approach is methodologically decisive. It establishes the relational character of the concepts and yields a more adequate historical reconstruction of politico-economic processes.

In this formulation, these categories and the relations they represent appear neither as isolated and separable fragments nor as undifferentiated particulars subsumed under a single dominant general category (whether production or exchange). Production and exchange are no longer conceived as discrete entities divorced from their broader contexts, separated from and opposed to each other as external objects; nor are they treated as identical. Rather, production and exchange are understood as relations that presuppose, condition, and are formative of one another as distinct parts of a whole. If we conceive of the social economy in this way, the relevant unit of analysis is defined by the extent of the interrelated processes of production, distribution, exchange, and consumption. As a general category, production is defined through its relation to the other moments of this process; its coherence, scope, and significance are defined within this conceptual field. If production is to be treated as determinant, it is determinant with regard to the totality of these relations.

From this perspective, it is possible more adequately to conceptualize the interrelation of production and exchange in the formation of the modern world economy. The creation of a world market beginning in the sixteenth century may be understood as the establishment of a unified network of commodity production and exchange, varying in scope and degree of intensity, on a world scale—a distinct historical social economy. Systematic and sustained exchange of commodities on a world scale implies and requires the organization of commodity production and relations, direct or indirect, among producers, i.e., social labor, on a world scale. Production is an attribute and constitutive element of the world economy as a social historical whole. But, of course, there is no general and undifferentiated production, only particular branches of production and individual producers whose activities and relations are organized through distinct social forms. Thus, in the modern world economy, commodity production and exchange unite multiple forms of labor and diverse groups of producers at the same time as they establish specific conditions of material and social interdependence among them. Production as a general systemic relation is realized and expressed through the division of labor on a world scale.

Within such a framework, the market appears neither as a secondary element outside of particular "primary" production relations nor as an abstract universal over and above particular production relations. Rather, it is understood as a constituent element of global production relations. By providing the systemic link between definite groups of buyers and sellers, producers and consumers, the market establishes the interrelation and interdependence of various forms of social labor across national boundaries. Exchange continues and completes commodity production and is the condition of renewed production for both particular units and the system as a whole. Of course, distribution, exchange, and consumption themselves entail distinct labor processes (production!) conducted through specific social forms, and various aspects of theses processes are subject to state or private appropriation as well as diverse types of formal organization outside of the exchange relation (Weber 1978, 63–126). The market thus may be viewed as a substantive, historically formed, social and political relation that integrates the diverse relations of production forming the division of labor. By equating the products of these various forms of social labor with one another, the market contributes to the "systemic" unity of this historical social economy. It thereby delineates the parameters of the system as a whole and gives it spatial expression as world economy.

This approach allows us to understand production and exchange—the world market and the division of labor—not as discrete and separate entities but as mutually dependent relations: as moments of an ongoing process of social production and reproduction on a world scale (Sayer 1987). Each conditions the other. The expansion of the world market requires an increase in the volume and variety of commodities to be exchanged. It encourages the development of new points of production to be integrated into the division of labor, and it stimulates the transformation of labor and labor processes. In turn, such large-scale, specialized production is only possible with the social and political organization of adequate trading networks. These networks must be capable of coordinating the movement of goods, money, and information, often across great distances and over periods of long duration; they must be able to reduce the costs of exchange, that is, transaction and transportation costs; they must provide stable and regular markets for specific quantities and types of merchandise; and they must establish social conventions and institutions that guarantee exchange. The rationalization of exchange and the development of trade and the world market create conditions for expanding the scale of production and encourage greater specialization and efficiency of labor (Torras 1993, 198–202). They thus promote the deepening of the division of labor, greater material and social interdependence, and increasing subordination of labor to commodity production.

These interdependent relations of production and exchange—the division of labor and world market—at once define the unit of analysis and the most general relations of the capitalist world economy. At this stage of the analytical procedure, however, they do not yet adequately disclose the structure of the world economy as a whole. They remain abstractions that presuppose as yet unspecified relations among the various forms of social labor integrated into the world economy and the structures that mediate their interrelation. Different productive relations—master and slave, lord and serf, bourgeois and proletarian—organize and structure the labor process in distinctive ways. As scholars writing in the

Marxist tradition have long argued, each such form specifies a particular relation to nature, particular forms of surplus production and appropriation, and particular class relations and conflicts. Specific forms of social relations of production thus come to define distinctive patterns of socioeconomic development (Marx 1976, 325; Wolf 1982, 73–76). Attention to the specificity of forms of social production allows us to comprehend the world economy not simply as the sum of its parts or as an abstraction over and above them, but as distinct relations among particular social forms and material processes of production, integrated with one another through definite modes of exchange and political power— as a structured and differentiated whole changing over time. Conversely, the system as a whole defines labor. Specific forms of commodity production presume exchange relations and are constituted through them within a distinct division of labor. Each such form of labor is subject to multiple determinations and mediations.

This approach enables us to account for the systemic interrelation and interdependence of diverse material processes and social forms of production and to avoid the difficulties entailed in conjoining separate entities. Specific production relations appear as constituent parts of a global system of labor, not as empirically distinct, mutually exclusive labor systems (McMichael 1991, 10). Each form of labor, waged or unwaged, is defined through its relation to the others. Similarly, the market may now be understood as the concrete historical mediation between specific forms of social production and political organization. Within this theoretically constructed historical economy, specific forms of production, exchange, and political power shape one another and are understood in relation to one another. Taken together, these diverse yet interdependent relations form a system, a totality that is the outcome of their mutual interaction. By establishing the specific relations among these various forms of material and social production, social interaction, and political power, all varying through time and in relation to one another, it becomes possible to clarify the development of the world economy as a concrete historical entity.

From this perspective it is possible to reevaluate the role of the capital–wage labor relation in the historical formation of the world economy. Both Marx and Weber have called attention to decisive features of this relation as a general theoretical category. With the commodification of labor power, land, labor, and capital are organized through market relations. Production for the purpose of exchange may be conducted through purchase and sale of its constituent elements. Labor power, instruments of labor, and raw materials all take the form of commodities: each is related to the others through its value. This relation gives meaning to concepts of labor cost, labor time, and labor productivity. Exact calculation in time and money becomes the basis for the organization and systematic transformation of the labor process. The labor supply can be rationally adjusted to production requirements through the labor market. These conditions facilitate technological change, the socialization of labor, and the division of labor within the productive unit (Marx 1976, 439–639; Weber 1978, 90–116, 137–38, 160–64).

From the perspective presented here, however, the importance of the capital–wage labor relation is not that it is itself coterminous with capital as a historical relation. It is neither the most frequent form of production nor the teleological end point of the evolution of all production in the world economy (McMichael 1991). Rather, its significance is determined by its position within the interdependent network of relations of production and exchange—its relation to other forms of labor. The formation of the capital–wage labor relation as an historical social relation presupposes, among other things, the growth of markets, the expansion of commodity production either through the transformation of existing forms of nonwage production or the creation of new ones, the concentration of wealth, and the dispossession of peasantries and independent artisans. Where wage labor could be established on a sufficient scale, its productive superiority transformed commodity circuits throughout the world economy. Its competitive advantage over other forms of production allowed it to become the key form of labor and the pivot of the world economy, altering the conditions of labor elsewhere.

Here Polanyi's account of the formation of a "market society" in nineteenth-century Britain is extremely suggestive. Polanyi links the formation of land, labor, and capital markets in Britain—that is, the creation of a self-regulating market society and liberal state—with the transformation of global commodity and money circuits and the creation a world market based on free trade (Polanyi 1957, 33–134). While he is most concerned with the commodification of land, labor, and capital within Britain, it must be remembered that Britain was at the confluence of world trade. Its strategic position in the world division of labor, hence its relation to various forms of unwaged labor throughout the world economy, contributed to the emergence of market society and the capital–wage labor

relation in Britain, and imparted world historical significance to their subsequent development. (Interestingly, it is precisely in the leading world
commodity circuits of the day—tobacco, sugar, shipbuilding, and maritime
transport—that the confrontation between capital and labor resulted in
the regularization of the wage relation as a means of imposing effective
labor discipline on workers [Linebaugh 1992, 153–83, 371–441].) Viewed
in this light, Polanyi's account prompts consideration of how the consolidation of a "market society" and the capital–wage labor relation in Britain
imposed new conditions and rhythms on production and exchange in the
world economy as a whole. The wage labor regime and industrial production resulted in the demand for new products, the expansion of markets, and an increased velocity of circulation. Free trade, the gold standard,
and the "self-regulating market" (in conjunction with the reorganization
of the interstate system and the rise of British hegemony) reorganized and
reintegrated production and exchange on a world scale.

Under these circumstances, the world division of labor was at once
expanded, diversified, and more tightly integrated, and the various forms
of unwaged labor within the world economy were subjected to new conditions. The creation of markets for new products, the expansion of old
ones, and new technologies of production and transport increased the
sheer scale of the demand for labor. The integration of markets and
increased velocity of circulation put pressure on labor productivity and
required producers to valorize production in new ways. These systemic
changes produced specific effects on particular forms of labor, both waged
and unwaged, and altered relations between classes in ways contingent
upon local conditions and their position within the division of labor. In a
complex movement of global pressure and local response—engendering
and conditioned by a variety of political and social conflicts with contingent local outcomes—new zones of production, forms of labor, groups
of laborers, and products were created while old ones stagnated or were
transformed (Tomich 1988, 1991, 1994; Trouillot 1988; Samuel 1977). The
scale and intensity of commodity-producing labor was increased throughout the world economy. Cheap food products and industrial raw materials produced by unwaged labor become the condition of the renewal on
an expanding scale of the capital–wage labor relation (Wolf 1982, 310–53;
Hobsbawm 1968, 134–53).

Wage labor and capital in Britain may thus be seen as the crucial
productive node of the nineteenth–century world economy, tying

together global commodity circuits through the national market society, while the restructured free trade world market subordinated producers everywhere to new conditions of valorization. Although forms of unwaged labor may have remained unchanged—slavery, serfdom, peonage, sharecropping, independent commodity production—their role, internal composition, and significance in the development of the world economy were redefined through the capacity of the capital–wage labor relation to transform the particular constellation of relations of production and exchange forming the world economy and to recast the division of labor and world market around itself. The predominance of the capital–wage labor relation thereby established a new hierarchy among forms of labor within the world economy and marked a decisive step in its historical evolution.

Attention to the specific forms of production relations allows us to explicate the structure of the world economy as a whole. However, within the premises of the argument presented here, it would be fundamentally distorting to treat particular empirical production relations—for example, wage labor in England or slavery in Brazil—as if they were analytically prior to the world market and division of labor, and formed in themselves the "real material basis" of social development, as conventional Marxist approaches would have it. Rather, any particular form of production relations presupposes the existence of *already historically given* relations of production, distribution, exchange, and consumption. Such particular class relations and forms of labor are themselves socially constructed within the division of labor and world market—that is, within the social historical whole. Rather than independent entities that simply exchange commodities with one another, they represent interdependent processes of social production.

The world economy develops by means of the incorporation of distinctive geographical zones and natural environments. These environments are transformed by selective material processes of production organized through specific forms of social relations of production. Although each form of social labor embodies distinctive patterns of political economic organization and conditions of production, the particular organization of labor is, in each instance, constituted in relation to other material processes and social forms of production within the division of labor. Through the market and the division of labor, each interacts with the others. Although the character, scope, and intensity of

interaction may vary, at every stage in their historical evolution, particular production relations are structurally conditioned and constrained
by the other relations comprising the whole. The nature and composition of production processes and class relations within each particular
form incorporate the relation of this particular form to the others and
to the world economy as a whole. Each represents a distinctive position and constellation of material processes and social relations within
the division of labor at a given point in its development.

Thus, systemic processes produce specific and irreducible "local
faces" (Tomich 1990; Mintz 1977, 1978). Each individual form is simultaneously constitutive of the global system and a particular manifestation
of its processes. Its course of development is dependent upon its position
within the division of labor (that is, its relation to forms of production
elsewhere, or to changes in exchange, distribution, or consumption). Differences in the demand for specific goods and the material conditions of
their production, differences in the social conditions of labor (levels of
production costs, productivity, etc.), and the capacity of states and enterprises to organize circuits of production and exchange at once profoundly
shape the fate of individual production zones and the scope and complexity of the division of labor.

From this perspective, specific forms of production relations cannot
be presumed to form discrete, coherent units that develop autonomously
from their own unique "inner processes." Rather than seeing each form
of class relation or national economy as an internally stable and externally bounded unit that is brought into relation with other such units,
particular class relations and social conflicts may be better understood as
the product of multiple and diverse yet interrelated relations and processes of varying intensity, extent, and duration. Viewed from the vantage point of the world economy, particular relations of production
appear as points of convergence and concentration within the broader
political economic network. Each represents a contingent "unstable
equilibrium" of processes that are spatially and temporally uneven, overlapping, and noncoincident with one another in the range of their effect.
Consequently, particular class boundaries appear to be inherently plural,
heterogeneous, and unstable, the product of the interaction of multiple
relations and processes operating simultaneously across varying spatial
and temporal scales. Rich, many-sided, and historically dense and complex concentrations of diverse elements, they are not comprehensible in

terms of their apparently "intrinsic" characteristics, but rather through their relation to the whole.

This emphasis on the social construction of production processes and on the historical specificity of relations of production permits a more historically and sociologically adequate understanding of processes of world economy and world class formation. Such a perspective requires us to address the formation over time and in space of the social-political frameworks through which commodity production and exchange occur in order to account for their specific character within the unifying whole. It thereby enables us to theoretically reconstruct at once the historical unity and interdependence of specific forms of social labor and of particular political economic units through the division of labor and world market and the world economy as the concrete relation of diverse forms of social relations of production, exchange, and power—a structured, historical whole.

By calling attention to production and exchange as general, systemic, yet abstract relations, the approach presented here allows diverse forms of social labor to be theoretically integrated into a conception of a world-scale political economy, without artificially separating the general from the particular, the global from the local, production from exchange. It draws attention to the material and social interdependence of diverse relations and processes united through the division of labor and the world market (Tomich 1990). If the *object* of analysis is particular class relations, the appropriate *unit* of analysis is the totality of relations forming the historical world economy. This perspective permits the disclosure of the complex, uneven and contingent processes within the totality of interdependent relations that form particular class relations as an historical outcome. Such a reconstruction of the historically specific character of particular relations also contributes to an understanding of the unity and diversity of the multiple forms of waged and unwaged labor that constitute the world economy. By seeing the whole as the unity of global and local, this perspective seeks to avoid the reification of world, national, or regional units and, consequently, either the construction of false necessity or premature emphasis on local agency or particularity. Rather, relations are seen as at once necessary and contingent: necessary because of the systemic unity imposed by the interdependence of forms of commodity production and exchange and political power; and contingent because the particular character of those forms are always the product of specific, complex, uneven historical processes within the relational network. Comprehension of empirically given relations, whether of the world economy as a whole or its particular forms, is the result of theoretically informed inquiry that is capable of reconstructing these relations and processes in their historical complexity.

Following the logic of the approach presented here, production remains an abstract and general category unless and until we are able to theoretically specify and historically reconstruct its various material processes (extraction, cultivation, manufacture, transport and communications, information) and social forms (the varieties of waged and unwaged labor) in their relation to one another through the division of labor and mediating structures of market and state. (Of course, the same may also be said for distribution, exchange, consumption, and, indeed, the "whole" itself.) Our knowledge of such relations only becomes concrete as we establish their historical interrelation and interdependence, that is, establish the social economic system as an historical, not an abstract entity. Therefore, the problem, from this perspective, is to develop methodological procedures and analytical frameworks that concretize theoretical categories, not to create abstract models (McMichael 1991, 15). Here the role of theory is to reconstruct this social economic whole in its historical complexity by specifying relations, establishing their historical interconnections and contexts, and ordering narrative accounts. Its purpose is neither to discover repetitive causal regularities nor to reveal paradigmatic or exceptional cases, but rather to identify significant difference within a spatially and temporally unified historical whole.

References

Aston, T. H., and C. H. E. Philpin. 1985. *The Brenner Debate: Agrarian Class Structure and Economic Development in Pre-Industrial Europe.* Cambridge: Cambridge University Press.

Brenner, Robert. 1977. "The Origins of Capitalist Development: A Critique of Neo-Smithian Marxism." *New Left Review* 104 (July–August): 25–92.

Corrigan, Philip. 1977. "Feudal Relics or Capitalist Monuments? Notes on the Sociology of Unfree Labor." *Sociology* 11 (3): 435–63.

Dobb, Maurice. 1947. *Studies in the Development of Capitalism*. New York: International Publishers.

Frank, Andre Gunder. 1967. *Capitalism and Underdevelopment in Latin America*. New York: Monthly Review Press.

Hilton, Rodney, ed. 1976. *The Transition from Feudalism to Capitalism*. London: New Left Books.

Hobsbawm, Eric. 1968. *Industry and Empire*. Harmondsworth, England: Penguin Books.

Laclau, Ernesto. 1971. "Imperialism in Latin America." *New Left Review* 67 (May-June): 19–38.

Linebaugh, Peter. 1992. *The London Hanged: Crime and Civil Society in the Eighteenth Century*. Cambridge: Cambridge University Press.

Marx, Karl. 1973. *Grundrisse*. Harmondsworth, England: Penguin.

———. 1976. *Capital*. Vol. 1. Harmondsworth, England: Penguin.

McMichael, Philip. 1991. "Slavery in the Regime of Wage Labor: Beyond Paternalism in the U.S. Cotton Culture." *Social Concept* 6 (1): 10–28.

Merrington, John. 1976. "Town and Country in the Transition to Capitalism." In Hilton 1976.

Mintz, Sidney W. 1977. "The So-called World System: Local Initiative and Local Response." *Dialectical Anthropology* 2 : 253–70.

———. 1978. "Was the Plantation Slave a Proletarian?" *Review* 2 (1): 71–98.

Polanyi, Karl. 1957. *The Great Transformation: The Political and Economic Origins of Our Time*. Boston: Beacon Press.

Samuel, Raphael. 1977. "The Workshop of the World: Steam Power and Hand Technology in Mid-Victorian Britain." *History Workshop* 3: 6–72.

Sayer, Derek. 1987. *The Violence of Abstraction: The Analytical Foundations of Historical Materialism*. Oxford: Basil Blackwell.

Sweezy, Paul. 1976a. "A Critique." In Hilton 1976.

———. 1976b. "A Rejoinder." In Hilton 1976.

Tomich, Dale W. 1988. "The 'Second Slavery': Bonded Labor and the Transformation of the Nineteenth-Century World Economy." In Francisco O. Ramirez, ed., *Rethinking the Nineteenth Century*. Westport, CT: Greenwood Press.

———. 1990. *Slavery in the Circuit of Sugar: Martinique in the World Economy, 1830–1848*. Baltimore: Johns Hopkins University Press.

——. 1991. "World Slavery and Caribbean Capitalism: The Cuban Sugar Industry, 1760–1868." *Theory and Society* 20 (3): 297–320.

——. 1994. "Small Islands and Huge Comparisons: Caribbean Plantations, Historical Unevenness, and Capitalist Modernity." *Social Science History* 18 (3): 340–58.

Torras, Jaume. 1993. "The Building of a Market." In *Els Espais del Mercat: 2on Col.loqui Internacional d'Història Local*. València, Spain: Diputació de València.

Trouillot, Rolph. 1988. *Peasants and Capital: Dominica in the World Economy*. Baltimore: Johns Hopkins University Press.

Wallerstein, Immanuel. 1974. *The Modern World System: Capitalist Agriculture and the Origins of the European World-Economy in the Sixteenth Century*. New York: Academic Press.

——. 1979. *The Capitalist World-System*. New York: Cambridge University Press.

Weber, Max. 1978. *Economy and Society*. Berkeley: University of California Press.

Wolf, Eric R. 1982. *Europe and the People Without History*. Berkeley: University of California Press.

CHAPTER 10

Class Location versus Market Interests in Macropolitical Behavior: The Social Origins of the German Nazi Party

William Brustein

THERE APPEARS TO BE A GROWING CONSENSUS AMONG SOCIAL SCIENTISTS that class-based models of political behavior no longer offer an accurate explanation of political behavior. R. Inglehart (1987, 1289) posits a tendency in political behavior for postmaterialist motivations to supplant economic self-interest or class-based motivations as advanced industrial society emerges. He adds that whereas previously the politics centering on the ownership of the means of the production engendered a class-based polarization between the working class and the middle class, this is no longer the case in present-day advanced industrial societies (1295).

Inglehart may or may not be correct about the motivations of voters in contemporary advanced industrial societies, but implicit in his argument is an assumption that class-based models provided valid explanations of political behavior in earlier historical periods. Inglehart's assumption is indeed consistent with the claims of S. M. Lipset and others (Lipset 1981; Minkenberg 1992; Weakliem 1993, 382) who argue that the rise of industrial capitalism and democracy resulted in social class replacing religion as the strongest predictor of voting behavior.

What is the class-based model of political behavior? Marx employed the concept of class to demarcate groups in terms of their location within the productive process. Although Marx understood the existence of subclasses, he concentrated on the emergence within different historical epochs of two opposing classes—opposing by virtue of their relationship to the means of production. Within the bourgeois or capitalist mode of production Marx identified the nonowning working class (or proletariat) and the owning middle class (or bourgeoisie). For Marx, individuals' social class stood for more than their locations within the productive process; Marx believed that people's social being—that is, their social outlook, values, beliefs, and behavior—is shaped by their social class. When individuals within a class recognize their common socioeconomic interests and undertake to change or defend them, they affiliate with political parties or organizations that they perceive to reflect their common or (class) interests (Marger 1987, 35). This kind of political behavior came to be referred to as class-based. On the other hand, individuals within a class who fail to vote for or join their class party were seen as possessing a "false consciousness."

The central argument of this chapter is that class-based models stressing people's relationships to the means of production (e.g., Wright 1978) fail to capture the complexity of individuals' material interests and, consequently, their political behavior. People's relationship to the means of production (class) is a necessary but not sufficient determinant of their political behavior; individuals' political preferences are shaped by additional structural locations. Following Max Weber, some scholars have suggested that Marxist class or economic models of political behavior ignore a person's relationship to the marketplace (Collins 1986, 132–38; Kerbo 1991, 110–11; Hall, Introduction to this book). Of course, there are many models of class-based politics (e.g., Aminzade 1993; Gould 1995; Hanagan 1994; Tilly 1992). Here, instead of disputing their details, I want to propose an alternative approach. In this chapter, I concentrate on individuals' relationship to the marketplace as a principal determinant of their political behavior. My usage of "marketplace" refers to the forms of economic production in which individuals are engaged, taking into consideration the extent to which these forms are market oriented and profitable, that is, produce a surplus (Brustein 1988a, 1988b, 1991). My argument is that individuals' market location plays as important a role in shaping their political choices as does their social class.

In previous writings I demonstrated the usefulness of a model of market interests to explain regional variation in peasant participation in antistate rebellion in France, Spain, and England between 1500 and 1700 (Brustein 1985; Brustein and Levi 1987), the persistence of right-wing voting patterns in Western France and left-wing patterns in Mediterranean France (Brustein 1988b), and regional variation in support of interwar fascist movements in Belgium and Italy (Brustein 1988a; Brustein 1991). Here, as an alternative to a class-based explanation, I will attempt to demonstrate the appropriateness of a market-interests model as an explanation of the social origins of the Nazi Party joiners between 1925 and 1933.

The reigning class-based theory holds that German Nazism was a reaction of the German lower middle class (independent artisans, shopkeepers, farmers, and white-collar employees) to the growing influence of big labor and big business in Germany. Lipset (1981) posits that every social class or stratum is associated with an extremist form of political expression: communism or Peronism in the working class, traditional authoritarianism in the upper class, and fascism or Nazism in the lower middle class. For proponents of the lower-middle-class thesis of Nazism, the strain from the processes of concentration and centralization of production resulting from the late-nineteenth- and early-twentieth-century modernization in Germany was primarily responsible for this class's embrace of Nazism. However, individual-level data on Nazi Party joiners reveal that the Nazi Party was not strictly a lower-middle-class phenomenon but instead a catchall party gaining adherents from all social classes.[1] Moreover, the data demonstrate significant intraclass variation regarding joining the Nazi Party. For example, in Weimar Germany

1. See Brustein 1996. The primary and richest source of information on Nazi Party membership is the NSDAP *Zentralkartei*, or Master File, containing approximately 7.2 million original and official individual German Nazi Party membership cards from the reconstitution of the party in February 1925 to its demise in May 1945. The cards are arranged alphabetically on every member of the Nazi Party. The files are believed to be nearly 90 percent complete. Some cards are believed to have been destroyed by Nazi Party officials before they were captured by the U.S. military. The Master File, which is housed at the Berlin Document Center, holds two separate files. The larger collection is the *Ortskartei;* the smaller, the *Reichskartei*. Originally these two files were intended to duplicate one another for the purpose of cross-referencing. The *Ortskartei* was originally arranged alphabetically by *Gau* (administrative region) and then within each *Gau* alphabetically by county, local group, and member's last name. The *Reichskartei* was arranged alphabetically by last name, regardless of membership location. After these files were captured by the U.S. military in Munich in 1945, they were moved to Berlin, where both files were rearranged alphabetically by last name regardless of geographical designation.

Each membership record includes the individual's first and last names, gender (via first name), party number, birthplace, birthdate, marital status, occupation, residence (and subsequent residences), local membership affiliation, *Gau* affiliation, dates and location of joining, exiting, and rejoining, and remarks on the member by party leaders. As a source of information on the social origins of the Nazi Party, the Master File is incomparable.

(1919–1933), although both independent livestock farmers and wine-pro-
ducing farmers owned property, and although both blue-collar laborers
engaged in export-oriented (chemical and electro-technical) industries
and blue-collar workers involved in domestic or import-oriented industries (foodstuffs, construction, and woodworking) shared a similar relationship to the means of production, in each case they frequently held
divergent views on important issues like free trade and tariffs. Indeed,
many livestock farmers and domestic sector industrial workers opposed
free trade and were more likely to join the Nazi Party, while many wine-
producing farmers and export sector industrial workers favored free trade
and were less likely to join the Nazi Party. That the Nazi Party recruited
successfully across all social classes, and that there were significant divergences within specific social classes with respect to joining the Nazi Party
point to obvious weaknesses in a class-based explanation of Nazi Party
joiners (Childers 1983; Falter 1991; Hamilton 1982; Kater 1983).

The German Old Middle Class and the Nazi Party

There is a general consensus that the German lower middle class of self-
employed farmers, shopkeepers, merchants, and independent artisans was
a major constituency of the Nazi Party before 1933. Figure 1 shows that
the old middle class was overrepresented among Nazi Party joiners compared to the population. During each year between 1925 and 1932 the old
middle class constituted between 30 and 35 percent of the Nazi Party joiners, with the exception of 1926 and 1927, when it declined to 29 percent.

But why did the German old middle class embrace Nazism so
wholeheartedly, and why did the various groups constituting this class
really uniformly support Nazism? In contrast to the standard explanation
of the old-middle-class endorsement of Nazism, which highlights its reac-
tive character, my analysis stresses its proactive nature; that is, old-middle-
class Germans joined the Nazi Party because they perceived the party's

---

Aware of the significance of the NSDAP Master File for a study of the Nazi Party as well
as the lacunae in earlier examinations of the file, J. W. Falter and I jointly organized and supervised in 1989 the largest and most systematic collection of Nazi Party membership data from
both the *Ortskartei* and the *Reichskartei*. Our total sample of pre-1933 members consists of
42,004 observations. Our sample contains nearly 3,000 cases for each of the early years (and
for 1933) and roughly 8000 cases for each of the years 1930 to 1932. For a more detailed
description of the data and the method of sampling, see Schneider-Haase 1991.

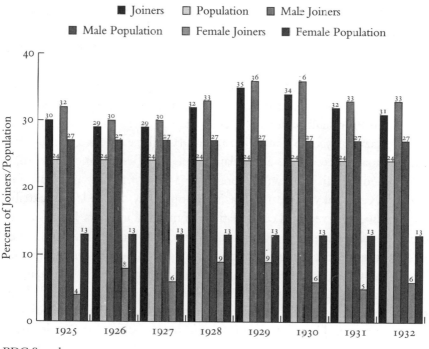

BDC Sample

FIGURE 10.1 NSDAP old middle class joiners, *1925–32*

programs as meeting their material interests best. Moreover, because of
the heterogeneity of interests within the German old middle class, not
every old-middle-class group was equally inclined to join the Nazi Party.
For instance, by forcefully advocating economic protectionism, resettlement, impartible inheritance, and tax relief, while attacking Weimar policies on reparations and subsidies to large East German grain growers, the
Nazi Party should have obtained stronger support from Protestant livestock farmers than from Catholic livestock farmers or from large grain
growers and export-oriented vegetable and fruit farmers.

That Protestant livestock farmers were more predisposed than grain,
fruit, or vegetable producers to join the Nazi Party before 1933 should
help explain another interesting puzzle about the rise of Nazism: the
degree to which German regions varied in terms of Nazi Party membership. Like German classes, German regions varied in their attraction to
the Nazi Party. On the one hand, the areas of Schleswig-Holstein, Lower
Saxony, and Danzig manifested exceptionally high Nazi Party voting and

membership, while, on the other hand, the areas of North-Westphalia, Württemberg, Cologne-Aachen, and Coblenz exhibited relatively weak attraction to the party. In fact, the ratio of Nazi Party members to the total population was more than five times greater in the state of Schleswig-Holstein than in the state of North-Westphalia (*Partei-Statistik*, 1935). Why did the Nazi Party fare better in some German regions than in others? We know that Protestant regions of Germany displayed a greater attachment to the Nazi Party than Catholic regions. But the existence of religious confessional differences as an explanation is insufficient, since Nazi support varied significantly within predominantly Protestant and Catholic regions. Regional variation in Nazism's popularity can be largely attributed to divergent regional constellations of material interests. For instance, the close fit between the regional distribution of people's material interests and the specific programs of the Nazi Party played an important role in the party's ability to attract supporters in northwestern Germany—particularly in the states of Schleswig-Holstein and Lower Saxony. Here, the typical farmer was a small landowner engaged in highly speculative dairy farming and hog fattening (Heberle 1951; Loomis and Beegle 1946; Stoltenberg 1962). During the final years of the Weimar Republic, many of the farmers of Schleswig-Holstein and Lower Saxony protested against what they perceived was the government's insensitivity to their economic plight. They demanded a German trade policy that would eliminate foreign sources of food, an immediate state takeover of mortgage interest payments, a law lowering the rate of interest, governmental financial assistance, lower taxes, and less expensive fertilizer and electricity (Tilton 1975, 52; Pridham 1973, 124). It was exactly these concerns that the Nazi Agrarian Program addressed with specific solutions.

Farmers in other German regions were less eager to support the Nazis because the Nazi program did not correspond to their needs. Farmers in Germany's more prosperous regions—many of whom were less affected by price changes in the international market for dairy and beef—were less susceptible to Nazi promises and the Nazi message of economic autarky, that is, national independence from any imports (Moeller 1986, 15–16; Kater 1983, 58). For example, in parts of Rhineland-Westphalia, Baden, Bavaria, and Württemberg, many farmers specializing in the production of highly exportable cash crops like tobacco, beer, wine, and fruits favored free-trade policies and worried more about foreign retaliation if Germany imposed agricultural tariff barriers.

East German large grain producers were not won over by the Nazi agrarian program either. Unlike the government's apparent insensitivity to the plight of the dairy and meat farmers, the government enacted a series of policies between 1928 and 1930 that largely benefited the large grain producers in East Germany. The East German estate owners also became the beneficiaries of massive state aid in 1931 under the Eastern Assistance Program. These farmers continued to rely on the conservative German National Peoples Party as their political voice.

Many farmers in Germany's more prosperous regions had an additional reason to look unfavorably upon the Nazi agrarian program. The Nazi promise to halt the sale of farms to nonfamily buyers meant that owners could not sell their property or offer it as collateral against a loan (Farquharson 1976, 63–68). While this policy should have received support in the economically depressed Northwest, where farmers were fighting to prevent foreclosure on their properties, it should not have been well received by farmers in the relatively prosperous zones of Rhineland-Westphalia, Baden, and Bavaria. There the sale of land was still a source of profit, and putting up one's property as collateral against a loan was seen as a suitable means to obtain capital to expand one's holding.

Also, in many Catholic parts of southern Germany, Hesse, and Rhineland-Westphalia, farmers had a particular problem with the Nazi proposal for a compulsory system of impartible inheritance. If implemented, this would have terminated the practice of dividing land holdings among heirs, a practice that was in effect in much of the region and was guaranteed by regional laws (Farquharson 1976, 63–68). Since many farmers' children counted on their portion of fixed and moveable property as an inheritance, the Nazi pledge to eliminate partible inheritance did not elicit enthusiasm.

Many farmers in Schleswig-Holstein and Lower Saxony, by contrast, had no problem with the Nazi position on inheritance, since impartible inheritance was already in practice there. Moreover many of these farmers enthusiastically welcomed the fact that accompanying the Nazi policy on inheritance was the promise of a settlement program through which disinherited farmers' sons would receive land parcels in Eastern Germany (Farquharson 1976, 13–15; Noakes 1971, 124–25). The settlement program offered young farmers the hope of owning a piece of land. While there were other impartible inheritance areas in Germany, the Nazi settlement program had a special significance for the

farmers of northwestern Germany. Traditionally, in Germany's impartible inheritance regions, the noninheriting children received a monetary compensation. However, in the economically depressed farming
areas, older farmers did not have sufficient cash to pay off their
younger sons. By promising to set aside land in Eastern Germany for
the disinherited, the Nazi program offered both parents and children
an appealing exit from their dilemma (Noakes 1971, 127; Farquharson 1976, 240).

Insofar as livestock farmers more than grain or grape farmers favored
national independence from imports, the market interests argument predicts that Nazi Party joiners were more likely to come from agricultural
regions that specialized in livestock than from cereal or fruit cultivation
regions. Yet all livestock farming areas should not have equally embraced
the Nazi Party. In particular we would expect that people residing in
Protestant livestock farming areas would have joined the Nazi Party in
greater numbers than those residing in Catholic livestock farming areas.
The old middle class in Catholic livestock farming communities found
the Nazi Party's positions on tariffs, credit, foreclosures, and governmental subsidies consistent with their own interests, but they objected to the
Nazi Party's inheritance proposals, which would force them to abandon
the practice of partible inheritance. Moreover, the old middle class residing in Catholic livestock communities had a viable alternative to the Nazi
Party. The Bavarian People's Party's agricultural positions mirrored the
Nazi Party's positions, and, what is more, the Bavarian People's Party promoted the interests of the Catholic Church in Germany, which to many
Catholic Germans made it a better choice than the Nazi Party. Figure 2
shows that as the proportion of farmland devoted to livestock farming
increases in Protestant German counties, the proportion of the eligible
population that joined the Nazi Party also rises (the proportions are quite
small because party joiners constitute a relatively minor proportion of
total eligible voters). In those majority Protestant counties with less than
20 percent of the farmland devoted to livestock use, only .11 percent of
the total eligible voting population in those counties joined the Nazi
Party, compared to .16 percent in those majority Protestant counties with
more than 41 percent of the farmland devoted to livestock use. In countries with a Catholic majority, an increase in the proportion of farmland devoted to livestock farming does not correspond to a rise in the
proportion of Nazi Party joiners.

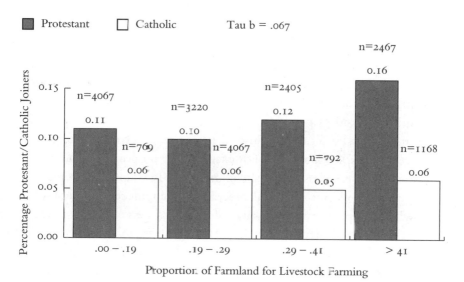

BDC Sample; WRCD; 1933 Statistik des Deutschen Reichs. Percentages are based on a ratio of n joiners divided by total farming population in the four farming groups.

FIGURE 10.2   NSDAP joiners from majority Protestant/Catholic counties, by county farming mix

The German Working Class and the Nazi Party

Like the old middle class, the blue-collar class included groups with divergent interests. Although all workers likely desired higher wages, a shorter workday, and improved health and retirements plans, workers frequently disagreed over the benefits accruing from free trade or protectionism, unionization, and the ownership of private property. Much of the divergence in support for the Nazi Party among German workers stemmed from differences in their skill level and factors related to their particular industrial contexts. Workers' interests were shaped by whether they were skilled, semiskilled, or unskilled laborers, whether they worked in large or small plants, and whether they worked in export-oriented or domestic-oriented, dynamic or stagnant industries.

Consider how German labor differed in terms of skill level. In 1925, for instance, 83 percent of the laborers employed in the mining industry—as compared to only 15 percent of the labor in the rubber and asbestos industries—were classified as skilled labor. Moreover, by 1933 many of the industries employing a high proportion of skilled labor experienced a significant shift from skilled to semi and unskilled labor, principally as a result of German industrial rationalization. In particular, between 1925 and 1933 the proportion of all industrial jobs classified as skilled fell from 83 percent to 46 percent in mining, 70 percent to 54 percent in woodworking, 44 percent to 17 percent in textiles, 54 percent to 30 percent in iron and steel, and 55 percent to 35 percent in leather and linoleum. In other industries, by contrast, industrial rationalization hardly affected the proportion of skilled labor jobs. For example, the proportion of all industrial jobs that were classified as skilled between 1925 and 1933 remained at 59 percent in electro-technical, precision and engineering, and optometry, while the proportion actually rose from 23 percent to 25 percent in the chemical industry (Preller 1949, 119).[2] In short, many skilled workers employed in industries that had witnessed the erosion of skilled jobs may have looked quite favorably upon the promises of job creation and economic autarky.

In addition to workers' levels of skill, the market orientation and profitability of the industrial branch where workers were located shaped their material interests. Although he is primarily interested in the views of industrial elites, D. Abraham (1986) focuses on the division within German industry between an import/domestic and a export/dynamic sector. The import/domestic sector was characterized by the older, more monopolistic, and more labor-intensive branches of heavy industry, such as mining, steel, iron, and coal. This sector suffered from a relatively low rate of profit and a relatively high level of expenditure for wages, salaries, and social insurance.

The import/domestic sector pushed for higher prices for its goods, lower employee costs, expansion into "Mitteleuropa" (central and eastern Europe), and a larger share of the domestic market. For instance, quotas enacted by the international iron cartel in 1925 closed the door to further international expansion for Germany's iron makers. These iron makers, consequently, turned inward and saw promise in an expanded domestic market. As a group, the import/domestic sector favored limiting imports, introducing protective tariffs, lowering taxes, reducing social

---

2. L. Preller (1949) compiled his 1925 findings from the occupational census reporting male and female workers, including apprentices, and his 1933 findings from the census of German firms reporting only males without apprentices. Although the two reporting procedures differed, the magnitude of the results support his overall finding about the effects of industrial rationalization.

welfare expenditures, and terminating reparation payments imposed by the Allies at the end of World War I (Gourevitch 1986, 142; Abraham 1986; Smith 1986, 211).

Abraham (1986) describes the export/dynamic sector as decentralized and capital intensive. Machine, metal-finishing, electro-technical, and chemical industries belonged to this sector. The export/dynamic sector enjoyed relatively higher rates of profit and relatively lower employee costs. Its industries favored reduced prices on imports, free trade, expanded markets, and Germany's fulfillment of her reparations payments. The export/dynamic sector's support for measures to improve exports made sense in the light of its international competitive advantage. For instance, Germany's chemical industry held 43 percent of the world market in chemical exports in 1928, while Germany's coal industry—producing for domestic consumption, and stagnating—maintained a 10 percent share of the world market in coal (Abraham 1986, 140; Gourevitch 1986, 22–23, 141–42; Calleo 1978, 63). By agreeing to the allies' reparation demands, advocates of the export/dynamic sector believed that Germany would obtain much-needed foreign credits and that German industry would benefit from a "most favored nation status" that would open doors to the world's richest markets. They believed this because the major markets for many of the high-quality and high-cost goods manufactured by the export/dynamic sector were in the United States, Britain, Netherlands, Belgium, and France and because many industries in this dynamic sector depended on these nations for vital imports (Gourevitch 1986, 141–42; Abraham 1986; Smith 1986, 211).

During the first two years of the Depression, the gap between the two sectors grew. While the situation for import/domestic industries deteriorated between 1929 and 1931, Germany went from the world's number three exporter in 1929 to number one in 1931 (Abraham 1986, 139).

Abraham provides an informative glimpse into the rivalry between competing sectors of German industry. However, his dichotomous separation of industrial branches assumes incorrectly that domestic industrial branches are inherently stagnant and export industrial branches are inherently dynamic. Careful analysis suggests that this is not necessarily so. For example, if we define the export value of an industrial branch as the value of the branch's exports divided by the ratio of workers in that branch to all German workers, and if we measure whether a branch was dynamic by its profit ratio, we find that while some export industrial branches were dynamic, others were stagnant. In particular, while the chemical industry scored high on export value and profit ratio, the machine industry scored high on export value but had a negative profit ratio. Conversely, not all import/domestic branches were stagnant. The coal industry and the food and food-processing industrial branch ranked low on export value (29 and 45.6 respectively) but had positive profit ratios (2.22 and 2.84 in 1932). A more accurate separation of German industrial branches would situate branches along a two-dimensional continuum: one ranging from production for export to production for import and the other ranging from positive profit ratio to negative profit ratio (Sweezy 1940, 384–98; Hoffmann 1965, 522–23).[3]

Abraham's examination of industrial sectors in Weimar Germany has an additional limitation. It focuses exclusively on the role played by elites—industrial leaders and political leaders—rather than on the implications of industrial policy for blue-collar labor interests. Regarding labor's interests, Abraham implies that they were inherently at odds with those of management. This claim is misleading. Although labor and management would have held dissimilar positions on wage levels, unionization, collective bargaining, and unemployment compensation, they would have shared a stake in the economic health of the industry. Workers, after all, were more likely to lose jobs in an unprofitable industry than in a profitable industry, and a profitable industry was more likely to accede to labor demands of higher wages and improved benefits. Not only did workers in the more profitable branches of German industry maintain relatively high wages throughout the Weimar era, the leaders of the more profitable German industries were substantially more agreeable to labor's demands than leaders of the less profitable sector (Gourevitch 1986, 141–42; Abraham 1986, 137).[4] If, therefore, free-trade policies were favored by a particular industrial branch, then both workers and management in that branch would likely support free trade; if protectionist policies were favored, however, then workers and managers within that branch would most likely support protectionism.

What becomes amply clear from this cursory examination of blue-collar labor material interests during Weimar is that workers did not con-

3. For a detailed critique of Abraham's bipartite categorization and data see Hayes 1987, 452–72.

4. Gourevitch (1986, 141–42) notes that foreign economic policy interests drove some German industrialists to establish more amicable relations with labor. He also observes that by 1932 major elements of both German labor and domestic and heavy industry favored a policy of domestic reflation (144).

stitute a single homogeneous class. The Nazi Party received differential support from various sectors of the working class. The Nazi Party membership data show clearly that the Nazi Party drew substantial support from the blue-collar working class (Brustein and Falter 1994). What we need to ask is: What kinds of workers should have been most attracted to the Nazi Party? Four major points stand out.

1. In comparison to the Social Democratic Party (SPD) and the Communist Party (KPD), the Nazi Party was clearly the most nationalistic. Throughout Weimar the Nazis steadfastly opposed the government's fulfillment policy of reparations and German compliance with the stipulations of the Versailles treaty. Furthermore, in contrast to the Communists' and Social Democrats' avowed sympathy for the international working class, the Nazis promoted solely the interests of the German working class, and they linked their opposition to reparations and the Versailles treaty to the economic interests of German workers. The Nazi Party, therefore, should have appealed to nationalistic German workers more than the SPD and KPD.

2. Throughout Weimar the Nazis stood out as a strong proponents of autarkic economic development. The party opposed free-trade measures and supported protective tariffs, the expansion of the domestic market, and the development of a continental economic zone in southeastern Europe. The Nazi positions on protectionism and autarkic economic development corresponded closely to the economic interests of workers in the import-oriented industrial sector. On the other hand, the Nazis condemned free-trade policies and expressed no sympathy for improved relations with Germany's western European and North American trading partners. Thus, the Nazis' positions were at variance with the interests of many workers in the export-oriented industrial sector, who perceived benefits from free-trade policies. We should expect, therefore, to find higher rates of Nazi Party affiliation among workers in industries producing primarily for the domestic market (e.g., food production, construction, mining, clothing, and woodworking) and lower rates among workers in German industries producing primarily for the export market (e.g., chemical and electro-technical industries, machinery, and textiles).[5] Figures 10.3a through 10.3d list the

5. My classification of industries as either import- or export-oriented is based on information taken from Hoffmann 1965, 522–23; Svennilson 1983, 187, 335–36; and Abraham 1986. In examining world market shares or total exports of seven major European countries and the United States for 1928, Svennilson (1933, 187) shows that German chemical industry exports commanded 42.8 percent of world exports while German foodstuffs held 9.3 percent of world exports.

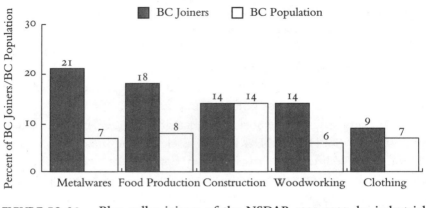

FIGURE 10.3a Blue-collar joiners of the NSDAP, 1925–1932, by industrial branch

seventeen principal industrial branches found in the 1925 German census.[6] I have calculated the proportion of working-class individuals who joined the Nazi Party from each industrial branch. The proportions represent each industrial branch's share of the total Nazi Party working-class joiners of at least eighteen years of age. These figures provide substantial support that German workers in import-oriented branches were more likely to join the Nazi Party than workers in the export-oriented branches. In particular, the figures show that four of the five major import-oriented industrial branches (food production, construction, woodworking, and clothing) have significantly high proportions of Nazi Party joining, while two of the four chief export-oriented industrial branches (chemical and textiles) have exceptionally low proportions.

3. The National Socialist German Workers' Party (NSDAP) emerged in 1931 as a very forceful proponent of pump priming and job creation. Therefore, we should expect that after 1931 the NSDAP should have recruited relatively successfully both among employed workers who feared the loss of their jobs and among the growing numbers of unemployed workers. In particular, since the NSDAP job creation program called for mass construction of public housing, highways, dams, and canals, we would expect the party to recruit especially successfully among workers who would get these new jobs: principally, workers in the construction and woodworking industries. The evidence appears to support

6. The Tau b of 0.056 was calculated across all seventeen branches of industry.

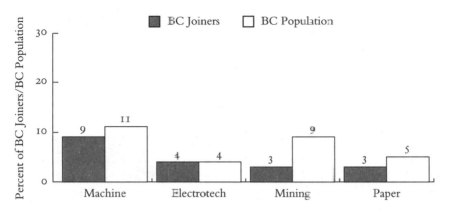

FIGURE 10.3b Blue-collar joiners of the NSDAP, 1925–1932, by industrial branch

this conclusion. The highest unemployment levels between January and July 1932 were in the construction industry (77.3 percent in January 1932 and 77.2 percent in July 1932) and the woodworking industry (66.1 percent in both January and July 1932), and these two industrial branches ranked among those branches with higher proportions of Nazi Party working-class joiners. The lowest unemployment levels were in mining (18.3 percent in January 1932 and 17.6 percent in July 1932). The mining industry ranked far below the woodworking and construction industries in terms of Nazi Party affiliation (*Wirtschaft und Statistik* 1932, 147–48, 471–73, 541–42, 740–41; Brady 1933).

4. Most importantly, among the working-class parties, the Nazi Party subordinated an exclusively working-class orientation to a non-class-exclusive societal outlook. By promoting the interests of private property and small business, the Nazi Party likely alienated many workers who were convinced that private ownership and profit were unacceptable evils. Although many workers decided to stick with the "real" working-class parties (the Social Democrats or Communists), however, other workers who aspired to climb the social ladder (own a home, become a salaried employee, or start their own business) supported the Nazi Party precisely because they saw it as a working-class party that favored social mobility. H. A. Turner (1985, 64–65) has argued that the Nazi Party sought to achieve social equality through a process of upward leveling, that is, absorption of workers into the middle class. In particular, skilled workers, more than semiskilled or unskilled ones, were likely to possess a strong

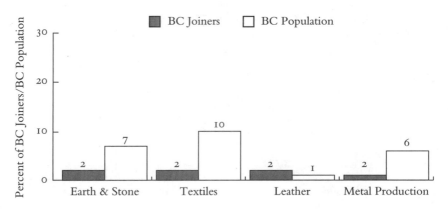

FIGURE 10.3C   Blue-collar joiners of the NSDAP, 1925–1932, by industrial
branch

social mobility aspiration. Skilled workers thought of themselves as both
socially and economically superior to semiskilled and unskilled laborers.
Unlike semiskilled and unskilled workers, they believed that a middle-class
existence was a viable possibility (Kater 1983, 34–38).

Some might claim that laborers in Weimar Germany had few
prospects of social advancement. But for much of the Weimar period,
German labor experienced a rise in real hourly and weekly earnings.
Measured by an index of hourly and weekly earnings (1913 = 100), German labor's hourly earnings climbed from a level of 86 in 1924 to 125
in 1932, while weekly earnings rose from a level of 70 in 1924 to a peak
of 110 in 1929 and dropped to 94 in 1932 (Abraham 1986, 238). The social
and economic gains achieved by workers between 1924 and 1929 should
have persuaded many workers that further social advancement was possible. Ironically, by fighting for and gaining improvements for the working class, the Social Democratic Party may have prepared the ground
for the Nazis to recruit many workers. Many workers had prospered from
the social and economic legislation of the mid-1920s and began to dream
of a middle-class life. They found the Social Democratic Party's opposition to private property and capitalism distasteful and turned instead to
the Nazis because they perceived that the Nazis would help them up the
next rung of the social ladder. All told, the human desire for economic
advancement—and the perception that the Nazi Party, alone among the
working-class parties, reflected that desire—made the Nazi Party a likely
choice for millions of German workers.

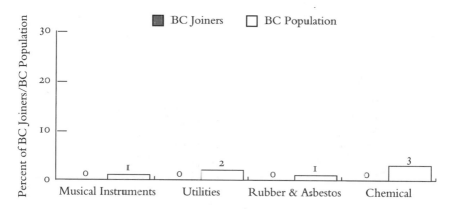

FIGURE 10.3d   Blue-collar joiners of the NSDAP, 1925–1932, by industrial branch

If my argument about the link between social mobility aspirations and joining the Nazi Party is correct, then we should find that more skilled workers than semiskilled and unskilled workers joined the party. By virtue of their social status and wage level, skilled workers should have perceived social advancement as an achievable goal. Figure 4 compares the proportions of skilled blue-collar NSDAP joiners to semiskilled and unskilled blue-collar joiners for the years between 1925 to 1932. As predicted, skilled blue-collar joiners were overrepresented in the Nazi Party, while unskilled and semiskilled were underrepresented.

The market interests argument is a valuable one not just because it predicts that the Nazi Party was a catchall party—that finding has received considerable attention elsewhere (Childers 1983; Falter 1981)—but because it offers an explanation of why the Nazi Party became a catchall party and, equally important, which groups within each class were overrepresented or underrepresented in the party.

This chapter examined the material interests of the German old middle class and blue-collar working class. Guided by the argument that individuals' market interests play a central role in shaping their political behavior, we found that the Nazi Party's emphases on protectionism, autarkic economic development, tax relief, resettlement, and a mandatory system of impartible inheritance positioned the party to recruit successfully among the old middle class of artisans, merchants, and small independent farmers (especially Protestant livestock farmers). The results of the data on Nazi Party

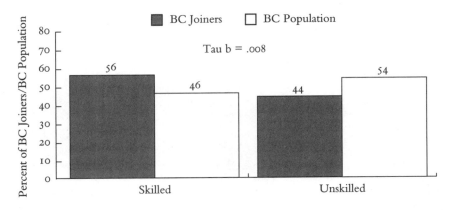

FIGURE 10.4   Blue-collar joiners of the NSDAP, 1925–1933: skilled versus unskilled

joiners between 1925 and 1932 generally confirm the importance of market interests for explaining the political behavior of the old middle class. The market interests argument also offers a materialist explanation for the often cited (but seldom explained) relationship between a population's religious confession and its support for the Nazi Party. It suggests that the absence of livestock farming and the presence of partible inheritance in many Catholic communities shaped attitudes vis-à-vis the Nazi Party.

The Nazi Party's working-class programs—stressing protectionism, autarkic economic development, job creation, and social advancement—strengthened the party's appeal among patriotic workers, workers employed in import-oriented industrial branches, and skilled workers. The findings of the data strongly support the importance of workers' market interests for explaining their political behavior. The data show the highest proportions of Nazi Party joining in several import-oriented industrial branches, and they reveal an overrepresentation of skilled workers compared to an underrepresentation of semiskilled and unskilled workers.

All told, an empirical examination of the social composition of the Nazi Party between 1925 and 1933 points to a weakness in a class-based explanation. The data strongly suggest the existence of both intraclass differences and interclass commonalities of political behavior. The market interests argument of political behavior holds that intraclass divergences and interclass commonalities are not ascribable to a "false consciousness" within classes but rather to self-interests which emerge from differences in individuals' market interests.

References

Abraham, D. 1986. *The Collapse of the Weimar Republic*. 2d ed. New York: Holmes and Meier.

Aminzade, R. 1993. *Ballots and Barricades: Class Formation and Republican Politics in France, 1830 - 1871*. Princeton: Princeton University Press.

Brady, R. A. 1933. *The Rationalization Movement in German Industry; a Study in the Evolution of Economic Planning*. Berkeley: University of California Press.

Brustein, W. 1985. "Class Conflict and Class Collaboration in Regional Rebellions, 1500–1700." *Theory and Society* 14: 445–68.

——. 1988a. "The Political Geography of Belgian Fascism: The Case of Rexism." *American Sociological Review* 53: 939–50.

——. 1988b. *The Social Origins of Political Regionalism: France, 1849 to 1981*. Berkeley: University of California Press.

——. 1991. "The Red Menace and the Rise of Italian Fascism." *American Sociological Review* 56: 652–54.

——. 1996. *The Logic of Evil: The Social Origins of the Nazi Party, 1925–33*. New Haven: Yale University Press.

Brustein, W., and J. W. Falter. 1994. "The Sociology of Nazism: An Interest-Based Account." *Rationality and Society*. 6: 369–99.

Brustein, W., and M. Levi. 1987. "The Geography of Rebellion: Rulers, Rebels, and Regions, 1500–1700." *Theory and Society* 16: 467–95.

Calleo, D. 1978. *The German Problem Reconsidered*. Cambridge: Cambridge University Press.

Childers, T. 1983. *The Nazi Voter: The Social Foundations of Fascism in Germany, 1919–1933*. Chapel Hill: University of North Carolina Press.

Collins, R. 1986. *Max Weber*. Beverly Hills: Sage.

Falter, J. W. 1991. *Hitlers Wähler*. Munich: C. H. Beck.

Farquharson, J. E. 1976. *The Plough and the Swastika: The NSDAP and Agriculture in Germany 1928–45*. London: Sage.

Gould, R. V. 1995. *Insurgent Identities: Class, Community, and Protest in Paris from 1848 to the Commune*. Chicago: University of Chicago Press.

Gourevitch, P. 1986. *Politics in Hard Times: Comparative Responses to International Economic Crises*. Ithaca, N.Y.: Cornell University Press.

Hamilton, R. F. 1982. *Who Voted for Hitler?* Princeton: Princeton University Press.

Hanagan, Michael P. 1994. "New Perspectives on Class Formation: Culture, Reproduction and Agency." *Social Science History* 18: 77–94.

Hayes, P. 1987. "History in an Off Key: David Abraham's Second *Collapse*." *Business History Review* 61: 452–72.

Heberle, R. 1951. *Social Movements*. New York: Appleton-Century-Crofts.

Hoffmann, W. G. 1965. *Das Wachstum der deutschen Wirtschaft seit der Mitte des 19. Jahrhunderts*. Berlin: Springer Verlag.

Inglehart, R. 1987. *American Political Science Review* 81: 1289–1303.

Kater, M. 1983. *The Nazi Party*. Cambridge: Harvard University Press.

Kerbo, H. R. 1991. *Social Stratification and Inequality*. 2d. ed. New York: McGraw Hill.

Lipset, S. M. 1981. *Political Man* Baltimore: Johns Hopkins University Press.

Loomis, C., and L. P. Beegle. 1946. "The Spread of Nazism in Rural Areas." *American Sociological Review* 11: 724–33.

Marger, M. N. 1987. *Elites and Masses*. 2d edition. Belmont, Calif.: Wadsworth.

Minkenberg, M. 1992. "The New Right in Germany: The Transformation of Conservatism and the Extreme Right." *European Journal of Political Research* 22: 55–81.

Moeller, R. G. 1986. *German Peasants and Agrarian Politics, 1914–1924*. Chapel Hill: University of North Carolina Press.

Noakes, J. 1971. *The Nazi Party in Lower Saxony, 1921–1933*. London: Oxford University Press.

NSDAP Partei-Statistik. 1935. Vol. 2. Munich: Reichsorganisationleiter der NSDAP.

Preller, L. 1949. *Sozial Politik in der Weimarer Republik*. Stuttgart: Franz Mittelbach Verlag.

Pridham, G. 1973. *Hitler's Rise to Power: The Nazi Movement in Bavaria, 1923–1933*. New York: Harper and Row.

Schneider-Haase, T. 1991. "Beschreibung der Stichprobenziehung zu den Mitgliedern der NSDAP vom 27. März – 7. September 1989 im Berlin Document Center." *Historical Social Research* 16: 113–51.

Smith, W. D. 1986. *Ideological Origins of Nazi Imperialism*. New York: Oxford University Press.

Stoltenberg, G. 1962. *Politische Strömungen im schleswig-holsteinischen Landvolk 1918–1933* Dusseldorf: Droste Verlag.

Svennilson, I. 1983. *Growth and Stagnation in the European Economy.* New York: Garland Publishers.

Sweezy, M. 1940. "German Corporate Profits, 1926–1938." *Quarterly Journal of Economics* 54: 384–98.

Tilly, L. A. 1992. *Politics and Class in Milan, 1881–1901.* New York: Oxford University Press.

Tilton, T. A. 1975. *Nazism, Neo-Nazism and the Peasantry.* Bloomington: Indiana University Press.

Turner, H. A., Jr. 1985. *German Big Business and the Rise of Hitler.* Oxford: Oxford University Press.

Weakliem, D. 1993. "Class Consciousness and Political Change: Voting and Political Attitudes in the British Working Class, 1964 to 1970." *American Sociological Review* 58: 382–97.

Wirtschaft und Statistik. 1932. Vol. 12.

Wright, E. O. 1978. *Class, Crisis and the State.* New York: Schocken.

CHAPTER 11

Social Class and the Reemergence of the Radical Right in Contemporary Germany

George Steinmetz

IN RECENT YEARS THE RADICAL RIGHT HAS REEMERGED AS A SERIOUS threat across the advanced capitalist world. Right-wing movements and political parties have gained strength in Austria, Italy, Japan, Sweden, Norway, Denmark, and Flanders, and since the end of the 1980s they have made gains in Russia, Romania, and other parts of Eastern Europe (Betz 1994; Merkl and Weinberg 1993; Kirfel and Oswalt 1991). Jörg Haider's Austrian Freedom Party has been the most successful right-wing electoral force, attracting over 22 percent of the electorate (one million voters) in the December 1995 national elections and 28 percent in the 1996 Austrian elections for the European Parliament. Le Pen's National Front has gained somewhat smaller percentages—15.3 percent in the most recent French presidential elections—but a larger overall number of voters (4.5 million). In Italy the neofascist Movimento Sociale Italiano actually became part of a coalition government in 1994. And in the United States, at least 250 right-wing paramilitary organizations were operating by mid-1995, forty-five of them with ties to neo-Nazi or other white supremacist groups.[1]

---

1. Cf. *Klanwatch Intelligence Report*, no. 78 (June 1995); and deposition by Brian Levine, Southern Poverty Law Center, before the Militia hearings of the Crime Subcommittee of the House Judiciary Committee, 2 Nov. 1995. Thanks to Anne O'Neill for tracking down these figures.

Should Germany still have a privileged place in the study of right-wing radicalism, fifty years after the downfall of Nazism? Hasn't the final chapter on German "exceptionalism" been written, at least since the collapse of East Germany (Kocka 1990; Steinmetz 1996)? Wasn't the thesis of a "German mind" peculiarly disposed to fascism discounted long ago? All "reasonable" observers have agreed that the Federal Republic has proven itself to be a stable, exemplary democracy. By singling out Germany for a study of the radical right, are we not perpetuating an unfair and obsolete stigma? The single most deadly incident of right-wing violence in recent years took place not in Germany but in Oklahoma City. Radical right-wing parties have been less successful electorally in Germany than almost everywhere else in Europe, and no radical right-wing party has managed to clear the 5 percent hurdle required for representation in the Bundestag.[2] Comparative European survey data rarely find Germans to be the *most* ethnocentric group of Europeans, even if they usually rank near the top of the list (Willems et al. 1993, chap. 2).

Nonetheless, there are good reasons for focusing on Germany. Right-wing violence has been more brutal and sustained in Germany than elsewhere in Western Europe during the past five years. Hate crimes reached a peak in June 1993, with around fifty incidents reported daily (Willems et al. 1993, 100). The German right has specialized in collective pogroms and deadly nocturnal firebombings directed against migrant laborers and asylum seekers. The German case also presents a methodological advantage in that Germany's "unique" relationship to historical fascism throws into sharp relief the continuities and discontinuities between the contemporary far right and the interwar period. Worries about the Nazi past are also responsible for the relative wealth of information on contemporary radical right-wing activities and opinions in Germany. These data allow us to identify the social class location of right-wing voters and hate crime participants, revealing an overwhelming preponderance of male workers. This information then provides us with the question guiding this paper—why the class base of fascism has become more proletarian over the course of the twentieth century.

2. The right-wing Republikaner (Republicans) received 7.5 percent of the vote in the 1989 West Berlin elections, 10.9 percent in the state of Baden-Württemberg in 1992, and 7.1 percent in the 1989 European elections; and they are represented in other local political assemblies. See Falter 1994, 18–21.

There has been a flood of writing on the radical right in recent years, but the explanatory problem has rarely been framed in a satisfactory manner. Many analysts ignore evidence about the movement's social base. Some have traced right-wing violence to the antiauthoritarian educational practices of the sixties generation,[3] even though arrest data show an almost complete absence of children from the more educated social strata within the movement (Willems et al. 1993, chap. 6). Moreover, those writers who do emphasize the movement's proletarian base have typically not been able to say exactly why it is anomalous. Traditional Marxism and political sociology assume that there are certain timeless features of working-class existence or objective class interests which make the turn to fascism paradoxical (e.g., Lipset 1963). But the overrepresentation of manual workers in the movement is a surprise for historical, not sociological, reasons. Until recently, German far-right movements have had less success recruiting workers than other social groups.

A further shortcoming of much of the existing literature is that its explanations tend to focus on the far right in either western or eastern Germany, but cannot make sense of both. The most influential approach in current German sociology explains right-wing radicalism in terms of the pressures on the "victims of modernization" of contemporary "risk society" (Heitmeyer 1988, 1992a; Beck 1986). This perspective must resort to ad hoc explanations to explain the rise of a radical right-wing movement in the socialist German Democratic Republic (GDR), where pressures of competition and hyper-individualization were minimal (cf. Heitmeyer 1992b). Another set of explanations apply *only* to the east. The radical right-wing leanings of some East Germans have been traced to their experience of cradle-to-grave social security or to the GDR's authoritarianism, parochialism, and homogeneity (e.g., Farin and Seidel-Pielen 1992). The exclusive focus on the east was intelligible in the period immediately following German unification, when the most egregious violations seemed to be occurring in the eastern *Länder* (provinces). But the eastern emphasis became implausible with the firebombing atrocities in Mölln, Solingen, and other western cities. Bifurcated approaches cannot make sense of the similar rates of violence in both halves of Germany, the greater number of deaths attributable to right-wing attacks in the western states, the weaker electoral success of far-right parties in the east

---

3. "Linke Lehrer, rechte Schüler," *Der Spiegel* 47, no. 4 (1993): 41–45.

since 1990, or the fact that most far-right propaganda has come from the west.[4] Undeterred, some West German authors continue to insist that "the new right-wing extremist violence originated in eastern Germany" (Veen, Lepszy, and Mnich 1993, 71) or that the violence was "transferred" from the east to the west (Bergmann and Erb 1994, 9).[5]

The challenge, however, is to come up with a theoretical framework that can account for the similarities in radical right-wing politics in east and west, including the central role played by workers in both movements. One option is to focus on historical continuities with the shared pre-1945 German past. But can forty years of separate history in two radically different political systems really have mattered so little? Did it make any difference that some Germans were socialized into a "liberal-democratic" culture and others into an "antifascist" one? Did East and West German families somehow bequeath Nazi ideologies to their children and grandchildren in ways that went largely unnoticed for decades? Or was there a "convergence" between capitalist and socialist systems with lasting effects on political behavior?

These questions bring us back to the issue of German peculiarity. We need to explain not only the similarities between eastern and western Germany, but also why "racist violence in Germany [has been] more sustained and brutal than in every other West European country" (Rommelspacher 1995, 26). We need to account for the unique *form* of right-wing violence in Germany, especially its choice of targets, which range from disabled people to Holocaust memorials. Why is anti-Semitism so prominent in a country that destroyed most of its Jews? Does the current movement simply represent a resurgence of "incurable Germanness" (Sichrovsky 1993)?

4. During the first half of the 1980s, almost all of the radical right-wing rock bands originated in the western Länder (Giessen 1993). The largest number of right-wing offenses have occurred in the western state of Nordrhein-Westfalen (see *Süddeutsche Zeitung*, 15 January 1995). Comparative assessments depend heavily on how rates of right-wing violence are operationalized. For example, eastern states have shown higher rates of antiforeigner violence *per foreigner*, while western states have had greater *absolute* numbers of attacks. Surveys have often found that antiforeigner attitudes are higher in the east and anti-Semitism higher in the west (see Bergmann and Erb 1995). See Steinmetz 1994 for a discussion of the contending methods of measuring violence and the problems with hate crime statistics in general.

5. Some of these "eastern"-oriented explanations may of course have a partial validity; after all, disparate causes can produce similar results. Indeed, the account I sketch below identifies different western and eastern pathways to a common intermediate outcome (Fordism), which then partially explains similarities in right-wing militancy.

Although non-German observers are quick to connect the current movement to the Nazi past, many German writers dismiss continuity arguments, criticizing a "one-sided orientation toward past forms of right-extremist movements, particularly the Nazi regime" (Kowalsky and Schroeder 1994, 55). This dismissive stance stems as much from an effort to appear "scientific" as from German resentment against being reminded of Nazi crimes. In light of the fact that the far right has arisen simultaneously across Europe, we obviously need to explore the relationship between "uniquely German" factors and more general ones.

The account developed here is historical in three main respects. First, I describe the transition from Fordist to "flexibilized" post-Fordist forms of production, consumption, and culture within a regulation-theoretical framework. Regulation theory is deeply historical in terms of its concepts and its approach to explanation. Second, the present account is historical insofar as it revolves centrally around constructions of memory and identity. Contemporary right-wing violence can be understood as driven in part by a working-class "moral economy" generated by East and West German Fordism and by a nostalgia for an idealized version of this Fordist era. But the specific ideology of the radical right and its array of enemies cannot be explained entirely in terms of a declining, idealized Fordism. A third historical dimension must be introduced, involving the survival and reactivation of even older, pre-Fordist ideological materials. The ideological glue that binds together contemporary far-right ideology is rooted in historical Nazism, but this third aspect of historical causality also includes strands of political culture that predate Nazism.

The account is developed as follows. I begin with a discussion of the concept of right-wing radicalism. The second section summarizes what we know about the far right in contemporary Germany, especially its social class base, and compares this to the social composition of earlier German right-wing movements. The third section sketches a model of West and East German Fordism and their contribution to working-class subjectivity and to the overall salience of social class. The fourth section links these constructions of Fordism to contemporary neofascism, drawing on E. P. Thompson's concept of the "moral economy." The fifth section considers the role of earlier ideologies, especially classical Nazism, in the contemporary movement. I conclude with some comments on the implications of contemporary working-class participation in far-right movements for theories of social class.

The Contemporary Radical Right

Right-wing radicalism is constituted in relation to the rest of society, and cannot be defined in a timeless, abstract fashion. *Contemporary* right-wing radicalism—a historical phenomenon—can be defined as a cluster of six linked elements (cf. Heitmeyer 1988, 1992b):

(1) A view of the world as consisting of incompatible groups defined by essential, incommensurable differences rooted in biology and/or culture; this sociological map is typically linked to *racist* and *nationalist* ideologies;

(2) A *social Darwinist* belief in the ubiquity (and positive functions) of the struggle for existence;

(3) Demands for the *exclusion* or elimination of "inferior" groups from the community through policies ranging from apartheid to expulsion to physical destruction;

(4) Support for *nondemocratic*, authoritarian styles of decision making and governance;

(5) Acceptance of private vigilante *violence* against enemies;

(6) Hatred of the "left," however that is currently defined.

But this definition is only partial, containing ideological codes, or clusters of "ideologemes," that recur across contemporary geographical settings. Right-wing radicalism in Germany, France, and the United States shares these six items. This definition thus does not refer to contemporary right-wing radicalism in a specific country or region. Two additional specifications must be added for a definition of contemporary German right-wing radicalism:

(7) A positive stance towards the Nazi past, ranging from unequivocal admiration for the Third Reich to a more nuanced sympathy, along the lines of "it was generally a good idea with a few negative sides" or "it was good during the 1930s, bad thereafter." By contrast, some right-wing movements outside Germany have a more ambivalent view of the Third Reich, and a few are actively hostile to it (cf. Sprinzak 1993).

(8) A vicious form of anti-Semitism. Because of the Holocaust and Nazism, anti-Semitism plays a unique role in the contemporary German far right. German neo-Nazis regard Jews as their primary enemies (cf.

interview with Ingo Hasselbach, former leader of the neo-Nazi National Alternative Party, in *Die Woche*, 28 July 1994).

Found in isolation, these individual elements do not necessarily constitute right-wing radicalism. Conservative parties may endorse the first two items and support mild versions of the third and seventh while continuing to embrace democracy and the rule of law. Positive memories of the Nazi period are widespread among the older generations, even among Social Democratic workers (Niethammer 1986). It is the *combination* of these eight elements that defines German right-wing radicalism.

The Return of the Repressed

Xenophobic attitudes and violent hate crimes began to increase in West Germany during the early 1980s, and right-wing skinhead attacks soon appeared, somewhat unexpectedly, in the GDR as well.[6] German unification marked a sharp increase in right-wing offenses. Between January 1990 and early October 1995, there were at least 1,955 right-wing offenses resulting in injury or death, or almost one incident daily in all of Germany (*Berliner Zeitung*, 30 October 1995, 6). Right-wing hate crimes rose from 7,684 in 1992 to 10,561 in 1993 and then fell slightly to 10,000 in 1994 and 8,000 in 1995.[7] At the same time, the "baseline" level of hate crime between peaks of right-wing violence has crept up steadily (Ohlemacher 1994; Willems et al. 1993, 99–100). The number of specifically anti-Semitic attacks has also increased sharply since unification: from 367 in 1991 to 656 in 1993, to 1,366 in 1994, and to 1,155 in 1995 (*Süddeutsche Zeitung*, 6 July 1995; Verfassungsschutzbericht 1995). Although at the time of this writing the radical right is no longer the German media's favorite theme, almost every weekend sees a renewed explosion of violence.

Even more startling than the *quantity* of hate crime is the extraordinary range of right-wing targets and enemies. The German right's victims

6. See "Die Ausländerfeindlichkeit wächst," *Frankfurter Allgemeine Zeitung*, no. 214 (16 September 1982), 6. The first Neo-Nazi murders occurred in 1985 in Hamburg (Seidel-Pielen 1993; Zimmermann and Saalfeld 1993, 63). For an overview of right-wing extremism in the GDR before 1989, see Brück 1991.
7. See *Neue Zürcher Zeitung*, 7 July 1995; and interview with BKA (Federal Crime Bureau) head Hans-Ludwig Zachert in *Süddeutsche Zeitung*, 1 January 1996.

include Jews (or people believed to be Jewish), leftists, Turkish families who have lived in the Federal Republic for several generations, Gypsies (Sinti and Roma), Africans, Poles, Vietnamese, immigrant workers and seekers of political asylum, the homeless, physically disabled people, or anyone else who is deemed an outsider. Other common targets of right-wing wrath are inanimate objects such as Jewish cemeteries, Holocaust memorials, left-wing youth centers, or squat houses. Many incidents are smaller in scale, hovering ambiguously between vandalism or provocation and hate crime but still contributing to an atmosphere of uncertainty.[8]

There are around 50,000 right-wing activists in Germany today, with many more far-right sympathizers and voters (Steinmetz 1994). The Republikaner Party alone has about 20,000 members according to recent estimates (*Süddeutsche Zeitung*, 6 July 1995). Membership in far-right and neo-Nazi parties and groups is extremely difficult to determine, but is thought to have grown from around 19,000 in 1982 to 64,500 in 1993, and then to have fallen back slightly to 56,600 in 1994 (Verfassungs-schutzbericht 1995). Far rightists have also made inroads into the German fraternities (*Burschenschaften*), with their 26,000 members.[9]

What is the social background of the right-wing radicals? Recent German electoral surveys indicate that skilled and unskilled blue-collar workers are much more likely than better-educated or better-paid strata to vote for the radical right, as are the unemployed (Falter 1994, 65, 99–100; Pfahl-Traughber 1993, 180). Farmers and the self-employed also give above-average levels of support to German radical right-wing parties (Falter 1994, 38–39, 99–100; Pfahl-Traughber 1993, 170–81). Voting patterns also differ in the eastern and western states. The typical radical right-wing voter in the west is a married male worker over forty-five, living in a small or medium-sized town, and with a below-average level of income and education. In the east, the typical far-right voter is younger, single, and more likely to be a skilled worker (*Facharbeiter*) than an unskilled one (Falter 1994, 99, 106).

8. This unsettling mix is illustrated by a recent incident involving an installation at the Anhalter Bahnhof in Berlin, a train station from which prisoners were deported to concentration camps during World War II. Sixteen gaunt, Giacometti-style figures, wearing different-colored triangles, were positioned as if walking toward the station's ruined portal. By late October 1995, half of the sculptures had been seriously damaged, and the installation had to be removed. *Zitty*, no. 22 (1995), 12.

9. *Süddeutsche Zeitung*, 17 April 1993. According to Ingo Hasselbach, the Burschenschaften have helped "educate" new Neo-Nazis (*Tageszeitung*, 18 April 1993).

The most extensive study of participants in xenophobic hate crimes is based on all police investigations in six western and three eastern Länder between January 1991 and April 1992. The majority of the perpetrators were skilled (63.7 percent) or unskilled (29.9 percent) workers or apprentices. Almost all were male (96 percent) and under twenty-five, with a modest level of education. Most participants in hate crimes are from mainstream social backgrounds, not marginal ones. Almost 76 percent of the perpetrators came from households headed by two married parents. The percentage of participants who were unemployed at the time of arrest was high (18 percent), but not dramatically higher than the average jobless rate for young men in Germany in this period (Willems et al. 1993, 122, 116, 124). As in other studies, only a minority of hate crime participants (25.2 percent) were formally connected to far-right organizations, even if many were exposed indirectly to neo-Nazism through right-wing rock bands. Indeed, only 12 percent of the identified perpetrators of anti-Semitic offenses during the first half of 1994 belonged to right-extremist groups, according to the German Federal Crime Bureau (*Süddeutsche Zeitung*, 19 October 1994).

There is no a priori reason to expect workers to be less racist or xenophobic than people from any other social class. But the disproportionately working-class base of contemporary right-wing extremism is historically unique, at least in Germany.[10] The German working class proved relatively immune to right-wing radicalism and anti-Semitism from the late nineteenth century through 1933. Workers continued to be underrepresented within the radical right throughout the Nazi period and during the first two decades after the war in West Germany.

Most historians have concluded that the working class "remained almost untouched" (Jochmann 1988, 161) by anti-Semitic agitation during the Kaiserreich (1870–1918).[11] The court chaplain-turned-politician Adolf Stoecker tried unsuccessfully in the late 1870s to lure workers away from the Social Democrats to his anti-Semitic movement, but soon shifted his focus to the middle classes, university students, and committed Protestants (Brakelmann, Greschat, and Jochmann 1982). Workers' relative immunity to anti-Semitism during this period is trace-

---

10. The same holds for Italy: the Italian Fascist Party "had an even lower percentage of workers in it than the NSDAP"—only about 17 percent in 1921 (Poulantzas 1979, 219).

11. An important exception to this was the increasing use after 1890 of anti-Semitic stereotypes in cartoons and jokes in the Social Democratic popular press. See Leuschen-Seppel 1978, esp. 252ff.; also Massing 1949, 151–69.

able partly to Social Democratic agitation.[12] Discrimination against Polish-speaking workers in the industrial Ruhr came from the general population as well as state officials, but there was little violence against immigrants of the sort seen in France during the same period.[13] German workers also showed little support for the other ideologies and policies during this period that generated some of the "raw materials" for twentieth-century Nazism, such as colonial racism, racial eugenics, and the jus sanguinis that governed German citizenship.[14]

Workers were also underrepresented within the ranks of the Nazi Party (NSDAP) relative to their percentage in the labor force.[15] Certainly, recent historical research has refuted the long-standing view of the NSDAP as a party of the petty bourgeoisie, indicating that the Nazis drew support from all social classes and strata, including the proletariat (Falter 1991, Kater 1983). But voting statistics show that the Nazis received less support in districts with larger percentages of industrial, service-sector, and white-collar workers (Falter 1991, 224). There was an especially strong negative relation between Nazi voting and the unemployment rate in a given electoral district (Falter 1991, 292–314). Once in control of the state, the Nazis were able to gain the compliance of many workers through economic recovery, social and leisure programs, and massive political repression (Lüdtke 1994, 190; Zimmermann 1986). Membership among wage earners increased (Mason 1995, 246), and Hitler himself was just as popular among workers as in the general German population (Kershaw 1989). Many older West German workers later looked back on the 1930s as a sort of golden age (Herbert 1987). Yet workers were never *overrepresented* among the strong supporters of Nazism, and "there is very little evidence that German workers became enthusiastic anti-Semites" (Mason 1995, 243–44, 258).[16]

12. Brakelmann, Greschat, and Jochmann 1982, 161. Protestant workers' growing alienation from the church also played a role.
13. Klessmann 1978. Of course, most "Polish" workers in the Ruhr came from Prussian, not Russian, Poland, and were therefore officially German citizens. On popular anti-immigrant violence in pre–World War I France, see Néré (1959).
14. Indeed, before 1914 the SPD was the only major opponent in the Reichstag of overseas colonialism and the racializing jus sanguinis; see Kautsky 1907; Schröder 1979; Hyrkkanen 1986; Brubaker 1992, 120. Some SPD thinkers embraced eugenics (cf. Steinmetz 1993, 202).
15. See Kater 1983, 243–63; Falter 1991, 227. According to official party statistics, workers constituted 28–33 percent of Nazi Party membership between September 1930 and March 1933.
16. See the evidence on Nazi Party joiners between 1933 and 1945 in Kater 1983, 252–53. Mason also shows that militant workers engaged in "countless acts of workplace indiscipline and insubordination" (Mason 1995, 23), but it is unclear whether this should be read as resistance to the regime.

Nazism thus does not seem to have rearranged the relations between class and politics to such an extent that German workers were in the forefront of the right wing after 1945. Indeed, the Social Democrats typically attracted over 50 percent of the working-class vote in West German national elections from 1953 through the end of the 1980s, especially in the economically decisive Ruhr valley region (cf. Ballerstedt and Glatzer 1979, 451; Cerny 1990, 284). And until the end of the 1960s, most "neo"-Nazis were actually former Nazis (Lewis 1991, chap. 2). The first signs of change appeared during the economic recession of the late 1960s, when the far-right NPD (National Democratic Party of Germany) experienced a sudden burst of electoral success. In contrast to the Nazi voter of the 1920s, the typical NPD voter was now a manual worker with low educational attainment (Falter 1994, 61; Scheuch and Klingemann 1967).[17] The radical right's strongly proletarian base is thus a relatively recent phenomenon; the theoretical challenge is to explain this change.

The influential "victims of modernization" perspective cannot explain why the contemporary movement receives stronger support from skilled and employed workers than from workers whose "losses" are more immediate, especially the unskilled and unemployed. Nor can this approach make sense of the rise of right-wing radicalism in the still socialist GDR during the 1980s or explain why rates of hate crimes have been roughly the same in both parts of postunification Germany, despite the worse economic conditions in the east. Nor can current versions of "modernization theory" illuminate the historically specific form and contents of radical right ideology.

To understand the forms of subjectivity generating the current right-wing rebellion, it is necessary to make a detour through West and East German society during the 1960s and 1970s. Specifically, we need to examine the constitution of working-class identities and expectations— the cultural process of working-class formation—during the period of Fordism in West and East Germany.

---

17. It is much more difficult to assess right-wing tendencies in the GDR before 1989, since they were officially nonexistent. Workers in East Germany were at least superficially resocialized into antifascism, and many East German workers went through the motions. Yet there is also growing evidence of anti-Semitism within the SED, especially in the 1950s. See Hell forthcoming; Herf 1994; Wolffssohn 1995.

The Golden Age of Fordism in East and West Germany

The concept of Fordism (defined below) is based in regulation theory.[18] As we will see, regulation theory is especially useful in the present context because it permits a nonreductionist understanding of the effects of economic change on working-class interests and subjectivities. Regulation theory is a quasi-Marxist approach to explaining macrosocial change which attempts to overcome many of the shortcomings (e.g., teleology and functionalism) of older versions of Marxism without abandoning the Marxian emphasis on the dynamics of capital accumulation. Regulation theory exchanges the figure of historical necessity for the figure of contingency and accident in politico-economic change. Its only general assumption is that profit rates eventually decline when the social arrangements underpinning capitalist accumulation begin to fall apart (Lipietz 1990, 153). A "regulatory crisis" typically provokes a diverse array of social actors to begin searching for specific and general solutions. General structural features of capitalism virtually assure that a solution will be pursued but not that one will be found. The outcome of a regulatory crisis is the product of multiple actors and institutions intersecting in unpredictable ways.

The most abstract concept within regulation theory is the notion of *regulation* itself, which refers to institutions and norms that permit the reproduction of conflictual or contradictory social relations. Although the concept of regulation has no specific historical content, most regulation theorists are concerned with capitalist societies. A *regime of accumulation* is a set of rules determining the distribution and allocation of the social product between investment/accumulation and consumption. A *mode of regulation* is a set of rules and procedures, norms, institutions, and modes of calculation through which the accumulation regime is secured (cf. Jessop 1989, 262). In addition to predominantly economic institutions (such as banks or money), a mode of regulation typically encompasses institutions such as social policy, political parties, cultural and family forms, schools, and systems of interest intermediation.

At an intermediate level of abstraction are *specific* modes of regulation such as Fordism and post-Fordism. Fordism is based on a regime of accumulation involving a systematic relation between mass produc-

---

18. Key works of regulation theory include Aglietta 1987, Boyer 1990, Lipietz 1986 and 1990, and Jessop 1989; its different schools are discussed in Jessop 1990a.

tion and mass consumption. Economically Fordism involves, inter alia, the centrality of the wage as the main mechanism for securing the reproduction of labor power; monopolistic price regulation; and the predominance of mass consumption of standardized commodities and the collective consumption of goods and services supplied by the state (Jessop 1989, 1990a). The prevailing cultural forms under Fordism are productivism and consumerism (Hirsch and Roth 1986). Culture is institutionally centered around the mass media. An ideology of individualization is combined in a potentially contradictory way with a narrow range of "normal" lifestyle orientations. Fordism's central political forms are neocorporatism and the Keynesian welfare state. According to Hirsch and Roth (1986, 37), Fordist politics are based on "social-democratic, bureaucratic societalization, strong unions, reformist parties of mass integration, corporatist institutionalization of class contradictions, and Keynesian state interventionism." The economic rudiments of Fordism took shape in the United States during the interwar period (Gramsci 1971, Aglietta 1987), but Fordism was only consolidated as a full-blown mode of regulation after the Second World War. Fordism then began to unravel during the 1970s. The advanced capitalist world today is in the midst of a transition to a still vaguely defined "post-Fordist" mode of regulation centered around "flexible accumulation" (Harvey 1989; Bonefeld and Holloway 1991).

At the most concrete level, regulation theory describes geohistorically specific variants of modes of regulation such as Fordism. Fordism is thus a description of the *general* features of the advanced capitalist world during a certain period, and not some sort of model that was installed in a complete and unvarying form in every country. The specific kind of Fordism that developed in a given country was shaped by local historical legacies, such as antecedent patterns of industrialization and the level of state strength. The timing of the rise and decline of Fordism also depends upon nationally specific conditions (Lipietz 1984; Jessop 1989). Fordism is argued to have emerged relatively late in West Germany, due to postwar reconstruction, but Germany eventually came to exhibit a more "complete" form of Fordism than Britain or the United States (cf. Jessop et al. 1991, 137–42). Although Henry Ford pioneered several of the key economic components of Fordism—the high wage, the assembly line, the idea that workers should be consumers as well as producers—American Fordism remained "incomplete" due to the weakness of institutions like

collective bargaining and the welfare state (Lipietz 1986, 19). The decline
of Fordism also set in later in Germany, taking hold in the 1980s.

The importance of regulation theory in the present context is that it
allows us to understand why class became a crucial determinant of consciousness in "Fordist" West and East Germany, without insisting that class
always has this effect. As a form of societalization, Fordism was organized
around various institutions that continually ratified the existence of the
working class and produced substantial homogeneity in its conditions
of existence. Regulation theory also sheds light on the contents of right-
wing workers' grievances, many of which are based on the implicit social
contract of Fordism.

The contemporary German context raises specific difficulties, however, because regulation theory has only rarely been applied to "socialist"
or Soviet style societies (see Lipietz 1991 and Murray 1990). Events in the
GDR during the 1980s make it clear that "socialist" societies were perfectly
capable of generating right-wing radicalism, as does the speed with which
many former East Germans shifted to the right after 1989. The question
is whether regulation-theoretical concepts can be of any help here. The relative neglect of state-socialist societies by regulation theorists is due partly
to a traditional Marxist belief that social classes only exist where the means
of production are in private hands.[19] Many Marxists also believe that the
law of value imparts a distinctive historical dynamic to capitalist societal
development. Yet regulation theory immediately begins to look more
applicable to socialist societies once we conceptualize the latter within the
context of a capitalist world system (Wallerstein 1986; see also Hobsbawm
1994). It has become impossible since 1989 to ignore the extent to which
socialism's "internal" dynamics were intertwined with global economic,
political, and cultural forces. This suggests that we need to rethink the ways
in which socialist societies were shaped by the capitalist West even during
periods in which they seemed internally stable. This does not imply a
return to earlier "convergence" approaches. Indeed, it would be impossible to explain the collapse of "eastern" socialism without reference to a
whole range of social-structural *differences* from western capitalism. But the
official ideology of the Cold War should not prevent us from exploring the
penetration of socialist societies by local "translations" of Western-capital-
ist military, economic, cultural, and political institutions.

19. Erik Wright (1985) elaborated a system of neo-Marxist class analysis that applies with equal
force to socialist societies.

Regulation theory seems ideally suited for such an analysis. Governing elites in socialist societies, like those in the west, had an interest in raising levels of production and productivity, in stabilizing the long-term allocation of the net product between production and consumption, and in warding off social conflict. To attain these goals, they too tried to forge a *dispositif* of appropriate institutions, norms, and habits. As in the west, these institutions and norms operated fairly smoothly for some time before entering into crisis. There is ample evidence that the GDR achieved a certain degree of stability in production, consumption, and everyday life during the 1970s (Bude 1993, 272; Niethammer 1994, 110). We can also trace the adoption of various Fordist practices by the GDR, especially in the 1960s and 1970s, just as we can plot the resonance of the crisis of western Fordism during the 1980s.

East Germany borrowed both from Soviet "iron Fordism" (Lipietz 1991, 88–89; Murray 1990) and from Western Fordism to come up with its own unique regulatory form. Ulrich Voskamp and Volker Wittke find that "socialist planning elites in the GDR during the 1950s and 1960s were enamored of the Fordist production principles that dominated Western industrial production and organization," resulting in the "continuous extension of the division of labor, the creation of ever more specialized production tasks, the centralization of resources, and vertical integration" (Voskamp and Wittke 1991, 344; see also Schneider and Troder 1985). The East German economy came to resemble West German Fordism in other respects. Exports were a central component of both economies and constituted a similar percentage of the national product, even if they were directed at different markets. Both countries even emphasized similar economic sectors, such as mechanical engineering and chemicals (Dennis 1988, 136–39). Another significant feature of "pan-German" Fordism was what might be called its economic nationalism. Citizens in both countries were proud of their economies' leading position within their respective economic regions.

There are also parallel developments between West and East German Fordism in the areas of work and labor relations, resulting from postwar rivalry, explicit modeling, and the two countries' shared history. Perhaps the most important similarity lies in the overall ideological importance of work, workers, and the economy in the self-understanding of both the Federal Republic and the GDR. The official communist heroizing of the working class in East German political culture (Hübner 1994) had its less blatant West German counterparts in the widespread pride in the "economic miracle" and in older German ideologies of "quality work" (Lüdtke 1994).[20] Job security became nearly absolute in the east, while workers in the west benefited from low levels of joblessness, generous unemployment benefits, and extensive job retraining programs. East German workers' "right to work" gave them a considerable degree of structural veto power over managerial decisions in the form of work slowdowns and absenteeism (Hübner 1993; Bahro 1981); West German practices of industrial codetermination granted workers a certain measure of influence over production decisions. Workers' wages were lower in the east than in the west, but they were partly compensated by the GDR's minimal degree of overall wage stratification (Lötsch 1993, 117). East German workers' wages also rose more rapidly than productivity during the Honecker era. One effect of these ongoing wage increases was to stimulate workers' disillusionment with the system, given the paucity of consumer goods. Seen from a different perspective, however, many East German workers came to view rising wages and relative income equality as normal, and carried these beliefs into the united post-Fordist Germany.

There are also surprising parallels in the use of immigrant labor on both sides of the Wall. West Germany began importing workers in 1955, first drawing on southern Europe and then reaching into North Africa and Turkey. By 1980, a third of the nearly four million foreign residents in West Germany were Turkish (Bade 1992). The GDR began to import migrant laborers from other East European countries during the 1960s, followed in the 1970s and 1980s by immigrant laborers from Vietnam, Cuba, Mozambique, Angola, China, etc. The number of foreigners in the GDR remained much smaller than in the west, reaching only 166, 419 at the beginning of 1989 (Jasper 1991, 171; Broszinsky-Schwabe 1990). Foreign workers performed similar functions in the two societies. Just as immigrant laborers in the GDR were expected to return home within a fixed number of years, immigrant workers in West Germany were referred to as "guests" (*Gastarbeiter*) to underscore their temporary status, and faced numerous restrictions in the areas of civil rights, citizenship, and social policy. The revelation in 1973 that thousands of Turks were working in the GDR underscored a pragmatism that was not fundamentally different from West German policy (Jasper 1991, 163–64).

20. The GDR partially replaced the ideology of "quality work" with a focus on quantity during the Stakhanovite "Hennecke" movement in the late 1940s (Lüdtke 1994, 192–93), but started emphasizing "quality" again in the mid-1950s (Hübner 1994, 179).

Strong parallels can also be found in the field of social policy. From the 1960s onwards, the East German Socialist Unity Policy (SED) tried to emulate West Germany by making rising living standards the key component of legitimation (Weber 1993, 198). Honecker opened his nineteen-year reign (1971–89) with an emphasis on social policy, which in practice entailed a rise in social consumption spending (McAdams 1985, 137). East Germans came to expect an all-embracing system of "social security"; *Geborgenheit* (security) became the key term of Honecker's social-political discourse (cf. Weber 1988, 97; Spittmann 1990, 48). As the economy slowed down during the second half of the 1970s, the regime began insisting on "the growth of productivity as the precondition for social policy" (Spittmann 1990, 45, 70; Meuschel 1993, 12; Weber 1988, 77), but social security programs continued to expand. The social programs of the Honecker period included maternity leave, youth centers, free contraception and abortion, day care, universal health care, and the subsidization of essentials such as housing and food at very low prices (Dennis 1988, 42–78; Scharf 1989). Especially significant in the context of the present analysis is the fact that workers remained the central addressee of the state's social policies (Hübner 1990, 260).

Mass culture was a final sphere in which unexpected similarities emerged between east and west. Postwar SED cultural policy was rooted in the earlier socialist tradition of rejecting mass culture and bringing "bourgeois" culture to the working class. Workers were given privileged access to higher education; books and theater tickets were subsidized. By the early 1960s, however, the SED was torn between opposing Western mass culture as decadent and using it to pacify discontent (Rauhut 1991). Under Honecker the state became more tolerant of light entertainment, jazz and rock music, and films from the capitalist west (Dennis 1988, 176). East Germans experienced a "discount version of western consumerism" (Hübner 1994, 181), but it was consumerism nonetheless. The most extensive oral history project in the GDR found that East Germans recalled the 1970s—the golden age of German Fordism—as the "good old days" (Niethammer 1994, 110). Although consumer goods in the east were typically in short supply and of lower quality (though not as uniformly bad as many in the west assumed), there was also a form of vicarious consumerism that should not be underestimated. Against challenging odds, many East Germans tried to emulate Western consumerism (see Bornemann 1991, 71–79). Private viewing of West German television became the most common leisure-time activity in the last two decades of the GDR and was undoubtedly the most significant source of convergence with Western consumerist expectations.

East and West Germany also differed in many important respects, but it is not clear that these would affect the forms of popular subjectivity under investigation here. One major area of differences has to do with women and the family. The extreme labor shortage in the GDR led to a much more extensive integration of women into the labor force, such that 85 percent of adult East German women were working by 1985, as opposed to only 51 percent in West Germany (Hübner 1994, 177). This means that the nuclear family centered on the male breadwinner was always an even less realistic ideal for East German workers than for their western counterparts. Secondly, the GDR was not able to respond to the crisis of Fordism with comparable moves away from gigantism and inflexibility. Only the SED had a real structural incentive to find a stable model for economic growth, yet that same elite depended on an extreme degree of centralization in order to stay in power.[21] As Charles Maier notes, "the superiority of Western economies lay not in their immunity to these systemic challenges, but in their capacity to overcome them" (1991, 39).

The Fordist "Moral Economy"

My argument, then, is that there was enough convergence between East and West German Fordism to have endowed workers on both sides of the wall with similar expectations, especially in the areas of work, wages, social policy, foreigners, and consumerism. At a more basic level of social ontology, both cultures emphasized the very existence of the working class. These similarities account for the strong class-based reaction by some German workers to the present processes of post-Fordist restructuring. They also explain why some of these workers are attracted to radical right-wing "solutions." (It hardly needs mentioning that the majority of German workers do *not* support or participate in the radical right; we are concerned here with an extremely visible minority.) Right-wing opposition to present conditions is based on an idealized recollection of a time in which

---

21. The question whether socialism's lack of regulatory problem-solving capacity was rooted in the weakness of private property and the profit motive, in political repression, or in functional "dedifferentiation" (Luhmann 1989) is tangential to the present paper.

- there were abundant jobs corresponding to workers' skills;
- manual workers' wages were comparatively high and rising;
- social policy provided a comforting buffer during periods of impaired work ability and raised working-class consumption levels;
- foreigners were barely visible "guests" doing the work that Germans shunned, rather than competitors for scarce jobs and resources;
- the economy was defined in national rather than global terms;
- leisure time was spent consuming homogenized mass-cultural goods and not struggling for distinction in a stratified market of symbolic goods;[22]
- the gender ideal revolved around a male-headed nuclear family with women taking care of domestic tasks.

As noted above, these Fordist conditions were often ideals rather than realities, especially in the east, and since the 1980s they have become increasingly elusive. German unification provided an opportunity to accelerate the ongoing erosion of wages and job security and the "flexibilization" of labor markets and industrial organization. The opening up of international borders and the disruptions throughout eastern and southeastern Europe led to a rapid rise in the number of people seeking work or political asylum in Germany—an influx that was slowed but not halted by the drastic curtailment of the right to asylum in 1993. European integration and economic globalization threatened an already tenuous mainstream German national identity whose only solid base was a nationally defined economy. For most workers, the ideal of a male-headed nuclear family has become even more chimerical than during the 1960s or 1970s (Chopra and Scheller 1992). Coherent, ascriptive class-based cultures have been replaced by ephemeral "scenes" populated by self-selected participants. The processes described by British studies of youth subculture (e.g., Hebdige 1979), in which identities are "taken" rather than "given," increasingly characterize identity formation in general. Although some workers may welcome the increased opportunities for reflexive self-construction (Lash and Urry 1994), others simply feel less secure.

22. The Fordist consumer game of "keeping up with the Joneses" was one-dimensional and quantitative, differing sharply from the post-Fordist game of qualitative struggle for distinction *tous azimuts*. While many Fordist subjects tried to escape from cultural homogenization, they did so *against* the system's imperatives; post-Fordism virtually requires such "inventiveness" of its flexible consumers (contrast Lüscher n.d. with Lash and Urry 1994). Even in the GDR, the stratification of cultural consumption proceeded apace during the 1980s; cf. Bisky and Wiedemann 1985, 147ff.

We can now refine our earlier critique of arguments that depict the radical right as "losers in the process of modernization." We cannot make sense of the right-wing revolt simply by attending to current economic depression. E. P. Thompson long ago criticized the "abbreviated and 'economistic' picture of the food riot as a direct, spasmodic, irrational response to hunger," noting that "*of course* food rioters were hungry. . . . But this does not tell us how their behavior is 'modified by custom, culture and reason'" (1993, 258, 262). By the same token, to understand contemporary workers' responses to decline, we need to reconstruct their preexisting views of society, economy, and justice.

Thompson's notion of the "moral economy of the crowd" refers to an informal set of customary rights and usages embedded within popular consciousness and culture, the "expectations, traditions, and, indeed, superstitions of the working population" (1993, 260). In hierarchical nonmarket societies, the moral economy is a popular translation of official discourse, from which it draws its legitimacy (208). These customs and usages are made conscious only when they are threatened by monetary rationalizations, giving rise to indignation and collective efforts to enforce justice (340). To make sense of the logic underlying inarticulate crowd actions, one therefore needs to reconstruct the moral economy, sometimes looking back "several hundreds of years" (224). In the case of German rightists, we also need to look back for an origin, but first to the 1960s and 1970s.

There are obvious differences between the threats of dearth and starvation discussed by Thompson and the dangers facing workers in the present-day transition to post-Fordism. Yet there are important structural similarities as well. In both periods, the familiar life conditions of the laboring classes are undermined by massive socioeconomic transformations. Thompson's analysis focuses on the encroachments of the monetary economy on peasant and early industrial communities in which "many 'economic' relations are regulated according to nonmonetary norms" (1993, 340). Analogously, the present-day transition is one in which hypercompetitive market logics replace institutions that weakened the disciplinary iron grip of the market. Under Fordism, reproduction was partially *decommodified* and market transactions were subjected to extensive regulatory controls; post-Fordism, by contrast, involves massive *recommodification* and deregulation. Once again, a "tissue of customs and usages" is "threatened by monetary rationalizations."

The dynamic interaction between German state officials and the current right-wing movement also recalls Thompson's analysis. The moral economy involves not just a plebeian culture but also a web of informal mutual relationships with rulers. In Thompson's account, there are no *formal* institutions regulating the relationship, such that the poor have no choice but to communicate with their rulers through riot. Again, the contemporary situation reveals unexpected parallels. Nowadays, of course, nonextremist parties can organize for electoral competition and adult citizens can vote. But there is also an uncanny sense of a return to early-modern politics, as the extraparliamentary right wing appears to communicate with the country's political rulers through rioting. The best illustration of this dynamic process can be seen in the Bundestag's decision to curtail foreigners' access to political asylum in 1993, following two years of antiforeigner pogroms.[23]

Like other objects of nostalgia, imagined Fordism is not so much directly recalled as it is reconstructed, mentally and emotionally. This point is underscored by the fact that most radical right-wing activists are too young to have personally experienced the golden age of Fordism. But they are still able to construct a picture of what they missed. Like all effective ideologies, however, the moral economy of Fordism has a partial basis in present-day reality. Since the social transition is not abrupt, there are still many vestiges of the older system. These include regions, industrial branches, and individual firms where Fordist practices survive; and in Germany, many aspects of the Fordist welfare state still exist. Also important are the older Fordist "veterans" who can convincingly evoke the advantages of the past and provide encouragement to the young right-wing thugs from the sidelines.[24] We can make sense of the German right-wing activists' "immoral" social movement in terms of the reproduction and ongoing violation of this moral economy.

The Other Far Right

In what might first appear to be an act of intellectual contortionism, one author has made out the neofascist thugs to be part of a "post-Fordist class

23. I am grateful to an anonymous reviewer of an earlier version of this chapter for calling attention to this aspect of Thompson's analysis, although my extension to the present case is one this reviewer would probably not accept.
24. The best example of this was provided by the applauding crowds during the Rostock pogrom; see also the interview with "Willi D." in Sichrovsky 1991, 123–38.

bloc" (Roth 1992). How can eighteen-year-old workers with only a basic education be called "post-Fordist"? But the argument is not so much wrong as incomplete. Roth suggests that "the formation of a wider social basis [for German neofascism] is still in its beginning stages" (9), because the collapse of Fordism is still an ongoing process. The "post-Fordist bloc" consists of small- and medium-sized employers, highly skilled workers, and young academics in the new postindustrial sectors. Not surprisingly, in most European countries one segment of this bloc has embraced a variant of neofascism. As Roth notes, neofascist modernizers want to "cast aside the bothersome ballast with dictatorial methods" (8). The Italian Northern Lega is the most obvious example of the move to embrace hypercompetitive post-Fordism by expelling obsolete populations (Betz 1995, 7–10; Schmidtke and Ruzza 1993).

Such tendencies exist in Germany, but they have not yet been able to assume control of entire right-wing organizations.[25] Electoral support for the Republikaner is strongest in states like Bavaria and Baden-Württemburg, where many self-employed and blue-collar workers have recently "risen to middle-class status" (Veen, Lepszy, and Mnich 1993, 39).[26] Within most of these organizations, the boundaries between the reactionary and the modernizing branches of neofascism are blurry, and backward-looking ideology is still dominant.[27] The differences between the post-Fordist winners and the "reactionary radicals" within the Republican Party are partially overshadowed by shared opposition to "multiculturalism" and immigration. We should expect a division of political labor to emerge among radical right-wing parties, with the Fordist stream eventually disappearing altogether.

25. The most likely carriers of a modern neofascist project in Germany are the university-educated ideologues around periodicals like *Junge Freiheit* (cf. Pfahl-Traughber 1993; Lange 1993) and successful small employers and middle employees in the emerging high-tech sectors. Again, I am not suggesting that radical right-wing politics will be the dominant political stance among post-Fordist winners. For some in Germany (and in the United States), communitarianism has become an attractive strategy for managing the social disasters produced by the end of Fordism.

26. According to the Verfassungsschutz (the German Office for the Protection of the Constitution) the majority of the Republican Party's members are in Baden-Württemburg and Bavaria, and not in the declining industrial regions. See *Süddeutsche Zeitung*, 20 April 1995.

27. Interestingly, the electoral base of the French Front National has become *less* petty bourgeois and more proletarian in recent years. In the 1995 French presidential elections, 30 percent of French workers (and 35 percent of the unemployed) voted for Le Pen, more than for any other candidate. See *Süddeutsche Zeitung*, 29 January 1995.

In Hitler's Shadow

Let me clarify both the extension and the limits of the explanation presented so far. Because regulation theory was not originally developed as a theory of social movements, it is ill suited to account for individuals' microlevel decisions to participate, or to explain the fluctuating "opportunity structures" for extraparliamentary mobilization. Nor am I claiming that right-wing extremism is the only, or even the predominant working-class response to current social changes. Other reactions include resignation, psychological disorders, progressive collective resistance, and successful individual adaptation to the demands of post-Fordism. What the regulation-theoretical account does illuminate (when supplemented by the notion of the moral economy) is the construction of a specific form of class subjectivity and a specific view of society. This Fordist "moral economy" explains the apparent viability of right-wing radicalism for many workers and accounts for some of the neofascist movement's goals.

But even at this general level, regulation theory cannot explain the specific contours of the German far-right political movement. For many of the far right's victims have no relationship at all to post-Fordist restructuring. Regulation theory cannot make sense of the German movement's peculiar catalogue of enemies. Nor can the general regulation-theoretical model account for the greater brutality of right-wing violence in Germany, as compared to other societies undergoing similar transitions, or for its "repertoire" of collective action (Tilly 1978).

In order to construct a more complete explanation of the contemporary radical right, we need to thematize the relationship between layers of ideology rooted in different historical epochs. We need to understand how these ideologies have been reproduced over decades and how they are being woven together with Fordist ideologies originating in more recent periods. This entails paying particular attention to the conservation of ideological material from the period of "classical" Nazism, but there is a role for even older ideologies as well.

Despite the differences in the social composition of the current radical right and the NSDAP, there are some striking continuities at the level of ideology. Key elements of classical Nazi discourse included the biologically grounded national *Volk*; hatred of Gypsies, homosexuals, Communists, blacks, and especially Jews; biological racism, eugenics, and social Darwinism; the need for *Lebensraum*, or "living space," for the Germans;

a disdain for democracy and liberalism; worship of war and violence; and a reversal of the roles of victim and perpetrator. A sizable minority of Germans, especially among the younger generations, seem to be embracing these ideas with enthusiasm (cf. Zimmermann 1986). The only way to understand the peculiar constellation of neofascist enemies in Germany is in terms of ideological continuity with classical Nazism.

Nazi ideology is reproduced selectively, of course. Certain elements of classical Nazism are less salient today or, like anti-Bolshevism, have lost their referents. The Holocaust makes a huge difference for contemporary German right-wing radicalism, but its effects are far from uniform. Some right-wing extremists distance themselves from Hitler and the Holocaust for strategic reasons (Kowalsky 1993, 18), while others focus on Holocaust denial propaganda.[28] The individual elements of Nazi ideology are also recombined and given different weights. For example, there is greater stress within contemporary neo-Nazism on the "socialist" ideas of the Nazi "national revolutionary" wing represented by Ernst Röhm and Gregor Strasser (Stöss 1991, 169).

Fragments of classical Nazi ideology continue to circulate far beyond the ranks of the neo-Nazis. There has been a consistent solid core of West Germans with extreme right-wing views throughout the postwar period.[29] Public opinion polls during the postwar period showed that a rising proportion of Germans condemned Hitler and the Holocaust and rejected other specific Nazi policies, yet there was also widespread continuing approval of certain aspects of Nazism, especially among the older generations. The assumptions of Nazi culture were reproduced intact in some sectors of postwar German society. Lutz Niethammer and his col-

28. Many German neo-Nazis privately acknowledge the reality of the Holocaust but publicly propagate denial propaganda. Holocaust denial is often seen as tactically necessary for lowering peoples' inhibitions toward the far right (Schmidt 1993). Other German right-wingers are attempting to develop a "respectable" new rightist movement that accepts the reality of the Holocaust; see the interviews with "a student" in Sichrovsky 1993, 149–65, and with a young writer for *Junge Freiheit* in Tenner 1994, 217–37. An even more typical approach, not restricted to the extreme right, is to avoid the topic of Nazi genocide altogether in favor of the more "benign" features of the Third Reich, or to skip over the Nazi period in the narration of personal or national history (cf. Fisher 1995). Still another position is taken by historians who shift responsibility for the Holocaust to the "Asiatic" USSR or relativize the Holocaust through comparisons with other atrocities (see the interview with a history teacher in Sichrovsky 1993, 19–40). In light of these ideological contortions, therefore, it is not implausible to suggest that the actual Nazi past is not just a boon to the German radical right but also a liability.
29. On the right-wing mainstream, see Assheuer and Sarkowicz 1992; Noelle-Neumann and Ring 1985; SINUS-Institut 1981.

leagues found evidence of such continuity among workers in both the West German Ruhr valley (Niethammer 1986) and in three regions of the GDR (Niethammer 1991).

The availability of historical Nazism as an indigenous ideological system provides the far-right movement with several advantages. Even if Nazi ideologemes are rejected, they are at least familiar to most Germans. Thus while many members of the immediate postwar generations explicitly rejected their own Nazi-educated parents, right-wing radicals today often emphasize the importance of their *grandfathers* in the formation of their right-wing views and identities. This differentiates Germany from a country like the United States, where Nazi ideology is typically regarded as foreign or is not even "understood." Indigenous Nazi ideology gives the German movement a degree of coherence, even when its formal organization is weak. Another of the German neofascists' advantages, perversely, is the "realism" of their program, since it was actually put into practice during the Nazi era. Historical Nazism is thus a cultural resource for the contemporary right-wing social movement in Germany.

The German far right is also shaped by strands of national political culture that predate the Nazi era. For example, most Germans believe that their country is harboring more "foreigners" than other OECD countries. This is formally true, but only as a result of Germany's ethnically based citizenship laws and restrictive understanding of national identity, both of which date from before the Nazi regime. If France (or the United States) had applied these rules they would currently be harboring more "foreigners" than Germany (Terkessidis 1995; see also Renault 1991; Brubaker 1992). Older ideologies concerning the state and its relation to its subjects also influence the German radical right. Unlike their American counterparts, for example, German far-rightists typically want to strengthen, not eliminate, the central government.

Traditional political sociology, which analyzed fascism as the extremist politics of the middle class (Lipset 1963; Trow 1966), has been at a loss to understand the reemergence of the far right.[30] Many leftists have also been hesitant to acknowledge the extent to which the radical right wing has become one of the few sites of vigorous working-class politics. This chapter has attempted to apply some of the more interesting recent devel-

---

30. For an exception from the 1960s, see Scheuch and Klingemann 1967.

opments in neo-Marxist theory to these political developments. At the same time, theoretical discussions within Marxism during the past two decades have systematically eroded the concept of social class.

Some theorists have responded to the critique of class by inverting the proletarian messianism of traditional Marxism, viewing the working class as a symptom of all that is wrong with capitalism, as a "replica of capital" (Gorz 1982) rather than its negation. This position seemed to ignore the numerous instances in which working-class struggle has played a crucial role in the expansion of political and economic democracy (see Rueschemeyer, Stephens, and Stephens 1992 on political democracy and Steinmetz 1993 on the expansion of social protection). Other Marxists followed Manuel Castells (1978) in arguing that the new urban movements were rooted in social cleavages that cut across class boundaries, even if they were explicable in terms of the dynamics of capital accumulation. Although this approach seemed appropriate for many of the new social movements, it was unable to explain why some social movements continued to present themselves as class based. Another alternative involved various "pluralist" critical perspectives that simply gave class equal explanatory billing with social cleavages like race and gender (e.g. Albert and Hahnel 1978). While these approaches seemed descriptively plausible, they could not explain why class mattered in some contexts and not in others, or why workers were on the left in some settings and on the right in others. Finally, post-Marxists like Ernesto Laclau and Chantal Mouffe (1985) argued that class has no socially consequential extradiscursive reality at all, and that one can speak of a "working class" only where hegemonic articulations bring it into existence culturally.

The regulation-theoretical explanation elaborated in this chapter might seem to agree that one cannot speak of class as a universal feature of capitalist societies; one finds it only in societies where regulatory hegemony underscores class identities. Against this reading, I would agree with Erik Wright (1985) that social class is more than just a contextually variable cultural category. Class is also a *real* mechanism producing systematic effects, regardless of whether people are aware of it, regardless of whether regulatory institutions exist to channel practices and consciousness along class-based tracks. As an analytic category, class refers to positions within a matrix of asset distribution (or "ownership of the means of production") and is therefore intrinsically related to outcomes like income. The extent to which class determines beliefs or political practices, however, is a function of contingent hegemonic articulations. Certainly class structure makes some hegemonic articulations more likely to be successful than others. Yet "while the probability of assembling a set of agents . . . rises when they are closer in social space . . . alliance between those most distant from each other is never *impossible*" (Bourdieu 1985, 726, 741).

Regulation theory can accept Wright's "critical realist" understanding of class, just as it posits certain features of capitalist accumulation as common to all capitalist societies. But regulation theory also seems to offer a more systematic way of explaining the geohistorical variability in the cultural importance of social class and in workers' political proclivities. Put simply, regulation theory helps explain why working-class identities are more systematically generated in some sociohistorical contexts than others. Regulation theory can explain why Fordist class formation was salient enough to continue to shape workers' subjectivities even after the disappearance of Fordism. Regulation theory does not claim to account for the entirety of social life, however, but only those aspects that are brought under the sway of a regulatory mode. In explaining social movements, one will usually have to bring in causal mechanisms foreign to regulation theory, mechanisms that are not even partially articulated with a mode of regulation.[3] Two such concepts which may be important in accounting for contemporary right-wing radicalism, in Germany and elsewhere, are the moral economy and historical political culture.

References

Aglietta, Michel. 1987. *A Theory of Capitalist Regulation: The US Experience*. London: Verso.

Albert, Michael, and Robin Hahnel. 1978. *Unorthodox Marxism*. Boston: South End Press.

Assheuer, Thomas, and Hans Sarkowicz. 1992. *Rechtsradikale in Deutschland*. 2d ed. Munich: Beck.

---

31. Bob Jessop (1990b, 12) has proposed the term "contingent necessity" to describe this epistemological and explanatory stance. It is also discussed in Steinmetz 1993.

Bade, Klaus. 1992. "Einheimische Ausländer: 'Gastarbeiter—Dauergäste—Einwanderer.'" In Klaus Bade, ed., *Deutsche im Ausland—Fremde in Deutschland*. München: Beck.

Bahro, Rudolf. 1981. *The Alternative in Eastern Europe*. London: Verso.

Ballerstedt, Eike, and Wolfgang Glatzer. 1979. *Soziologischer Almanach*. Frankfurt: Campus.

Beck, Ulrich. 1986. *Risikogesellschaft*. Frankfurt: Suhrkamp.

Bergmann, Werner, and Rainer Erb. 1994. "Neonazismus und rechte Subkultur." In Werner Bergmann and Rainer Erb, eds., *Neonazismus und rechte Subkultur*. Berlin: Metropol.

———. 1995. "Wie antisemitisch sind die Deutschen? Meinungsumfragen 1945–1994." In Wolfgang Benz, ed., *Antisemitismus in Deutschland: Zur Aktualität eines Vorurteils*. Munich: Deutscher Taschenbuch Verlag.

Betz, Hans-Georg. 1994. *Radical Right-Wing Populism in Western Europe*. New York: St. Martin's Press.

Bisky, Lothar, and Dieter Wiedemann. 1985. *Der Spielfilm—Rezeption und Wirkung: Kultursoziologische Analysen*. Berlin: Henschelverlag.

Bonefeld, Werner, and John Holloway, eds. 1991. *Post-Fordism and Social Form*. London: Macmillan.

Bourdieu, Pierre. 1985. "Social Space and the Genesis of Groups." *Theory and Society* 14: 723–44.

Boyer, Robert. 1990. *The Regulation School: A Critical Introduction*. New York: Columbia University Press.

Brakelmann, Günter, Martin Greschat, and Werner Jochmann. 1982. *Protestantismus und Politik. Werk und Wirkung Adolf Stoeckers*. Hamburg: Christians.

Broszinsky-Schwabe, Edith. 1990. "Die DDR-Bürger im Umgang mit 'Fremden'—Versuch einer Bilanz der Voraussetzungen für ein Leben in einer multikulturellen Welt." In Sanem Kleff et al., eds., *BRD-DDR/ Alte und neue Rassismen im Zuge der deutsch-deutschen Einigung*. Frankfurt: Verlag für interkulturellen Kommunikation.

Brubaker, Rogers. 1992. *Citizenship and Nationhood in France and Germany*. Cambridge: Harvard University Press.

Brück, Wolfgang. 1991. "Skinheads—Vorboten der DDR-Systemkrise." *Freitag*, 26 July.

Bude, Heinz. 1993. "Das Ende einer tragischen Gesellschaft." In Hans Joas and Martin Kohli, eds., *Der Zusammenbruch der DDR*. Frankfurt: Suhrkamp.

Castells, Manuel. 1978. *City, Class and Power*. London: Macmillan.

Cerny, Karl H. 1990. *Germany at the Polls*. Durham, N.C.: Duke University Press.

Chopra, Ingrid, and Gitta Scheller. 1992. "'Die neue Unbeständigkeit.' Ehe und Familie in der spätmodernen Gesellschaft." *Soziale Welt* 43 (3): 48–69.

Dennis, Mike. 1988. *German Democratic Republic: Politics, Economics and Society*. London: Pinter.

Falter, Jurgen. 1994. *Wer wählt rechts? Die Wähler und Anhänger rechtsextremistischer Parteien im vereinigten Deutschland*. Munich: Beck.

Farin, Klaus, and Eberhard Seidel-Pielen. 1992. *Rechtsruck. Rassismus im neuen Deutschland*. Berlin: Rotbuch.

Fisher, Marc. 1995. *After the Wall: Germany, the Germans and the Burdens of History*. New York: Simon and Schuster.

Giessen, Hans W. 1993. "'Ich sing ein deutsches Lied.' Chauvinistische Poptexte und der neue Rechtsradikalismus." *Soziale Welt* 44: 555–69.

Gorz, André. 1982. *Farewell to the Working Class: An Essay on Post-Industrial Socialism*. Boston: South End Press.

Gramsci, Antonio. 1971. "Americanism and Fordism." In *Selections from the Prison Notebooks*. New York: International Publishers.

Harvey, David. 1989. *The Condition of Postmodernity*. New York: Basil Blackwell.

Hebdige, Dick. 1979. *Subculture, the Meaning of Style*. London: Methuen.

Heitmeyer, Wilhelm. 1988. *Rechtsextremistische Orientierungen bei Jugendlichen*. 2d ed. Weinheim: Juventa.

———. 1992a. "Die Wiederspiegelung von Modernisierungsrückständen im Rechtsextremismus." In Karl-Heinz Heinemann and Wilfried Schubarth, eds, *Der antifaschistische Staat entläßt seine Kinder*. Cologne: PapyRossa.

———. 1992b. *Die Bielefelder Rechtsextremismus-Studie*. Weinheim: Juventa.

Hell, Julia. Forthcoming. *Postfascist Fantasies: Psychoanalysis, History, and the Literature of East Germany*. Durham: Duke University Press.

Herbert, Ulrich. 1987. "Good Times, Bad Times: Memories of the Third Reich." In Richard Bessel, ed., *Life in the Third Reich*. Oxford: Oxford University Press.

Herf, Jeffrey. 1994. "East German Communists and the Jewish Question: The Case of Paul Merker." Occasional Paper No. 11. Washington, D.C.: German Historical Institute.

Hirsch, Joachim, and Roland Roth. 1986. *Das Neue Gesicht des Kapitalismus: Vom Fordismus zum Post-Fordismus.* Hamburg: VSA-Verlag.

Hobsbawm, Eric. 1994. *The Age of Extremes.* New York: Vintage Books.

Hübner, Peter. 1990. "Von unten gesehen: Krisenwahrnehmung durch Arbeiter." In Jochen Cerny, ed., *Brüche, Krisen, Wendepunkten. Neubefragungen von DDR-Geschichte.* Leipzig: Urania-Verlag.

———. 1993. "Balance des Ungleichgewichtes: Zum Verhältnis von Arbeiterinteressen und SED-Herrschaft." *Geschichte und Gesellschaft* 19 (1): 15–28.

———. 1994. "Die Zukunft war gestern: Soziale und mentale Trends in der DDR-Industriearbeiterschaft." In Kaelble et al. 1994.

Hyrkkanen, Markku. 1986. *Sozialistische Kolonialpolitik: Eduard Bernsteins Stellung zur Kolonialpolitik und zum Imperialismus, 1882–1914.* Helsinki: SHS.

Jasper, Dirk. 1991. "Ausländerbeschäftigung in der DDR." In Marianne Krüger-Potratz, ed., *Anderssein gab es nicht: Ausländer und Minderheiten in der DDR.* Münster: Waxmann.

Jessop, Bob. 1989. "Conservative Regimes and the Transition to Post-Fordism: The cases of Great Britain and West Germany." In M. Gottdiener and Nicos Komninos, eds., *Capitalist Development and Crisis Theory.* London: Macmillan.

———. 1990a. "Regulation Theories in Retrospect and Prospect." *Economy and Society* 19: 153–216.

———. 1990b. *State Theory.* University Park: Pennsylvania State University Press.

Jessop, Bob, et al., eds. 1991. *The Politics of Flexibility: Restructuring State and Industry in Britain, Germany and Scandanavia.* Brookfield, Vt.: Edward Elgar.

Jochmann, Werner. 1988. *Gesellschaftskrise und Judenfeindschaft in Deutschland 1870–1945.* Hamburg: Christians.

Kaelble, Hartmut, Jürgen Kocka, and Hartmut Zwahr, eds. 1994. *Sozialgeschichte der DDR.* Stuttgart: Klett-Cotta.

Kautsky, Karl. 1907. *Sozialismus und Kolonialpolitik: eine Auseinandersetzung.* Berlin: Buchandlung Vorwärts.

Kershaw, Ian. 1989. *The Hitler Myth.* Oxford: Oxford University Press.

Kirfel, Martina, and Walter Oswalt, eds. 1991. *Die Rückkehr der Führer. Modernisierter Rechtsradikalismus in Westeuropa.* 2d ed. Vienna: Europaverlag.

Klessmann, Christoph. 1978. *Polnische Bergarbeiter im Ruhrgebiet 1870–1945.* Göttingen: Vandenhoeck & Ruprecht.

Kocka, Jürgen. 1990. "Revolution und Nation 1989: Zur historischen Einordnung der gegenwärtigen Ereignisse." *Tel Aviver Jahrbuch für deutsche Geschichte* 19: 479–99.

Kowalsky, Wolfgang. 1993. "Rechtsextremismus und Anti-Rechtsextremismus in der modernen Industriegesellschaft." *Aus Politik und Zeitgeschichte* B2-3 (January 8): 14–25.

Laclau, Ernesto, and Chantal Mouffe. 1985. *Hegemony and Socialist Strategy.* London: Verso.

Lange, Astrid. 1993. *Was die Rechten lesen.* Munich: Beck.

Lash, Scott, and John Urry. 1994. *Economies of Signs and Space.* London: Sage.

Leuschen-Seppel, Rosemarie. 1978. *Sozialdemokratie und Antisemitismus im Kaiserreich.* Bonn: Verlag Neue Gesellschaft.

Lewis, Rand. 1991. *A Nazi Legacy: Right-Wing Extremism in Postwar Germany.* New York: Praeger.

Lipietz, Alain. 1984. *L'audace ou l'enlisement: Sur les politiques économiques de la gauche.* Paris: La Découverte.

———. 1986. "New Tendencies in the International Division of Labor: Regimes of Accumulation and Modes of Regulation." In Allen J. Scott and Michael Storper, eds., *Production, Work, Territory.* Boston: Allen and Unwin.

———. 1990. "La trame, la chaîne at la régulation: Un outil pour les sciences sociales." *Economies et Sociétés*, Série Théorie de la Régulation, R no. 5: 137–74.

———. 1991. "Die Beziehungen zwischen Kapital und Arbeit am Vorabend des 21. Jahrhunderts." *Leviathan* 19 (1): 78–101.

Lipset, Seymour Martin. 1963. *Political Man.* Garden City, N.Y.: Anchor Books.

Lötsch, Manfred. 1993. "Der Sozialismus: Eine Stände—oder eine Klassengesellschaft?" In Hans Joas and Martin Kohli, eds., *Der Zusammenbruch der DDR.* Frankfurt: Suhrkamp.

Lüdtke, Alf. 1994. "Helden der Arbeit'—Mühen beim Arbeiten: Zur mißmutigen Loyalität von Industriearbeitern in der DDR." In Kaelble et al. 1994.

Luhmann, Niklas. 1989. *Ecological Communication.* Cambridge: Polity.

Lüscher, Rudolf M. n.d. [1988]. *Henry und die Krümelmonster: Versuch über den fordistischen Sozialcharakter.* Tübingen: Konkursbuch Verlag C. Gehrke.

Maier, Charles. 1991. "The Collapse of Communism: Approaches for a Future History." *History Workshop* 31: 34–59.

Mason, Tim. 1995. *Nazism, Fascism, and the Working Class.* Edited by Jane Caplan. Cambridge: Cambridge University Press.

Massing, Paul W. 1949. *Rehearsal for Destruction: A Study of Political Anti-Semitism in Imperial Germany.* New York: Harper and Brothers.

McAdams, A. James. 1985. *East Germany and Detente: Building Authority after the Wall.* Cambridge: Cambridge University Press.

Merkl, Peter H., and Leonard Weinberg, eds. 1993. *Encounters with the Contemporary Radical Right.* Boulder: Westview.

Meuschel, Sigrid. 1993. "Überlegungen zu einer Herrschafts- und Gesellschaftsgeschichte der DDR." *Geschichte und Gesellschaft* 19 (1): 5–14.

Murray, Robin. 1990. "Fordismus und sozialistische Entwicklung." *PROKLA* 20 (4): 91–122.

Néré, Jacques. 1959. *La crise industrielle de 1882 et le mouvement boulangiste.* 2 vols. Paris: Thèse de lettres.

Niethammer, Lutz. 1991. *Die volkseigene Erfahrung: Eine Archäologie des Lebens in der Industrieprovinz der DDR.* Berlin: Rowohlt.

———. 1994. "Erfahrungen und Strukturen: Prolegomena zu einer Geschichte der Gesellschaft der DDR." In Kaelble et al. 1994.

———, ed. 1986. *"Die Jahre weiss man nicht, wo man die heute hinsetzen soll": Faschismuserfahrungen im Ruhrgebiet.* 2d ed. Berlin: Dietz.

Noelle-Neumann, Elisabeth, and Erp Ring. 1985. *Das Extremismus-Potential unter jungen Leuten in der Bundesrepublik Deutschland 1984.* 2d ed. Bonn: Bundesminister des Innern.

Ohlemacher, Thomas. 1994. "Public Opinion and Violence against Foreigners in the Reunified Germany." *Zeitschrift für Soziologie* 23 (3): 222–36.

Pfahl-Traughber, Armin. 1993. *Rechtsextremismus: Eine kritische Bestandsaufnahme nach der Wiedervereinigung.* Bonn: Bouvier.

Poulantzas, Nicos. 1979. *Fascism and Dictatorship.* London: Verso.

Rauhut, Michael. 1991. "DDR-Beatmusik zwischen Engagement und Repression." In *Kahlschalg: Das 11. Plenum des ZK der SED 1965.* Berlin: Aufbau.

Renault, Alain. 1991. "Logiques de la nation." In Gil Delannoi and Pierre-André Taguieff, eds., *Théories du nationalisme: Nation, nationalité, ethnicité.* Paris: Kime.

Rommelspacher, Birgit. 1995. "Warum Frauen rassistisch sind." In Petra Wleckik, ed., *Frauen und Rechtsextremismus.* Göttingen: Lamuv Verlag.

Roth, Karl Heinz. 1992. "Europa der 'Völker'? Sozialstruktur und Perspektiven der neuen Rechten in Westeuropa." *1999: Zeitschrift für Sozialgeschichte des 20. und 21. Jahrhunderts* 4: 7–10.

Rueschemeyer, Dietrich, Evelyne Huber Stephens, and John D. Stephens. 1992. *Capitalist Development and Democracy*. Chicago: University of Chicago Press.

Scharf, C. Bradley. 1989. "Social Policy and Social Conditions in the GDR." In Marilyn Rueschemeyer and Christiane Lemke, eds., *The Quality of Life in the German Democratic Republic: Changes and Developments in a State Socialist Society*. Armonk, N.Y.: M. E. Sharpe.

Scheuch, Erwin, and Hans D. Klingemann. 1967. "Theorie des Rechtsradikalismus in westlichen Industriegesellschaften." *Hamburger Jahrbuch für Wirtschafts- und Gesellschaftspolitik*, 11–29.

Schmidt, Michael. 1993. *The New Reich: Violent Extremism in Unified Germany and Beyond*. New York: Pantheon Books.

Schmidtke, Oliver, and Carlo E. Ruzza. 1993. "Regionalistischer Protest als 'Life Politics.' Die Formierung einer sozialen Bewegung: die Lega Lombarda." *Soziale Welt* 44 (1): 5–29.

Schneider, Gernot, and Manfred Troder. 1985. *Zur Genesis der Kombinate der zentralgeleiteten Industrie in der Deutschen Demokratischen Republik*. Berlin: Osteuropa-Institut.

Schröder, Hans-Christoph. 1979. *Gustav Noske und die Kolonialpolitik des Deutschen Kaiserreiches*. Berlin: Dietz.

Sichrovsky, Peter. 1993. *Unheilbar Deutsch: Rechte Schicksale und Lebensläufe*. Cologne: Kiepenheuer & Witsch.

SINUS-Institut München. 1981. *Fünf Millionen Deutsche: Wir sollten wieder einen Führer haben*. Reinbek: Rowohlt.

Spittmann, Ilse. 1990. *Die DDR unter Honecker*. Cologne: Verlag Wissenschaft und Politik.

Sprinzak, Ehud. 1993. "The Israeli Radical Right: History, Culture, and Politics." In Merkl and Weinberg 1993.

Steinmetz, George. 1993. *Regulating the Social: The Welfare State and Local Politics in Imperial Germany*. Princeton: Princeton University Press.

——. 1994. "Fordism and the 'Immoral Economy' of Right-Wing Violence in Contemporary Germany." In Frederick D. Weil, ed., *Research on Democracy and Society*, vol. 2. Greenwich, Conn.: JAI Press.

——. 1996. "German Exceptionalism and the Origins of Nazism: The Career of a Concept." In Ian Kershaw and Moshe Lewin, eds.,

Dictators Unleashed: Historical Approaches to Nazism and Stalinism. Cambridge: Cambridge University Press.

Stöss, Richard. 1991. *Politics against Democracy.* New York: Berg.

Tenner, Franziska. 1994. *Ehre, Blut und Mutterschaft: Getarnt unter Nazifrauen heute.* Berlin: Aufbau-Verlag.

Terkessidis, Mark. 1995. *Kulturkampf: Volk, Nation, der Westen und die Neue Rechte.* Cologne: Kiepenheuer & Witsch.

Thompson, E. P. 1993. *Customs in Common: Studies in Traditional Popular Culture.* New York: The New Press.

Tilly, Charles. 1978. *From Mobilization to Revolution.* Reading, Mass.: Addison-Wesley.

Trow, Martin. 1966. "Small Businessmen, Political Tolerance, and Support for McCarthy." In Lewis Coser, ed., *Political Sociology.* New York: Harper and Row.

Veen, Hans-Joachim, Norbert Lepszy, and Peter Mnich. 1993. *The Republikaner Party in Germany: Right-Wing Menace or Protest Catchall?* Westport, Conn.: Praeger.

Verfassungsschutzbericht (Annual report of the Office for the Protection of the Constitution). 1995. Bonn: Bundesministerium des Innern. Online version at Bundesamt für Verfassungsschutz WWW site.

Voskamp, Ulrich, and Volker Wittke. 1991. "Industrial Restructuring in the Former German Democratic Republic (GDR): Barriers to Adaptive Reform Become Downward Development Spirals." *Politics and Society* 19 (3): 341–71.

Wallerstein, Immanuel. 1986. *The Capitalist World-Economy.* Cambridge: Cambridge University Press.

Weber, Hermann. 1988. *Die DDR 1945–1986.* München: Oldenbourg.

———. 1993. "Die Geschichte der DDR: Versuch einer vorläufigen Bilanz." *Zeitschrift für Geschichtswissenschaft* 41 (4): 195–203.

Willems, Helmut, et al. 1993. *Fremdenfeindliche Gewalt.* Opladen: Leske + Budrich.

Wolffsohn, Michael. 1995. *Die Deutschland Akte: Juden und Deutsche in Ost und West: Tatsachen und Legenden.* Munich: Ferenczy bei Bruckmann.

Wright, Erik Olin. 1985. *Classes.* London: Verso.

Zimmermann, Ekkart, and Thomas Saalfeld. 1993. "The Three Waves of West German Right-Wing Extremism." In Merkl and Weinberg 1993.

Zimmermann, Michael. 1986. "Aufbruchshoffnung: Junge Bergleute in den Dreissiger Jahren." In Niethammer 1986.

CHAPTER 12

Class Analysis and Social Movements: A Critique and Reformulation

J. Craig Jenkins and Kevin Leicht

O VER THE PAST TWO DECADES, THE CLASS ANALYSIS OF SOCIAL MOVEMENTS has experienced a crisis. In the Western capitalist democracies, working-class movements have declined and become less militant; and with the breakup of the Soviet system and the international decline of Marxism, the relevance of class to social movement theory has come under question. Several observers have argued that we are witnessing an end of class-based movements. With the growth of the welfare state, postindustrialization and the resurgence of ethnic and alternative identities, class issues have waned relative to concerns with the life space of the local community, the natural environment, and the private household. Nevertheless, we think class remains a potent factor in contemporary social movements. In the West, economic restructuring and postindustrial modernization have created new economic and political inequalities and a growing clash between the winners and losers of this process. Although not class-based in the traditional sense, these movements and countermovements are structurally based and address basic distributional issues. In Eastern Europe and the Third World, economic development and political crises have stirred new class conflicts and democratization movements, which have put the question of class inequality on the political agenda.

Our aim in this essay is to show that class analysis remains central to an understanding of contemporary social movements. First we outline a theory of class formation, arguing that social movement development is the central process in class formation. As E. P. Thompson (1963) argued some time ago, classes do not simply exist; they are "made." At the center of this "making" process are social movements that articulate a distinctive identity, define collective interests that are opposed to other classes, and mobilize political and economic struggles against these antagonists (Hobsbawm 1984, 18). As Thompson argued, this "making" process entails agency and cannot be understood in terms of the classic "class-in-itself/class-for-itself" transition. Drawing on the historical contingency approach outlined by Katznelson and Zolberg (1986) and the resource mobilization theory of social movements (Tilly 1978; McAdam 1982; Jenkins and Klandermans 1995), we argue that class formation is largely shaped by the pace and organization of economic development and by the political opportunities created by the centralization and autonomy of the state.

We illustrate this argument with international comparisons. Although unionization and the welfare state have largely resolved traditional class conflicts in the Western capitalist democracies, new questions of class inequality are emerging. Industrial restructuring and postindustrial modernization are creating new divisions and protests. These movements, however, do not typically present their claims in class terms but instead adopt neopopulist ideologies. Postindustrial modernization has undermined traditional working-class organization and created a "new class" of salaried professionals who support various new movements pursuing an expanded set of social protections. On the right, economic insecurity and favorable opportunities have nurtured a set of New Right movements protesting these state interventions. These movements are also shaped by the legacy of past class struggles. Where "old" class struggles remain alive, the political space for these new challenges has remained limited. In the Third World, rapid industrialization combined with strong repressive states has stirred a new wave of industrial militancy and democratization movements. In a strikingly similar fashion, the economic crisis of the former Soviet Union and its satellites has likewise targeted blame at the state and political elites, producing broad challenges to the sociopolitical order. State-directed industrialization, whether organized privately or through state-owned enterprise, creates a centralized target. It also fuses workplace and political grievances, making for broad-gauged oppositional struggles.

Class Formation and Social Movement Development

Over three decades ago, E. P. Thompson (1963) launched his famous attack on structuralist theories of class. Arguing that classes do not simply exist but are *made* through collective action, he argued that we need to understand the historical processes by which community institutions, cultural outlooks, and political mobilization shape class formation. Applying this to the making of the English working class, he argued that classes are collective actors whose identity and solidarity are forged through collective action itself. Hence there is no preexisting class structures or institutions that explain this pattern but rather a need to trace the historical development of working-class movements (see also Thompson 1991). The major virtue of this argument was that it put social movement development at the center of class analysis. It lacked, however, a coherent theory of class formation. Why are some classes "made" while other remain "unmade"? Why do some workers support socialist parties while others support multiclass political machines? Without a sociological explanation of political outcomes, Thompson's scheme merely substituted an historicist approach for a simpleminded structuralism.

A more useful approach has been the historical contingency theory developed by Ira Katznelson (1986) and Aristide Zolberg (1986). Drawing on a comparative analysis of four Western countries (Britain, the United States, France, and Germany), they argued that working-class formation has two major dimensions: (1) the general moral outlook or "disposition" towards politics, including the adoption of reformist vs. radical ideologies and a unified vs. divided approach to work and community; and (2) the mobilization of collective action in terms of union strength and class support for political parties. Arguing that these are two independent two dimensions, they traced the major variations in working-class formation to two historically anterior dimensions of class formation: (1) the pace and organization of industrialization, and (2) the centralization and autonomy of the state. The core of their argument was a series of paired comparisons, highlighting the importance of these dimensions. Where industrialization was rapid and centralized (the United States and Germany, but not France), working-class solidarity was strong. Where proletarianization rested on immigrant workers (the United States, but not the others), work and community were treated as separate spheres and ethnoreligious rivalries were predominant. Where democratization occurred prior to industrialization and the state was relatively weak (the United States), preexisting multiclass parties based on region, religion, and ethnicity prevailed, and political and economic grievances tended not to overlap, thus discouraging the mobilization of broad oppositional challenges. In contrast, where the state was highly centralized and autonomous (e.g., France and Germany), class conflicts became politicized, producing a radical and well-organized movement.

This scheme provided a coherent explanation of the historical development of working-class movements in the West. Its relevance to the contemporary setting, however, is unclear. Many see either an end to class politics or at least a new politics of class resulting from economic restructuring and postindustrialization. It is also unclear how these arguments apply to working-class movements in the Third World or to state socialism. Will these follow a parallel experience, or are there distinctive aspects of these challenges?

In this essay, we draw on this "contingency" theory and ideas drawn from Adam Przeworski (1977, 1985), neo-Weberian stratification theory (Giddens 1973; Parkin 1979; Bonacich 1976), and the resource mobilization theory of social movements (Tilly 1978; McAdam 1982; Jenkins and Klandermans 1995). Our argument is organized by five premises. We begin with the premise that class formation is a dual process (Therborne 1983) in that social movement development is simultaneously shaped by objective and subjective processes. On the objective side, structural economic changes interact with changing political opportunities to shape the development of class-based movements. Just as industrial development created the industrial working class, so postindustrialization is currently creating a "new class" of salaried professionals in the West. Likewise labor market institutions and proletarianization created workplace solidarities that provided a basis for working-class mobilization. Political opportunities also facilitated the development of these movements, channeling them into reformist or oppositional challenges. On the subjective side, classes are also *made*, in the sense that people exposed to these objective processes develop distinctive life styles, solidarities, and identities that set them off from other groups and mobilize around these interests. Hence, to borrow from Weber (1968), classes may exist as objective market positions, but to become conscious social actors, they have to become *social classes* with a distinct corporate identity and an awareness of opposed interests that leads them to contest the power and interests of other classes.

This entails mobilization, which cannot be understood simply from an objective viewpoint but requires an independent subjective element.

Our second premise is that class formation is a product of class struggles that come together in a concrete nexus of economic, political, and ideological relationships between specific actors. Central to this nexus are specific institutions that create mobilization potentials, including the division of labor and authority relationships within the firm as well as distributive groupings such as neighborhoods and status communities. This "proximate structuration" (Giddens 1973) creates both specific relationships between those with power and authority and those without, as well as specific solidarities and identities that shape the prospects for mobilization. Institutionalization also creates the ability to reproduce social advantages, allowing status communities to establish market monopolies of specific resources, such as cultural and social capital, and thus enforce social closure in terms of mobility and life chances (Giddens 1973; Parkin 1979). Typically social closure is organized around property or claims to technical skill, but as split labor market theory (Bonacich 1976) contends, such market monopolies can also be organized around skilled manual positions. The class identities and ideologies attached to these positions are not forged in isolation but in concrete struggles with opposing class actors. As Marc Steinberg (1993) argues, there is no pure working-class consciousness per se but rather a set of identities and ideological outlooks that have been defined by their interaction and opposition with powerful groups. And, as Doug McAdam (1982) has argued, new political opportunities frequently provide the impetus for the construction of new identities, providing for a cognitive liberation in which subordinated groups are able to identify the sources of their oppression and devise tactics for challenging and altering it.

Third, this class struggle depends critically on the political context, especially the political opportunities and alliances that shape the mobilization of new contenders. As comparative studies have shown, the timing of democratization relative to industrialization was key to working-class formation (Zolberg 1987). In the United States, mass parties and associations, such as fraternal societies and churches, were founded several decades before industrialization, thus creating multiclass parties that were centered on regional, ethnic, and religious loyalties. Hence, once industrialization occurred, the working class was mobilized around these preexisting regional, ethnic, and religious identities. The strongest bases of oppositional mobilization were limited to immigrant workers who imported their radical political traditions, while native workers supported multiclass urban political machines and populist candidates (Rosenblum 1973; Blee and Gedicks 1980; Katznelson 1981). By comparison, in Western Europe, industrialization occurred before democratization, thus forming the working class through a political struggle for citizenship that simultaneously targeted the state and the industrial capitalists. Class identities and organization were forged in the process of wresting power away from the state as well as the upper classes, creating an oppositional consciousness and strong class-based associations and political parties.

In line with this reasoning, working-class formation also is critically shaped by the centralization of the state and its autonomy. In France, a highly centralized state that was involved as a copartner in industrialization adopted an exclusionary stance towards unions and working-class associations. Hence the working class adopted anti-statist or syndicalist strategies (Birnbaum 1988). However, industrialization in France was relatively slow and organized around smaller enterprises than elsewhere, creating weaker working-class solidarity . By contrast, the more politically permeable laissez faire United States nurtured a narrow "business unionist" labor movement. Even within the United States, labor strategies evolved depending on the political context. As Howard Kimmeldorf (1988) shows, the centralization and repressiveness of the shipping companies on the west coast produced a more radical longshoreman's union, while the more decentralized and less violent east coast shipping industry spawned a moderate "business unionist" labor movement.

Likewise, the making of the new middle class was shaped by political traditions and the threat of working-class movements. In Germany, strong bureaucratic and corporate state traditions coupled with the threat of an emerging radical working class encouraged the development of corporatist exclusionary conservatism among the middle class. By contrast, the laissez-faire tradition and the autonomy of professional associations in the United States interacted with a moderate working-class movement has encouraged neopopulist liberalism among the middle class that has, at times, supported the welfare state and broad inclusive definitions of citizenship (Wacquant 1991).

Political institutions shape the persistence of class identities. In the United States, presidential government and a two-party system rooted in a winner-take-all, single-member district electoral system have discouraged third parties and thus muted the potentials for oppositional challenges. As a result, socialism has never been a powerful electoral force, and this weakness, combined with the importance of ethnic and religious cleavages, led the working class to develop a split or dualistic consciousness. It responded to class inequalities in the workplace, but in the electoral arena it supported regional, ethnic, and religious appeals (Katznelson 1981). By contrast, parliamentary government and proportional voting systems have encouraged multiparty systems and thus greater ideological diversity, allowing class-based ideological parties to persist.

Fourth, no class is ever completely formed in the sense that it is fully mobilized around a single coherent identity and set of political organizations. Instead, capitalist development continually transforms the structure of locations in the social system, simultaneously facilitating the mobilization of some groups and class segments while demobilizing others. Hence industrial workers during one period may be highly mobilized and play a critical part in leftist political coalitions and, during another, become demobilized and largely irrelevant to political struggles. Or as Jeff Manza, Michael Hout, and Clem Brooks (1995) argue, working-class voting may follow a pattern of trendless fluctuation shaped by election-specific issues and personalities.

Fifth, capitalist development simultaneously hinders the formation of class-based social movements at the same time that it facilitates them. In classical Marxian theory, the assumption was that the centralization of industry and the polarization of the class structure, coupled with the growth of the factory system, would contribute to working-class solidarity. While accepting these arguments, contemporary analysts contend that these structural trends are not necessary features of capitalist development. Capitalist development may render more people dependent on the capitalist system as market relations spread to ever broader spheres of life, but this is not the same as creating structural places for proletarians. Nor does it insure that their loyalties and solidarities will be available for oppositional politics. Capitalist development also displaces people from definite locations in the relations of production at the same time that it creates new places for others, and these structural changes do not always fit into a neat package that one can label "proletarianization." In the current period, the self-employed middle class has experienced significant growth, reflecting the advantages for large corporations of subcontracting and maintaining a more flexible workforce. Moreover, as

Michael Burawoy (1985) has argued, the joint dependence of worker and capitalist and the institutionalization of labor-management relations in the new competitive global marketplace has undermined industrial militancy and "manufactured" a new type of political consent. Hence much of the unevenness of class mobilization depends on historical contingencies and institutional specifics rather than on uniform processes of socioeconomic development. We must incorporate these socially and politically contingent processes if we want to understand when class movements form and when they do not.

The New Politics of Class in the West: Working-Class Disorganization and the Rise of the "New Class"

The crisis of Marxism and the general decline of working-class movements in the Western capitalist democracies are often cited as evidence of the growing irrelevance of class (see Vanneman and Cannon 1987). However, our discussion above should have made it clear that this outocome is a historical contingency. The more relevant question is, What are the economic and political conditions that facilitate the development of class-based movements, including the persistence of oppositional working-class challenges? Here we examine both the general structural trends that are currently undermining traditional class conflicts, as well as the emergence of a new division between the "winners" and "losers" of postindustrial modernization, a division that prefigures a new politics of class. These processes are also historically contingent, however. In France, for example, the persistence of traditional class mobilization has limited the opportunities for the development of these new social movements of the left and the right. Hence the decline of working-class politics and the rise of a new politics of class are historically variable rather than structurally determined.

We begin by arguing that there are strong structural tendencies towards the decline of working-class movements throughout the Western capitalist democracies. First, the number of proletarianized industrial workers has stabilized and in many countries declined as a proportion of the labor force. This has placed pressure on working-class parties to forge multiclass alliances, making appeals to the new middle class and other marginalized groups. This in turn has tended to demobilize workers and blunted the significance of class, thus opening the way to new electoral alignments and protest movements.

Second, postindustrialization and the accompanying economic restructuring have set in motion a series of forces that undermine working-class cohesion and create new types of social identities that are not conducive to class mobilization. The traditional Fordist system of standardized mass production provided fertile ground for the development of labor and related movements whose members were interested in securing economic justice for themselves and occasionally acting in the name of workers as a whole. Although the actual effectiveness of labor movements as class actors has always been questioned (Davis 1980; Form 1987, 1995), there is no doubt that the labor movements of the West were generally effective at improving the working lives of those they represented (Freeman and Medoff 1984). Union movements also provided a structural space within which potential appeals in the name of all members of the working class could be made, even if this avenue was infrequently used. Wage and hours legislation, occupational safety and health, and social insurance programs in most industrial capitalist economies all bear the strong stamp of organized labor movements, which either initiated these policies or significantly modified legislation once it was introduced (Western 1995).

The development of a post-Fordist production system, however, has transformed this organizing environment. By post-Fordism, we mean a system of flexible production for specialized markets in which capital is highly mobile and the links between workers and firms are transitory and indirect. This system has had several implications for labor movements. First, as union movements became institutionalized, they increasingly have had to operate in market relationships as providers of "goods" to workers as "consumers" of union benefit programs rather than as all-encompassing social movements with political and ideological platforms that had general public appeal (Cornfield 1986; Leicht 1989a). This institutionalization of class struggle left the labor movement structurally vulnerable to employer efforts to weaken worker loyalties. Cut off from broad public support, unions had to survive through their ability to mobilize support from workers in a specific plant or industry. They could no longer rely on general public support, including that of potential strikebreakers and consumers. Hence, all employers needed to do to prevent union organizing was to provide pay and benefits that approached those that unionized employers provided (Freeman and Medoff 1984; Leicht 1989b; Leicht, Wallace, and Grant 1993) or threaten to withdraw from the economic relationship via capital flight. This hegemonic production regime, as Burawoy (1985) has called it, yielded worker consent and loyalty to the firm in its market competition against its rivals. This company identity has in turn undermined broader working-class loyalties and reinforced the importance of class identities in politics.

With new technologies, employers have also been able to lower the transaction costs associated with capital mobility and thus had the option of relocating plants to other regions and countries instead of acceding to union demands. Even in plants that still rely on a Fordist system of production, unions have been weakened and find themselves fighting defensive efforts to block "outsourcing" and similar methods of decentralized production. In addition, there has been a "new class war" in which employers used new legal tactics and personnel policies to destroy union organizing drives and create new loyalties among workers (Freeman and Medoff 1984). The Fordist managerial ideology, as it is reflected in human relations management and other systems oriented toward the control of the industrial workforce (Gordon, Edwards, and Reich 1984; Edwards 1979; Baron, Dobbin, and Jennings 1986), has gradually given way to a new managerial ideology in the 1980s and 1990s. This ideology is rooted in such terms as "downsizing", "rightsizing", "lean organizations," and "outsourcing." For want of a better term, we refer to this ideology as "neo-entrepreneurialism" (Skaggs and Leicht 1995).

Neo-entrepreneurialism has several features that distinguish it from Fordist production processes. Instead of control and dependency as the central organizing dynamics of production, neo-entrepreneurial production stresses independence and diversification. The combination of sophisticated flexible technologies and global competition has eliminated much of the structural slack that allowed large employers to survive in the Fordist production system. In place of this is a conception of the environment surrounding production as "turbulent" and "ever-changing" (Boyett and Conn 1992). The practical result from the standpoint of class-oriented social movements is that the implied social contract that existed between large employers and their workers (the consent that Burowoy [1985] and others have discussed) is destroyed and replaced by networks of temporary and cursory relationships with subcontractors and temporary help agencies. In effect, the working class is disaggregated and disorganized on an unprecedented scale (Hyman 1992).

One might argue that this opens the way for the emergence of a new class consciousness, as workers, denied their traditional rights to secure employment and related fringe benefits, rebel against the new factory regime. This, however, assumes that they have the organizing space and solidarity to forge a new consciousness and act against their employers. If our picture is correct, disorganization and a politics of resentment are more likely, fueling right-wing populist movements that work against traditional working-class unions and leftist politics.

Let us look in more detail at the structures of solidarity and identity created by the new "global" workplace. In the neo-entrepreneurial environment, a small core of permanent managerial employees purchases skilled human capital through subcontracting and consulting arrangements and unskilled human capital through temporary help services. The skilled are paid through "fee-for-service" arrangements, much as professional services are paid for in the United States. The unskilled workers are employed by temporary help agencies that subcontract employees to the neo-entrepreneurial firm on a short-term basis. Added to this is the increase in administrative and personal service workers who, personally identifying with supervisors or providing services to upper-class consumers, are more likely to identify with their superiors than with a working-class community (Stinchcombe 1990, 303).

The political consequences are profound. Neo-entrepreneurialism produces a more fragmented labor market as it also shrinks the number of established places for members of the working class. The traditional unskilled working class is thus severed from its direct links with employers and thus is denied direct leverage as a mobilized group. It also undermines the workplace solidarities that have provided for collective action in the past. At the same time, the established group of managers shrinks through corporate downsizing and is replaced by outside contracts and temporary hiring offices. This managerial class and the new middle class find it necessary to market their services as consultants and subcontractors, adopting an entrepreneurial self-image that militates against professional norms. Managers no longer direct the activities of a stable pool of workers; and at the same time, a stable group of workers is no longer structurally connected to these managers. Further, the neo-entrepreneurial firms' commitment to flexible production and capital mobility makes workplace linkages even more tenuous because there is increasingly "no workplace to organize" (see Cornfield 1986).

This neo-entrepreneurial production system also creates spatial fragmentation in terms of urban space. Production is no longer locality dependent and makes use of the diversity of existing ecological spaces. This means, on the one hand, that capital can maximize its leverage against local communities, demanding tax abatements, public works concessions, and special investments in training a labor force as a condition for investment. It also means that communities are powerless to oppose these demands and must increasingly concede or be pushed to the side and become economic backwaters. In the United States, this occurs in the midst of significant racial segregation in which minorities are concentrated in specific neighborhoods and have little or no structural access to employers against whom they could press collective grievances (Wilson 1987). Their energies are thus directed towards the life space of the urban community or, in the case of the urban underclass, towards immediate survival in the social anarchy of discarded and unneeded neighborhoods (Massey and Denton 1993) .

In practical terms, the spatial fragmentation of the postindustrial economy combines with the service orientation of many postindustrial enterprises to structurally cut off most of the poor and underprivileged from access to productive employment of any kind. Marginal work is increasingly suburbanized, which spatially separates low-wage work from those who have traditionally performed it. The service orientation of much of this new low-wage work means that from the standpoint of the institutional environment surrounding the postindustrial firm, workers are expected to take on the characteristics of the customers they serve. Both trends enhance the attractiveness of temporary employees who are spouses or children of either the "new class" or of the new subcontracting entrepreneurial elite.

These combined developments mean that in large segments of the West (and especially the United States) there is no locally dependent employer class against whom protest can be directed. The bourgeois no longer is available as a coherent target or is no longer located in the sites where production actually takes place. In extreme cases such as homeworkers, there is literally no production site against which protests and grievances can be directed. The result of all of these changes is a "structural softening" of economic life. The groups most likely to press for grievances on the basis of class appeals cannot mobilize because, as Schwartz (1976) has argued, one cannot protest effectively against a system to which one has no structural access. Furthermore, even if the economically disenfranchised could mobilize, their employers have the option of moving overseas or to another locale, thus blunting the workers' leverage.

This is a stark scenario. It is by no means fully developed yet, but it marks the direction of change. The practical consequence of neo-entrepreneurial, postindustrial development, with its downsizing, rightsizing, and subcontracting, is the creation of a new and, we think, enduring market-intensive method of organizing production, one that presents major barriers to class-based mobilization. In class terms, the neo-entrepreneurial economy has created a group of relatively secure, upwardly mobile subcontractors and consultants whose well-being is based on both earnings and investment income; a second group of fragmented, economically insecure, intermittently employed workers who are only tenuously connected to the labor market and are encouraged to disinvest in it emotionally; and a third group, growing in most western countries that is not attached to the labor force at all. Reinforcing this, a "new class war" against the poor and unemployed has been launched to strip away the safety net of the welfare state. The result is a widening split between the "winners" of this process, both the entrepreneurs and the new entrepreneurial professionals, and the "losers," the temporary workers and the unemployed as well as those who are threatened by these developments. This split creates the potential for a profoundly different politics of class.

One group whose position has not changed are the civil servants and culture workers. Although postindustrialism creates cultural fragmentation (as many postmodern writers have argued) similar to the economic fragmentation, it ironically does not appear to threaten the structural positions of most culture workers, civil servants, and members of the "public intelligentsia" who are government subsidized or protected and thus relatively secure. These groups still harbor considerable emotional and psychic investments in their work roles and are often in frequent conflict with their employers because of strong occupational and professional identities. Furthermore, these groups represent coherent occupational communities. They work in relatively stable, permanent positions in physical proximity to others with the same commitments, and these commitments spill over into their nonworking lives in terms of friendship networks, social involvements, and intermarriage patterns. Because these workers have precisely what the old working class once had (and which large segments of the new working class lack), namely strong solidarity and structural access to important positions that are ideologically and socially necessary, they can still be mobilized. We expect them to become increasingly important sources of leftist politics in this new entrepreneurial environment.

The question is, What type of leftist politics will they support? In contrast to this disenfranchised working class, these relatively secure "new class" workers are more likely to support general public interest and lifestyle movements that reflect their status concerns and conceptions of citizenship. Such challenges constitute the major focus of the new social movements. Instead of conducting a battle against the bosses, this "new class" is more likely to support general humanitarian campaigns such as minority rights, animal rights, and conservation, and attempts to reclaim control over private life. This "new class" mobilization does not center on economic themes because (1) the vast majority of the professional workers are still economically secure, (2) most have considerable bargaining power in their human capital and hence leverage against their employers, and (3) they are relatively privileged compared to their clients or to the disadvantaged victims of the neo-entrepreneurial economy and hence do not have a strong sense of relative deprivation. Because of their structural leverage in the production system and urban social space, we think the new movements of these "new class" workers are likely to have considerable political, ideological, and economic clout.

In this setting, new social movements have developed that in various measures mobilize these "new class" professionals and various marginalized groups. Using a broad neopopulist rhetoric of citizen rights, the women's movement, racial minorities, the ecology and peace movements, and homosexuals and other stigmatized groups have mobilized to claim the mantle of democratization and progressive social change. In response, a heterogeneous coalition of religious fundamentalists, housewives, threatened industrial workers and the new entrepreneurial professionals and managers have mobilized around conservative campaigns to restore individual responsibility and conformity to traditional social norms.

What then is this new politics of class? First the "new class" appears to be a potent source of protest and of support for new social movements throughout the advanced capitalist democracies (Kriesi 1989; Wallace and

Jenkins 1995). These protests are also supported by the young, the better educated, and those of secular orientations, and they tend to be led by representatives of the new class. Second, there appears to be a growing divide within the new class, broadly defined, between, on the one hand, the sociocultural professionals who maintain strong identities with their clients and with traditional conceptions of professional responsibility and, on the other hand, what Alvin Gouldner (1979) calls the technical intelligentsia. The latter are increasingly under the sway of the new entrepreneurial identities and thus align with the "old class" of managers and entrepreneurs. Hence there is a growing split, with the sociocultural professionals supporting the new liberation movements and the technical intelligentsia rallying around moral campaigns of the New Right (Eder 1993; Jenkins and Wallace 1996; Hout, Brooks, and Manza 1995). Third, there also evidence of what Gouldner calls the "flawed universality" of this new class, namely, its simultaneous commitment to the new liberation movements alongside commitments to protecting its economic privileges and the social institutions (such as restricted access to higher education) that protect its claims (Brint 1985, 1994). Fourth, there is the growing resentment by the losers of postindustrial modernization, especially the de-skilled workers and those threatened by the new post-Fordist production system, and this creates a base that can be mobilized for the New Right's campaigns.

Overall, the losers of neo-entrepreneurialism and postindustrial modernization are unlikely to mobilize without the assistance of conservative entrepreneurs and managers. However, some have sufficient solidarity and resources to mount independent challenges from the New Right. In Germany, neo-Nazi groups in the unemployed working-class youth have mounted violent attacks on immigrants and refugees. In the United States, right-wing extremists based in small business, displaced industrial workers, and the lower middle class have mounted a neopopulist "sagebrush rebellion," challenging the state's policing and tax powers and claiming a natural right to bear arms and hold private property free from government control (Lo 1986). Even more significant is the potential that these groups may provide an electoral base for right-wing campaigns mobilized by other groups. Hence, as Hanspeter Kriesi (1995) has shown in Western Europe, those who are most threatened by these economic changes have supported right-wing candidates appealing to nationalistic sentiments against immigrants and culturally diverse groups. Although it seems unlikely that these candidacies will prevail politically, the scope of their support will depend on the pace of economic changes and the ability to forge multiclass alliances in support of these solutions.

Thus far, we have emphasized general structural trends creating a new division between "winners" and "losers," unleashing a new type of class politics in which class identities per se are submerged in the name of either general citizens' rights or the restoration of moral purity. Yet, as we have argued, this outcome is politically contingent. It depends on the pattern of political alignments, especially the pacification of the traditional class cleavage and the development of new political opportunities for these new social movements.

Let us begin with the pacification of the "old" class struggle. As Adam Przeworski and John Sprague (1986) argue, the decline of working-class solidarity is not a structural given but a product of political choices made by party strategists in the context of existing class solidarities and political alliances. Although all working-class parties are structurally limited by their inability to mobilize an electoral majority based on industrial workers, and hence are encouraged to resort to some type of middle-class electoral strategy, their willingness to engage in this strategy and the political consequences of it vary significantly. In countries where working-class solidarity and union centralization are strong and the bourgeois parties have failed to mobilize workers around particularistic appeals to religion or ethnicity, the strategy of appealing to middle-class voters has not undermined working-class solidarity. Hence in the Nordic countries, class solidarity has remained strong, and the middle class has developed a working-class identity, joining unions and supporting social democratic parties (Brooks 1994). In this context, alliances between the middle and working classes have been dominant. In contrast, in countries where industrial workers have never mobilized broadly as a class (e.g., the United States) or have lost their organizational position (e.g., Britain)— or in countries where bourgeois parties have mobilized workers as members of religious and ethnic communities (e.g., Belgium)—class solidarity has weakened with the adoption of middle-class electoral strategies, and leftist parties have typically been weak. Here, the middle class's support for the new social movements has flourished, and the new politics of class outlined above has become central. In short, the structural trend towards working-class decline and the displacement of the "old" by the "new" politics of class depend on political opportunities and processes.

This switch to the new politics of class also depends on the political cohesion and traditions of the left. In France, the left has remained divided between the Communists and the Socialists, with the former maintaining a strong class rhetoric, due in part to the exclusionary tradition of the French state, inherited revolutionary ideology, and the experience of the Resistance during World War II. This has forced the Socialists, who have been more adept at mobilizing the new middle class and other groups, to compete in the same terms, thus perpetuating a strong class rhetoric. This political rivalry has also prevented the unions from integrating into stable policy networks and thus abandoning their traditional commitments to class conflict (Golden 1986). At the same time, the state has frequently used market forces to modernize the economy, thus preventing the pacification of industrial relations and politicizing the use of the strike. In this setting, French unions have used the strike as a political weapon to bargain with the government as well as with employers, perpetuating the long-standing tradition of politically regulated strikes (Shorter and Tilly 1976). At the same time, French unions are organizationally weak, meaning that they cannot enter into stable bargaining relations with employers. As a result, traditional class cleavages have remained highly salient, and the organizing space for the new social movements has been limited. Protest remains largely centered in traditional class cleavages, and the new movements are relatively weak and ill organized (Kriesi et al. 1995).

Together, these arguments suggest factors that facilitate or discourage the switch to a "new politics" of class. Where traditional working-class solidarities remain strong and politically relevant, whether by the persistence of a divided left (France) or the continued strength of unions and the social democratic party (Sweden), the "old politics" of class will remain relevant. In this setting, neo-entrepreneurialism and postindustrial modernization will make fewer inroads and the "new class" is likely to maintain a coalition with industrial workers. In contrast, where working-class mobilization has been weak or been undercut by economic changes, social movements of the New Left and the New Right have been more likely to flourish.

State Industrialization and New Working-Class Militancy: The Third World and the Crisis of State Socialism

A second new arena of class politics is in the Third World and the former state socialist countries where state-led industrialization has created new contradictions and working-class militancy. These could be looked at as successor struggles, in the sense that they mirror the historical experience of the industrialized West. Yet some have also argued that they display a new working-class militancy and radicalism.

First, some parallels. The most obvious parallel is structural. Industrialization creates a growing manual working class which, especially if it is centered in large-scale, capital-intensive enterprises, yields a cohesive and politically influential working class. Insofar this working class is cohesive in terms of both workplace solidarities and those formed around stable residential neighborhoods, and is relatively homogeneous in terms of ethnicity and religion, then this working class will eventually mobilize and become an important political force. The questions is, What will this working class demand? Following European experience, this depends heavily on the reception working-class militants receive from the state and employers. If the militants face intense repression and a partnership between the state and employers, then they are likely to develop a radical consciousness. If instead they face a weak and more permeable state, then moderate "business unionist" demands and multiclass political coalitions seem more likely. At the minimum, the exclusionary nature of these states, both in the Third World and the former state socialist regimes, suggests that industrial workers will be a critical force in democratization struggles. Without rights to organize and press claims through unions and electoral politics, they cannot hope to organize. Insofar as they are met with state repression, they are likely to adopt a more oppositional stance, defining the state as well as employers as the enemy.

The most important structural factors are the pace and organization of industrialization coupled with the strength and legitimacy of the state. In the Western experience, economic growth eventually transformed the class struggle into a positive-sum game, giving workers a choice between continuing the high-risk strategy of supporting a radical program or the low-risk strategy of pursuing increased returns from an expanding economy. So long as the economy continued to grow, workers were more prone to accept the economic logic that moderate but certain gains were preferable, thus creating a material basis of consent (Przeworski 1985).

Does this fit the Third World experience? In some contexts, the economic success of industrialization has channeled working-class politics into moderate strategies. East Asian development is frequently held up as an example of how cultural solidarity coupled with effective state promotion of export-oriented industrial development has created a moderate working class that accedes to the paternalistic guidance of entrepreneurs and a strong state. The speed of industrialization, coupled with strong paternalistic ties and a relatively narrow range of inequality, has created a social contract that minimizes class conflict and deters militancy.

This portrait, however, may be atypical of Third World experience. Hagen Koo (1994) argues that rapid and centralized industrialization in South Korea has created a militant and highly mobilized working class. Despite significant economic growth and increases in industrial wages, a highly centralized and repressive state led by corrupt politicians—many of whom were former collaborators with the Japanese colonialists—has produced a militant and oppositional working class. In this setting, working-class mobilization has fed into a militant movement that has pressed for democratization and that threatens to undermine the political stability of the South Korea "miracle."

In Latin America, the strong role of the state in industrialization has created a similar pattern. Despite rapid industrialization in several countries, economic growth has generally been unmatched by comparable improvements in human development. Overurbanization, growing income inequality, and the expansion of the informal and tertiary sectors of the economy have produced a zero-sum game in which the high-risk strategy of radical redistribution has become more appealing. Many argue that this is due to the disadvantages of "third wave" industrialization, which has relied on foreign investment and the import of labor-displacing advanced technology, making these economies more dependent on the international marketplace (Evans 1979; Bornschier and Chase-Dunn 1985). Following a strategy that Alain Lipietz (1978) has called "global Fordism," many less developed countries during the 1950s and 1960s embarked on "hothouse" industrialization programs by importing foreign technology, mobilizing a semiskilled labor force, and implementing various protections in terms of export subsidies, infrastructure investments and direct state investment. These policies succeeded in creating new heavy-industry and consumer-durables manufacturing but at the expense of competing directly with the more advanced West. They also failed to import the more skilled production and engineering functions from the advanced countries and, insofar as production was for export, created a severe disarticulation between production and consumption, thus leaving these economies strongly exposed to international instabilities. Hence when the two "oil shocks" of the 1970s struck, these economies went into recession and, despite various attempts to restore accumulation by foreign loans and restructuring, many of them experienced protracted economic depressions.

In many respects, this scenario fits the classic Marxian argument about class polarization and the emergence of a sharply divided mode of production in which a large number of "have-nots" confront a small number of "haves." Insofar as these Third World societies have experienced polarizing inequality and the increasing cohesion created by urbanization and industrial centralization, they have experienced higher rates of political rebellion and violence (Jenkins and Schock 1993). Urbanization, the debt crisis, and the imposition of austerity policies in the 1980s have likewise spurred urban protests and lower-class mobilization (Walton and Ragin 1990). However, there are also strong political elements that need to be incorporated into this story.

First, states have adopted alternative strategies in attempting to control working-class mobilization. As Valenzuela (1992) has outlined, many Third World states have sponsored unions and used patronage to harness them to a hegemonic mass party, thus preempting autonomous unionization and converting union leaders into loyal allies of the regime. The first Peronist government in Argentina and the PRI in contemporary Mexico represent examples of this pattern. Although strikes and labor protest will occur, they will be contained and largely work to increase the bargaining leverage of co-opted union leaders. In other countries, states have adopted a labor-repressive strategy of outlawing all types of union organization, repressing strikes, arresting union organizers and confiscating strike funds. Although this has worked in the short run to prevent independent unionization, it has not suppressed all working-class mobilization and, paralleling the German experience in the nineteenth century, has typically produced militant and oppositional unions. Alternatively, where worker militancy has been too strong to control with repression (especially in heavy industry, such as metalworking, mining, and petrochemicals), employers and the state have experimented with negotiating with independent unions, attempting to insure the economic privileges of these workers to secure labor peace. This, however, has been limited by the constraints of the debt crisis and international competition, which have tended to undermine these limited class compromises, thus producing militant leaders of broader social movements.

In addition, the social origins and community ties of industrial workers have fostered a broad definition of worker interests. Comparing Brazil with South Africa, Gay Seidman (1994) argues that both have experienced a rapid growth of "social-movement unionism," meaning that industrial workers have supported a general democratization program alongside union protections. These industrial workers are typically recent immigrants from the countryside or former workers in the informal sector and hence are less constrained by craft union traditions. Likewise, they are less likely to support split labor market institutions that would shelter privileged workers from other workers; or, as in the South African case, mobilization is centered on the minority workers themselves, thus attacking racial privilege in addition to pressing for the right to organize. In addition, the close partnership between the state and employers in these settings, plus the international economic vulnerability of these regimes, creates a strong likelihood for elite divisions to emerge over how to control working-class militancy. Under pressure from abroad but unable to institute labor control through simple repression, employers are likely to support reforms, thus creating political opportunities for unionization. Once developed, these challenges have frequently become central to broad democratization struggles.

A third and surprisingly similar experience has been that of state socialist regimes. This experience reinforces the point about the centralization and autonomy of the state, which in these countries has been the central agent of industrialization. Turning Marx on his head, Burawoy (1985; also Burowoy and Lukacs 1992) argues that state socialism is more vulnerable to working-class militancy. Without the "hidden hand" of the market, social control is more visible, and hence workers can blame their troubles on the Communist Party and the central ministries responsible for planning the system. This politicizes everyday grievances, ranging from inferior merchandise to long food queues and housing scarcity. Meanwhile, political rituals that were meant to legitimize the regime by emphasizing it as a "people's state" ironically work to remind people of its failures to live up to its ideals. Hence, in contrast to the "market despotism" of early industrial capitalism and the "hegemonic regimes" of post-Fordist capitalism, state socialism has created employment guarantees that preclude the threat of loosing one's job as a means of extracting cooperation. Nor are institutional rules, such as collective bargaining or management-initiated games, adequate to insure worker consent. Socialist managers

have instead turned to a new set of controls, using wage insecurity introduced through piece rates, bonuses, fines, and premiums to extract cooperation. These remunerations are subject to continual change and are
wielded arbitrarily, thus creating a "bureaucratic despotism." By simultaneously mobilizing around the rituals of socialism, which keeps the
ideals of "to each according to need," while operating in a capricious and
arbitrary fashion, state socialist regimes have delegitimized themselves.
Thus, when threatened by economic crisis, such as occurred during the
1980s, and by growing dissidence among the intelligentsia, these regimes
became highly vulnerable to working-class challenge.

During the 1980s, several East bloc countries experienced major
working-class insurgencies which eventually produced a crisis of socialism. In Poland, independent unions and a Catholic subculture provided
the political space for working-class insurgency. In Hungary, middle-class
intellectuals and students played more critical roles in provoking resistance, while in East Germany popular insurgency was irrelevant. These
states, however, were internationally dependent on the Soviet Union, and
when it became evident that the Soviet Union was not going to inter-
vene militarily to stave up failing socialism, the economic and political
crises spawned a wave of democratization movements that eventually
transformed these societies. Under pressure from the Solidarity movement in the early 1980s, the Polish state responded initially with repression and military rule, thus stripping away its pretensions to a workers'
state. Later, under international military pressure from the West, the Soviet
Union embarked on an ill-fated economic modernization program,
which eventually destroyed the Communist Party and the Soviet system as well as the military empire that had maintained them. Once it
became evident that the Soviet troops would not back up illegitimate
regimes, working-class militancy and student/intellectual revolt undermined these regimes.

Whither Class Analysis?

What conclusions flow from this discussion? Social movements are central to class formation and cannot be treated as the dependent outcomes
of an automatic or structurally determined process. As Katznelson (1986)
and Zolberg (1986) and others have argued, class formation is a histori-

cal process shaped by social institutions and political processes. For example, the sharp division between home and work in the United States facilitated a bifurcation between urban and workplace politics (Katznelson 1981). Likewise, electoral institutions have channeled the structure of political choice, thus facilitating the development and persistence of reformist or radical working-class parties. To echo E. P. Thompson (1963), the struggle itself is also a crucible of new identities. As Fantasia (1988) has argued, conflictive interactions create emergent collective identities—or as he calls them, "local cultures of solidarity"—that help form class identities and movements. A persistent history of state repression has been a critical ingredient in the formation of oppositional working-class movements. Hence the development of social movements should be understood as an historically contingent process that entails multiple factors and various outcomes. At the same, the major sociological task is to understand the social and institutional factors that shape these contingencies and work to create specific outcomes. Simple cultural or linguistic analyses (e.g., Thompson 1991; Jones 1983) that fail to address the "why" of movement development are thus inadequate.

We have identified two major structural contexts that shape the development of social movements. First, the pace and organization of economic development: rapid centralized industrialization creates a cohesive working class capable of sustaining mobilization against employers and the state. In a similar fashion, rapid postindustrialization and the spread of neo-entrepreneurialism are currently undermining the "old" politics of class and creating the possibility for a new politics of class. Second, class-based movements are critically shaped by the political opportunities defined by political alignments and the centralization and autonomy of the state. Just as state centralization and repression radicalized the industrial working class, creating an oppositional challenge, so the development of a new politics of class is regulated by the persistence of "old" class politics. Where the working class has remained highly mobilized and where traditional class-based party alignments have persisted, there has been little political space for the development of these new social movements of the left or the right. By contrast, in decentralized and permeable regimes like the United States, a weak reformist working class has created extensive space for middle-class organizing and hence the development of a wide variety of new social movements that frame their demands in general neopopulist terms.

Reflecting these processes, the rapid industrialization and economic changes in the Third World and Eastern Europe have created a new relevance for class analysis. Centralized autonomous states have created "hothouse" industrialization that spawned working-class movements. State repression and a centralized target have radicalized these movements, creating a new wave of "social movement unionism" (Seidman 1994). By forging coalitions with middle-class and urban groups, working-class insurgency has been a central force in the democratization of these states. In a strikingly similar fashion, working-class movements have also been central to the democratization struggles in Eastern Europe. By joining forces with students and the intelligentsia, the working class has been central to the dismantling of state socialism. Turning Marx on his head, state socialism has proven to be as radicalizing as authoritarian capitalism.

In recent decades, the discussion of class and social movements has been the scene of sharp theoretical disputes. Structuralist ideas (Poulantzas 1975; Wright 1985) have come under attack for providing only a thin skeleton picture of the process of class formation. By neglecting the social institutions and political processes that shape the development of social movements, these approaches capture only a limited aspect of the potential for development. At the same time, the retreat into semiotics and cultural analysis (Jones 1983; Thompson 1991) is even more limiting. Although these studies might provide an understanding of the political vision of actors, they fail to capture their social and political context. For this type of understanding, we need to link our analyses of class structure and identity construction to the historical contingencies that shape the course of social movements. The key contingencies lie in the pace and organization of industrialization and the structure of political opportunities.

References

Aminzade, Ronald. 1981. *Class, Politics and Early Industrial Capitalism.* Albany: State University of New York Press.

Baron, James N., Frank R. Dobbin, and P. Devereaux Jennings. 1986. "War and Peace: The Evolution of Modern Personnel Administration in U.S. Industry." *American Journal of Sociology* 92: 350–83.

Birnbaum, Pierre. 1988. *States and Collective Action*. New York: Cambridge University Press.

Blee, Kathleen, anc Al Gedicks. 1980. "The Emergence of Socialist Political Culture Among Finnish Immigrants in Minnesota." In Maurice Zeitlin, ed., *Classes, Class Conflict and the State*. Cambridge: Winthrop.

Bonacich, Edna. 1976. "Advanced Capitalism and Black/White Relations: A Theory of the Split Labor Market." *American Sociological Review* 41: 34–51

Bornschier, Volker, and Chris Chase-Dunn. 1985. *Transnational Corporations and Underdevelopment*. New York: Praeger.

Bourdieu, Pierre. 1984. *Distinction: A Social Critique of the Judgement of Taste*. New York: Cambridge University Press.

Boyett, Joseph. H., and H. P. Conn. 1992. *Workplace 2000: The Revolution Reshaping America*. New York: Dutton.

Brint, Steve. 1985. "Political Attitudes of Professionals." *Annual Review of Sociology* 112: 389–414.

———. 1994. *In an Age of Experts*. New York: Oxford University Press.

Brooks, Clem. 1994. "Class Consciousness and Politics in Comparative Perspective." *Social Science Research* 23: 167–95.

Burawoy, Michael. 1985. *The Politics of Production*. New York: Verso.

Burawoy, Michael, and Jaros Lukacs. 1992. *The Radiant Past*. Chicago: University of Chicago Press.

Calhoun, Craig. 1982. *The Question of Class Struggle*. Chicago: University of Chicago Press.

Castells, Manuel. 1983. *The City and the Grassroots*. Berkeley: University of California Press.

Cornfield, Daniel. B. 1986. "Declining Union Membership in the Post–World War II Era: The United Furniture Workers of America, 1939–1982." *American Journal of Sociology* 91: 111–53.

Davis, Mike. 1980. "The Barren Marriage of American Labour and the Democratic Party." *New Left Review* 123: 43–84.

Eder, Klaus. 1993. *The New Politics of Class*. Newbury Park, Calif.: Sage.

Edwards, Richard. 1979. *Captured Terrain*. New York: Basic Books.

Evans, Peter. 1979. *Dependent Development*. Princeton: Princeton University Press.

Fantasia, Rick. 1988. *Cultures of Solidarity*. Berkeley: University of California Press.

——. 1995. "From Class Consciousness to Culture, Action and Social Organization." *Annual Review of Sociology* 21: 269–87.

Form, William. 1987. *Divided We Stand: Patterns of Working Class Stratification in the U.S.* Urbana: University of Illinois Press.

——. 1995. *Segmented Labor, Fractured Politics.* New York: Plenum.

Freeman, Richard B., and James L. Medoff. 1984. *What Do Unions Do?* New York: Basic Books.

Giddens, Anthony. 1973. *The Class Structure of Advanced Societies.* New York: Barnes and Noble.

Golden, Miriam. 1986 "Interest Representation, Party Systems and the State." *Comparative Politics* 28: 279–301.

Gordon, David M., Richard Edwards, and Michael Reich. 1984. *Segmented Work, Divided Workers.* New York: Cambridge University Press.

Gouldner, Alvin. 1979. *The Future of Intellectuals and the Rise of the New Class.* New York: Oxford University Press.

Hobsbawm, E. J. 1984. *Workers.* New York: Pantheon.

Hout, Michael, Clem Brooks, and Jeff Manza. 1995. "The Democratic Class Struggle in the United States, 1948–1991." *American Sociological Review* 60: 805–28.

Hyman, Richard. 1992. "Trade Unions and the Disaggregation of the Working Class." In Marino Regini, ed., *The Future of Labour Movements.* Newbury Park, Calif.: Sage.

Jenkins, J. Craig, and Bert Klandermans. 1995. *The Politics of Social Protest.* Minneapolis: University of Minnesota Press.

Jenkins, J. Craig, and Kurt Schock. 1993. "Global Structures and Political Processes in the Study of Domestic Political Conflict." *Annual Review of Sociology* 18: 161–85.

Jenkins, J. Craig, and Michael Wallace. 1996. "The Generalized Action Potential of Protest Movements: The New Class, Social Trends and Political Exclusion Explanations" *Sociological Forum* 11: 183–207.

Jones, Gareth Stedman. 1983. *Languages of Class.* New York: Cambridge University Press.

Katznelson, Ira. 1982. *City Trenches.* New York: Pantheon.

——. 1986. "Working-Class Formation: Constructing Cases and Comparisons." In Ira Katznelson and Aristide Zolberg, eds. *Working-Class Formation.* Princeton: Princeton University Press.

Kimmeldorf, Howard. 1988. *Reds or Rackets? The Making of Radical and Conservative Unions on the Waterfront.* Berkeley: University of California Press.

Koo, Hagen. 1994. *State and Society in Contemporary Korea.* Ithaca, N.Y.: Cornell University Press.

Kriesi, Hanspeter. 1989. "New Social Movements and the New Class in the Netherlands. *American Journal of Sociology* 94: 1078–117.

———. 1995. "Movements of the Left, Movements of the Right." Department of Political Science, University of Geneva, Switzerland. Unpublished paper.

Kriesi, Hanspeter, Ruud Koopmans, Jan Willem Duyvendak, and Marco G. Giugni. 1995. *New Social Movements in Western Europe.* Minneapolis: University of Minnesota Press.

Leicht, Kevin T. 1989a. "Unions, Plants, Jobs and Workers: An Analysis of Union Satisfaction and Participation." *The Sociological Quarterly* 30: 331–62.

———. 1989b. "On the Estimation of Union Threat Effects." *American Sociological Review* 54: 1035–47.

Leicht, Kevin T., Michael Wallace, and Don Sherman Grant II. 1993. "Union Presence, Class, and Individual Earnings Inequality." *Work and Occupations* 20: 429–51.

Lipietz, Alain. 1987. *Mirages and Miracles: The Crisis of Global Fordism.* New York: Verso.

Lo, Clarence. 1986. *Small Property vs. Big Government.* Berkeley: University of California Press.

Manza, Jeff, Michael Hout, and Clem Brooks. 1995. "Class Voting in Capitalist Democracies Since World War II: Dealignment, Realignment or Trendless Fluctuation?" *Annual Review of Sociology* 21: 137–62.

Massey, Douglas, and Nancy Denton. 1993. *American Apartheid.* Cambridge: Harvard University Press.

McAdam, Doug. 1982. *Political Process and the Development of Black Insurgency.* Chicago: University of Chicago Press.

Parkin, Frank. 1979. *Marxism and Class Theory.* New York: Columbia University Press.

Poulantzas, Nicos. 1975. *Classes in Contemporary Capitalism.* London: New Left Books.

Przeworski, Adam. 1977. "Proletariat into a Class: The Process of Class Formation from Karl Kautsky's 'The Class Struggle' to Recent Controversies." *Politics and Society* 7: 343–401.

———. 1985. *Capitalism and Social Democracy.* New York: Cambridge University Press.

Przeworski, Adam, and John Sprague. 1986. *Paper Stones: A History of Electoral Socialism.* Chicago: University of Chicago Press.

Rosenblum, Gerard. 1973. *Immigrant Workers: Their Impact on American Labor Radicalism.* New York: Basic.

Schwartz, Michael. 1976. *Radical Protest and Social Structure.* New York: Academic Press.

Seidman, Gay. 1994. *Manufacturing Militance.* Berkeley: University of California Press.

Shorter, Ned, and Charles Tilly. 1976. *Strikes in France.* New York: Cambridge University Press.

Steinberg, Marc W. 1991. "Talkin' Class: Discourse, Ideology and Their Roles in Class Conflict." In Scott McNall, Rhonda Levine, and Rick Fantasia, eds., *Bringing Class Back In.* Boulder: Westview.

———. 1993. "The Labour of the Country is the Wealth of the Country . . .: Class Identity, Consciousness and the Role of Discourse in the Making of the English Working Class." Unpublished paper.

Stinchcombe, Arthur. 1990. *Information and Organization.* Berkeley: University of California Press.

Therborne, Goran. 1983. "Why Some Classes Are More Successful Than Others." *New Left Review* 138: 37–55.

Thompson, E. P. 1963. *The Making of the English Working Class.* New York: Vintage.

———. 1978. *The Poverty of Theory and Other Essays.* New York: Monthly Review Press.

———. 1991. *Customs In Common.* New York: New Press.

Tilly, Charles. 1978. *From Mobilization to Revolution.* Reading, Mass.: Addison-Wesley.

Valenzuela, Samuel J. 1992. "Labour Movements and Political Systems." In Marino Regini, ed., *The Future of Labour Movements.* Newbury Park, Calif.: Sage.

Vanneman, Reeve, and Lynn Weber Cannon. 1987. *The American Perception of Class.* Philadelphia: Temple University Press.

Wacquant, Loic J. D. 1991. "Making Class: The Middle Class(es) in Social Theory and Social Structure." In Scott McNall, Rhonda Levine, and Rick Fantasia, eds., *Bringing Class Back In.* Boulder: Westview.

Wallace, Michael, and J. Craig Jenkins. 1995. "The New Class, Postindustrialism and Neocorporatism." In J. Craig Jenkins and Bert Klandermans, eds., *The Politics of Social Protest*. Minneapolis: University of Minnesota Press.

Walton, John, and Charles Ragin. 1990. "Global and National Sources of Political Protest: Third World Responses to the Debt Crisis." *American Sociological Review* 55: 876–90.

Weber, Max. 1968. *Economy and Society*. Berkeley: University of California Press.

Western, Bruce. 1995. "A Comparative Study of Working-Class Disorganization: Union Decline in Eighteen Advanced Capitalist Countries." *American Sociological Review*. 60: 179–201.

Wilson, William J. 1987. *The Truly Disadvantaged*. Chicago: University of Chicago Press.

Wright, Erik Olin. 1985. *Classes*. New York: New Left Books.

Zolberg, Aristide. 1986. "How Many Exceptionalisms?" In Ira Katznelson and Aristide Zolberg, eds., *Working-Class Formation*. Princeton: Princeton University Press.

Index

Abraham, D., 322–24, 325n, 328
Abrams, Philip, 109n
Accumulation, capitalist, 14, 346–47, 360–61
Action, 88; class, xi, 5, 16, 18, 21–22, 25–26,
    97, 115, 138, 145, 262, 271, 314; collective,
    48, 50–52, 152, 190, 357; political,
    313–30. *See also* Strikes
Adams, Julia, 27
Age, 140, 214
Agency. *See* Action
Agriculture, 94, 121, 190, 267, 288, 294; in
    Germany, 315, 317–21, 329–30, 342
Alexander, Sally, 143–44
Alford, Robert, 16
Alonso, W., 109
Althusser, Louis, 8, 12–13
Ambition. *See* Attitudes
American Federation of Labor, 272
Aminzade, Ronald, 5, 314
Anderson, Margo, 110, 111n
Anderson, Perry, 74n
Annales school, 80–81
Anthropology. *See* Social sciences
Anti-Semitism, 338, 338n, 340–44, 345n,
    357–58, 358n
Arbeitskraft, 176, 189–90
Argentina, 388
Art. *See* Culture
Artisans, 94, 121, 134, 139, 143–45, 148, 171–
    72, 315, 329
Asia, East, 30, 386–87
Associations, voluntary, 277–78, 374. *See also*
    Employers, associations; Unions, labor
Attitudes, 197–216, 223, 225–38, 328
Austrian Freedom Party, 335
Authoritarianism, 315, 340
Authority, 29–30, 205, 373. *See also* Domina-
    tion; Power

Balibar, Etienne, 12
Barnes, Barry, 201
Baron, Ava, 74n, 247
Batenburg, R., 227n
Bauman, Zygmunt, 77
Bavarian People's Party (Germany), 320
Beekenkamp, G., 227n
Behavior. *See* Action
Bell, Daniel, 4, 247
Bendix, Reinhard, 147
Benenson, Harold, 147
Biernacki, Richard, xi–xii, 29
Biggart, Nicole, 30
Birmingham school, 215
Blackburn, R. M., 63n
Blacks, 142, 146, 153–54, 212–13, 217.
    See also Ethnicity
Blatchford, Robert, 185
Blau, Peter, 12, 12n
Block, Fred, 31, 75
Boltanski, Luc, 123–25
Bonacich, Edna, 24, 373
Booth, Charles, 118
Boundaries, 19, 22, 24, 151. *See also* Class
    boundaries; Ethnicity, boundaries
Bourdieu, Pierre, 27, 49–50, 150–51, 221–25,
    361
Brazil, 389
Brenner, Robert, 287–89, 293–95, 297
Britain, 153–54, 174; and capitalist develop-
    ment, 287, 304–5, 347; class formation
    in, 73–77, 91–97, 135, 141, 143–44,
    146–48, 151–52; labor compensation
    in, 170–90; and occupational statistics,
    109n, 110, 114–20, 122–26
Brittain, N., 62n
Brooks, Clem, 375
Brustein, William, 5, 23

Bulmer, Martin, 113n, 116
Burawoy, Michael, 29, 43n, 376, 378, 389
Burris, Val, 59n

Cadres, 123–26
Calhoun, Craig, 5, 77, 79, 246
California, state government, 250, 267, 270–71, 274
Canning, Kathleen, 74n
Capital, 27–28, 55, 221–38, 378; cultural and social, 27, 210–13, 221–38, 373. *See also* Morality
Capitalism, 13, 97, 124–25, 150, 391; mode of production, 11, 28, 30–31, 48–49, 134, 287–88, 313–14; political, 6–7; and production for market, 289, 296, 299–304; rise of, 287–300; transition from, 7, 50, 66, 147; and wage versus non-wage labor, 287–98, 301–6
Carchedi, Guglielmo, 53n
Castells, Manuel, 360
Catholicism, 124, 152, 187, 266, 317–21, 330, 390. *See also* Religion
Chartism, 148, 173–74
Children, 62, 225–30, 263
Citizenship, 93, 134, 136, 139, 148, 195, 213, 344, 350, 359, 374
Clark, Anna, 77, 148
Clark, Terry, 247
Class, 2, 4–5, 8–9, 17–20, 22–29, 43, 58, 87, 93, 108, 126, 138n, 139n, 150–51, 216n, 246–47, 262; bourgeois, 56–57, 124, 141, 143, 149, 188, 198, 205, 291, 351, 380; capitalist, 18, 48, 52–53, 64, 70, 94, 172, 185, 315; lower-middle, 315–16; managerial-bureaucratic, 56, 121, 198; new, 4, 6, 51–52, 53n, 376, 379–80, 382–83, 385; petty bourgeois, 19, 52–54, 65, 121, 124, 205, 315, 327, 329, 344, 356; professional, 118, 120–24, 126, 206–7, 217; propertied, 17–20, 27–29; ruling, 109n, 222, 227n, 236–38, 380; upper, 115, 315; upper-middle, 193, 195, 198, 208. *See also* Middle class; Workers; Working class
Class alliances, 21, 190, 330, 344, 360, 372–73, 376–77, 384–85, 392
Class associations. *See* Employers, associations; Unions, labor

Class boundaries, 63, 125, 170, 187–88, 197, 206–8, 213, 215–16, 218
Class conflict: and capitalist development, 2, 13, 18–19, 31, 194, 288, 293, 313–14, 378, 381; language of, 198–99, 204; in Monterey fishing industry, 266–74; and social movements, 124–25, 145, 151, 190, 373, 376, 384, 387–88; theories of, 11, 21–23, 43, 47, 50, 138, 140, 149, 153. *See also* Resistance
Class consciousness: and class formations, 137, 348, 373, 379; and statistical classification, 110, 115, 125; theorizing, 76–77, 79–80, 140, 142, 152, 216n
Class differences, 119, 185, 187, 193–218, 330
Class formation: processes of, 24, 109, 134–38, 142–54; theories of, 43, 56, 74, 76–78, 90–91, 96–97, 169, 289–90, 299–300, 308, 370–76
Class fractions, 222–36, 385
Class in itself. *See* Interests, class
Class location, 12, 44, 52–54, 57–58, 60–71, 62n, 69n, 313–14, 336, 375
Class mobilization, 4–6, 20n, 23, 28, 357, 373–74, 376, 381–82
Class relations, 52–54, 56, 62, 62n, 79, 111, 176, 215, 218, 292, 296–98, 305. *See also* Relations of production
Class structure, 208, 361; theories of, xi, 2, 11–16, 20, 31, 41–45, 47, 49–54, 56, 58–63, 138, 291–94, 371, 375
Class struggle. *See* Class conflict
Class theory. *See specific theories, theorists*
Classification, statistical. *See* Occupations, classification of
Cohen, Joshua, 46
Collective bargaining, 122, 124–25, 146, 190, 348, 389. *See also* Unions, labor
Collins, Randall, 5, 19, 27, 314
Commerce, 287–88, 293; export versus import orientation in, 316, 321–30, 387
Commodities, 17–18, 20–21, 294, 298, 301–8
Communism, 6, 124, 211, 325, 327, 385, 389. *See also* Socialism
Community: and class formation, 9, 24, 79, 134, 138n, 152–53, 169, 354; and Monterey fishing industry, 244–45, 249–50, 262–63, 268, 274; political, 92–96, 137, 340, 356n; and social movements, 371,

Community (*cont.*)
    373, 379–82; worker attitudes and values,
    193–218
Comparison, cross-national, 14, 97, 122–27,
    170, 175–90, 193–218, 227n, 229, 370–90
Conk, Margo. *See* Anderson, Margo
Connell, R. W., 12, 150, 152
Consumption, 5, 217, 233, 236, 300–1, 306,
    351–53, 353n, 377, 387
Contingency theory, 2, 14–15, 21, 370, 372,
    376
Core. *See* World economy
Corporatism, 124, 347, 374
Corrigan, Philip, 298
Credentials, 24, 29, 53, 55–58, 64
Cultural power. *See* Hegemony
Culture, xii, 15–16, 93, 116, 136, 147–51, 229;
    and class, 18, 194, 215, 391–92; and Ger-
    man right-wing radicalism, 338, 342n,
    343, 347, 351–53, 359, 361, 381; high, 211,
    217, 224–27, 238; and Monterey fishing
    industry, 244–45, 260, 266, 274–79; pop-
    ular, 153–54, 224n, 229–31, 236, 238; of
    production, 169–73

Dahrendorf, Ralf, 29–30, 246
Davidoff, Lenore, 74n, 143
Davies, Celia, 114
Davis, Kingsley, 11
Debt crisis, 388
Deconstruction, 7–8, 10, 80, 134
Democracy, 313–30, 360, 370–74, 391–92
Derrida, Jacques, xiii, 8
Deskilling, 144–45, 171, 383. *See also* Skills
Desrosière, Alain, 121–23
Determinism, 15, 20, 30, 172n, 295, 297
Development, economic, 6–7, 134, 138,
    287–88, 294–95, 370–73, 375–81, 383,
    385–92
Difference, social and cultural, 22, 24, 152,
    197, 383
Discipline, work. *See* Work discipline
Discourse, 15, 89, 148, 173–74, 189, 253;
    class, 151, 169, 170–71, 188, 193–218
Discrimination, 143, 147, 151–52, 225, 340
Distribution, 300, 306
Division of labor, 11, 24, 78, 120, 253–57,
    262, 304; global, 288, 290–92, 300–9,
    373

Dobb, Maurice, 287
Domination, 53–54, 206, 276. *See also*
    Authority; Power
Donnelly, Michael, 8
Dualism, xi, 295–99
Duncan, Otis Dudley, 12, 12n, 113
Durkheim, Emile, 248

Education, 19, 24, 206–11, 223, 225, 227n,
    228–32, 235, 351
Edwards, Alba, 111n, 119
Eley, Geoff, 78n, 147, 149
Elster, Jon, 11
Embeddedness, 150
Employees, 54–56, 61, 66–68, 71, 121. *See*
    also Workers
Employers, 54, 121, 186, 377–78, 380–82,
    385–86, 388–89; associations, 143,
    267–68. *See also* Class
Engels, Frederick, 140
England. *See* Britain
Entrepreneurialism, neo-. *See* Fordism
Environment, natural, 15, 250, 267, 269–72,
    278–79, 306
Epistemology, 2, 8, 78, 82, 96–97
Erikson, Robert, 16
Ethnicity: and class formation, 136, 139,
    148, 195, 212–15, 218, 371–72, 389; and
    inequality, 16, 22, 24, 27, 29, 150; and
    Monterey fishing industry, 244–45,
    249–58, 262–70, 274–76; non-white,
    144, 147, 212; and politics, 15, 357,
    360, 382, 384, 386; segregation, 218,
    380. *See also specific ethnic groups and*
    racial classifications
Ethnocentrism. *See* Racism
Eugenics, 115, 118, 120, 126, 344, 344n, 357
Europe, 294, 336, 383–85, 392
European Union, 204, 335
Exchange, economic, 291, 294, 299–301,
    303, 306
Exclusion. *See* Discrimination
Experience: class, 138, 144–45, 169, 215–16,
    246, 357; lived, 5, 48–52, 54, 186, 188, 314
Experts. *See* Professionals
Exploitation: social formations of, 170, 182,
    185, 186, 190, 198, 291; theories of, 11,
    13–14, 26–29, 46–47, 52–57, 59–60, 66, 70
Export orientation. *See* Commerce

Fascism, 315
Factories. *See* Production, culture and organization of
False consciousness, 314, 330
Falter, J. W., 316n
Family: class formation, 27, 135, 151–52; class location, 12, 24, 62, 62n, 352; and domestic relations, 26, 140–42, 144, 148–49, 207–8, 211, 237–38; and enterprises, 94, 122, 175; and politics, 92, 96, 382
Fantasia, Rick, 14, 151, 391
Farmers. *See* Agriculture
Feenstra, Robert, 30
Feminism, 15, 49, 135–37, 141–42, 147, 382
Feudalism, 55, 194, 287–88
Fink, Leon, 134
Fishing industry, 243–45, 249–62, 266–74, 278–79
Fordism, 5–6, 338n, 339, 346–57, 361, 377–85, 387, 391. *See also* Regulation theory
Foucault, Michel, xii
Fox, Pamela, 153
Frader, Laura, 77
Frames, collective-action, 151n
France: class formations, 94, 135, 371–72, 384–85; cultural capital in, 227n, 235; and occupational classification, 114–15, 117, 120–26; politics, 79, 143, 194–95, 213, 340, 356n; worker attitudes and values, 193–218
Frank, Andre Gunder, 287–88
Fraser, Nancy, 149
Friedland, Roger, 16
Functionalism, 8, 11–12, 69, 297, 346

Gallie, Duncan, 194
Galton, Frances, 118
Gans, Herbert, 246
Geertz, Clifford, 81
Gender, 15–17, 19, 49, 60n, 62, 62n, 135, 138–48, 150–51, 174, 360; discrimination, 22, 24, 27, 29, 214; and Monterey fishing industry, 244, 244n, 246 251, 253–58, 260–65, 272–73
Geography, 150, 291, 297–98, 300, 306–8, 317–20, 356, 372. *See also* Space
Germany: class movements in, 135, 371–72, 374, 388, 390; Fordism in, 347–58, 361; labor compensation in, 170, 175–90;

occupational categories, 124; political mobilization in, 315–30, 336–45, 348, 352, 354–59, 383; trade policy in, 316–18, 321–25, 329; Weimar Republic, 315–17, 324–25, 328
Gibson, Gloria, 80
Giddens, Anthony, 17–18, 22–24, 50, 246–47, 373
Gilroy, Paul, 153
Giroux, Henry, 237
Golden, Miriam, 25
Goldthorpe, John, 16, 50n, 58n, 62, 62n
Gould, Roger, 314
Gouldner, Alvin, 51, 383
Gourevitch, P., 324
Gramsci, Antonio, 248, 347
Granovetter, Mark, 112, 150
Guestworkers. *See* Immigrants
Guilds, 122, 190
Gusfield, Joseph, 27

Habermas, Jürgen, 136, 140n, 149
Habitus, 27, 50, 223–24, 226, 233, 237
Hacking, Ian, 107, 109, 113
Haider, Jörg, 335
Halbwachs, Maurice, 248
Hall, Catherine, 74n, 143
Hall, John R., xi, 314
Halle, David, 14, 194
Halsey, A. H., 112
Hamilton, Gary, 30
Hamilton, Richard, 194
Hanagan, Michael, 314
Harmsen, Ger, 234
Hartman, Heidi, 12
Hasselbach, Ingo, 341
Hate crimes. *See* Violence
Hauser, Robert, 12
Heath, A., 62n
Hechter, Michael, 24
Hegemony, 26, 57, 153, 225, 237, 248, 276–79, 360–61
Heredity, 118
Hindess, Barry, 17
Hirsch, Joachim, 347
Hirst, Paul, 17
Historical analysis: historicism in, 2, 9, 11, 14–15, 20, 371; methods of, xiii, 75n, 80–81, 119n, 137n; social constructionism

Historical analysis (*cont.*)
  and, 111, 247–48, 275–79 theory and,
    8–9, 13, 44, 55, 59, 74–78, 188, 295–97;
    universal, 2, 9
History: of concepts of class and classifica-
  tion, 108, 114, 127; labor, 9, 133–37, 134n,
  137n, 142, 144–47, 153–54, 169; social,
  246. *See also* Memory, collective
Hitler, Adolf, 344
Hobsbawm, Eric, 305, 348
Hodge, Robert, 12
Hoffman, W. G., 325n
Holism, 9, 11, 13–15, 19–20, 31, 89, 296
Home-ownership, 61n
Homosexuals, 357
Horan, Patrick, 12
Hoschshild, Jennifer, 217
Household, 62, 148–49. *See also* Family
Housewives, 49, 62, 62n
Hout, Michael, 375
Huddersfield, England, 177, 179
Hungary, 390
Hunt, Lynn, 81

Identity, 22, 215, 246, 262, 339, 359–60, 373;
  class, 134–36, 147–48, 194, 345, 360–61,
  372, 381, 391; narrative, 76, 86–89; political, 93–94, 151–53
Ideology, 31, 109, 136, 139, 141–42, 148,
  169–72, 276, 278, 377–78; of exploitation, 185, 188; German radical right,
  339–40, 344–45, 347, 349–51, 356–59;
  oppositional, 174–75
Immigrants, 148, 196, 213–14, 371, 374; and
  German right-wing radicalism, 336,
  338n, 342, 344, 350, 353, 356
Import orientation. *See* Commerce;
  Industries
Income, 67, 360, 381. *See also* Labor, com-
  pensation of
Indians, East, 213
Industrial society. *See* Society, modern
Industrialization, 75–79, 96, 119, 137, 145,
  170, 172; and class formation, 370–76,
  385–89, 391–92
Industries: export vs. import orientation in,
  316, 321–30. *See also* Fishing industry;
  Production, culture and organization of;
  Textiles

Inequality, 16, 22, 24, 117n, 134, 149–50,
  216–17, 387. *See also* Poverty
Inglehart, R., 313
Institutionalism, 1–3, 16–17, 24, 30–31, 89,
  122, 146, 355
Intellectuals, 19, 381, 383, 390
Interests: class, 5, 10–12, 20–22, 20n, 25, 30,
  48, 52–53, 61, 63, 87, 137, 324, 337; mar-
  ket, 2–3, 16–22, 27–29, 314–30; material,
  45–48, 51, 57, 59, 65, 76, 313; political, 11
Irvine, J., 109n
Italy, 335, 343, 356

Jackman, Mary, 217
Janiewski, Delores, 29
Japan, 146, 387
Jenkins, J. Craig, 6
Jones, Gareth Stedman, 15–16, 173–74,
  246, 391
Joyce, Patrick, 2, 77, 171–74

Kalmijn, M., 227n
Kammen, Michael, 81
Katznelson, Ira, 14, 16, 74n, 78–79, 96–97,
  134, 136, 194, 370–71, 375, 390–91
Kelley, Robin, 142, 153
Kerbo, H. R., 314
Kimmeldorf, Howard, 374
Knights of Labor, 144
Knowledge. *See* Education
Kondo, Dorinne, 146
Konrad, George, 51
Koo, Hagen, 387
Korea, South, 387
Kriesi, Hanspeter, 383

Labor, xii, 13, 49; compensation, 18, 29, 64,
  67, 148, 152, 170, 175–90, 260–62,
  267–73, 305, 321–22, 324, 328, 377, 390;
  control, 92, 291–94, 305, 347, 378, 386,
  388–90; immigrant, 148, 253, 350, 353,
  371, 374; markets, 17–26, 28–29, 53, 67,
  96, 185–86, 189–90, 199, 372–73, 379;
  power, 56, 184–88; social construction
  of, 181–83, 186, 188; surplus, 48–49, 179,
  185–86. *See also* Division of labor;
  Exploitation; Work discipline
Laclau, Ernesto, 15, 287, 360
Lamont, Michele, 24–25

Lancashire, England, 152, 175, 183–84, 188
Landes, Joan, 143
Language. See Discourse
Lash, Scott, 235
Laslett, Barbara, 49n
Latin America, 387–89
Latinos, 213
Law, 24, 28–29, 89, 92–96, 140; labor, 94, 122
Le Pen, Jean-Marie, 335, 356n
Left, political, 205, 215, 376, 382, 384–85. See also Politics
Leicht, Kevin, 6
Leisure, 230, 232–33, 352–54
Lembcke, Jerry, 9
Lewin, Linda, 27
Life, everyday, 24, 136, 147, 149–50, 154, 381–82
Lifestyle, 224, 226, 230, 232–34, 236, 246, 372, 382
Lipietz, Alain, 387
Lipset, Seymour M., 194, 247, 313, 337, 359
Lipsitz, George, 153
Locke, John, 139–40
Lockwood, David, 50n
Luddites, 171

MacLeod, Jay, 237
Maier, Charles, 352
Malasia, 146
Managers. See Workers, managerial
Mann, Michael, 89, 194
Manufacturing. See Industries; Production, culture and organization of
Manza, Jeff, 375
Markets, 6, 17–31, 31, 78, 89, 304, 314–30, 354; capacities in, 47, 247; in cultural capital theory, 27, 235. See also Exchange, economic; Labor, markets
Marshall, Gordon, 120
Marx, Karl, 16, 125–26, 140; on class, 10–11, 19, 50, 74n, 246, 314; on labor, 169, 183, 185–86, 188–89; on social change, 7, 73–74, 74n, 297, 300, 303
Marxian theory, 7–13, 15, 29, 31, 81, 139–41, 237, 376, 388; and capitalist development debates, 288, 297, 300, 303; and class debates, 1, 19–20, 24, 41, 43–45, 47,

55, 58–60, 60n, 64, 70, 144, 246, 314, 348, 360, 375; and fascism explanations, 337, 360; in labor movements, 185–86. See also Communism; Socialism
McAdam, Doug, 373
McMichael, Philip, 309
Megill, Allan, 89
Memory, collective, 8, 247–49, 275–79, 339, 352–53, 355, 358n
Men, 14, 49, 62, 136, 138–41, 143–48, 151–52, 336, 342–43, 352–53. See also Gender
Metanarrative, 2, 8–10, 15, 74–78, 80, 86–87, 97, 138, 145, 150
Methodology, 11, 17, 195n, 196, 196n, 226, 233n, 315n–16n, 316, 325n, 336
Mexico, 388
Michielse, H. C. M., 234
Middle class, 52, 55–56, 58, 60, 64–65, 66n, 70–71, 115, 124; attitudes toward, 194, 199, 206, 216, 218; and cultural capital, 222, 236; in Germany, 316–17, 321, 327–29, 343; organization and politics, 43, 125, 384, 390, 392; and separate spheres, 141, 143. See also Class
Miles, I., 109n
Mills, C. Wright, 246
Minkenberg, M., 313
Minorities. See Ethnicity
Mintz, Sidney, 307
Mobility: attitudes toward, 207, 236; inter-generational, 23, 63, 200–1, 216–17; occupational, 11–12, 22–23, 19, 113, 205, 327–29, 356, 381
Mode of production, 7, 10, 19, 44, 52, 55–56, 58–60, 69, 126, 293, 295, 297. See also Production
Modern society. See Society, modern
Modernization. See Development, economic
Monterey, California, 243–46, 249–79
Moore, Wilbert, 11
Moral economy, 92, 172, 339, 352, 354–55, 361
Morality, 27, 197–98, 210, 212–13, 217, 383–84
Mouffe, Chantal, 15, 360
Movimento Sociale Italiano, 335
Musson, A. E., 77

Nairn, Tom, 74n
Narrative, 74–78, 75n, 80–88, 90–91, 96–97, 174; statistics as, 114, 127
National Front (France), 335, 356n
National Peoples Party (Germany), 319
Nationalism, 148, 213, 325, 340, 349, 353, 383
Nazi Party, 315–21, 325–30
Nazism, neo-, 336, 338–45, 357–59, 383
Neighborhood, 149, 214, 223, 228, 231, 380, 386. *See also* Community; Space
Neithammer, Lutz, 358–59
Neitz, Mary Jo, 5
Netherlands, 228–36
Nicholson, Linda, 140
Nield, K., 78n
Nightingale, Carl, 217

Occupations: classification of, 107–22, 123–24, 126; in Monterey fishing industry, 244, 244n, 249–72; structure of, 20, 45, 113, 122
Ong, Aihwa, 146
Ontology, 8, 82, 84, 352
Organization, 27–28, 30–31, 55, 89
Orrù, Marco, 30

Pakulski, Jan, 15
Palmer, Bryan, 15
Parkin, Frank, 16, 373
Parti Communiste (France), 204
Passeron, Jean-Claude, 221, 225, 227n, 236
Pateman, Carole, 139–40
Patriarchy, 27
Patrimonialism, 30
Pay. *See* Labor, compensation of
Peasants. *See* Agriculture
Pensioners. *See* Welfare
Periphery. *See* World economy
Perkin, H. L., 77, 79
Piece rates. *See* Labor, compensation of
Poland, 390
Polanyi, Karl, 26, 75, 150, 304–5
Political economy, 15–16, 22–31, 188, 308
Political parties, 51n, 134, 314–30, 341–45, 356n, 357, 371–74, 384–85. *See also* Politics; specific political parties
Political theory, xii, 139–41, 359. *See also* specific theories, theorists
Politics, 21–22, 28, 43, 68, 92–93, 96, 142n, 150; of class, 313–14, 330, 359, 371, 384–85, 391; and class struggle, 136, 138, 140, 142–43, 147, 152–53; conservative, 382; liberal, 190, 374; radical, 15, 147, 171, 173–74, 199, 211, 386–87, 391; of recognition, 110, 115, 123–25. *See also* Left, political; Right, political
Populism, 370, 374, 379, 382–83, 391
Post-Fordism. *See* Fordism; Regulation theory
Post-industrial society. *See* Society, post-industrial
Postone, Moishe, 13
Post-structuralism, 9–10, 137n
Poulantzas, Nicos, 12–13, 17, 391
Poverty, 216, 380–81
Power, 29–31, 46, 43, 88, 204–6, 373, 391. *See also* Authority; Domination
Prandy, K., 63n
Prestige. *See* Status
Price, Richard, 172n
Private sphere, 136, 138–42, 149
Production: culture and organization of, 14, 28–30, 50, 62, 138–39, 169–73, 175–85, 188–90, 290–93, 297, 305, 378, 381; point of, 136, 138n, 144, 152, 170, 175, 185–86, 188. *See also* Mode of production; Relations of production; Restructuring, economic
Professionals, 29, 53, 55–56, 59, 64–65, 66n, 67, 70, 374, 379, 382–83
Profit, 185, 290–1. *See also* Relations of production
Proletarianization, 14, 76, 79, 97, 134, 138–39, 144, 148, 372, 375
Proletariat. *See* Working class
Property, 17–18, 53, 61, 64, 92, 139, 174, 274, 294, 327–28, 373; inheritance, 27, 319–20, 328–29
Protectionism. *See* Commerce
Protestantism, 152, 187, 317–18, 320–21, 329, 343, 344n. *See also* Religion
Przeworski, Adam, 14, 16, 21, 43n, 51, 51n, 151, 372, 384, 386
Public sphere, 95, 136, 138–44, 148–49, 189

Rabinbach, Anson, 137n
Race. *See* Ethnicity
Racism, 213–15, 340, 343–44, 357, 336
Ragin, Charles, 388

Rational choice theory, 23
Rationality and rationalization, 23–24, 26–27, 302, 354
Realism, 45, 360–61
Reddy, William, 18, 247
Reductionism, 170–75, 346
Regulation theory, 31, 92, 339, 346–47, 349, 357, 360–61. *See also* Fordism
Reid, Ivan, 119
Relational setting, xii, 75–76, 88–91, 93–94
Relations of production, 94, 137–43, 148; capitalist, 53, 55, 69–70, 360; and development, 290–99, 301, 306–7; social, 44n, 48, 67–68, 171, 314, 316. *See also* Production
Religion, 19, 24, 146, 245, 247, 313, 330, 371–73, 384, 386. *See also* Catholicism; Protestantism
Reproduction, 140, 142
Republikaner Party (Germany), 336n, 342, 356n
Resistance, 134–36, 138–39, 142, 145–46, 149–54, 169, 175, 190, 237. *See also* Class conflict
Resource mobilization theory, 372
Restructuring, economic, 4–6, 134, 377–81. *See also* Production
Rhine valley, Germany, 175, 177
Right, radical political, 370, 376, 382–83, 385; in contemporary Germany, 335–45, 348, 352, 354–59. *See also* Politics
Rights: employment, 29, 176; political, 92–94, 139, 382–83
Roediger, David, 24, 148
Roemer, John, 11, 28, 55
Rogers, Joel, 46
Rose, Sonya, xi–xii, 24, 74n, 77
Roth, Guenther, 19n
Roth, Karl, 355–56
Roth, Roland, 347
Runciman, W. G., 12
Rupp, Jan, 27

Samuel, Raphael, 305
Sanworth, M., 62n
Sartre, Jean-Paul, xi, 24, 134, 150, 152, 154
Saville, John, 77
Sayer, Derek, 16, 31, 302
Schluchter, Wolfgang, 19n

Schock, Kurt, 388
Schwartz, Michael, 381
Scott, James C., 139,
Scott, Joan, 15, 114n, 174, 247
Segregation, residential, 218, 380
Semiotics, 15, 391
Semiperiphery. *See* World economy
Serfdom. *See* Agriculture
Seriality, xi–xii, 24, 134, 150–54
Sewell, William, Jr., 7, 133, 246
Sex. *See* Gender
Sharecroppers. *See* Agriculture
Shorter, Ned, 385
Silesia, Germany, 188
Skills: and class, 24, 64, 135, 173, 373, 379; and exploitation, 11, 28–29, 55–58; and occupational classification, 115, 116n, 122–23; and political interests, 321–22, 327–30; and production, 4–5, 251, 253, 387. *See also* Deskilling; Workers, skills of
Smelser, Neil, 77, 142n
Social constructionism, 2, 8–10, 29, 111, 247, 308
Social Democratic Party (Germany), 325, 327
Social movements, 138n, 147; and class, 5, 29, 171, 360, 369–79, 382–85, 388–92; socialist, 185, 189; theory, 357, 369–70, 372, 390–92
Social sciences, 108–9, 111–14, 142, 144, 246–48, 391
Social security. *See* Welfare
Socialism, 12, 43, 50, 55, 147, 172n, 186–87, 348–49, 348n, 375, 385–86, 389–91. *See also* Communism
Society, 89; class, 78, 97; modern, 74–75, 80, 120, 126, 188, 190, 246; post-industrial, 4, 246, 313, 356, 370, 376–85, 391; traditional, 74–75, 80, 120
Sociology. *See* Social sciences
Solidarity, 14, 22, 134–35, 148, 151, 215, 263, 265, 267, 272–73, 371–77, 391
Solidarity movement (Poland), 390
Somers, Margaret, xi–xii, 10
Sørensen, Annemette, 12
South Africa, 389
Soviet Union, 348–49, 370, 390
Space, 22, 75, 82, 88, 90, 136, 149–54, 218, 380; social, 221–22, 225, 227, 235, 237. *See also* Geography
Split labor market theory, 24, 373

Sprague, John, 51n, 384
Stadman, Carolyn, 142
Starr, Paul, 109, 113n
State, the, 54–57, 62, 68, 78, 95, 122, 124,
    139, 141n, 349, 386–87; and economy,
    25–26, 30, 371–72, 385–89; employees,
    64, 67–68, 71; and Monterey fishing
    industry, 262, 266–67, 270–71, 274,
    277–78; policies, 25, 29, 31, 351–52, 377,
    383, 391; repression, 390–91; socialist, 30,
    385–86, 389–91; welfare, 215, 322–24,
    347–48, 355, 370, 374, 378, 381; and
    world economy, 288, 290, 306–7
Statistical classification. *See* Occupations,
    classification of
Statistics, 107–14, 116n, 119, 123, 126
Status, 11–12, 12n, 118–21, 197–98, 200–3,
    208–10, 214, 217; in Monterey fishing
    industry, 251, 253, 263
Status group, 12n, 19, 20n, 24, 27, 31, 246, 373
Stearns, Peter, 81
Steinbeck, John, 245–46, 263n, 274–78
Steinberg, Marc, 15, 74n, 77, 373
Steinmetz, George, 6
Stevenson, T. H. C., 115–19
Stewart, A., 63n
Stoecker, Adolf, 343
Stoianovich, Traian, 81
Stone, Lawrence, 81
Stratification, 8, 16, 11–12, 107–8
Strikes, 190, 267–70, 272–73, 385, 388. *See
    also* Action, class; Class conflict
Structuralism, 8, 11–16, 113, 138, 371, 391
Structuration, 22–24, 50, 373
Struggle, class. *See* Class conflict
Students, 62, 390
Subject, universal, 136, 138, 154
Success. *See* Attitudes
Surplus product, 46–47, 56, 68, 288. *See also*
    Labor, surplus
Svennilson, I., 325n
Sweezy, Paul, 287–88
Szelenyi, Ivan, 51
Szreter, Simon, 119

Taxation, 322, 329
Taylor, Charles, 83–84
Technology, 78, 144, 171, 172n, 173, 175, 188,
    290, 304, 378, 387

Teleology, 7, 76, 78, 97, 153, 346
Temporality, 22 53–65, 70, 75, 90; historical,
    82, 88, 110, 291, 298, 307–8; of work, 29,
    173, 176, 183–84, 190
Tenant farmers. *See* Agriculture
Textiles, 170–71, 175–88
Thelwall, John, 171
Therborne, Goran, 372
Third World, 288, 370, 385–89, 391
Thomis, M. I., 77
Thompson, E. P., 339, 354–55, 391; and
    English working class, 19, 74n, 77, 79,
    169–73; on history and theory, 8–9, 14,
    137–39, 145, 148, 246–47, 370–71
Tilly, Charles, 14, 77, 112, 357, 385
Tilly, Louise, 247, 314
Time. *See* Temporality
Tocqueville, Alexis de 238
Tomich, Dale, 13–14
Torras, Jaume, 302
Tourism, 250, 275, 277–78
Trade. *See* Commerce
Trouillot, Rolph, 305
Trow, Martin, 359
Turner, Ben, 186
Turner, H. A., 327

Underclass, 212, 380
Underdevelopment. *See* Development,
    economic
Unemployment, 62, 327, 342–45, 381, 383
Unions, labor, 5, 140, 186–7, 235, 347; and
    economic development, 371, 374,
    377–79, 384–85, 388–90, 392; in Ger-
    many, 315, 321; and labor movement,
    142, 144, 146, 151–52, 173, 215; in Mon-
    terey fishing industry, 245–46, 266–73
United States, 110, 114, 135, 141, 143–44, 146,
    335, 340, 347, 356n, 380; Census, 111n,
    114, 119–20, 124, 244, 251, 251n; and class
    movements, 371–74, 383; and culture, 153,
    227, 235; government, 261, 383; worker
    attitudes and values, 193–218
Urban society, 190, 275–78, 288, 360, 374,
    382, 387–88, 391

Valenzuela, Samuel, 388
Value-orientations. *See* Attitudes
Vernon, James, 143

Versailles, treaty of, 325
Violence, 336, 338, 338n, 340–43, 345, 354–55, 357, 388
Voskamp, Ulrich, 349
Voss, Kim, 25
Voting, 313–30, 375, 384, 390

Wacquant, Loïc, 227n
Wages. *See* Labor, compensation of
Wallerstein, Immanuel, 13, 287–92, 296, 348
Wallerstein, Michael, 25
Walton, John, 8, 26, 388
Waters, Malcolm, 13, 22, 247
Weakliem, D., 313
Wealth, 116
Weaving. *See* Textiles
Weber, Max, 1, 8, 221, 301; on class analysis, 12n, 13–14, 16–20, 22–23, 25–28, 30, 247, 314, 372
Weberian theory, 1–3, 9–11, 13, 16–31, 47, 50n, 58–60, 59n, 81, 237, 372
Welfare: attitudes and politics, 62, 212–13, 322–24, 337, 351; economic, 46–48; state benefit programs, 92, 203–4, 347–48, 350, 353–55
Whites, 136, 138, 143–45, 148, 193–215. *See also* Ethnicity
Willis, Paul, 237
Wittke, Volker, 349
Wolf, Diane, 146
Wolf, Eric, 303, 305
Women, 49, 135, 139–40, 142–43, 151, 196, 230, 352–53. *See also* Gender
Wood, Ellen, 15
Wood, George, 183
Work. *See* Production, culture and organization of
Work discipline, 146, 176, 183–84. *See also* Labor, control
Work ethic, 203

Worker, quintessential, 137, 139, 154
Workers, 48, 50, 141, 144–46, 148, 152, 189; blue-collar, 121, 172n, 194, 197, 199, 202, 206–7, 216–17, 316, 321–30, 384, 386; and German radical right, 336–37, 339, 342–44, 349–54, 356–57, 359–61; managerial, 52–57, 59, 63–67, 70, 121, 379, 382; self-employed, 65, 375; skills of, 134, 138–39, 144–45, 147, 342–43, 345; technical, 59, 121; temporary, 5, 29, 379–81; white-collar, 121, 193–95, 197–217, 315, 381. *See also* Class; Professionals
Working class, 19, 43, 49–50, 52–53, 64, 68, 70, 73–74, 76–80, 91, 94–97, 124–25, 348, 354; attitudes toward, 194, 199, 214–15, 373; and culture, 4, 215, 222–38; decline of, 4, 7, 13, 376; in Germany, 315–16, 321, 324–29, 348–49, 354, 357, 359–61; in Monterey fishing industry, 244–46, 249–50, 262, 266–74; organization and politics, 356n, 370–72, 374–79, 382–85, 391–92; and state socialism, 389–90; and world economy, 291–92, 296, 386–89. *See also* Class
Working-class history. *See* History, labor
World economy, 5–6, 13–14, 31, 175, 288, 290–92, 297–307
World-system theory, 13–14, 288–92, 296–97, 348
Wright, Erik O., 12–13, 246, 314, 348, 360–61, 391
Wupper valley, Germany, 175, 188

Yorkshire, England, 175, 183, 185–86, 188
Young, Iris M., 150–51
Youth, 342, 353, 358, 383

Zelizer, Viviana, 26
Zolberg, Aristide, 14, 74n, 78, 370–71, 373, 390

John R. Hall is Professor of Sociology at the University of
California at Davis and Visiting Fellow at New College,
Oxford University. He is the author of several books,
most recently *Culture: Sociological Perspectives,*
with Mary Jo Neitz.

Patrick Joyce is Professor of History at the
University of Manchester, England.